The Kachina and the Cross

The Kachina and the Cross

Indians and Spaniards in the Early Southwest

Carroll L. Riley

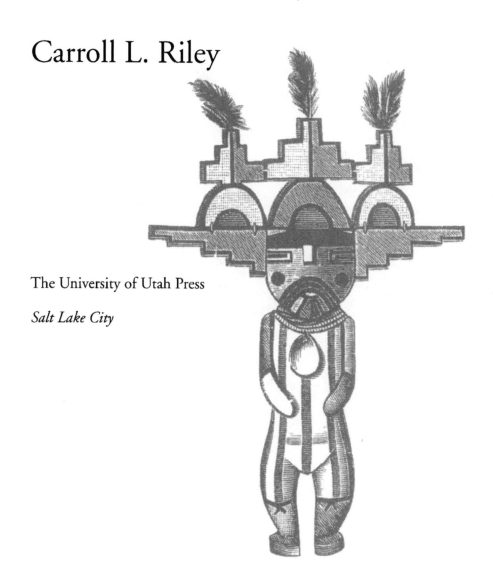

The University of Utah Press

Salt Lake City

Typography by WolfPack

Library of Congress Cataloging-in-Publication Data

Riley, Carroll L.
    The kachina and the cross : indians and spaniards in the early southwest /
Carroll L. Riley.
        p. cm.
    Includes bibliographical references and index.

    1. Indians of North America—Southwest, New—History—17th century.
2. Southwest, New—History—17th century. 3. Pueblo Indians—History—
17th century. I. Title.
E78.S7
979'.00497—dc21   99-22274

To the memory of
three great scholars
Eleanor B. Adams
France V. Scholes
Leslie Spier
Teachers   Friends

Contents

Illustrations

Preface

My interest in the seventeenth-century Southwest began at the University of New Mexico (UNM) in the late 1940s and early 1950s when I had the privilege of being a student of historian France V. Scholes. I had classes and seminars with France Scholes, and he was also the history member of my doctoral committee, ably chaired by anthropologist Leslie Spier. At the time I knew him, Professor Scholes was involved in a study of the complex struggles of church and state in the province of New Mexico during the turbulent seventeenth century. Scholes's interpretations were published in more than thirty articles, many in the *New Mexico Historical Review (NMHR)*. Today, Scholes's published work and his large collections of primary documents, now housed at the University of New Mexico and at Tulane University, represent major sources for any study of this subject.

I was aided in my Southwest work by other scholars, including Donald Brand, Florence Hawley [Ellis], W. W. Hill, and Dorothy Woodward at UNM; Harry Hoijer at UCLA; and at a slightly earlier period and somewhat more indirectly, Josiah Russell, the medievalist who directed my undergraduate Honors program at New Mexico. However, the individual who, next to Scholes and Spier, influenced me most was Eleanor B. Adams. Eleanor and I had the barest of nodding acquaintances during my student and early professional years. I came to really know Eleanor Adams around 1970 when she was editor of the *New Mexico Historical Review,* and I was returning to the Southwest after a long intellectual detour by way of Latin America, western Europe, and the Mediterranean. We were simpatico from the first, and to me Eleanor became not only a friend but also a mentor. Eleanor Adams had an extraordinarily fine mind, and she shared her knowledge and insights with generosity and flair. I was greatly influenced by her ideas on the Southwest and other subjects.

Study of the early historic Southwest has been largely in the domain of historians and has tended to concentrate on the Spanish presence in this region. As an anthropologist I am also very interested in the Native Americans, and I believe that any comprehensive study of the Southwest must take account of the lifeways of the various indigenous populations as well as the newcomers. The seventeenth-century Southwest cannot be understood only in Spanish or only in Indian terms. Much of the social energy of that century resulted from the complex interaction between these culturally distinct peoples. In this book I offer a new interpretation of the first century of Spanish control of the upper Southwest; that is to say, the Franciscan mission area of Pueblo New Mexico and Arizona. The extension of the Southwest, southward into Sonora and Chihuahua (what our Mexican colleagues call "el norte [or noroeste] de México") will be touched on only as it relates to the province of New Mexico.

In order to provide context to the reader, I begin by surveying the "Spanish century" in the New World, a period when Spanish arms and missionary effort created a vast new empire for the Spanish Crown. It was at the end of this period of heroic and legendary expansion that the colonization of New Mexico took place. I shall then give a brief sketch of Pueblos and pre-Pueblos in the prehistoric Native American world of the Southwest. A third chapter will be devoted to the pre-seventeenth-century Spanish penetration of the Southwest. The balance of the book basically concerns the seventeenth century in the Southwest (or more exactly, the final years of the sixteenth century to the beginning of the eighteenth).

The Spanish movement into the Greater Southwest began at a time when Spain's period of military and economic greatness had passed and the Spaniards at home and abroad were increasingly being challenged by other, rising European powers. The settlement of New Mexico as a Franciscan mission establishment took place over several generations, paralleled by the slow movement of Jesuit missionaries and their military support groups up the coast and into the interior valleys of Sonora. About the time that Spain established a more or less firm control over Pueblo New Mexico and Arizona, the Jesuits had finished their major penetration of the northern Sonoran heartland. The two conquest agendas, utilizing different strategies and somewhat diverse missionization aims, operated side by side but with relatively little interaction throughout the seventeenth century.

The seventeenth century in the province of New Mexico saw rapid, often forced acculturation of Native Americans. That very acculturation, however, created ripples of resentment that, as the century went on, became massive resistance, at first mainly passive, but with growing activism. This active resistance fed on the increasingly draconian Spanish reaction until in 1680 the province exploded into war. For a dozen years the Indians were independent, and even after the Spaniards returned in 1692, there was resistance and a second rebellion four years later. By the end of the seventeenth century, however, the Spanish government was again in reasonably complete control of the Rio Grande Basin. The western portion of the province never again became a firm part of the Spanish imperium, and the Hopi people were able to remain completely outside it.

The history of seventeenth-century New Mexico, as suggested by the title of this book, was first and foremost a product of missionization and Native American reaction to this intense and sometimes ruthless missionizing effort. It was at the center a struggle of two very different religious ideologies: the religion of the Pueblos, symbolized in Spanish minds by the kachina cult, and the zealous Christianity of the Franciscans. In large part (though by no means totally) because of this struggle, the colony's first hundred years were very troubled, not only in comparison to the quieter years of eighteenth-century New Mexico, discussed below, but also compared to contemporary history in other parts of New Spain. The unique set of circumstances in seventeenth-century New Mexico (considered in chapter 7) produced levels of disquietude that simply were not matched in other provinces. The nineteenth-century Southwest was also a time of troubles, but in this case the problems were external rather than internal. Early in that century, there began a sea change, an actual shift of governments from Spaniard to Mexican, and then (a few decades later) to American.

The eighteenth century, largely beyond the purview of this book, saw different problems and different solutions. The chances of another successful rebellion, at least on the Rio Grande, became increasingly remote. Still, the Pueblos had won a partial victory. The religious heart of Pueblo culture was no longer under direct attack; more and more the missionaries turned a blind eye to what they chose to characterize as "harmless superstitions." The complex accommodation in Pueblo culture of native and Spanish ideas was largely bonded in the eighteenth century—and it contained the basic elements of Pueblo religious and political life. To that extent the great rebellion of 1680 was not in vain.

In writing this book, I have relied heavily on the rich published materials: the Oñate documents edited by G. P. Hammond and A. Rey, the C. W. Hackett three-volume publication of the Bandelier collection from the Seville Archives, and the R. E. Twitchell two-volume compilation of the Spanish Archives of New Mexico. I have drawn extensively on the massive published contributions of F. V. Scholes, mentioned above—works that include both analysis and transcriptions of original documents. In that same period (1920s to 1950s) scholars such as E. B. Adams, L. B. Bloom, and Fray A. Chavez, among others, contributed to the baseline studies of Spanish and Pueblo life. Chavez, especially, pioneered genealogical studies of seventeenth- and eighteenth-century New Mexico. There were, of course, important writers of the colonization era, especially Torquemada near the beginning of the seventeenth century and Vetancurt and Sigüenza y Góngora at the end of it. The two Memorials of Benavides and the work of Zárate Salmerón shed light on the earlier decades of the century. There are also narrative poems from this era. One of these, alas containing very little real information, was commissioned by Juan de Oñate as tribute to his dead son, Cristóbal. Fortunately, the other poem, a famous epic description of the first days of the New Mexico colony by Gaspar Pérez de Villagrá, is filled with information on the nascent province. A splendid, heavily annotated new edition of this important work, with the Spanish text and English translation in parallel columns, was produced in 1992 by M. Encinias, A. Rodríguez and J. P. Sánchez. Another printed but strangely underutilized source for the period around A.D. 1600 is the two-volume work of Captain D. Bernardo de Vargas Machuca, *Milicia y descripción de las Indias*. Also valuable was the *Extracto de noticias* of Fray S. Vélez de Escalante, which I had available in a transcription from the Center for Southwestern Research (CSR) as well as in a translation by Eleanor Adams.

For the revolt and reconquest period there are several fine studies, especially those by C. W. Hackett and C. C. Shelby, and by J. M. Espinosa. No one writing on this period should be without the masterful multivolume study of de Vargas by J. L. Kessell and his associates R. Hendricks and M. D. Dodge. For the archaeology, genealogy, and history of the pre-revolt seventeenth century, I have greatly benefited from the various writings of, among others, J. A. Esquibel, R. A. Gutiérrez, S. M. Hordes, J. E. Ivey, F. Levine, M. Simmons, C. T. Snow, D. H. Snow, and L. Tigges.

I have also utilized the extensive Scholes collections at the Center for Southwest Research at the University of New Mexico in Albuquerque; the New Mexico State Archives, Santa Fe; and the Documentary Relations of the Southwest (DRSW) collection at the Arizona State Museum and University of Arizona in Tucson. I also had available the microfilm collection of New Mexico Spanish archives, and microfilm of the Parral archives at New Mexico Highlands University, and the Works Progress Administration (WPA) project transcription and translation of the New Mexico archives at the Laboratory of Anthropology, Museum of New Mexico, Santa Fe. In addition, the Museum of New Mexico History Library kindly made the collection of Martínez de Montoya papers available to me.

The general task I have set myself is to interpret seventeenth-century New Mexico as an anthropologist would see it. This was a land where several major ethnic groups cooperated and competed. There was a swirl of relationships among Pueblos, nomads and Spaniards—relationships that changed over time and differed from one part of the province to another. What really happened in New Mexico can only be understood as a nexus of these interacting forces and the dynamic that they produced.

Acknowledgments

A work such as this relies on many people with differing areas of expertise. Individuals who have read parts of the manuscript and given sage advice include Richard and Shirley Cushing Flint, Villanueva, New Mexico; James E. Ivey, National Park Service, Santa Fe, New Mexico; Edmund Ladd, Curator of Ethnology, Laboratory of Anthropology, Museum of New Mexico, Santa Fe; Charles H. Lange of Santa Fe; Richard V. Lee, Flagstaff, Arizona; Curtis F. Schaafsma, Curator of Anthropology, Laboratory of Anthropology, Santa Fe; and Margaret Vazquez-Geffroy of New Mexico Highlands University. Nancy P. Hickerson of Texas Tech University was most generous in sharing materials from the western Plains. Cordelia T. Snow of the Archaeological Records Management Section (ARMS) of the Laboratory of Anthropology, and David H. Snow of the Cross Cultural Resources Center, Santa Fe, read the entire manuscript, and their detailed and incisive comments were of great benefit. Other thanks go to John Kessell, director of the Vargas Project, for his generosity in sharing copies of the Extracto de noticias, and for giving me other timely advice and information. Stanley M. Hordes, former New Mexico State Historian, kindly shared his research on seventeenth-century New Mexico with me, as did genealogist José A. Esquibel of Santa Fe. Marianne L. Stoller, Colorado College, generously allowed me to use student papers from her research on the Sánchez site (LA 20,000). Dody Fugate at the Laboratory of Anthropology contributed from her vast store of information on dogs in the Southwest. Laura Holt and Orlando Romero, librarians respectively at the Laboratory of Anthropology and the History Library of the Museum of New Mexico, offered splendid and sustained assistance as did various members of the ARMS staff at the Laboratory of Anthropology. Louise Stiver, Curator of Collections at the Museum of Indian Arts and Culture/Laboratory of Anthropology (MIAC/LA), was most generous with her time and advice.

Dianne Bird, archivist at MIAC/LA, and Louanna L. Haecker of ARMS gave good advice on illustrations, and Richard Rudisill and Arthur L. Olivas, Museum of New Mexico Photo Archives, supplied many of the plates. Rowyn L. Evans of Tucson, Arizona, assisted with maps. I very much appreciate the insights provided by reviewers for this book: Patrick H, Beckett, Rick Hendricks, and Charles W. Polzer, S.J.

Ornithologist Charmion R. McKusick advised me on various aspects of macaw and parrot trade into the Southwest as well as the religious implications of such trade. I also appreciate the generous help of Superintendent Duane Alire and his staff at Pecos National Historical Park. I wish to thank my colleagues, Jay (Courtway) Jones of Las Vegas and Virgil Wyaco of Zuni Pueblo, for their critiques of work on early historic Zuni, and Nancy Brown of the Center for Southwestern Research, Zimmerman Library, Albuquerque, for help with archival sources.

I greatly benefited from discussions with my wife, Brent Locke Riley, and my daughter, Victoria Riley Evans, both experts on various aspects of Southwestern archaeology and history. As always, any errors and misinterpretations in the book are my sole responsibility.

CHAPTER ONE

Spain at the Flood

Spain's entry as a world power can reasonably be said to date from 1492, the year that the Muslims of southern Spain were finally defeated and, more important, that Columbus sailed to the New World. Of course, there was, technically speaking, no single political entity called "Spain" in 1492. Instead there were two more or less independent states, Aragón and Castile, united in the persons of their rulers, a married couple, Ferdinand and Isabella. Ferdinand (Fernando), the king of Aragón, also ruled Catalonia and Valencia on the east coast of Spain, while Isabella (Isabel), queen of Castile was the ruler of León, Asturias, and Galicia. Navarre, too, was to be incorporated into the Crown of Castile in 1515. The Islamic Kingdom of Granada, ruled by Abu Abd-Allah Muhammad (Boabdil), eleventh sultan of the Nasrid dynasty, surrendered to Ferdinand and Isabella in January 1492 ending almost eight hundred years of Islamic political power in Spain.

Under Ferdinand and Isabella's grandson, Charles I of Spain (Charles V of the Holy Roman Empire), the peninsula was largely united; only Portugal in the west—for the time being—maintained its independence. Greater Castile was the dominant partner from the beginning. With three times the area of Aragón in A.D. 1500 (225,000 square miles compared to 60,000) and more than six times the population (six and a half million to one million people), Castile was a dynamic warlike state honed by the long struggle with the Moors—austere, narrowly religious, and parochial.

Under Charles and, to a lesser degree, his son Philip II (the latter reigning from 1556 till his death in 1598), the Spanish Empire continued to grow. Portugal, along with its own large overseas domain, was added in 1580. At the time of his death Philip II ruled over all of South and much of North America, and indeed claimed both continents. His period in power had been marked by considerable military success including a major naval victory at Lepanto over the

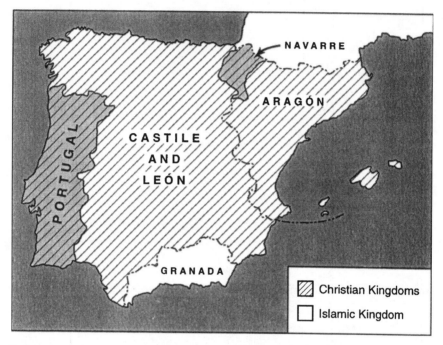

Spain, ca. 1490

Turks in 1571. Against this was the continuing rebellion of the Netherlands, whose navy was beginning to challenge Spanish control of the northern European seas. England also became a competitor with considerable naval success including destruction of the Spanish Armada in 1588. A rebellion in southern Spain by the Moorish inhabitants that began in 1567 was put down only after several years of bloody fighting.

The discovery and colonization of the New World was one—perhaps the foremost—of the seminal events in human history, and in a very short time changed the entire face of the globe. The two hemispheres had developed in relative isolation for millions of years, each producing specialized animal and plant forms. Human beings moved into the New World through a corridor by way of east Asia and Alaska very late in time, near the end of the last great period of earth glaciation, or ice age. Native American populations spread rapidly through North and South America and fitted themselves into a number of environments. From all evidence at hand it would seem that agriculture and animal husbandry were invented separately in the Eurasia-Africa continents and in the Americas. New World plant and animal domesticates were quite different in species (with a few exceptions) from those of the Old World. In isolation, a number of the agricultural societies of the Americas developed high cultures with cities, metallurgy, complex social organization, and in a few places written records. Other Indian societies remained hunters and gatherers, living much the same life as had their forefathers over the millennia.

The idea of sailing westward from Europe to find new lands or a shorter way to the great eastern polities of China and Japan was not at all new. An understanding that the earth was spherical was hardly an invention of Columbus; sophisticated people had believed it from the days of Pythagoras in the sixth century B.C. The real question was the circumference of the Earth. A number of estimates had been made; one by Eratosthenes of Cyrene in the third century B.C. was reasonably near the correct figure of about 25,000 miles. Columbus, however, accepted a smaller measure of the Earth's circumference, probably the one being promoted by the fifteenth-century Florentine cosmographer Paolo Toscanelli, which in turn drew from the maps of the second-century A.D. astronomer and geographer Ptolemy. Columbus believed that Asia extended farther eastward than was actually the case, and he also had his East Asian latitudes confused. In fact, he reached the edges of the New World at about the place he expected to find Japan.

Columbus was to a large degree a medieval man. He seems to have believed in the geographic correctness of the Judeo-Christian Bible even when it violated the canons of common sense. For example, Columbus took quite literally a statement in the Second Book of Esdras, which he read from the Vulgate. This passage, Columbus believed, proved that the earth was mainly dry land, so that the western ocean must be narrow: "On the third day You commanded the waters to be gathered together in the seventh part of the earth, but six parts You dried up" (2 Esd. 6:42).

There had been other explorations westward and southward before Columbus. For centuries the Europeans had listened to folk tales of lands off to the west. A group of seven Portuguese bishops fleeing the Moors in the eighth century were supposed to have founded seven cities in some new land to the west, a durable legend that—transplanted to northern New Spain—had considerable impact on the early exploration of the Southwest. Large islands, one called Antilia and another St. Brandan or Brendan (after a sixth-century Irish saint), appeared on certain maps in the fifteenth century. By that time Antilia was becoming fused with the older Seven Cities tale.

As opposed to these problematic lands, real islands were discovered by exploring parties from Spain and Portugal. But even earlier, the Canary Islands were contacted by Arab navigators in the twelfth century and may have been rediscovered in 1312 by a Genoese ship. Both Spain and Portugal claimed the Canaries, but they were ceded to Spain in 1477. At the time of Columbus a war of conquest with the native Guanches was still underway. By 1492 Spanish control of the islands was sufficient for them to be a base from which Columbus launched his voyage to the New World.

Two other sets of islands were taken over by the Portuguese in the fifteenth century. The uninhabited Madeira Islands, north of the Canary group, were colonized by Portugal sometime in the 1420s. Between 1431 and 1439 Portugal discovered and explored the Azores to the north and west of the Madeira Islands and some thousand miles directly west of southern Portugal. In 1443 serious colonization of these islands began. An attempt was made by Ferñaó Dulmo in 1486 to sail westward from the Azores, but because of adverse winds and currents, Dulmo failed to reach the North American coast. It is possible, however, that unrecorded voyages from the Azores and/or trips by fishing vessels from Bristol in western England reached the Newfoundland Banks or the coast of Newfoundland itself before Columbus's first voyage. It should be stressed, though, that the major Portuguese effort for a half-century or more had been sailing south and east, around Africa, with the idea of eventually reaching India and Indonesia. In this they were spectacularly successful, rounding the Cape of Good Hope and reaching the Indian coast in 1497–98.

In any case, the Vikings had touched the coast of North America five centuries before Dulmo and Columbus. In the year A.D. 1001, a Viking explorer named Leif Ericsson, sailing from Greenland, even attempted a settlement at L'Anse aux Meadows on the northern tip of Newfoundland, overlooking the eastern entrance to the Strait of Belle Isle. The site was visited by Leif's brother, Thorvald, perhaps in 1003, and Thorvald spent two winters there. In 1009, an Icelandic ship's captain named Thorfinn Karlsevni, having married Leif's widowed sister-in-law, shipped out from Greenland with both men and women to attempt a permanent colony at L'Anse aux Meadows. The expedition failed, and probably by 1012 the would-be colonists had returned to Greenland. A final attempt in 1014 to settle at Leif's old site failed miserably, partly due to infighting among the settlers. One footnote to history was a boy named Snorri who became perhaps the first European child born in the New World.

But the Viking attempts were bound to fail. They were launched from Greenland, whose peripheral position and lack of basic materials, including timber for ships, made it an unlikely seed bed for colonization. Indeed, the Greenland colonies themselves had failed and been deserted or destroyed by Columbus's time. A concerted colonizing effort launched from Norway or Denmark might possibly have succeeded, but the mainland countries were uninterested.

Christopher Columbus reached what became known as the Antilles, or West Indies, in the fall of 1492. Though he made three additional voyages over the next twelve years and explored parts of coastal South and Central America, Columbus seems to have gone to his death with the stubborn belief that he had explored the continent and islands of Asia. But even before he died in 1506, events had passed Columbus by. The Spaniards had exhausted the placer gold deposits and destroyed the native population on the main islands of the West Indies and were probing at various points on the mainland.

A Portuguese voyage headed around Africa had touched on Brazil in A.D. 1500, but Portugal's claim to that part of South America was based on the 1493 "donation" by Pope Alexander VI dividing the western Atlantic lands between Spain and Portugal in such a way that present-day eastern Brazil fell into the Portuguese sphere of influence. Although neither nation had any real idea what they were sharing, the division was codified in the Treaty of Tordesillas the following year. Portuguese expeditions in 1501–2 and again in 1503 under Gonçalo Coelho also carried a Florentine explorer named Americus Vespucci who reported the voyages. Coelho and Vespucci explored the Brazilian coast and contacted the Tupian-speaking natives of the area. Because of his skillful publicizing of these and other voyages, Americus Vespucci became very well known to mapmakers in Europe. One major result was that the name *America* was given to the new western lands.

Spanish exploration of the New World was very rapid. In 1513 Vasco Núñez de Balboa led a party to the Pacific shore of Panama. The mainland of Mexico was invaded by Hernán Cortés in 1519, and over the next two decades Mexico and Central America were largely overrun by Spanish arms. The viceroyalty of New Spain was set up in 1529 but was not fully functioning until 1535. In the early decades it included much of Mexico and Central America, the Antilles, and after their conquest (1565–71), the Philippine Islands.

Meanwhile Spaniards from the Panama settlements were planning exploration and conquest to the south. In 1532 Francisco Pizarro led an expedition against the Inca Empire, and within a few years his soldiers controlled most of the central Andes. In the thirty years that followed Pizarro, the Spaniards operating from Peru established control over Columbia and northern and central Chile. Venezuela was colonized in the 1560s, and colonies were founded in Argentina, Uruguay, and Paraguay well before the end of the century. Sailing from Spain in 1519, Ferdinand Magellan in 1520 discovered a way around the southern tip of South America, through the straits that bear his name. He then sailed on to the Philippines, where he was killed in an attack on a native chiefdom. One of his ships, however, managed to continue across southern Asia and

Sebastian Münster's map of the New World, Basel, 1540 (from facsimile in author's possession)

around Africa, reaching Spain in 1522—the first known circumnavigation of the world.

The great and mysterious Amazon River, whose mouth had been entered in A.D. 1500 by the Spanish explorer Vicente Yañez Pinzón, was explored throughout much of its length by Francisco de Orellana in 1541 and by Lope de Aguirre in 1561. Eastern Brazil was considered to be Portuguese, and settlers spread along the coast. Portugal and her empire merged with Spain in 1580.

Spain made several thrusts into what is now northern Mexico and the United States. There was an attempt to settle Florida by Ponce de León in 1521. An ambitious expedition by Pánfilo de Narváez, launched from Cuba in 1528, ended in disaster. Another, even larger expedition led by Hernando de Soto entered Florida in 1539 and explored the southeastern and part of the central United

States until 1543, when battered remnants of the expedition managed to reach Pánuco on the east coast of Mexico.

Probing into the lower Southwest began as early as 1533, and a major expedition to the upper Southwest and to the western Plains under Francisco Vázquez de Coronado took place from 1540 to 1542. The Greater Southwest was not brought under firm Spanish control, however, until the seventeenth century. (The sixteenth-century Spanish exploration of the Southwest shall be discussed in chapter 3.) A sea expedition in 1542–43 explored the West Coast as far as Oregon, but no settlements were made.

After 1580 the Spaniards considered all the New World to be theirs. This was not really a practical point of view, however, for the east coasts of present-day United States and Canada had received very early attention from both English and French explorers. John Cabot had rediscovered Newfoundland for the Europeans in 1497, reaching landfall probably only a few miles from L'Anse aux Meadows, the ill-fated settlement made by the Viking Leif Ericsson. This was likely an accidental conjunction since Cabot, who had probably never heard of the Viking voyages, was searching for a short northern route to Asia and the spice trade.

John Cabot was lost with his ships in a second attempt to find Asia in 1498. The English and Portuguese made a few more attempts in the next two or three decades to exploit the area. The Portuguese actually established a colony on Cape Breton Island sometime in the early 1520s, but it was deserted after a year or so. By that time fishermen from Brittany and England had discovered the Newfoundland Banks with their riches in cod. The French established a claim with voyages by Jacques Cartier in the 1530s. Returning to the St. Lawrence area in the autumn of 1541, Cartier established the town of Charlesbourg-Royal on the Cap Rouge River, which joins the St. Lawrence a few miles upstream from modern Quebec. However, reinforcements carried by Jean-François de La Roque, Sieur de Roberval, the nominal commander of the expedition, failed to appear, and Cartier deserted the town in June 1542, about the time Coronado was on the march home from the Southwest, and the remnants of the de Soto expedition were floundering their way through the Mississippi Valley. When Cartier met up with Roberval in Newfoundland, he declined to have anything further to do with the colony and returned home to France. Roberval then established his own town, France-Roy, near the deserted Charlesbourg-Royal, but this settlement, like its predecessor, lasted only a year.

In fact, no permanent colonies were established despite various attempts until the first decade of the seventeenth century, when the French at Port Royal (1604), now Annapolis Royal, and Quebec (1608) as well as the English at

Jamestown (1607) managed to put down settlements. It is interesting that Quebec, Jamestown, and Santa Fe, soon to be capital of the province of New Mexico, were founded within a year or two of each other. A second group of English towns in what became New England date from the 1620s, as does the Dutch settlement of New Amsterdam (later New York), the latter near the site of a failed 1615 fort and storehouse.

The Spanish domination of the New World was not only political and military but also religious. In no other colonizing power of the period did the religious organizations, intent on missionizing the native peoples, have as much power as in Spanish America. The English settlements were largely secular, as in Virginia, or were formed by religious refugees fleeing the control of the English official church, as in New England and, a few decades later, Pennsylvania, founded by William Penn's Quakers. The Dutch settlements along the Hudson were essentially stations for the fur trade. In all cases, attempts to missionize the native population were sporadic and halfhearted. Treatment of the Native Americans by both English and Dutch colonists (with the exception of certain remarkable individuals such as William Penn of Pennsylvania and Roger Williams of Rhode Island) was marked from the beginning with cruelty and double-dealing. Only in the French-controlled lands, where the Jesuit order was powerfully deployed, was there a more or less consistent and relatively benign Indian policy. Even the French colonies, however, did not have the close state and church partnership in exploration and settlement that developed during the sixteenth and seventeenth centuries in Spanish America. With it came a humane (though very paternalistic) attitude toward and treatment of the Native Americans, more so than exhibited by any other European colonial power.

Part of Spain's success in the sixteenth century lay in the makeup of Spanish society at the time of Columbus. The wars with the Moorish population of Spain were coming to an end, and Castile and Aragón had large numbers of footloose fighting men. The New World offered a young, militarily trained, and tough generation new military adventures and the chance of fame and fortune abroad. It also shored up the Spanish economy by exporting large numbers of idle soldiers to take part in entrepreneurial operations in the Americas. The Spaniards who took part in the early conquests in the New World had, in many cases, already been involved in a holy war against the Islamic Moors. During the first incredible century, Spanish armies were usually inspired by two driving forces: the search for wealth, especially gold, and the belief that Spaniards were part of a great crusade, doing God's work in heathen America. In Spain itself, this crusading spirit had a sinister side. At the instigation of the clergy, but apparently with strong public approval, Castile and Aragón launched a period of "purification" aimed at the non-Christian elements (Jews and Muslims) both on the Iberian Peninsula and overseas. Granada, the last Moorish stronghold, fell in 1492, and within a short time the program of mass, forced conversion to Christianity was underway. Those refusing conversion were killed or forced to flee the country.

The Spaniards' belief that they were on a divine crusade in the New World was certainly encouraged by the religious orders and by the Crown, which financed and backed these orders in their search for souls. Only in the first chaotic two decades in the New World was there little or no influence by the missionaries. Certain expeditions of a slightly later period—especially ones like those of Cortés and Pizarro, before the viceregal system was firmly in place—were relatively little influenced by the missionaries, but as the century wore on this became less and less the case.

The Franciscans were the first of the religious groups in the New World, at least on an organized and regular basis. There was a Franciscan on Columbus's second voyage, and twelve friars sailed with Ovando for Santo Domingo in 1502 with instructions to give the native Taino instructions in Christian doctrine. They do not seem to have had much effect on either Spanish or Indian behavior. The twelve Franciscans who reached Mexico after Cortés's conquest had greater success. They arrived in central Mexico in 1524 and were quickly involved in educating Aztec and Tlaxcalan youths, especially young noblemen. The missionaries soon began to learn Nahuatl, the major language of the region. These first Franciscans had considerable political clout; one of them, Pedro de Gante, was a kinsman of King Charles. Their missionizing work was made even easier when three years later a Franciscan bishop, Juan de Zumárraga, was sent to Mexico City. Hostile Spanish bureaucrats tended to act as a counterbalance to the missionaries until the arrival of first viceroy, Antonio de Mendoza, in 1535. Mendoza was an enthusiastic protector of Indian rights, and he and Zumárraga worked hand in hand. There were also Franciscans on the Pizarro expedition and with Coronado in the Southwest. In fact, the period from about 1530 to mid-century was a kind of golden age for the Franciscans. Their millenarian beliefs—that conversion of the New World people would hasten the Second Coming of Christ—led to a feeling of divine mission accompanied by frenetic efforts to fulfill that mission. It did pay an unexpected dividend. The Franciscan study of native languages and collecting of aboriginal histories and customs were to be of inestimable value to later anthropologists and historians; however, the early Franciscan agenda, especially the use of native languages to promote Christianity, fell out of favor in the latter years of the sixteenth century.

The Franciscans were the earliest workers in the Southwest and were given the province of New Mexico for their mission activities. They were in the region as early as 1539 and took part in a number of the sixteenth-century expeditions to the Southwest. In the seventeenth century, the main focus of this book, they dominated the religious life of the upper Southwest. The Sonoran region, however, was assigned to the Jesuits (see below). (For a further discussion of the Franciscan order and its development in the Southwest, see chapter 8.)

The second group of missionaries to reach the Americas was the Dominican order, whose first members arrived in Santo Domingo in 1510. They were instrumental in offering some protection to the remnants of the Taino groups, and the greatest of them all was Bartolomé de Las Casas, who joined the order in 1523 and became a compelling and powerful voice for protection of Native Americans everywhere.

The last major missionary group to come to the Western Hemisphere was the Society of Jesus, or order of Jesuits, founded in A.D. 1540. The Jesuits first reached the New World in 1549. By the latter part of the sixteenth century, they were operating in several areas, including the northwest of New Spain, where they continued to be a powerful missionizing force until the removal of Jesuits from the Americas in the mid-eighteenth century. As mentioned above, the Jesuit order was also the missionary group that functioned in French North America.

By the last decade of the sixteenth century the tide of Spanish affairs was definitely on the wane. It is often said that the Spanish golden age of empire ended with the death of Philip II in 1598. This date, coinciding with the beginning of colonization of New Mexico, is a useful marker. However, it must be pointed out that a general decline of the Spanish Empire—caused in part by continuing adventurism in Europe and overseas, ruthless religious repression, and a destructive economic policy at home—was already well advanced by the end of Philip's reign. The gold and especially silver from the American mines helped fuel an inflation that affected all of Europe. Prices in Spain in A.D. 1600 were four times what they were in A.D. 1500.

Parenthetically, the Spanish literary Siglo de Oro, or Golden Century, is generally considered to start in the mid-sixteenth and run to the mid-seventeenth century. Though brilliant in literature, this was also a period when both Spain's economy and her political fortunes were flowing downhill, slowly at first but then in a precipitous and disastrous torrent. The unstable coalition of Spain and Portugal broke apart in 1640; that same year Catalonia revolted and, with French help, remained outside the Spanish orbit for twelve years. The long de facto independence of the northern Netherlands was formally ceded by Spain in 1648.

A part of Spain's decline in the seventeenth century had its roots far back in the reconquista, that period of several centuries when the states of Christian Spain were gradually reclaiming the peninsula from the Muslims. At first the struggle centered on the *meseta* country of central Spain. At one time heavily agricultural, the back-and-forth surges of armies increasingly discouraged the maintenance of agricultural villages. More and more, people turned to herding in order to have a certain mobility of capital. Over time a powerful organization of sheep owners called the *Mesta* grew up, often able to dictate even to the state. The result, by the end of the reconquista, was the entrenchment of herding, especially in Castile, to the detriment of grain agriculture and to the environment generally. In southern Spain another but equally devastating trend took place after the fall of Seville and the rich Andalusian region in A.D. 1248. Hundreds of thousands of Muslims, perhaps the most skilled farmers in Europe at that time, were driven out. The land was quickly made into large estates (latifundia), ceded to important members of the Spanish nobility and to the Church. Agricultural production fell rapidly and remained low. At the same time as this destruction of agricultural potential by latifundia, Spanish cities were becoming static. The middle class of merchants, professions such as law and medicine, the building trades, and various kinds of manufacturing had drawn heavily on Jewish and Muslim elements. Many of these were now forcibly converted or driven out. Even though large numbers of both groups became converts, they were the object of constant suspicion and harassment by Church and Crown. Even in the vibrant sixteenth century these basic economic weaknesses could barely be glossed over. In the seventeenth century they rendered Spain increasingly feeble, especially in international affairs. Long before Turkey, Spain was the "sick man of Europe."

Though no longer a bona fide world power, Spain managed to stabilize her national life and policy in the eighteenth century; however, in the early nineteenth century most of the American colonies were lost to independence movements. Spain tenaciously clung to Cuba and Puerto Rico until the Spanish-American War of 1898. After a period of experiment with democracy, a regressive movement in the late 1930s—led by a brutal military *caudillo*, Francisco Franco, backed by elements in the Church, with active support of Nazi Germany and Fascist Italy, and tacit help from England—attempted to turn back the clock and re-create an earlier Spain. This had the incidental effect of alienating many of the Latin American nations, especially the ones tending to democracy. The Franco experiment collapsed in the 1970s, and in the post-Franco era, Spain, now a full economic and cultural partner within Europe, has redeveloped strong cultural and economic ties with her former colonies.

CHAPTER TWO

The Native Americans

The Southwest was occupied as part of that earliest migra-
tion out of northeast Asia near the end of the *Pleistocene,* or Ice Age. At that time
the climate of the Southwest was wetter than now with many lakes and large
rivers. The first *Paleo-Indians* to become, indisputably, an element in the
Southwestern landscape were people of the *Clovis* archaeological tradition who
probably reached the region about 11,500 years ago. There is increasing evidence
to suggest earlier settlements, but the Clovis Paleo-Indians with their fluted
stone points used to hunt the great Pleistocene elephants are fully documented.
Clovis sites are found over much of the Greater Southwest and extend beyond it
in every direction. Clovis peoples had a technology probably based on the
spear-thrower, sometimes called by its Aztec name, *atlatl.* The atlatl is a flattened
two-foot billet of wood, bone, or ivory, tapered at one end to form a hand grip,
with a notch at the other end into which is fitted the butt end of a short spear.
The spear is then cast with a rounded motion of the arm, sending the missile farther and faster than could be done with the arm alone. Clovis spears were often
tipped with a chipped stone point that was fluted; that is, a flake was removed
on either side of the point along its long axis. Fluting is a characteristic American
method of chipping and may have served to make the wound bleed more freely.

Clovis was replaced by a series of more topographically restricted cultures, the
best known of which is *Folsom,* whose hallmark was another type of fluted point.
By Folsom times, the various elephants (mammoth and mastodon) had largely
disappeared from the Southwest, and Folsom hunters concentrated on the large
Pleistocene bison. After Folsom came other hunting traditions, but the climate
was growing warmer and drier. By about 6000 B.C. it was becoming very difficult
to depend on big game hunting. Slowly, the Paleo-Indians adapted to this more
difficult climate, concentrating on a strategy of gathering wild plants and hunting
small and mid-sized game. This new era of human endeavor is called the *Archaic*

in the Americas. It is roughly equivalent in technology and economic strategy and overlaps to a certain degree in time with the group of post-Pleistocene societies sometimes called the *Mesolithic* in Europe and the Mediterranean region. The Southwestern Archaic involved very small family groups who wandered over the desiccated landscape searching for fruits, berries, roots, or grass seeds in season and hunting rabbits and other animals.

Several Archaic traditions eventually established themselves in what later became the Pueblo Southwest. In the Rio Grande Valley they included the *Oshara,* a largely indigenous development in the upper valley, while to the west was the *Cochise* and to the south a tradition called the *Chihuahuan,* both of which extended into the Rio Grande Valley south of Oshara. People of these various Archaic traditions had a tool kit somewhat like that of the Paleo-Indians: they used the atlatl and a variety of chopping and grinding tools. They lived in caves and rock shelters or had huts of jacal (interlaced poles and branches daubed with mud) or, perhaps, skin tents of some sort. Life in general was hard, and populations rose very slowly over the millennia.

About 2000 B.C., at a time when the climate was slowly ameliorating from the "long drought" of the previous several thousand years, a new and revolutionary idea began to penetrate the Southwest from the more advanced societies of Mexico to the south. This was the concept of plant domestication, which had begun some two thousand to three thousand years before in southeastern Mexico. The plants that spread into the Southwest were descendants of these early domesticates, a rather primitive form of maize (*Zea mays*), squash (*Cucurbita pepo* and *C. moschata*), and the bottle gourd (*Lagenaria siceraria),* the latter plant dried and used as a container. Two other plants of very great importance spread out of Mexico later, reaching the Southwest in the early post-Christian centuries: bean (*Phaseolus vulgaris*) and cotton (*Gossypium hopi*).

Maize and squash had become well-known food crops in various parts of the Southwest by the last centuries B.C., and beans and cotton by the early A.D. centuries. They demanded new skills and a considerable amount of time devoted to planting, weeding, guarding, and harvesting the crops. The importance of agriculture, once it took firm hold in the Southwest, was enormous; however, there continued to be gathering and hunting. For the latter, another invention, the bow and arrow, gradually spread across the Southwest, reaching the Basketmaker-Pueblo areas in the early A.D. centuries.

The term *Basketmaker-Pueblo,* or *Anasazi* (for the latter name, see below), refers to the peoples in the upper Southwest, descendants of the Oshara Archaic, who gradually developed their very distinctive culture in the period from around A.D. 300 to 400 and were the ancestors of the historic and modern Pueblo Native

Americans. Appearing in the same general time frame as the Anasazi were three other major cultural traditions that developed primarily from the Cochise Archaic. By the early A.D. centuries these traditions were established, and in one way or another they all affected the Anasazi. Farthest west were the *Patayan* peoples of the lower Colorado River. In southern Arizona lived the desert farmers known as the *Hohokam* who irrigated the basins of the Salt and Gila Rivers to raise their crops. In the mountain region of the modern New Mexico–Arizona border were other groups of Indians called *Mogollon,* and Mogollon-like villagers also extended eastward to the Rio Grande and deep into western Mexico. All these traditions had agriculture, and they all developed pottery, though the Patayan perhaps not until the latter part of the first millennium A.D. It was from the Mogollon area that simple red and brown hand-molded ceramics spread to the Anasazi. These latter people quickly began utilizing different clay sources and producing what became the typical late Anasazi black-on-white pottery. At about the time the Anasazi Indians began making pottery, they also began cultivating protein-rich beans that had made their way northward. Mogollon peoples and ideas were to strongly influence the western Anasazi region; in earliest historic times the Pueblo people of Zuni and Hopi were an amalgam of Mogollon and Anasazi.

Basketmaker-Pueblo began when groups of Archaic peoples who lived in caves and rock shelters turned agriculturist, growing maize and squash, and made sophisticated basketry. They inhabited both the Rio Grande and the San Juan river basins. These early farmers lacked pottery, the bow and arrow, and certain agricultural crops (beans and probably cotton). Their name comes from the well-made baskets used for food storage, transport, and probably to a limited degree, cooking. Around the time these Basketmaker II groups adopted pottery, beans, and probably the bow and arrow from Mogollon Indians farther south, they also began to build a relatively sophisticated type of structure called a pithouse. The idea for this structure, called a pithouse because a portion of it is excavated into the earth, probably also came from the Mogollon. Such cultural innovations led—by the period A.D. 500–700—to a new synthesis that we call Basketmaker III.

By the way, there is no Basketmaker I. When the term was first coined in the early part of the twentieth century, archaeologists felt that there should be an earlier, more primitive culture from which the Basketmaker II people derived. We can now say that Basketmaker I is late Oshara Archaic.

The alternate name, Anasazi, was suggested by A. V. Kidder in 1936 because the term Basketmaker-Pueblo was somewhat cumbersome. Kidder employed the name for the entire Basketmaker-Pueblo sequence beginning with Basketmaker

II and extending through Pueblo V (fig. 2). This is the way many archaeologists still use the term, though, personally, I prefer to call Anasazi only that period from Basketmaker III to the beginnings of historic times. It seems to me that Basketmaker III—with its new cultural inventory of pithouses, pottery, bow and arrow, and the incorporation of beans into the agriculture—represented a major cultural break. Of course, this was an ongoing process, and such things as pithouses and an early brown pottery actually begin in Basketmaker II times; still, the complex as a whole characterizes Basketmaker III. At the other end of the sequence, Pueblo V was the period of Spanish intrusion into the Southwest, with its accompanying drastic changes in the Pueblo world.

The word *Anasazi* is Navajo, and Kidder thought that it meant "Old People." Actually, *Anasazi* is a composite word meaning something like "non-Navajo ancestors," rather a contradiction in terms if used by a Navajo speaker. In any case, the name is now well embedded; in fact, it has entered the popular literature in the Southwest in a rather unfortunate way. A great deal is often made in magazine articles and especially on television about the "mysterious Anasazi" who disappeared from the Southwest, leaving only massive ruined towns. In reality, the direct descendants of the Anasazi, the Pueblo Indians of New Mexico and Arizona, are very much with us today.

Basketmaker III and the early Pueblo period were marked by a large expansion of population in various parts of the San Juan Valley. The Rio Grande, which became a major heartland of the Anasazi from about A.D. 1300 on, seems to have had only a small population in the early Anasazi centuries. As time went on, the Basketmaker experiment led to new building forms: aboveground structures, usually a series of contiguous houses made by setting stone blocks in mud mortar. These are referred to as *pueblos,* the Spanish word for "village" or "town." In certain areas the pithouse type of construction maintained itself for some centuries after the appearance of pueblos.

The early Pueblo period (what is sometimes called *Developmental Pueblo* in the Rio Grande Valley; see fig. 2) saw a gradual expansion in population, particularly in the region north of the San Juan River in southwestern Colorado and southeastern Utah. This area was, by Pueblo II times, heavily peopled. The turkey had joined the dog as an animal domesticate probably as early as Basketmaker III times, and a new food plant, cotton (its oil-rich seeds were eaten), had been established. Weaving of cotton was also presumably early, though a true loom may not have appeared until Pueblo III times. Fibers of yucca and, to some degree, apocynum (alternatively called black hemp or dogbane) also were woven. The black-on-white painted pottery became technically more advanced and artistically more sophisticated as time went on.

	PECOS CLASSIFCATION	ROBERTS CLASSIFICATION	RIO GRANDE CLASSIFICATION	
2000				2000
1800	Pueblo V	Historic Pueblo	Historic	1800
1600				1600
	Pueblo IV	Regressive Pueblo	Classic or Golden Age	
1400				1400
1200	Pueblo III	Great Pueblo	Coalition	1200
1000	Pueblo II	Developmental Pueblo		1000
800	Pueblo I		Developmental	800
600	Basketmaker III	Modified Basketmaker		600
400				400
200	Basketmaker II	Basketmaker	Basketmaker II?	200
AD BC				AD BC
200			Late Oshara	200

Classificatory schemes for the Southwest from Basketmaker to historic times

While still living in pithouses, the ancestors of the Pueblo Indians seemed to have used their dwellings for certain religious ceremonies. In Pueblo times the pithouse kind of structure was retained, often as a special ceremonial chamber within the pueblo courtyards or room blocks. This ceremonial house, found today in all pueblos, is generally referred to by its Hopi Pueblo term of *kiva*. In the earthen floors of pithouses were small holes rimmed with clay. These continued to be used in the kivas and, at least in historic and modern times, represented the opening to the underworld from which human beings emerged to populate the earth. The modern kivas are used for a variety of ceremonies central to Pueblo Indian religion. Presumably this was true in prehistoric times; at least the prehistoric kivas have many of the same structural features seen today.

Out of an early Pueblo base a brilliant development of Pueblo III Indian culture began around A.D. 1000 in the high, rather barren Chaco Canyon south of the San Juan River in northwest New Mexico. A century or so later the populous Pueblo II towns of the region north of the San Juan grew into the extensive Pueblo III settlements of which Mesa Verde is perhaps the best example but which stretched along the San Juan and its northern tributaries—the Mancos,

McElmo, and Montezuma Rivers—across southwest Colorado into southeastern Utah.

The Classic period in Chaco Canyon, called the *Bonito phase,* saw the rise of large pueblos several stories in height and including hundreds of rooms. Though they were built of stone and adobe like earlier pueblos, there was a certain sophistication in the stone structures. Over time there developed banded wall exteriors made with different sized stones. The core and veneer technique, possibly Mesoamerican in nature, allowed the massive lower walls at Chaco to support upper stories also built with stone and mud masonry. A new type of kiva, perhaps developing from a Basketmaker prototype in the Chaco area, was the *Great Kiva.* Such structures were huge, circular excavated areas, six to eight feet deep, the largest being almost eighty feet across. These enormous kivas were roofed by four massive timbers or by columns of alternating stone and wood resting on massive sandstone disks. They may have been used by large groups such as moieties, the two ceremonial units of the pueblo. There are also smaller kivas in the Chaco area, possibly clan or society kivas.

The large Chaco towns were connected in all directions by a series of roadways. Major roads are some thirty feet wide, and the road system stretched to the San Juan River on the north, to the Puerco drainage to the east, to the San José to the south, and to Coyote Wash (north of Gallup) to the west. Chacoan outliers reach well beyond the road system, being found as far north as Colorado and westward to the upper Little Colorado drainage. One important outlier was the Village of the Great Kivas in the Zuni region.

There was considerable trade reaching the Chaco towns. An important trade item was turquoise, some of it from the Cerrillos region south of modern Santa Fe, New Mexico, and some perhaps from other parts of the Southwest. Some trade was from more-distant places. There was shell from the Gulf of California and from the Pacific coast of California, copper bells from western Mexico, and the technique of pseudo-cloisonné (lacquering the surface of pottery or, in the case of Chaco, sandstone). The most dramatic of the imports was the scarlet macaw (*Ara macao*). This brightly feathered bird has been in great demand from at least Chaco times to the present day, the feathers being used in ceremonial dress and in ritual offerings. The macaws seem to have been traded from the jungles of eastern Mexico, and some came as immature birds to be caged and raised to adulthood by the Chaco people. It seems likely that turquoise was traded in return; stockpiles of turquoise representing some hundreds of thousands of pieces have been found at Chaco.

The upper part of the San Juan Basin had large and well-built stone and mud pueblos and a considerable level of technology. In the upper Rio Grande Valley there was a slow growth, though this area remained somewhat of a backwater through the Pueblo III period. About the time that the great pueblos of the Chaco region were beginning to fade, there was some quickening in the Rio Grande Valley, and populations became somewhat larger in what is called the *Coalition period.* In the lower portion of the upper Rio Grande, the Early and Late Elmendorf Indians, probably ancestral to the historic Piro, built fairly large masonry pueblos, some of them on fortified sites.

During the eleventh century, people from the region north of the San Juan River, the *McElmo phase* groups, moved into Chaco, where they seem to have intermixed with the Bonito peoples. For reasons not entirely clear, but probably including drought and overuse of scarce resources, the Chaco towns were in a state of decline after about A.D. 1100, and the dominant Bonito phase was largely gone by mid-century. Some of the McElmo phase peoples may have continued on to A.D. 1200 or later.

As mentioned above, the region along and north of the San Juan, the Four Corners, had a flourishing Pueblo III culture at Mesa Verde and in the McElmo and Montezuma Valleys and the Hovenweep region. This area did not share in the widespread Mesoamerican trade but was still prosperous. The Mesa Verde people maintained themselves for more than a century after Chaco, not deserting their cliff dwellings until around A.D. 1300. During the latter part of the thirteenth century, people were moving out of the San Juan. Some migrated to the west, but the major population probably settled in the upper Rio Grande Basin (see discussion below). Why this happened is not clear, though a drought period of more than two decades was likely one factor. Again, overuse of the land and stripping of forest cover, especially in the highlands of Mesa Verde, were surely other reasons for desertion.

The Hopi country also saw dramatic changes during the thirteenth century. At the beginning of that century there were small Pueblo III settlements on Black Mesa and in the region both to the north and to the south. The people made traditional Anasazi black-on-white pottery and had small round kivas. Though distinctive in some ways, the culture was basically related to the San Juan region to the north and east. By around A.D. 1300 there had been a drastic consolidation, with only eleven large pueblos remaining. These Pueblo IV towns, ancestral to the historic Hopi, were built around central plazas containing rectangular kivas, usually oriented to the northwest. The pottery quickly evolved into a series of brilliant orange- and yellow-based bichromes and then polychromes. One reason for the fine pottery was the utilization of seams of rather poor grade, but perfectly serviceable, coal that can be found along the southern edge of Black Mesa in the region of the Hopi mesas. This coal, which was employed for cooking and heating, was also introduced for firing pottery early in Pueblo IV times.

Generally speaking, the Pueblo IV peoples of southern Black Mesa seem to represent a mixture of cultural influences combining a basic Anasazi with an influx from the Mogollon region to the south, something that many archaeologists call *Western Pueblo*. The same thing was true of Zuni. The earlier period saw an intrusion of Chacoan culture with its large structures and Great Kivas onto an Anasazi-Mogollon base. After about A.D. 1300, however, even stronger influences from the Mogollon entered the Zuni region, bringing square kivas, a southern ceramic tradition, and the idea of cremation burial. By the early 1300s there were at least fifteen stone pueblos in the upper and middle Zuni River region.

It seems likely that in the Hopi region the Hopi language, a member of the *Shoshonean* branch of the Uto-Aztecan language family, was already established by A.D. 1300. Indeed, this language may have been spoken well before that time. It is also probable that the Zuni language was being used by at least the fourteenth century. Zuni may have been spoken in the area of the Zuni River from early, possibly Archaic, times. Alternatively, it may have been a part of the Mogollon intrusion in the late thirteenth or early fourteenth century. Zuni is a language isolate, related to other Southwestern languages only on a very distant level. Recent studies suggest that it is a member of a group called *Penutian*, which has a generally western distribution

In a previous book I suggested that the language of the Chaco region, going back into Archaic times, was *Keresan*, another rather isolated tongue but one with a more eastern series of relationships. Keresan languages spread to the Rio Grande Basin sometime in late prehistory. It also seems to me that the San Juan region and the Rio Grande had speakers of *Tanoan* languages, another of the Uto-Aztecan subgroups, dating back at least to late Archaic times. In the historic period, Tanoan languages were spread all along the upper and middle Rio Grande. (For further discussion of Southwestern languages, see chapter 3.)

Another factor that led to great changes in the Southwest—and probably indicated by the spread of the *kachina* cult, discussed below—was the rise of a series of large and small settlements in what is now Chihuahua and in extreme southwestern New Mexico. The best-known of these was the extensive center of Casas Grandes in modern west-central Chihuahua. The Casas Grandes towns rose partly from Mogollon roots but with dramatic influences from western Mexico, appearing within a matter of a few years around A.D. 1200 and creating a new Mesoamerican-Southwestern synthesis. This "Casas Grandes Interaction Sphere" influenced the last phase of the Jornada Mogollon of southern New Mexico and western Texas and, at further remove, the Pueblo world as well.

The area that gained the most Pueblo population in Pueblo IV times was the Rio Grande. The rise in population brought large pueblos, some with two thousand or even three thousand rooms. Most of these continued to be built of stone and mud mortar, but beginning in the twelfth century a second tradition emerged, likely from the Jornada Mogollon region to the south, of using coursed adobe in building houses—a building technique that also penetrated the Casas Grandes area and marked the Classic period of the Hohokam. This period in the Pueblo region has been called its golden age because of its vigor and growth, especially in the Rio Grande Basin, but also at Zuni and Hopi.

The food eaten in the Pueblo IV period was about the same as that available to the Pueblos for centuries. The premier crops were maize, the brown bean, and varieties of squash. By this time cotton was probably mainly used in weaving, but the eating of cotton seeds—with their rich oil content—was an ancient practice. The bottle gourd was used primarily as a container. These plants represented the basic agricultural component of Southwestern life. Although corn was paramount in the diet, wild foods were collected and eaten, including the chenopod goosefoot, whose seeds were ground and treated somewhat like maize in cooking. Purslane and clammy-weed likely were eaten, as were piñon nuts, wild chiles, and wild sunflower seed. The people also used medicinal plants including ephedra (Mormon tea) and the powerful hallucinogen datura. Yucca fruit was also consumed, and threads from the plant itself were used in weaving, as were the strands of black hemp, or apocynum.

Two animals were domesticated, the dog and the turkey, the latter valuable for both feathers and food. The dog was probably used mainly as a hunting companion. Seasonally, the diet of the Pueblos had a considerable amount of animal protein. The bow had been in use since Basketmaker times, and the Indians hunted a variety of game animals including deer and antelope. Bison were also hunted by organized groups that went out onto the Plains, but bison products may have been mostly received in trade with Plains Indians, the Apache Querecho, and the Teya (see below). The Pueblos harvested rabbits, probably the most common wild animal food, by surrounding an area and killing the various cottontails and jackrabbits with clubs or digging sticks, a technique that went back at least to Archaic times.

In the earlier centuries there was a tradition of black-on-white pottery that had been considerably influenced by the San Juan area, especially in the twelfth and thirteenth centuries; however, new types of ceramics were beginning to appear. Originating in the White Mountains of Arizona, west and south of Zuni, a series of red wares and then polychrome or multicolored wares spread eastward. One of these, St. Johns Polychrome (black and white on a red base) was widely copied well before A.D. 1300. Certain White Mountain wares began to be treated with metallic paste which, when fired, made a glaze over portions of the vessel's surface. Glazes were popular at Zuni and by around A.D. 1300 had begun their diffusion eastward into the Rio Grande Valley, where they continued well into the Spanish colonial period. At Hopi, the magnificent Jeddito pottery, bichrome and polychrome on a yellow base, began to be made around the same time.

The catastrophe(s) that forced the desertion of the San Juan Valley and other parts of the Southwest in the twelfth and thirteenth centuries led to new social, political, and religious ideas. Pressures of rising populations and the new large towns created a need for novel ways to integrate the pueblos and groups of pueblos. New modalities that crosscut the old kin-based structures began to appear around A.D. 1300. War, hunt, and medicine societies may have developed at this time, and the *kachina cult* certainly did.

Kachinas are masked figures that represent ancestors and which also bring rain. The modern name *kachina* (in Spanish orthography, *katsina* or *catzina*) itself is somewhat of a mystery. Scholars have generally considered it to have been Hopi and to have spread from Hopi to the more eastern Pueblos. However, *kachina* clearly seems to be a loan word into the Hopi language. As Charles Adams points out, there is no initial syllable *ka* in Hopi. Colorful kachina ceremonies, likely with the name attached, spread into the Pueblo area, quite probably from the Casas Grandes region, sometime around A.D. 1300. The word *kachina* as well as aspects of the ceremonies were extensively documented by the seventeenth-century Spanish missionaries. These Franciscans primarily identified kachina dances among the Rio Grande groups, and the actual term may have appeared among the eastern Pueblos before being picked up at Hopi. Kachinas are basically Mesoamerican in nature, representing Tlaloc, a widespread and ancient deity of Mexico. Even such esoteric aspects of the cult as the sacrifice of children to produce rain has an echo in Pueblo mythology. The cult bonded pueblos and groups of related pueblos, and it was found everywhere in the Pueblo area. Today, the kachinas are more important in the Western Pueblo world of Hopi and Zuni than they are in the east, but this is because in the seventeenth century there was a powerful and sustained attempt by the Franciscans to wipe out "diabolical" masked dances, the centerpieces of the kachina cult. The drive against the cult was more successful in the heartland of Spanish control, the Rio Grande Valley, than among the more isolated western Pueblos.

The changes in the Southwest that took place around A.D. 1300 were so drastic that it might be best to use new names. The Hohokam Classic period collapsed at about this time. A century or so earlier, southern and eastern portions of the Mogollon had become part of a larger Casas Grandes–dominated region.

In the Pueblo world, a name other than Anasazi or even Pueblo IV, with its idea of simple continuity, might better be used for this post-1300 period. Perhaps a distinctive term should be introduced. One possibility would be to extend the term *Classic Pueblo,* used primarily for the Rio Grande, to all the old Anasazi region. This does, however, lead to a certain confusion since so many Southwestern and Mesoamerican cultures have their "classic" periods. I suggest the phrase *Protohistoric Pueblo* or, in a wider context, the *Protohistoric Southwest.* The term *Protohistoric* is already rather widely used, though different scholars give different beginning and ending dates for it. It may stretch the chronology a bit to think of the fourteenth century as being protohistoric, but in fact a major wave of Mexican influence began a few decades after A.D. 1300 and continued unabated until it merged with the massive intrusion of the Spaniards. This Protohistoric period can be said to end with the Pueblo Revolt, the last attempt to assert political and cultural "Pueblo-ness."

To go back to the older chronology, the Pueblo IV period or, as it is sometimes called, the Golden Age in the Rio Grande was a rich mixture of San Juan and southern (Mogollon or Mogollon-derived) traits. The San Juan–type round kivas were found as well as the southern and western square kivas. A great deal of the iconography, especially that relating to the kachina cult, came from Mesoamerica. For example, a complex relating to the twin war-gods—with deer-sun and rabbit-moon associations, and fish to human transformations that are found as far south and east as Yucatán and Guatemala—now appears in the Southwest.

Some of these religious features came up a series of trails that also brought trade items to the Southwest. One of these originated at Casas Grandes and flourished from around A.D. 1200 for two and a half centuries. A major prehistoric road may have run northeast from the Casas Grandes Valley into the lower Río Carmén near present-day Villa Ahumada, then directly north to the Rio Grande near modern El Paso. However, the Casas Grandes trade was gradually taken over by a series of small entities in northeast Sonora that I have elsewhere called "statelets." These began operating around A.D. 1300 and were still functioning at the time of Coronado in 1540. They traded Gulf of California shell and coral, parrots and macaws and their brightly colored plumage, and copper objects into the Southwest while receiving Southwestern turquoise, bison products (trans-shipped from the Great Plains), garnets, peridots, and other semi-jewel stones, probably salt, and possibly slaves into the Sonoran region. Another series of trade routes ran from the Pacific Coast via the Lower Colorado Patayan (Yuman) population, bringing Pacific and Gulf shell to exchange for turquoise, cloth, and other goods. Still other trails ran eastward from the Pueblo area for exchanging shell, coral, turquoise, pottery, maize, and beans for bison products, bois d'arc (Osage orange wood) used for bow making, and the translucent schist fibrolite for axes. Additional trade routes may have run from eastern coastal Mexico, the Huasteca, though these have yet to be worked out. In that regard, it might be pointed out that the nearest source of the scarlet macaw, the most desired of all the bright feathered birds, is the lower Huasteca.

Other peoples were interacting with the Pueblo world during this golden age. The *Querechos,* met by Coronado in the sixteenth century in what is now northeast New Mexico and the upper Texas Panhandle, were Apachean-speaking groups who had probably moved into those regions sometime around A.D. 1300. They traded with the Pueblo world but also raided when feasible. A bit farther south were the *Teya,* on the Llano Estacado, who were also in a trade-raid relationship with the eastern Pueblos for at least a century before Coronado. These Indians seem to have spoken a language related to that of the Tompiro, a group of Tanoan-speaking Pueblos out in the area of salt lakes east of the Manzano Mountains. The relationships of the Querechos and Teyas with both Pueblo Indians and Spaniards lasted throughout the seventeenth century.

CHAPTER THREE

A Clash of Cultures

By the early sixteenth century the population of the Pueblo world was something on the order of sixty thousand Indians. Of those, some ten thousand to twelve thousand lived in the western pueblos of Cíbola and Hopi, probably a total of twelve towns. These Native Americans were distributed in four major linguistic groups. The furthest west, the Hopi of present-day northeastern Arizona, were and are Shoshonean-speaking, their language related to other Shoshonean groups in the Basin and Plateau regions of western America: the Utes, Paiutes, and Comanches. They are related at a more distant level to the Tepimans (Pima, Papago, and Tepehuan), the Taracahitans (Tarahumar, Opata, Yaqui, and Mayo among others) and even more distantly to such people as the Aztecs of Mexico. The large language family to which all these groups belong is called *Uto-Aztecan.* On an even wider level, according to the recent language classification of Joseph Greenberg, the Hopi belong to the Central branch of the great Amerind stock of languages.

In chapter 2, I mentioned that the Zuni spoke a language of the Penutian family. Greenberg considers Penutian to be part of the Northern branch of Amerind. Another language group, also originally considered an isolate, is that of Keresan, spoken in the sixteenth century by Acoma Pueblos on the San José River, a tributary of the Puerco, and by Zia and other Pueblos on the Jemez River. A second branch of Keresan was and is utilized by Pueblos along the main Rio Grande, including Santa Ana, Santo Domingo, and Cochiti. Greenberg believes that Keresan is related to Iroquoian, Siouan, Yuchi, and Caddoan in a Keresiouan stock and, like Zuni, a part of the Northern branch of Amerind.

The Tanoan speakers were contained in several branches in the sixteenth century. In the north were the Northern Tiwa speakers of Taos and Picurís. Along the Chama River, the main Rio Grande south of the Chama mouth, the mountain fringe in the Santa Fe River basin, and to the south in the upper waters of

Galisteo Wash were speakers of Tewa-Tano. To the south was the great Southern Tiwa-speaking province of Tiguex, on the main Rio Grande from about the junction of the Jemez River south to around Abó Wash, roughly the line of modern U.S. Highway 60. Tiguex was flanked by Towa-speaking Jemez and Pecos. To the south and east were speakers of Piro, a Tanoan language probably most related to Tiwa. Piro speakers extended in a line of villages down the Rio Grande south of Tiguex to about Milligan's Gulch near modern San Marcial. South of them were villages of the Manso, descendants of the Jornada Mogollon, whose language affiliation is uncertain but was perhaps Tanoan.

The Tompiro, whose language was a dialect of Piro, lived in the region east of the Manzano Mountains, today called the Salinas country. To the north of them, along the eastern slopes of the Sandia Mountains, were villages of Southern Tiwa, related to—but apparently not part of—the polity of Tiguex. The Tanoan and their linguistic kinsmen, the Kiowa, were distantly linked to Uto-Aztecan and were also members of Central Amerind.

The Querechos and Teya, mentioned in chapter 2, were both nomadic groups with rather complex relationships with the Pueblos. The Querechos were probably ancestral to all the later eastern and western Apaches as well as Navajo, but in the sixteenth century these may not have been totally differentiated. The Teya, who later in the sixteenth century were called the Jumano, seem to have been closely related linguistically to the Tompiro and had a series of trading relationships with them. Teya Indians also had trading interaction with the Patarabueye at La Junta and with the Suma and Manso who lived along the Rio Grande, upstream from the mouth of the Conchos River.

Information—at least significant information—about the Spaniards probably did not reach the Pueblo world until after the conquest of Mexico by the Spanish captain Hernán Cortés in 1521. This conqueror moved quickly to consolidate his control over central Mexico, reaching the west coast of Colima by 1522. Two years later one of his captains pushed northward from Colima to what is now southern Sinaloa. In 1530 another Spaniard, Nuño Beltrán de Guzmán, began an expansion along that coast, reaching as far north as Culiacán in central Sinaloa. Guzmán was partly motivated by stories he had heard of a gold-rich area to the north. One of his kinsmen, Diego de Guzmán, raided northward to the lower Yaqui River in 1533 searching for slaves.

By that time, news of the Spaniards was trickling up the trade routes and had probably reached the Pueblo area, though likely in a somewhat garbled form. That the Spaniards were powerful was obvious; that they were also vulnerable became known in 1532. In that year a ship sent northward by Cortés to explore the west coast of Mexico was wrecked, probably somewhere around the mouth

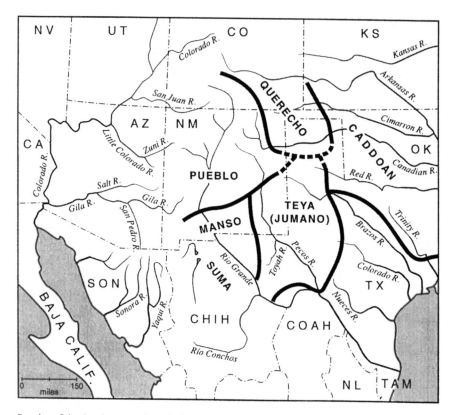

Peoples of the Southwest and High Plains found by early Spanish explorers

of the Sinaloa River. The crew reached the Fuerte River region, where they were killed by local Indians. Iron and other objects from the ship quickly entered the trade network and were spreading north and south when Guzmán arrived the following year.

A more dramatic series of contacts came in the years 1535–36 with the Cabeza de Vaca party. Alvar Núñez Cabeza de Vaca was treasurer in the expedition of Pánfilo de Narváez. This brutal and wildly incompetent commander had been sent to explore and conquer Florida, a vaguely known area that included the modern state and much territory beyond. Leaving Havana in 1528, Narváez floundered around northern Florida, committing a number of atrocities but finding little treasure. After sending his supporting ships back to the Cuban home base, he and his party built boats crafted from the skins of the expedition horses and coasted along the shore, hoping to reach the Spanish settlement of

Pánuco. The misadvised and misdirected expedition actually reached a point west of the Mississippi Delta before a storm blew Narváez away, leaving his men strewn dead or barely alive along the Louisiana-Texas coast.

The hundred or so survivors gradually dwindled from hardships, hunger, and Indian hostility until eventually only four remained: Cabeza de Vaca himself; two other Spaniards, Andrés de Dorantes and Alonso de Castillo Maldonado; and a black slave, Esteban, belonging to Dorantes. Of the four, Cabeza de Vaca was the clear leader and Esteban the most skilled traveler. Esteban was adept at languages and became the interpreter and general contact man for the group.

In 1535, these four men were in a region that sounds very much like La Junta de los Ríos, where the Rio Grande and Conchos Rivers meet. There they encountered an agricultural people and also a group that hunted bison. The latter, who were in all probability the Teya, told them of people farther upstream, most likely the Rio Grande Pueblos: "They informed us also that, all the way while we traveled upriver, we should pass among a people who were their enemies but who spoke their tongue and, though they had nothing to give us to eat, would receive us with the best of good will and present us with mantles of cotton, hides, and other articles of their wealth. However, they advised against going by this road."

If Cabeza de Vaca and his companions were, in fact, among the Teya, it seems that the people "who spoke their tongue" were Piro or possibly Manso. The Spaniards recorded some ethnographic information about their hosts, including a succinct account of stone-boiling, a technique used on the western Plains.

> Uncertain of what was best to do and of which trail to take we remained for two days with those Indians [at La Junta de los Ríos] who give us beans and squash to eat. Their method of cooking is so new that for its very strangeness I want to describe it. Thus it may be seen how curious and various are the uses and ingenuity of human beings. Those people have never obtained pottery, so in order to cook what they want to eat, they fill half a large calabash with water and toss on the fire many stones of a convenient type to absorb the heat. When the stones are hot they take them up with wooden tongs and drop them into the calabash until the water boils from the heat carried by the stones. Then they put in whatever they want cooked and continue taking out cooled stones and throwing in hot ones until it is cooked. In this way they boil their food.

Finally the Cabeza de Vaca party decided to push on westward, though their actual route is a matter of much disagreement. One scenario has the four men following the Rio Grande in a northwestern direction into the Mesilla Valley and then cutting westward across what is now southern New Mexico and

Arizona, finally going south to reach the Sonora River valley. Another possibility is that they traversed the desert westward, crossing the Carmén, Santa María, and Casas Grandes Rivers before finally reaching the Sierra Madre Occidental, perhaps in the Janos region. This route would in all probability have followed an ancient trade route running from Casas Grandes, but one likely deserted for a century. Proponents of this route are divided on whether the party went up the Rio Grande for a time and then swung off westward or whether they left the Rio Grande at La Junta.

One way Cabeza de Vaca clearly did not go: "Two days being spent [at La Junta de los Ríos] while we waited we decided to go in search of the corn. We did not want to continue along the trail leading to the bison for it was to the north and would lead us in a great loop since we were sure that going toward the sunset we would find what we desired." This "trail leading to the bison" (Camino de las Vacas) was the major trail used by Teya going from La Junta by way of Toyah Creek to the Pecos River, and then up the Pecos to the eastern Llano Estacado, where they lived, and the Tompiro Pueblos, where they traded and may also have resided part-time. Coronado, six years later, found the Teya in the Llano Estacado and heard stories about Cabeza de Vaca. In the 1580s, Espejo was to utilize Jumano (Teya) guides to travel over the Camino de las Vacas going south. In the sixteenth century Spanish lexicon, the term *vaca* [cow] was also used for bison.

Whatever the route, Cabeza de Vaca and his companions arrived in the region of the Sonora River, near the Ures Gorge, in the spring of 1536. There they were welcomed at a town they called Corazones (Hearts), the natives presenting them with six hundred dried deer hearts. This seems a rather curious offering, but the deer was and is a sacred animal throughout northern Mesoamerica and the Southwest. The real name of the settlement is unknown.

The little Spanish party also found evidence of a flourishing trade with peoples to the north who lived in large apartment-like houses several stories high and who traded turquoise and other semiprecious stones for bright-colored feathers of macaws and parrots. Cabeza de Vaca was on a major trade route running from western coastal Mexico to the Pueblo Southwest. He was in the region of the Sonoran statelets: small polities, each consisting of a primate town and associated villages along given stretches of the Sonora and Yaqui Rivers and some of their tributaries. The statelets were relatively sophisticated entities, organized especially for trade and warfare. They seemed to have welcomed Cabeza de Vaca and his companions, perhaps considering them traders who had lost their way or their goods. Although the inhabitants of most of the statelets spoke dialects of the Opata language, Corazones seems to have been a Pima-speaking area. Going farther south, Cabeza de Vaca was guided by Pima speakers, and a number of them remained in west Mexico for several years, learning Spanish and becoming guides for the expeditions of 1539–42.

Cabeza de Vaca and his companions reached Mexico about the time that news of Pizarro's conquest of the gold-rich Inca Empire of western South America was spreading to Mexico. The possibility that the Pueblo area might also be rich in gold stimulated the new viceroy, Antonio de Mendoza, to plan an expedition into the unknown north. He was further motivated when he found that one of Pizarro's captains, Hernando de Soto, was in the process of launching his own expedition, entering the new lands at Florida with the intention of marching westward. After two years in the planning and organizing stage, de Soto's expedition left Cuba in the spring of 1539 and spent the next several years exploring the southeastern region of the present-day United States. After de Soto's death in 1542, his lieutenant, Luis de Moscoso, reached as far west as the Trinity River area of east Texas. This expedition was, however, a disaster, and more than half of its soldiers failed to return.

Of course, Mendoza did not know this when in the spring of 1539 he sent the first probing party into the Southwest. The party was led by a Franciscan friar named Marcos de Niza who had been with Pizarro in Peru and could be expected to know gold if and when he saw it. With Marcos was the black slave from the Cabeza de Vaca party, Esteban de Dorantes, and a number of Indians including some from central Mexico and Piman speakers who had come south with Cabeza de Vaca and now wished to return home. A second friar started the journey but soon dropped out due to illness.

Marcos's route north in 1539 has been much disputed, but I think that he stayed close to the coast, crossing the lower sections of the various rivers. On reaching the Sonora River in west-central Sonora, Marcos stayed on a northward course though the coastline veered off to the northwest. Eventually he arrived at a place called Vacapa, which I believe was in the Altar or Magdalena Valley, probably near the confluence of the two rivers. Here he sent Esteban on northward with some of the Indians. In a few days word came back from Esteban that the party was traveling toward the "Seven Cities of Cíbola."

Esteban eventually did arrive at some Zuni town, assumed by earlier scholars to be Hawikuh but which probably was K'iakima, and for reasons still unclear was killed there. Possibly he was mistaken for a witch and/or a spy for the Europeans. Stories told in Zuni the following year do seem to indicate that the Zuni people already had heard stories of Europeans and were very mistrustful of them.

Marcos, at any case, went on to Zuni, observing from a distance the town outside of which Esteban had been killed. He then retreated to Mexico, taking time on his return to make a short trip up the Sonora Valley in the direction of the Ures Basin. He reported gold in that area, and, indeed, some was found by Coronado's men, the only gold discovered by the Coronado expedition.

Viceroy Mendoza was intrigued by the report of Marcos, and the expedition plan went forward. In November of 1539, he sent a reconnaissance party northward commanded by Melchior Díaz, a pioneer of the border country and mayor of the newly founded settlement of Culiacán. With fifteen horsemen, Díaz penetrated the region of Sonora and reached as far as a large ruined town the Spaniards called *Chichilticalli,* a term that means "Red House" in the Nahuatl language of the Aztecs. The exact location of this site is unknown, but it seems to have been one of the large Salado ruins somewhere south of the Gila River. He returned in time to be with the Coronado vanguard the following spring.

Meanwhile, the viceroy had appointed a young protege named Francisco Vázquez de Coronado, already governor of the far west province of Nueva Galicia, to lead an expedition to the north. Coronado launched his expedition from near modern Tepic with a force of around 350 Spanish soldiers, 1,200 to 1,300 native allies (Aztecs, Tlaxcalans, Tarascans, and probably Otomí and other groups), a large number of horses, burros, sheep, and probably cattle. Pigs were also purchased for the trip, but whether taken as salted pork or on the hoof is unknown. At Culiacán in April 1540, Coronado divided his forces, moving on northward with perhaps 200 to 300 men, with the main party following at a slower pace.

In the period 1540–42, Coronado made an extraordinary number of discoveries. He explored the northeast Sonoran valleys, especially the statelet area of Corazones and Señora, and parts of the Gila drainage in Arizona and New Mexico. One of his parties reached the Hopi mesas, and another penetrated as far west as the Grand Canyon. Coronado's men explored the Rio Grande as far north as Taos and perhaps as far south as modern Hatch. His army ventured onto the Great Plains and reached the Llano Estacado, where the army camped for a time in Blanco Canyon just north and east of present-day Lubbock. With a small party, searching for the supposedly gold-rich region called Quivira, he journeyed north and eastward to the Arkansas River in modern central Kansas. The sea wing of the expedition, under Hernán de Alarçón, explored the lower Colorado River to the mouth of the Gila.

Though it led to new geographic knowledge, the Coronado expedition was basically a failure. The Spaniards created enemies at various of the Rio Grande pueblos, in the Sonoran area, at Hopi, and at Pecos. Tiguex, the large Tiwa-speaking confederation on the Rio Grande, was badly mauled in a war that raged for the first three months of 1541. Coronado's way station at Corazones in the Sonora Valley was wiped out with considerable loss of Spanish lives. And, with the exception of some deposits in the Sonora Valley, no gold was found. Following a fall from his horse, resulting in a severe head injury, Coronado decided to retreat from the Southwest. In the spring of 1542, he returned to Mexico. Left behind were a number of disaffected central and west Mexican Indians and a Franciscan lay brother, Luis de Ubeda, who dreamed of converting the native southwesterners. With Fray Luis was a herd of sheep, presumably to teach the Pueblo Indians animal husbandry. One of the priests on the expedition, Juan de Padilla, insisted on returning to Kansas, where he believed that Quivira was on the edge of that fabled kingdom of Antilia founded by the Portuguese a thousand years before. Padilla was killed in Kansas, but certain other members of his party escaped back to Mexico.

The Mexican Indians settled in the Southwest and may have introduced a number of Mesoamerican traits to the area. Ubeda, however, seems to have been killed, as likely were his sheep. No new animal domestication came out of the Coronado expedition, although certain new plants, cantaloupes and watermelons, may have entered the Southwest during this period.

Coronado had approached the Southwest from the west coast of Mexico. As late as the time of Francisco de Ibarra in the early 1560s there were attempts to explore in that direction. Ibarra, who became governor of the new province of Nueva Vizcaya, crossed the central Sierra Madre Occidental in the Topia region and then worked his way north along the coast, exploring the Sonoran statelets and fighting a fierce battle with the people of Señora in the middle Sonora Valley. He then recrossed the Sierra into what is now Chihuahua, being the first European to view the great ruins of Casas Grandes, which had been deserted for a century or more but whose crumbling adobe walls were still an impressive sight. Ibarra returned to the Sonoran valleys and eventually moved back down the coast.

By this time, however, the Spaniards were well on their way to an advance up the intermontane interior of Mexico. Lured there by great silver strikes in Zacatecas beginning in 1546, the newcomers quickly moved into the modern Durango, where both silver and rich riverine grasslands for cattle ranches were to be found. Indé in northern Durango was settled by a lieutenant of Ibarra's named Rodrigo del Río in 1567, and that same year saw the colonization of the rich silver mining region of Santa Bárbara on the Río Florido, a tributary of the Conchos. Two years later the population of Santa Bárbara was enlarged by Tlaxcalan tribesmen, and around 1570 the Franciscans moved into the area establishing a center at San Bartolomé, the modern Allende.

Silver mining was labor intensive, and Indians were needed to work the mines. Slave raiding into the still largely unknown north became common despite attempts by officials in Mexico City and Spain to control it. In the process of this slave raiding, the Spaniards rediscovered the Rio Grande, probably first at La Junta where the Conchos and Rio Grande join. During the 1570s it became ever more clear to the Spaniards that they were on the edge of the great area explored by Coronado.

It was only a matter of time before exploring parties would penetrate the southwestern mystery once more. Even though Coronado had discovered no precious metals, rumor continued to have it that such riches existed in the Southwest. There was also the matter of the Coronado friar Luis de Ubeda, who had remained to missionize the Pueblo region. The Franciscans were eager to find out what had happened to Ubeda. Had he succeeded in producing a Christian Pueblo world? If so, there must be numbers of converted Indians badly in need of priests.

In 1542–43 Spain had made a serious attempt to control abuses to the native populations of the Americas with a series of sweeping "New Laws." These had been only partly successful, and the Crown in 1573 promulgated a second series of colonization reforms. These forbade "conquests" and set down rules for the peaceful contact and missionization of the Indians. No new area would be settled without a specific license from the king, and the missionaries and their agendas were to be favored over those of the civilian colonizers. It was under the aegis of the 1573 laws that later exploration of the upper Southwest was carried out.

The first persons to receive permission for a southwestern expedition were Fray Agustín Rodríguez and Captain Francisco Sánchez Chamuscado, who headed a small party leaving Santa Bárbara in June 1581. There were two other friars, Francisco López and Juan de Santa María. With them were nine soldiers and nineteen servants plus some six hundred head of stock and ninety horses. In spite of the pious intentions of the Franciscans, it was also to be an explorative outing with an eye to finding new mines.

The party made its way down the Conchos to La Junta, where the Spaniards met the sedentary Patarabueyes and probably also the nomadic Jumanos, a group who wintered at La Junta and spent the more clement months hunting bison on the southwestern Plains. These Jumano, clearly, were the same people called Teya by the Coronado expedition.

There can be little doubt that the Jumano were in trading contact with the eastern Pueblos, especially the Salinas group, the Galisteo pueblos, and probably Pecos. That the Patarabueyes also had Pueblo contacts is indicated by a later statement of Juan de Oñate. According to the Oñate contract to colonize New Mexico, written in 1595, only fourteen years after Chamuscado left for the Southwest: "They must give me the Indians that are to be found in this City of

Mexico of the nation [Patarabueyes], for they are the nearest to that province, and in particular an Indian woman who was brought from New Mexico, so that they may serve as interpreters on this expedition." The Patarabueye-Pueblo connection seems to have been a common assumption among the Spaniards. I shall discuss the Indian woman from New Mexico in chapter 4. Despite the proximity in the wording, she likely was not connected to the Patarabueyes.

The Chamuscado expedition worked its way northward along the north side of the Rio Grande from La Junta to what is now southern New Mexico. In fact, it was Chamuscado who gave the name San Felipe de Nuevo México to that section of the Rio Grande and, by extension, to the entire upper Southwest. The San Felipe portion of the name, possibly introduced in honor of Philip II of Spain as well as the saint, quickly dropped out, and the area became known simply as Nuevo (or Nueva) México. The first Piro town, also named San Felipe by the Spaniards, was on the west side of the Rio Grande south of Milligan's Gulch. It was in ruins, but as the party went on upstream, they found occupied settlements from which the Piro had fled at sight of the Spaniards. I have suggested that there may have been unrecorded Spanish slave raids into the area, perhaps in the early 1570s, which caused the Piro Indians to react with fear to this small Spanish party.

Continuing north, the Chamuscado party reached the Tiguex country and in the next few months explored to the west as far as Zuni and to the east into the edge of Querecho country. In September 1581, one of the friars, Juan de Santa María, decided for reasons unknown to return to Santa Bárbara. Leaving from Tunque Pueblo east of the Rio Grande, he attempted to make his way south along the eastern slopes of the Sandia and Manzano Mountains and was killed by hostile Pueblo Indians. In spite of this example of Pueblo unfriendliness, the two other friars, Agustín Rodríguez and Francisco López, decided to remain at Puaray in Tiguex country. This pueblo was most likely the Tiguex town of Arenal, burned and sacked by the Coronado expedition around the beginning of the year 1541. Chamuscado's two friars were killed a few days after the Spaniards began their march southward. Chamuscado also died on the way home.

Concern about the two missionaries left at Tiguex and a continuing desire to find rich mines in New Mexico led to the launching of another expedition in November 1582. This was led by Antonio de Espejo with fourteen soldiers and a number of servants plus one Franciscan missionary, Bernardino Beltrán. This group again followed the Conchos to its juncture with the Rio Grande and then went up the latter river to Piro country. Reaching the Tiguex towns, it found Puaray (called Puala by the Espejo chroniclers) deserted. The Espejo expedition explored widely even though dissension in the ranks led to desertion by the friar and about half the party. The little group reached Zuni and Hopi and then westward into the Verde Valley region of central Arizona. Returning, they had a brief but violent battle with a group of Querechos camped in the Acoma area. Reaching the Rio Grande, they found that about thirty of the Puala inhabitants had moved back into the pueblo. Espejo's men massacred these people and burned the pueblo. The expedition then departed the Southwest via the Pecos River valley, eventually reaching La Junta. Espejo, led by a Jumano guide, contacted Teya-Jumano somewhere in the middle Pecos drainage.

Expeditions to the Pueblo world were now coming at an accelerated rate. Beginning in July 1590, there was an unauthorized expedition from the new Spanish settlements in Nuevo León, headed by Gaspar Castaño de Sosa, the lieutenant governor of that province. Castaño led a party of some 160 to 170 settlers, including women and children, from Almadén (present Monclova) to the Southwest. There were ten or more carts or wagons, the first wheeled transport into the region. The Castaño expedition angled north and west, crossing the Rio Grande somewhere around modern Del Rio then traveling northwest to the Pecos River, perhaps in the present-day Sheffield area. Following the Pecos upstream, Castaño eventually arrived in the vicinity of Pecos Pueblo in late December 1590. Leaving his main party and the wagons somewhere around the junction of the Gallinas and Pecos Rivers, he pushed on with some forty men to Pecos, attacking the pueblo and occupying part of it on December 31, 1590. The Indians maintained themselves in certain of the house blocks for two or three days, but on the night of January 2, 1591, they fled to the mountains, leaving Castaño in charge.

From Pecos, Castaño de Sosa led his advance guard into the Rio Grande Valley. He explored portions of the Tewa and Keresan region, appointing officers at various pueblos. He hardly visited the Tiguex area, and the Piro not at all. Santo Domingo (actually so named by Castaño) in the Keresan region was chosen as a center of government. In late January he returned to the main camp, bringing those who had been camping on the Pecos back to the Rio Grande. Castaño presumably intended to settle New Mexico, to allot the native population in *encomienda* (grants of Indian tribute), and set up a government.

Castaño's ambitions came crashing down when Juan de Morlete arrived in mid-March 1591 to arrest him and to return the expedition to New Spain. Morlete led the two groups, including the wagons, down the Rio Grande to around modern El Paso and then apparently on to La Junta and up the Conchos. Because of the wagons, his expedition may have been forced to traverse the Jornada del Muerto, if so, making it the first Spanish party to go by that route.

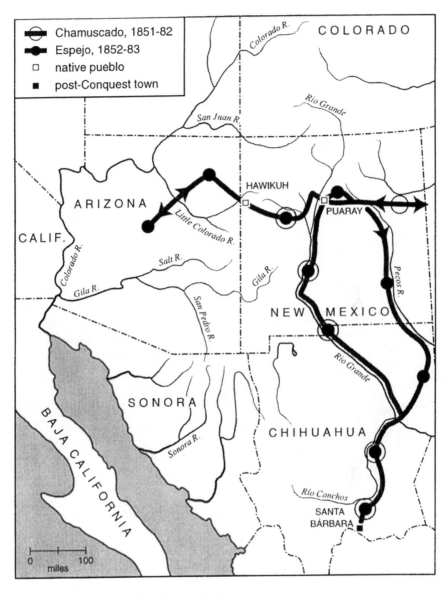

Spanish exploration in the Southwest, 1581–83

The Spanish government was now beginning to consider a long-term colonization plan for the Southwest. As early as 1568, Juan de Troyano of the Coronado expedition, who had brought home a Pueblo girl and married her, pleaded for a chance to take part in a new expedition to the north. In 1583, King Philip II of Spain issued a call for a wealthy settler who would undertake the settlement of the new area. Several individuals responded, including Cristóbal Martín, Antonio de Espejo, and Francisco Díaz de Vargas. In 1589, a well-to-do citizen of Nueva Galicia named Juan Bautista de Lomas y Colmenares actually had his proposal approved by the viceroy. Like the earlier proposals, however, it eventually died of neglect in the Spanish royal court. Castaño's attempt to settle New Mexico in defiance of the government was quickly checked, but it indicated the rising interest in the Southwest on the part of Spanish frontier settlers.

While the various government officials in Spain and Mexico pondered the fate of the Pueblo world, at least one other clandestine expedition thrust itself into the Southwest. In 1593 the governor of Nueva Vizcaya, Rodrigo del Río de Losa, sent the entrepreneur Francisco Leyva de Bonilla from Santa Bárbara northward on a trip to punish Indians who had been raiding border ranches. Marching with Leyva was a small group of soldiers and a vice-commander (or perhaps co-commander) Antonio Gutiérrez de Humaña. The expedition unilaterally and illegally extended its field of operation to the Pueblos, spending about a year, mostly at San Ildefonso in Tewa country.

The party then departed to look for Quivira and reached perhaps as far as the Arkansas River, where there was a large Indian settlement. Humaña murdered Leyva in a quarrel, and the group seems to have been eventually dispersed by the Indians. At least nothing else was heard of it except for an Indian servant of Humaña named Jusepe, who fled after the murder and was held captive by the Apaches for a year before escaping "near a pueblo of the Pecos," perhaps a Pecos summer town. Jusepe was still in that area when Oñate arrived in 1598, as were Cristóbal and Tomás, two Indians from somewhere in northern New Spain who remained at Santo Domingo after the collapse of the Castaño expedition.

CHAPTER FOUR

Oñate

The struggle for the honor and profit of settling New Mexico was long and bitter. There was little doubt from the time of Castaño that sooner or later such an attempt would be made. The different players in this southwestern sweepstakes had various reasons for wanting a part in the colonization. Later in this chapter I talk about the geopolitical considerations of the Crown, based on faulty geography but nonetheless real to the Spaniards. The primary reason for settlement, however, was silver, the engine that drove the expeditions of the 1580s and 1590s. Rich strikes of this precious metal had been found in Nueva Vizcaya; why not in New Mexico? Also important was the now well-known fact that the Pueblo Indians consisted of large numbers of peoples living in compact towns. The possibilities of exploiting this economic source must have played an important role in Spanish planning. One way was through the encomienda, an institution introduced at the very beginning of the Spanish period in the New World through which individual Spaniards were given grants of the labor and tribute of specific Indian groups. Encomiendas, though frowned on more and more by the Spanish government, were still granted in such frontier areas as New Mexico. In that colony they were to last throughout the seventeenth century.

A third factor was that of available arable or grazing lands. The expeditions from Coronado on seem to have given a somewhat exaggerated view of the fertility of New Mexico, but it was a country well suited for the rough-wooled and hardy *churro* variety of sheep bred in the northern Mexican area. Cattle were somewhat less adaptable to the New Mexican landscape, but still they were imported, and *estancias,* or ranches, quickly grew up in the riverine areas. It was not until the nineteenth century, however, that the great cattle herds were introduced in that large region where the Great Plains and Southwest merge—and that involved U.S. citizens rather than Spaniards or Mexicans.

A fourth possible source of wealth was trade. Spaniards had been carrying on an active trade along the northern frontier for decades. They needed certain northern products, especially hides and other products from bison, antelope, and deer; slaves for the mines and ranches (though slaves may have seemed a chancy business in view of the recent colonization laws); and minerals and semi-precious stones.

In addition to those considerations, the Franciscans had in mind the conversion of large populations. They already had martyrs—three from the Chamuscado expedition alone. Forty years before Chamuscado, Father Juan de Padilla had been killed as a direct result of his southwestern trip, and probably Fray Luis de Ubeda as well. There was another reason why the Franciscans wished to go to the Southwest. The ecclesiastical province of New Mexico would surely resound to the missionaries' glory both in this world and the next. In this world it might lead to a Franciscan diocese.

The region of New Spain that had the most direct interest in colonization of New Mexico was the north, especially the province of Nueva Vizcaya (the new "Basque-land"). This had been formed out of the fuzzy northern boundaries of Nueva Galicia in 1562, and the governorship was given to Francisco de Ibarra, who spent four years (1562–66) exploring his new domain. Nueva Vizcaya included essentially what were later to be the states of Durango, Chihuahua, and for a time Sinaloa. Its capital, Durango, was located in the rich Guadiana Valley in the southern portion of the modern state of Durango. The town, which was often called Guadiana in the sixteenth and seventeenth centuries, was formally founded in 1563 apparently on or near a mission station established by the Franciscans a few years earlier. It quickly became a center for ranches that supplied agricultural goods and especially cattle and sheep products for the miners.

The Basques, whose homeland contributed the name Nueva Vizcaya, were an ethnic group living in the mountainous north of Spain and in southwestern France. They spoke, and still speak, an isolated language called Euskera, quite unlike the various Indo-European languages of historic and modern Europe. Indo-European, the family that includes most modern European languages, spread through the continent within the last three to four thousand years. The place of Basque in a classification of world languages is still unsure, but the Basque language represents a remnant tongue isolated in the rugged Pyrenees, possibly from Upper Paleolithic times. Some linguistic specialists even believe that Basque is related to Apache and Navajo languages, though of course on a very distant time level.

In any case, the Basques were important in the settlement of Nueva Vizcaya and surrounding regions of northern New Spain. Ibarra himself was Basque, as were such influential families as the Oñates, the Tolosas, the Urdiñolas and the Zaldívars. True to their mountain heritage, the great Basque families developed sheep ranching and mining interests in various parts of the north. They also entered politics; Ibarra, of course, was the first governor of Nueva Vizcaya, and Cristóbal Oñate served as acting governor of Nueva Galicia during Coronado's expedition to the Southwest in 1540–42. His son Juan would be the first governor of New Mexico.

As mentioned in chapter 3, interest in settling New Mexico went back to the 1560s, but it reached fever heat by the 1590s. It was not all mining and missionary zeal, for the Spanish Crown also had a geopolitical interest. Crown officials had just heard of an English settlement at a latitude near that of New Mexico and were fearful that the English might eventually flank New Spain to the north, or that they might intrude on Spanish territory.

With our sophisticated map knowledge of today, this seems ludicrous, but it was taken seriously by the Spaniards. The English colony, though hardly successful, was real enough. It was Sir Walter Raleigh's settlement on Roanoke Island off the North Carolina coast, where a town was attempted in 1585–87. Roanoke, near the thirty-sixth parallel, does lie directly east of the Santa Fe–Río Chama area. But despite the de Soto explorations of the eastern United States a half century before, the Spanish authorities seemed not fully to comprehend the region between North Carolina and New Mexico. Though on the same east-west parallel, these two places were nearly two thousand miles apart, separated by a wilderness of mountains, forests, rivers, swamps, plains, and desert. More to the point, the easy water passage that sixteenth-century Europeans thought connected the Atlantic and the Pacific Oceans simply did not exist. The contract made with Juan de Oñate contains a striking indication of Spanish ignorance of North American geography. Originally it allowed him, to bring two ships across the Atlantic to the province of New Mexico "to provision the land and exploit the mines." This section of the contract was later canceled, not because of its topographic unreality, but for legal reasons having to do with royal control of the Atlantic shipping.

It is not clear just when Oñate first decided to make a bid for the New Mexico honor, though it may have been soon after the royal announcement of 1583 (see chapter 3). But the initial struggle to obtain this northern prize seems to have been between Juan Lomas y Colmenares, who had powerful ranching interests in central Nueva Vizcaya, and a former lieutenant-governor from the eastern part of Nueva Vizcaya named Francisco de Urdiñola. In 1594 Urdiñola was asked by Viceroy Luis de Velasco to head a New Mexican colonizing expedition. This plan fell through when Urdiñola was accused of wife-murder, apparently through the machinations of Lomas y Colmenares. By the time Urdiñola had cleared his name, the settlement contract had already gone to Oñate.

This latter man was the first generation of the Oñate family born in the New World. His father, Cristóbal de Oñate, originally from the Basque area of northern Spain, had come to New Spain as a young man. Born around 1504–5, he sailed to New Spain in 1524 as assistant to Rodrigo de Albornoz, the newly appointed accountant of New Spain's royal treasury. Oñate prospered in the new colony, following the savage Nuño de Guzmán to the west coast and becoming part of the brutal pacification of that region in the early 1530s. Oñate survived Guzmán's disgrace and eventually became Francisco Vázquez de Coronado's lieutenant governor of the new province of Nueva Galicia. In 1549 or 1550 he married Catalina de Salazar y de la Cadena, the daughter of a former royal factor, Gonzalo de Salazar. It was a second marriage for Catalina, and a daughter by her first marriage gave birth to the Zaldívar nephews who were so important to Juan de Oñate in New Mexico. This was an extremely tangled kin relationship, for these two nephews also had as a grandmother the sister of Cristóbal de Oñate. Catalina was interesting in another way. Like many upper-class Spaniards of the time, Doña Catalina had a converted Jewish ancestor, in her specific case on the maternal grandmother's father's side.

The Oñate couple had seven children, including Juan de Oñate. Juan was born probably in 1550, though by one account it was as late as 1552, at Pánuco near the Spanish mining town of Zacatecas. Juan de Oñate spent part of his boyhood in the Zacatecas area and part in the capital of Mexico City. The Oñate family was extremely wealthy, not only from silver mining but from ranches and encomiendas. This was the time of the "Chichimec" wars, when various groups of the hunting-gathering and marginally agricultural peoples of northern Mexico were actively resisting Spanish intrusion into the interior north of Mexico. Juan de Oñate, from a very early age (ten years, according to his friend and later comrade of arms Gaspar Pérez de Villagrá), accompanied his father on expeditions against the Chichimecs. This intermittent warfare was to rage on for many years.

By the time he was in his twenties, Juan de Oñate was outfitting, financing, and leading excursions against the Chichimecs. Around 1574 he pioneered the opening of the silver mines of Charcas a hundred miles northeast of Zacatecas, this in territory claimed by the Guachichiles, a particularly warlike Chichimec group. In the late 1580s, Oñate married the daughter of his father's old companion and partner Juan de Tolosa. Juan's daughter, Isabel de Tolosa Cortés Moctezuma had an extraordinary ancestry. Her grandmother was Isabel de Moctezuma (born Tecuichpotzin), the only surviving legitimate child of the Aztec emperor Moctezuma II. Her grandfather was Hernán Cortés. In sixteenth-century Mexico,

Juan de Oñate's coat of arms (courtesy of the Museum of New Mexico, neg. no. 14388)

the royal Aztec ancestry counted for something, as did descent from the conqueror of Mexico. In addition the marriage was between two of the wealthiest families on the north Mexican frontier. Their first child, Cristóbal, was born in 1590, and a second child, a girl named María, probably in the latter part of 1598.

In 1592 Juan de Oñate was appointed *alcalde mayor* (mayor) of the new Spanish settlement of San Luis Potosí. By this time he was already actively thinking of the New Mexico venture. Wealthy, in early middle age but still vigorous, and a favorite of the viceroy, Oñate was in a strong position to capture this honor. Viceroy Luis de Velasco had originally favored Urdiñola for this task, but the collapse of the Urdiñola proposal in 1594 led him to quickly find another claimant for the New Mexico expedition. Juan de Oñate moved rapidly and in September 1595 signed a contract to lead that expedition. Oñate was to recruit two hundred men and to have a certain minimum of supplies and livestock. He had already launched an ambitious project of signing up recruits.

The Oñate-Velasco agreement was a bit premature, however, for the viceroy was suddenly transferred to Peru, and in October 1595 another man, Gaspar de Zúñiga y Acevedo, Count of Monterrey, took over the reins of government of Mexico. Just before relinquishing his office, however, Velasco issued two additional documents, one appointing Oñate governor and captain-general of New Mexico, and the other giving him a set of rules to guide his operations in that area. Oñate was also promised the honorific title of *adelantado*. This much-coveted appellation (from the Spanish verb *adelantar,* "to advance" or "go forward") had been used in Spain since the Middle Ages. Christopher Columbus was the first New World explorer to receive this status. Oñate's designation as adelantado was not formally ratified by the Crown until February 1602.

Monterrey accepted the documents vis-à-vis Oñate but otherwise moved cautiously in planning the New Mexico venture. He made a number of modifications to the contract, the most important one being that Oñate must report to the Mexico City viceroy rather than directly to the Council of the Indies in Seville. Oñate was restricted in the future recruitment of soldiers, and also in the appointing of royal officials in New Mexico and in determining the tribute paid by Indians. The right of colonists to become gentrified—that is, to obtain the rank of *hidalgo*—originally had been granted to all on the expedition but was restricted to those who spent five years in the new land. Oñate protested these modifications but to no avail.

At this point a new player appeared, not in Mexico but in Spain. In the early part of 1596, the Count of Bailén, Pedro Ponce de León, petitioned to be given the New Mexico contract. At the request of the king, the Council of the Indies began a series of negotiations with Ponce de León, and in September 1596 the

Crown accepted his terms. The Oñate expedition, already on the Río Nazas, some seventy-five miles south of Santa Bárbara, was suspended and would seem to have died before it was properly born.

But events quickly took another turn. Ponce de León failed to obtain sufficient funds to finance the colonization effort, and Oñate received strong backing from the viceroy. Eventually, in December 1596, even though the contract was still in limbo, an inspection of Oñate's volunteers and supplies on the Nazas was made by a viceregal appointee, Lope de Ulloa y Lemos. This inspection showed that Oñate had recruited 205 men, slightly more than the agreed goal, and his supplies and stock animals met the demands of the contract.

The waiting was beginning to tell on Oñate. In a letter to the viceroy dated September 13, 1596, the colonizer complained that he could have had a thousand men under his command but for the delays and uncertainties. However, several more months of lobbying went by before a royal document lifting the suspension on Oñate was produced. It was actually issued in April 1597 but did not reach the viceroy in Mexico City until summer. Viceroy Monterrey ordered a second inspection, and a second inspector, Juan de Frías Salazar, arrived in November. By this time Oñate had moved his men and supplies to Santa Bárbara, the official jumping-off spot for the expedition.

Finally, on January 26, 1598, the expedition was launched. Oñate had failed to meet his quota of men, with only 129 (at least, officially) remaining from earlier head counts. Actually, a number of soldiers were named as receiving equipment from Oñate or, in a few cases, supplying their own equipment who were not listed on the muster roll. In addition, according to Frías Salazar, there were "some men in the neighborhood of the camp who had absented themselves because of some offenses and did not dare to appear before him and he was sure that they would join the expedition." Because of the shortfall in men, an in-law of Juan de Oñate, Juan Guerra de Resa, pledged a recruitment of eighty additional men. It is not entirely clear when these men joined the Oñate party, but they may have been part of the reinforcements that reached Oñate in 1600.

A number of the soldiers had families with them. Oñate's eight-year-old son Cristóbal was given the honorary rank of lieutenant, but his wife, Isabel, remained behind, her pregnancy perhaps already evident. The two Zaldívar nephews held important offices under Oñate: Juan was named *maestro de campo* (in this case, adjutant), and Vicente, *sargento mayor* (major).

Most of the soldiers whose names are on the Frías Salazar lists gave their ages, and it was a relatively young group. Some 39 percent of the group were twenty-five or under, while only around 26 percent were over thirty-five years old (the three oldest soldiers all being around sixty years of age). They were a rather mixed lot, some from Spain or other parts of Europe, others from New Spain. One listed himself as a mulatto. The two most trusted sub-commanders, Vicente and Juan de Zaldívar, were twenty-five and twenty-eight years, respectively. Oñate, himself in his mid to late forties, depending on which birth date is chosen, was one of the senior men on the expedition. More than half (about 62 percent) of those individuals who signed on at the Ulloa inspection do not show up on the Salazar lists. The long wait and uncertainty had certainly taken its toll.

A considerable number of people went with Oñate. Not only did officers and soldiers have wives and children, but there were also servants and slaves including Indians, mestizos, and blacks. The population of this border area in the seventeenth century was quite diverse, consisting of native Indians and mixtures of European, black, and Indian under various names (mestizo, mulatto, *cambujo,* etc.). This was likely the case in the late 1590s, so a large number of non-Europeans, especially in the servant groups, would not be surprising on the Oñate venture. In a careful combing of the extensive documents of the period, archaeologist David H. Snow has counted approximately 560 individuals with Oñate, not including the missionaries. The expedition personnel were drawn from Mexico and from European countries, primarily Spain and Portugal, though three soldiers gave their place of origin as Belgium, Italy, and Greece. Women made up about 20 percent of the group, a fair percentage of them unmarried. There were a number of children, but they are seldom mentioned by name and their sex is normally not given. Many of the Indians were from central Mexico, though curiously enough no Tlaxcalans were mentioned. Some 25 Indian, black, mulatto, or mestizo men and 26 women, mostly Indian, were listed by name.

Extraordinarily diverse goods were brought north with the expedition, partly owned or supplied by Oñate himself, partly brought in the baggage of other party members. The inventory included crude iron and iron tools of various kinds: plowshares, hoes, axes, saws, chisels, augers, blades, picks, mallets, hammers, and anvils. The governor brought with him an estimated 13,500 nails. There were many articles of clothing as well as rolls of cloth. The expedition also carried tailoring equipment including scissors, thimbles, needles, and thread. There were mirrors, knives, earrings, rings, and beads. Listed were grinding stones and large amounts of maize and wheat, oil, wine, and sugar. Oñate brought a number of medicines and medical equipment including lancets, syringes, and a variety of medicines including laxatives, astringents, soothing balms, and various rose concoctions (see chapter 9 for a more complete list). Mining and blacksmithing equipment included quicksilver (mercury) for extracting ore, bellows, tongs, files, and a vise for taking harquebuses apart. Eighteen barrels of gunpowder and considerable amounts of sheet lead were brought for ammunition. Artillery included three bronze field pieces and large numbers of harquebuses, swords, and both personal and horse armor. The term *harquebus* might refer to any sort of powder and ball weapon, but generally it meant a specific kind of matchlock, heavy enough so that the barrel needed an iron fork rest.

Oñate had trade in mind. He carried some 80,000 glass beads as well as rosaries and sacred images on tin. The party traveled with perhaps 1,200 head of horses, some thousands of sheep and goats, and around 1,500 head of cattle. The equipment was carried in eighty wagons and carts, drawn for the most part by oxen though mules were also employed. Oñate himself brought two mule-drawn coaches. The expedition on the trail was said to have been spread out over two miles.

The Salazar inspection had ended at the San Gerónimo River north of Santa Bárbara. On January 26, 1598, the expedition began its northward trek to New Mexico, reaching the Conchos on January 30. Here Oñate halted for eight days, reviewing the army and preparing for the march ahead. On February 10 the group reached the San Pedro River, an east-draining tributary of the Conchos. At that point the expedition made camp and remained for a month while Sargento Mayor Vicente Zaldívar was sent northward with seventeen men to "discover a road for carts." Oñate was pioneering the route across the Chihuahuan Desert that later became the *Camino Real*, the Spanish lifeline from the New Mexican province to New Spain. There is some possibility that in 1591, seven years before, Morlete had also taken this route, but most likely he bore to the southeast from the El Paso area and followed the Rio Grande to the Conchos, a route that had been taken by earlier expeditions. In all probability, however, the Morlete party *was* the first to venture across the Jornada del Muerto (see below).

During the wait at the San Pedro, the Franciscan missionaries joined the group, escorted by Captain Marcos Farfán de los Godos. The missionaries, eight in all, under the command of Fray Alonso Martínez, arrived at the San Pedro camp on March 3. In addition to the friars, two lay brothers were listed. There also seems to have been a third lay brother, Juan de Dios, who later was sent to Pecos (see below). One of the friars, Francisco de San Miguel, had planned to go on the Espejo expedition of 1582–83 but was forced to drop out at the last moment.

Meanwhile, Zaldívar explored northward, looking for likely routes for the carts and for available water, with (probably Concho) Indian guides. These guides quickly became lost, but Zaldívar found another Indian group and kidnapped four natives who may also have been Concho or perhaps Suma. Using these new guides, Zaldívar reached the Rio Grande on February 28. He then turned back to make his report to Oñate, reaching the San Pedro on March 10.

One branch of the Concho Indians lived in the vicinity of Santa Bárbara and had been interacting with the Spaniards for three or more decades. Conchos were on the expedition of Chamuscado and probably that of Espejo. Both the Concho Indians and the Suma lived in small scattered bands. They were basically hunters and gatherers, using the bow and arrow in hunting and collecting vegetable foods such as mesquite beans and various cacti. Hunting focused on a variety of animals including rabbits, deer, and along the Rio Grande, bison. There is some evidence that certain groups had a simple agriculture of maize, beans, and squash. I think that those Suma living on the Rio Grande probably had a marginal agriculture since they were on a major trail from La Junta to the Pueblo country and were well acquainted with the uses of agriculture. The same was probably true of the Concho Indians in the upper Conchos drainage because they too were on an old and established trail. In fact, Espejo in 1583 mentioned meeting a Concho Native American living among the Manso in the El Paso area.

The southern Concho Indians, by Oñate's time, may have begun to pick up animal husbandry. By the mid-seventeenth century, horses, often obtained by raiding, were becoming important throughout the area, and likely this was also true in Oñate's time. The more northerly groups, contacted by Zaldívar, whether Concho or Suma, were largely unacculturated. The Concho were probably Uto-Aztecan-speaking, perhaps related to the Taracahitan subgroup of languages.

The route of Oñate northward is not securely known. He seems to have swung somewhat to the west of the later Camino Real, probably rejoining it just to the south of modern Chihuahua City. He then moved slightly west of north, reaching the Río Carmén not too far from the modern Villa Ahumada and near the large pre-Columbian sites of Loma de Montezuma and El Carmén. From there northward, Oñate was on an old trail leading to the Rio Grande. In mid-April he reached the great expanse of Médanos de Samalayuca, the extensive sand dunes some forty miles south of the El Paso area. He seems to have gone through the dunes before swinging off to the northeast in the vicinity of the later mission of San Elisario, southeast of El Paso. Oñate, basically, was on one of the seventeenth-century routes of the Camino Real. During that century an alternate route was developed that turned northeastward at Ojo Lucero, the modern Lucero, north of Villa Ahumada. On reaching Tinajas de Cantarrecio, the direction was north to the Rio Grande at a point some twenty miles southeast of San Elisario.

Oñate, with an advance party, reached the Rio Grande on April 20, remaining there until April 26 to allow the army to catch up. He sent Captain Pablo de Aguilar Inojosa, a Spanish-born officer, with a few men to scout out the road ahead. The Spanish army slowly ascended the river, pausing on April 30 to take formal possession of New Mexico in the name of Felipe II and Spain. They continued along the south bank until May 4, when they reached the ford adjacent to a narrow pass on the opposite bank, the site of present-day El Paso. Oñate was now in Manso Indian territory (see chapter 5 for discussion of this group).

At the El Paso ford, Oñate made the statement that the site was "in 31° exactly." Considering the crudeness of the Spanish surveying instruments, this is reasonably correct, being off by less than a degree of latitude. On May 4, near the ford, Oñate noted the wagon tracks left seven years before by Morlete. The following day he moved through the pass, traversing what is now urban El Paso, and pushed on north along the east bank of the Rio Grande. The expedition proceeded slowly, reaching the Organ Mountains, called by Oñate the Sierra del Olvido, on May 13. Oñate was slowly losing expedition members: on May 17 the party lost a child, and on May 21, one of the officers, Pedro Robledo, approximately sixty years and one of the oldest members of the expedition, was buried. The region of his burial became known as the Paraje Robledo (the Robledo stopover or camp) and kept that name to the end of the colonial period. It is in the modern Rincon area, the southern entry to the Jornada del Muerto.

Meanwhile, on May 12 Captain Aguilar was sent ahead again to scout out the Piro area. He returned May 20 after having entered the first Piro village, a direct violation of Oñate's order of secrecy. The governor wanted Aguilar to avoid even being seen by any Indian group he might come across. This secrecy was important to Oñate because in previous expeditions the Indians had fled the invaders, taking their food supplies with them. The governor was furious and had to be dissuaded from ordering Aguilar's execution.

On May 22, Oñate, the Franciscan commissary, Alonso de Martínez, along with another friar, Cristóbal de Salazar, the Zaldívar brothers, and some sixty men pushed on ahead of the slowly moving wagons to contact the nearest Piro town. This is the point where the Rio Grande describes a curve westward and flows between rugged mountain ranges to the east and a highly dissected plateau country to the west. As Morlete had found out several years before, it was not practical for carts and wagons to follow the river at this point. Oñate likely followed Morlete's trail, perhaps even saw signs of his wagons as he moved through this flat, arid region. On his way he marked water holes, but even so his soldiers and especially the main army following slowly behind became very thirsty.

The party reached the north end of the Jornada on May 27 at a point near historic San Marcial. The next day the advance group reached the Piro town of Qualacú on the east bank of the Rio Grande near Black Mesa, bypassing the large pueblo later called San Pascual. As Oñate feared, the Piro had fled their towns, but they were coaxed back with gifts. Fray Alonso de Martínez was now very ill with gout, so Oñate camped in the Qualacú area for a month. During that time his purveyor general, Diego de Zubía, collected maize for the main army. According to Oñate, he "bought the provisions," though what was used to pay for the foodstuffs is not clear. Probably trade goods were used. Meanwhile, Oñate went back to help the wagon train, returning on June 13. Two of the black servants, Luis and Manuel, who were presumably with the advance party, wandered away and disappeared. On June 14, the party reached the riverbank opposite a pueblo that Oñate called Teypana (later known as Pilabó), which the Spaniards renamed Socorro (succor) because they received a great deal of maize there. On June 15 they reached a small Piro town on the east side of the river that they referred to as Nueva Sevilla (New Seville), the later Sevilleta, "because of its site." They camped there for a week and then pushed on northward. At a newly built pueblo they called San Juan Bautista, the people had fled, leaving large stores of maize. Here, Indians from various parts visited them, in Oñate's opinion probably acting as spies. Among them was a person the Spaniards called "Don Lope." He had been sent by Tomás and Cristóbal, "Indians who had remained [in Tiguex country] since the time of Castaño."

Leaving San Juan Bautista on June 25, the day following John the Baptist's feast, the group pushed on, "passing many pueblos, farms and planted fields on both banks of the river, most of them abandoned on account of fear." The governor was marching toward Puaray and at some point entered Tiguex country, probably on June 26. The party reached Puaray on June 27, for some reason assigning it the patronage of Saint Anthony of Padua, whose feast day was earlier that month. Oñate, with the maestro de campo, Juan de Zaldívar, and a small party then moved on to Santo Domingo, a pueblo that had been chosen by the missionaries for the Franciscan headquarters. The immediate purpose, however, was to seize Tomás and Cristóbal, who were taken by surprise and carried off to Puaray. On June 29, Juan de Zaldívar and Fray Cristóbal de Salazar pushed on to Zia, the pueblo that had befriended Coronado's group almost sixty years before. The town was given as patrons Saints Peter and Paul, whose day it was. This casual religious renaming of native villages signaled the Franciscan strategy of massive acculturation that was to ensure a century of turmoil between the Pueblos and the missionaries.

Oñate quickly explored other portions of the Rio Grande Valley. On July 7 he met at Santo Domingo with seven "Indian chieftains of different provinces of this New Mexico" and obtained a voluntary pledge of obedience to the king. Who these chieftains were, what pueblos they were from, and what they thought they were pledging are not known. During this period, Oñate brought Doña Inés, the Indian woman who had been living in Mexico City, to her natal village of San Cristóbal in the Galisteo country. She was, according to Oñate, "like a second Malinche"—that is, like María, the mistress of Cortés and his translator to the Aztecs. Unlike María, however, Inés no longer remembered the native languages, and her family and almost all her relatives were dead. According to Oñate, Inés had been brought south by Castaño de Sosa, something most unlikely since Castaño had been returned to Mexico in chains. I have suggested that Inés's removal to Mexico might possibly date to the Coronado expedition. We know that Juan Troyano brought a woman, presumably Pueblo, back from that expedition (see chapter 3). Troyano's wife was living in Mexico City in 1568. If she married Troyano in her teens, something not at all unlikely, she would have been in her seventies in 1598.

Another Pueblo Indian for which we have a clearer provenance was Pedro Oroz. He had been brought back to Mexico by Espejo but had died there. However, he had been taught Nahuatl and baptized, his sponsor perhaps being the Franciscan commissary-general, Pedro Oroz. While in Mexico, the Pecos native taught the Towa language to the lay brother Juan de Dios, and this man was escorted on July 26 to Pecos Pueblo, where he was left with Fray Francisco de San Miguel.

Oñate quickly settled on the region around the mouth of the Chama River for his capital. He took over the Tewa town of Okeh, the future San Juan Pueblo. The wagon train with the main Spanish party arrived on August 17, and Oñate made plans to visit all the major groups of Pueblos and to allot them among the missionaries. The first phase of the conquest and settlement of the upper Southwest was now underway.

CHAPTER FIVE

The Pueblos and Their Neighbors in 1598

The native world of the Southwest in 1598 had changed somewhat from the cultural landscape seen by Coronado six decades before. At the time of Coronado there was an east-west extension of the Pueblos from Pecos and the Salinas towns to the Hopi mesas. The most northern town was Taos, and settlements extended southward down the Rio Grande and its tributaries to Milligan's Gulch Pueblo, some thirty-five miles north of modern Truth or Consequences. Downriver from Milligan's Gulch were the rancherías of the Manso Indians (discussed later in this chapter). To the east were the Querecho, ancestors to the Apache and Navajo, and the Teya, who may well have spoken a language similar to that of the Piro/Tompiro. The Querecho held the plains in the Canadian and upper Red River drainage in what is now the upper Texas Panhandle, the Oklahoma Panhandle, and sections of northeast New Mexico and southeast Colorado. The Teya lived on the Llano Estacado south of the Querecho and also along the Pecos River valley below the Santa Rosa–Fort Sumner area.

West of the Pueblo world lived the various Pai groups and the lower Colorado River Yumans, both probably active in trade to the Hopi and Zuni towns, and both helping to form a link with the Pacific coast of California. To the southwest were the various Piman groups of the Gila River drainage, and south of them the Sonoran statelets, middlemen in an active trade network that extended throughout the Pueblo world and far to the south in western Mexico. On the northern frontier, there is a good possibility that Utes were situated in the Four Corners area, a region they held in later historic times.

During the fifty-six years between the time Coronado left the Southwest and Oñate arrived, the various Pueblos had pretty much continued living in the territories they held in Coronado's time. The Teya, now called Jumano, continued to control the southern part of the Llano Estacado and the Pecos River valley. During this period, however, the Querecho (ancestral Apacheans) began a series of migrations, still not clearly understood but reminiscent of those that had first brought them into the northeastern corner of the Southwest three centuries earlier. They started a move westward and at least by the early 1580s had reached the region around the Acoma and Hopi. It seems possible that Querecho began filtering into the Chama drainage at about this time. These Apachean forebears were also spreading southward in a line west of and paralleling the Jumano. The Apacheans gravitated to the mountains that fringe the Tularosa Basin to the east, and, indeed, some of them remain there today. As of Oñate's time, this penetration of the eastern New Mexico mountains may still have been in process. A little later on, Apaches were to threaten the Camino Real, especially along the Jornada del Muerto. During the seventeenth century the Apache continued to move southward, both to the east and to the west of the Pueblo world. They infiltrated groups such as the Jumano, Suma, Jova, and Jocome and gradually absorbed them. By the end of that century, the Apache were pressing on the Pima of what is now southern Arizona.

The Comanche as of the time of Oñate were still west of the Great Plains and made little or no impact on the Pueblo region. This Uto-Aztecan-speaking group did not reach the Plains and begin their love affair with the horse, and their reputation as fierce raiders, until after A.D. 1700. The Comanche did become important in the struggle for control of the western Plains in the eighteenth century, and they were a chronic threat to New Mexico. In the nineteenth century, Comanche war parties were deflected somewhat from the latter province, but they harried both northern Mexico and the Anglo-American settlements of Texas. They were not finally defeated until the 1870s.

The two Spanish expeditions of the 1580s found large numbers of pueblos, some thirteen or fourteen in the Piro area alone. In Tiguex there seems to have been at least fifteen and perhaps twenty or so pueblos, up from the twelve counted by Coronado forty years earlier. Individual pueblo size may have been somewhat less, however, for it seems unlikely that the aggregate population had increased—though from the Spanish figures one might think so. Since large numbers of Indians (and for the Church, large numbers of converts) inflated the importance of the new province in Spanish governmental eyes, there was always some inclination on the part of the governors and the Franciscans to exaggerate populations. This was true especially in the early period of Spanish control when dreams of establishing an important Spanish presence in New Mexico were high. For example, Oñate in a letter dated March 2, 1599, commented, "Here [among the Tewa] and in the other above-mentioned provinces there must be, being conservative in my reckoning, sixty thousand Indians, with towns like ours and with houses built around rectangular plazas." Fray Alonso de Benavides in his 1630 Memorial was even more generous, counting more than 68,000 Pueblos, not to mention vast numbers of Apaches who "form the largest tribe in the world."

What the population was at the time of Chamuscado and Espejo is unknown, but the population estimates of Espejo suggest that the Pueblo area was still flourishing as of the early 1580s. Whether there had been a drop in numbers is uncertain because of the considerable inflation of the Espejo figures. But if Spanish impact caused the population drop in the second half of the sixteenth century, much of that impact must have been due to the large Coronado expedition rather than the smaller ones of the 1580s and 1590s. Coronado's soldiers surely introduced some diseases, though perhaps not smallpox, which became such a killer in later decades. Probably, depopulation of the Pueblo area by Coronado's party was caused as much by war and the looting of food supplies as by disease.

The Chamuscado and Espejo expeditions were disruptive, but unless there was a introduction of epidemic disease for which we have no records, they likely did not significantly affect the demography of southwestern peoples. However, diseases may have crept northward from the interior of Mexico, brought by slavers or even by traders. Such diseases could have reached the Suma, Manso, and such southern Pueblos as the Piro before the Spanish entradas of the 1580s.

My own estimate for the Pueblo population of the Southwest in Coronado's time is around 60,000. In other parts of Spanish America, populations fell drastically when native peoples were first introduced to Euro-African disease. Although firm figures are lacking, I believe that this most likely happened in the Southwest. Here I will give a very tentative estimate of 50,000 Pueblo Indians at the end of the sixteenth century. This decline, as said above, was due partly to disease and partly to the economic disruptions of the Coronado and later expeditions.

Another factor could have been weather. Beginning about 1560 and lasting through the 1580s, there were a number of years with below-average rainfall. If climatic patterns from other parts of the Northern Hemisphere are any indication, the sixteenth-century Southwest likely had winters that increased in severity as the century wore on. It is not clear what effect, if any, these climatic hard times had on population. Certainly, this "Little Ice Age" changed a number of economic and social patterns in Europe.

In 1935, archaeologist Frederick W. Hodge compiled an astonishing list of pueblo names in the Oñate documents, more than 150 in all, even when duplicate names are taken into account. They were surely not all occupied towns; indeed, some may have been place-names rather than settlements. A certain confusion is also indicated by the Enrico Martínez map, apparently done at the direction of Viceroy Monterrey and included in the viceroy's letter to the king dated May 14, 1602. In this map, only 32 pueblos are numbered for the Rio Grande Valley, although some 56 pueblo markers are scattered on the map. Most of the numbered pueblos are named, though in one case some 11 or 12 pueblos are grouped under the heading *Pueblos del valle de Puará,* which probably represents those Tiguex towns on the east side of the Rio Grande. A separate Tiguex town, Santiago, is placed on the west bank. The large Mann-Zuris site in the Albuquerque area does not appear on this map, and this pueblo may well have been deserted by Oñate's time. A complete count of towns is probably impossible, although Torquemada's figure, published in 1615 but referring to the Oñate period, of 112 or more pueblos seems too high.

Oñate's count of pueblos in the Piro area and the archaeological evidence for such sites suggest about the same number of pueblos as listed by the Chamuscado and Espejo parties. The large pueblo of San Felipe, the southern-most of the Piro towns, was deserted by Oñate's time, but San Pascual, probably Senecú (since it became a mission station thirty years later), Qualacú, Pilabó, and Sevilleta were occupied, as were several others. Additional Piro archaeology will help clarify the occupation picture as of 1598.

What today we call the Tompiro—those Piro-speaking pueblos across the Manzano Mountains and in the Salinas region—Oñate referred to as Jumano. There were five towns including Quelotetrey (Gran Quivira), Cenobey or Genobey (perhaps Tenabó), and Pataotrey (perhaps Tabirá). Abó is listed separately as "Piro." The use of the term *Jumano* is especially interesting, for I have suggested that Jumano-Teya spoke a language similar to Tompiro. Certainly, there was extensive trade between the nomadic Jumano and the sedentary Tompiro.

For the Keres region, the Oñate documents list some eleven towns. Included are Guipui (Santo Domingo), Tzia (Zia), Cochiti, Acoma, Katishtya (San Felipe), and Tamaya (Santa Ana), all important towns of later times. By Benavides's day, in the 1620s, this number had fallen to eight, including the six listed above. For the Tano of the Galisteo Basin, and possibly in the Santa Fe River drainage, ten towns are listed. Some of these may have been temporary villages since a quarter of a century later Benavides mentions only five pueblos, probably San Marcos, San Lázaro, San Cristóbal, Ciénega, and Galisteo.

The Tewa towns included, of course, Okeh (San Juan) and Yungue in the lower Chama drainage; from the latter town, Oñate formed his first capital, San Gabriel del Yungue. Oñate lists a number of other towns including the pueblos of San Ildefonso and Santa Clara. It seems likely that the large towns upriver on the Chama and its tributaries—Tsamauinge, Pesedeuinge, Kuuinge, and Teeuinge—

had been deserted by Oñate's day, probably even by Coronado's day, and there had been a movement from the Chama Basin to the Rio Grande. Several of the upland towns south of the Chama and Rio Grande junction may have been occupied in Oñate's time.

As I said earlier, what may have happened between the time of Coronado and that of Oñate was that the Rio Grande area lost population but actually had a greater number of smaller pueblos. Acoma and the Pecos, Taos, and Picurís areas, however, continued to have their unitary pueblos as they did in Coronado's day. The Zuni towns, as in Coronado's time, enumerating roughly from southwest to northeast, included Hawikuh, Kechibawa, Kwa'kina, Halona (the modern Zuni), Matsakya, and K'iakima. The Spaniards talked of the "seven cities of Cíbola," but in all likelihood there were only six. By 1598 they were not all equally prosperous. Seven years after Oñate arrived, Father Escobar noted that while all the Zuni towns were occupied, "four of them [were] almost completely in ruins." The two flourishing towns were no doubt Halona and Hawikuh.

The Hopi town names in the Oñate documents are a bit confused, but in all likelihood they were the same as earlier in the century: Awatovi on Antelope Mesa, and Walpi, Mishongnovi, Shongopavi, and Oraibi at the edge of the three Hopi mesas. There is some possibility that two additional pueblos—Kawaika-a on Antelope Mesa, and Sikyatki on First Mesa—were occupied in Coronado's time, as that expedition had also reported a magical seven pueblos. In any case, these latter towns were deserted by the time Oñate arrived in New Mexico.

The fact that the Pueblos had regular towns is indicated by the Spanish use of the word *pueblo,* which in Spanish simply means "town." These pueblos were grouped around rectangular courtyards, and often the house structures rose several stories above the courtyards. Sometimes the room blocks offered a blank wall to the outside, entryways being through the courtyard, the area in which many of the ceremonies and much of the everyday work was carried out. The kivas or ceremonial rooms were often (though not always) within the courtyards. The traditional building material of the Anasazi was squared-off sandstone laid in mud mortar, with the walls then being plastered over with fine clay. By A.D. 1150 or a little earlier, an alternate method of house building was spreading from southern New Mexico. This was the use of coursed adobe to form house walls. The idea of adobe buildings probably originated somewhere in the Casas Grandes world and became popular during the Golden Age of the Pueblos, though most pueblos continued to be built the old-fashioned way with stone and mud mortar.

The language distribution of the upper Southwest in Oñate's time was very similar to what it was in the Coronado period and for perhaps two or two and a half centuries before Coronado. The major linguistic movement, discussed above, was the spread of the Querechos southward and westward, something that would have considerable consequence in the seventeenth and eighteenth centuries.

One important group, living in the El Paso area, not only figured in the Oñate accounts but was probably contacted as early as Coronado. Here were the various settlements of Manso Indians who for the purposes of missionization were considered part of the New Mexico province throughout the seventeenth century. Oñate first contacted the Manso on May 4, 1598, when forty of them came to the Spanish camp opposite modern El Paso:

> They had Turkish bows, long hair cut to resemble little Milan caps, headgear made to hold down the hair and colored with blood or paint. Their first words were *manxo, manxo, micos, micos,* by which they meant "peaceful ones" and "friends." They made the sign of the cross by raising their thumbs. They told us clearly by signs that the settlements were six days distant, or eight days along the road. They mark the day by the course of the sun; in these things they are like ourselves. We gave them many presents, and they helped us to transport the sheep across the river, which was forded on this day at the crossing which we named Los Puertos, because it is used by them to go inland. There is no other road for carts for many leagues.

By the time of Fray Alonso de Benavides, thirty years after Oñate, the term *Manso* had clearly become a Spanish-imposed tribal name. The word itself is an old Spanish term from the Latin *mansuetus,* meaning in both Latin and Spanish "tame" or "gentle." An alternate name, occasionally used, was *Gorretas,* meaning small caps, and referred to the peculiar style of haircut mentioned by Oñate. Since the Indians actually used the term *manso* in speaking to Oñate, it suggests a certain amount of previous contact with the Spaniards, and indeed the Manso were on the main trail taken previously by Chamuscado, Espejo, Morlete, and Leyva. I doubt if the Indians meant *manso* as a group name at this early date; they probably were only indicating their friendliness or neutrality. Luxán, with the Espejo party in 1582, referred to the group as *Tanpachoas,* a name of uncertain origins. Castañeda in the Coronado expedition probably was talking about the Manso when he referred to the downriver pueblos where the river turned to the east.

The evidence for Manso language is very scanty; only a handful of possibly Manso words have survived. There are, currently, two different theories as to the Manso language. One states that the Manso were closely related, perhaps identical, to the Jano and Jocome, who lived off to the west in and around the New Mexico bootheel, and that all three groups spoke one of the languages of the Taracahitan branch of Uto-Aztecan. Another theory holds that the Manso, along with the Suma and Jumano-Teya, spoke a Tanoan language, or closely related languages, probably most closely related to Tiwa and Piro-Tompiro. As discussed in chapter 3, I tend to accept this latter position, but it should be emphasized that language relationships in this area are decidedly unclear.

Whatever the language situation, the Manso seem to have been the lineal descendants of the archaeological El Paso phase of Jornada Mogollon, itself related to the great Casas Grandes culture to the south and west. The El Paso phase collapsed (as did Casas Grandes tradition in general) sometime around or perhaps a bit before A.D. 1450. The collapse of the Casas Grandes interaction sphere left in its place a series of marginal agricultural and hunting-gathering peoples in the Casas Grandes–Janos region and in the stretch of Rio Grande around El Paso and on southward to the Río Carmén. Only at La Junta, at the junction of the Rio Grande and the Conchos, did substantial towns with considerable agriculture continue on into Spanish times, and even there the sophisticated pottery was replaced by simple brown wares.

The Mansos at the time of Oñate had given up the substantial adobe structures of the El Paso phase of the Jornada Mogollon. It is generally thought that they no longer made the polychrome and black-on-white ceramics of their El Paso ancestors. It seems possible, however, that some of the pottery typical of El Paso phase sites persisted beyond the collapse of the El Paso phase as a recognizable entity, perhaps into the sixteenth century. A site in the Hueco Bolson, northeast of El Paso, which contains El Paso Polychrome, yielded a thermoluminescence date of A.D. 1561, though the excavator, Michael Whalen, doubts its validity. Another survivor was perhaps the durable and popular Chupadero Black-on-white, produced farther to the north but widely traded in protohistoric southern New Mexico.

The major difficulty for modern archaeologists in discovering Manso sites is that they are often impossible to recognize with any certainty, at least from surface survey. Without pottery, they basically resemble Archaic sites. When simple El Paso brown wares are found, they resemble the Mesilla phase of Jornada Mogollon culture, dating some centuries earlier. It may even be that by Manso times, the tradition of pottery making—whether plain ware, black-on-white, or polychrome—had ended. Nor are we sure whether the Manso practiced agriculture, though a statement in the Espejo account of 1582 suggests that they at least grew maize. A great deal more archaeology, directed specifically at the Manso, is needed.

What is known of Manso culture is very scanty. Gallegos's account from the Chamuscado expedition tells of receiving "two bonnets made of numerous macaw feathers." This certainly implies trade, which is not too surprising considering that the Manso were on a major north-south trade route. Luxán, the following year, tells of receiving "mesquite, corn and fish, for they fish much in the pools with small dragnets" from those Mansos that he called Tanpachoas. According to Luxán, they were similar to the Otomoacos and Caguates (Suma), but it is not clear if they spoke the same language as the two latter groups. Espejo claims to have met some one thousand Indians in the El Paso area, though it must be remembered that Espejo's numbers tend to be somewhat inflated. The Indians lived in scattered settlements or rancherías, probably made up of *jacal*-type houses: mud-plastered brush structures that date back thousands of years in the Southwest. The Indians performed their ceremonial dances for the Spaniards and presented them with mesquite, beans, and fish.

The Manso costume was mentioned briefly in some of the accounts. According to Luxán, men wore some sort of penis sheath or strap. Benavides, who described the group in some detail, said that the men were naked but that women wore two deerskins gathered at the waist, one in front and the other behind. Both Luxán and Oñate noted the use of "Turkish bows," apparently some sort of composite bow. Later southwestern Indians backed their bows with sinew or with yucca fiber held on by piñon gum. Possibly one of those methods was employed here.

The social organization of the Manso is unknown except that with a basically hunting and gathering economy and residence in scattered rancherías, it was likely a band organization consisting of no more than a few families. Except for the dances noted above, nothing is known of their religion.

The trade that I mentioned briefly in chapter 3 was still an important part of the southwestern economy in 1598. It is true that the Spanish conquest, devastation, and subsequent colonization of the west coast of Mexico had impacted the trade routes running northward through the Sonoran statelets and on into the Cíbola-Zuni towns. The statelets themselves were still actively trading as late as the time of Ibarra in the decade of the 1560s. Indeed, trade to eastern Sonora, though not exactly flourishing, was still reported as late as 1630. Feathers of the scarlet macaw had been in demand from at least Chaco Bonito phase times (see chapter 2). The source of the birds in Chaco times was probably southeastern Mexico and may have followed a trade route up the arid northern interior of Mexico. It seems quite possible that the route went by way of the Casas Grandes Valley, even though the city of Casas Grandes developed as an important center only after the fall of the Chaco culture. Archaeological finds from the post-Chaco period at Pecos, Gran Quivira, the García site (Pojoaque Pueblo), and Picurís as well as sites in southwest Arizona indicate that at least some of the birds reaching the Southwest during the Pueblo IV period were scarlet macaws. A likely source would have been Casas Grandes, where these macaws had been bred from perhaps A.D. 1200 on into the fifteenth century.

But Casas Grandes, too, had fallen by the time of the first Spanish entradas into the Southwest, and most of the southern trade was routed to the region west of the Sierra Madre Occidental. That various parrots and macaws were being traded northward from the Sonoran area is well known from early Spanish accounts, but the species cannot be determined from the historical records. I have an idea that this west coast trade was mainly in military macaws (*Ara militaris*) and the thick-billed parrot (*Rhynchopsitta pachyrhyncha*). The military macaw ranges into the mountains of Sonora on the southern edge of Sonoran statelet territory, while the thick-billed parrot's range extends through the northern part of the Sierra Madre Occidental, occurring as far north as southern Arizona and New Mexico. However, it must be pointed out that actual archaeological specimens of the military macaw are very rare in the Southwest except at Casas Grandes.

Be that as it may, it seems likely that much-desired scarlet macaw feathers continued to reach the Southwest; in fact, finds at Pojoaque most likely postdated the Casas Grandes period, and those at Pecos and Picurís may well have done so. The nearest home range of the scarlet macaw is the lowlands of southern Tamaulipas, southward on the Mexican east coast, and Oaxaca on the west coast. There seems a good chance that *Ara macao* specimens and feathers continued to be traded from the south and east along a route that was later utilized for the Camino Real, even after the collapse of Casas Grandes.

The post-Columbian trade into the Pueblo area not only involved parrots and macaws but also shell, which had been in great demand for centuries. Especially desirable were the tubular olivella shells that came both from the Gulf of California and from the Pacific coast of California. Glycymeris shell, made into bracelets, came from the Gulf of California, as did coral and a number of other shells. Abalone (*Haliotis* sp.) was traded from the California coast. Some of these shells were transshipped eastward to the Plains, where such items—along with pottery, turquoise, obsidian from sites in the Jemez Mountains, Glazes V and VI (E and F in the Rio Grande sequence), and maize—were exchanged for bison products, Osage orange (*bois d'arc*) bow wood, and riverine shells such as *Lampsilis purpurata*, a freshwater bivalve used mainly in pendants and beads. Alibates dolomite, a flinty material used for various stone tools that came from quarries in the northern Texas Panhandle, was popular at Pecos, but relatively little was traded farther west.

This trade with the Plains was still flourishing in Oñate's day, as indicated by information received by Zaldívar in 1599 and comments in the Valverde report of 1602. Pecos at that time seemed especially important for the trade to the Plains, but the Salinas Tompiro towns were surely also involved. As the seventeenth century wore on, eastern Apachean groups would increasingly become the middlemen for this trade to the Plains, and by 1598 they may have begun their slow squeeze-out of the Jumano. As the Sonoran area collapsed in the early seventeenth century, the supply of shell and parrot/macaw feathers dwindled, though the lower Colorado and west coast routes continued to be open throughout much of the century.

In the east, a new pattern of trading developed within two or three decades after Oñate. This was a partnership arrangement between the Spaniards and the Pueblo Indians. Turquoise continued to be traded, and even shell, but increasingly Spanish goods—including metal objects, cloth, and jewelry—entered the trade picture. By the end of the seventeenth century this kind of trading operation was beginning to penetrate northward to the Utes.

Within the Southwest, a trade situation like that of pre-Coronado days extended into the Spanish period. The cotton grown by the Hopi, often dyed with bright colors obtained from the central Arizona area, continued to be in demand among the Rio Grande Pueblos, as did the extraordinary Jeddito bichrome and polychrome pottery. Around 1550 an eastern contribution to native pottery, the beautiful Sankawi Black-on-cream, developing out of the earlier Biscuit wares, became popular in the upper Rio Grande. Glaze E (Glaze V at Pecos) persevered at various Pueblos. It should be stressed that these names for ceramic wares are the modern archaeological ones. We do not know what the sixteenth-century Pueblos called them.

Turquoise from the Cerrillos mines was traded both east and west, and the mineral fibrolite continued to be popular throughout the Pueblo world. Fibrolite, or sillimanite, is a fibrous, schistose mineral that has an extraordinary hardness and takes an exceedingly high polish. Depending on the minerals in the makeup, fibrolite can be brown or red with black or dark green inclusions, or it may be bluish black, mottled black and white, or gray. Fibrolite was extremely popular in the Pueblo Southwest, especially for making axes. The nearest outcroppings of this much desired material are in the mountains north of Pecos Pueblo, and that pueblo seems to have controlled the trade in fibrolite.

Generally, the material culture of the Pueblos of Oñate's time was not significantly different from that of the Coronado period. As discussed under trade, the Hopi Indians manufactured the Jeddito potteries, and these wares were copied by the Zuni. Among the eastern Pueblos, Glaze E was being manufactured south of the Chama region, while in the Tewa area Sankawi Black-on-cream was still being made. With the addition of a red underbody, it would develop into the seventeenth-century Tewa Polychrome. Pueblos from Taos to the Salinas group manufactured various micaceous plain wares for use at home and for trade into the western Plains.

There is little indication that the earlier Spanish expeditions to the Southwest had significantly changed the culture, material or otherwise, of either the Pueblo Indians or their nomadic neighbors. Although Coronado probably brought some of that utility pottery known by archaeologists as the "olive jar," and the senior officers of the expedition may well have carried a setting or so of Spanish majolica pottery, there is absolutely no evidence that these, or any other Spanish pottery, influenced the native pottery traditions. The copying of Spanish pottery forms by Pueblo Indians would not appear before the seventeenth century. No metallurgical tradition caught on in the Southwest. The Pueblo house type was not significantly affected by Spanish or Mexican Indian architectural ideas. The beehive ovens that are a feature of later historical pueblos were basically introduced in the seventeenth century or perhaps even later. The idea of heating the interior of houses with fireplaces rather than hearths also seems to have been a seventeenth-century idea. Weaving practices were probably much the same in 1598 as they had been in pre-Spanish times. Only after Oñate was the weaving of wool added to that of cotton, and minor Spanish-introduced technical improvements made to the Puebloan loom. A number of Spanish objects, however, did remain in the pueblos from Coronado's time. For example, a trunk and a book (subject unknown) were found by the Espejo party at Zuni. The latter group also reported seeing crosses. These may actually have been star symbols, since a star with four points was common in Pueblo iconography and symbolized the morning star with its kachina and twin war-god implications. We have no other evidence that Christianity took hold in the sixteenth-century Southwest, and the possibility of it seems vanishingly remote.

The economy of the Pueblo world of 1598, like that of previous decades and centuries, was based on agriculture of maize, beans, squash, and cotton, the latter crop grown only in part of the area but traded widely. Another old domesticate was the bottle gourd, used primarily as a container. It seems likely that Spanish watermelons and cantaloupe melons had taken hold in the Pueblo area from Coronado's time. Oñate reported melons at a time when his own colonists could hardly have planted and reaped their own crops. It is also possible that domesticated chile peppers had arrived in the Southwest before Oñate; Obregón mentions that chile seeds were brought to Pecos by Espejo, and a few years later Castaño lists "herbs, chile and calabashes" at that pueblo. This plant, however, really took hold in the seventeenth century.

Domesticated animals in Oñate's time were limited to the dog and the turkey, both many centuries old in the Pueblo area. According to one nearly contemporary

Pueblo star symbol near San Cristóbal, Protohistoric period (photograph by the author)

account, Coronado had brought Spanish chickens to the Southwest. If so, they do not seem to have survived the latter part of the sixteenth century, though imported chickens became popular after Oñate. The domesticated turkey, on the other hand, was well established and remained an important protein source into modern times.

It is known that Coronado left a flock of sheep with Fray Juan de Ubeda, who remained at Pecos and in the Galisteo area when Coronado left the Southwest. No sheep seem to have survived his expedition despite the fact that some of the Mexican Indians who "jumped ship" to remain with the Pueblos likely knew about sheep herding. The sheep became vastly popular among Spaniards and Indians alike in the seventeenth century, but sheep could hardly be counted as "native" as of Oñate's arrival.

There was continued emphasis on hunting, important from the earliest times. Such animals as bison (especially among the eastern pueblos), artiodactyls (deer and antelope), and smaller creatures such as lagomorphs (rabbits and hares) were important not only for the larder but also for their skins. Communal rabbit hunts are likely to be very old in the Southwest; from the evidence of the ubiquitous "rabbit stick," they date from Archaic times. Recent analyses suggest that in the Rio Grande Valley and westward, the harvest of rabbits and hares was considerably

higher than that of deer and antelope, while on the edge of the Plains a larger percentage of artiodactyls were utilized. Fish were probably eaten in the east, though
there is little evidence for this usage. Among the western Pueblos there was a taboo
against fish for food.

The Pueblos had extensive gathering and used a variety of plants for food and
medicine. Examples both from archaeology and from later historical pueblos—
the latter probably or certainly going back into prehistoric days—include piñon
nuts, Rocky Mountain beeweed, various garden greens that also in some cases
had edible seeds (cañaigre or wild dock, lambs quarters or goosefoot, pigweed,
saltbush, tansy mustard, and purslane among others), wild potato, cattails, wild
chile, wild currants, wild mint, sunflower, chokecherry, and in areas where they
grow, mesquite beans and the fruits of various cacti. Certain of these contain significant vitamin C and other vitamins, and some have considerable mineral content, including iron. There was a variety of medicinal and ceremonial plants,
including tobacco (*Nicotiana rustica* and other species)—which was sometimes
mixed with point-leaf manzanita, thoroughwart, or sumac and employed in
rainmaking ceremonies. Medicinal plants included Mormon tea (*Ephedra* sp.)
used as a stimulant, and the psychoactive plant datura with its antiseptic and
pain control uses. Golondrina (*Euphorbia* sp.) was a treatment for cuts or burns,
with paste from the ground-up plant being spread on the affected area.
Doveweed (*Croton texensis*) was useful as a treatment for earache, the moistened
leaves being packed into the ear, while a tea made from plumahilla or western
yarrow (*Achillea lanulosa*) was used to combat chills. Smoke from the burned
hulls of piñon nuts was inhaled by a patient experiencing difficult childbirth,
and piñon gum mixed with ground squash seed was packed into wounds. Roots
of the cañaigre (*Rumex hymenosepalus*), mentioned above, were also boiled and
the water used for treating head colds, as was a tea made from the "white medicine," the boiled roots of *Erigonum fasciculatum*. This latter medicine was also
applied to wounds.

This is a small selection of plants recorded for later times; some of them, perhaps most or even all of them, were part of the Archaic heritage of the Pueblos.
However, a cautionary note should be introduced here. Certain foods and medicines used by Pueblo Indians in historic times, including accidentally introduced
"field weeds," are plants that have a wide geographical distribution and may possibly have been brought by Hispanics or Mexican Indians in the colonial period.
Likely there was borrowing back and forth, and certain plants of the historic
Pueblos definitely came from the European and Mexican Indian settlers. For
example, chile peppers were almost certainly introduced by the Spaniards but in
the later historic period were used medicinally by settlers and Pueblos alike. The

"buttons" from the peyote cactus, containing psychoactive alkaloids including mescaline, may conceivably have arrived in pre-Hispanic times, but the first record of them dates to the 1630s, and they probably came with the early Spanish settlers. In northern and western Mexico, peyote was and is used both in religious ceremonies to produce visions and for medicinal purposes. In the United States it has become the focus of a Native American religion, but one not particularly popular among the Pueblos.

There was always a strong ceremonial component among the Pueblos and their neighbors in the matter of food procurement. In agriculture, for example, it is clear that food plants with their enormous implications for culture change came already intertwined with considerable ceremonial baggage. Such large-scale movement of religious ideas, tied specifically to food production, is reflected, historically, in the similarities in mythology and ceremonialism between the Southwest and Mesoamerica. Some of the hunting rituals found around the Pueblo world today probably go back to an Archaic, possibly even a Paleo-Indian, time horizon. Such things as hunt societies, however, may represent Mesoamerican organizational influence at about the beginning of the Golden Age. Collecting seems to have attracted less ceremonial baggage, but it certainly had some.

Part of the planting ceremonialism had to do with the seasonal movements of heavenly bodies and the shifting of seasons. Observations of the heavens to trace out the seasons, a *calendar* approach to heaven and earth, was strongly developed in Mesoamerica. Important deities were personifications of the sun, moon, and the planet Venus in its appearances as morning and evening star. The importance of these celestial bodies, probably always in their aspects as deities, can be demonstrated in the Southwest. There we find, archaeologically, Quetzalcoatl and Venus associations, and of course the sun and moon were both important in marking the seasonal and agricultural round.

As early as the Anasazi Pueblo II times, measurements of the solstices can be demonstrated archaeologically at places like Yellowjacket in southwestern Colorado. The great Classic sites of Chaco Canyon and the Pueblo III period at Mesa Verde and Hovenweep also show evidence of such measurement. Siting lines, sometimes originating in the pueblos, or in shrines specifically built for that purpose, were used to observe the sunrise or sunset. All that is necessary is that a reasonably distant eastern skyline (or western skyline, if the observation is of the sunset) be available, one that has sufficient horizon features to measure, day by day, the slow apparent movement of the sun northward or southward as it rises or sets.

The moon was also important. For example, at Chimney Rock in the Piedra drainage of southern Colorado, some ninety miles north of Chaco Canyon, two adjoining spires rise from a rather barren sandstone plateau. Here was built a Chacoan outlier, apparently to take advantage of the northernmost declination of its 18.6 year lunar "cycle," at which time the moon, as seen from the site, rises between the two spires. The site itself was constructed in A.D. 1076 at the time of a northern "standstill" of the moon.

We know very little of the calendar calculations made by Pueblos as of the time of Oñate. But calendarial observations were part of their heritage and continued on into the future. Pueblos in the later historic period were especially interested in the summer and winter solstices. Both were important. The summer marked the end of the planting season and the beginning of the summer ceremonial round, but perhaps the winter solstice, with its "turning" and renewal of the sun, was most critical. The priestly observers, especially at Zuni, attempted to make the winter solstice correspond to the full moon—alas, something that they could not always do. The historic Pueblos also studied the night skies for other signs of the changing seasons with observations of the Pleiades, Sirius, and Venus as morning and evening star.

In recent times, although the winter solstice remains important, eastern Pueblos do not have the complex star and calendar lore of their Zuni and Hopi cousins. This was probably *not* the case in Oñate's time. In colonial days, the intense Spanish occupation of the Rio Grande Valley and the heavy Christianization of the ceremonial life and use of the handy Gregorian calendar permitted some of the old calendar ways to be discarded. This dependence on an alien calendar cannot have been the situation in A.D. 1598.

In the upper Rio Grande Valley, the sun sets earlier and earlier in the evening until around the middle of December, when the evenings lengthen. The situation is asymmetric as regards sunrise, however. The sun continues to rise later each day until around mid-January. The absolute *shortest* days of the year (clockwise) are the handful around December 21. Of course, neither the Pueblos nor Oñate's Spaniards had the chronometric capabilities to measure the *times* of sunrise and sunset, but the farthest south position of the sun on the eastern horizon also comes in the period around December 21. The various pueblos varied in desirability of their locations for solstice dawn or sunset observations, depending on the height of mountains on the eastern or western skylines. But the balance of the evidence is that they made such observations, and that these were important in the ceremonial and the agricultural year.

The religious and ceremonial life of Pueblos of Oñate's time must largely be reconstructed by archaeology and by analogy with nineteenth- and twentieth-century practices. The early Spaniards gave very little specific information. Still, a number of early Europeans do mention masked dances, almost certainly dances of the kachina cult. Kachinas are ancestor figures who visit the Pueblos and perform ceremonial weather control and fertility dances, with the kachina being embodied by masked individuals. The kachinas, as discussed in chapter 2, were everywhere in the Pueblo world. Cognate words for the cult appear in the Keresan languages and in the Towa and Northern Tiwa. The Tewa and Zuni use different terms, however; at Zuni, for example, the kachina are called *kokko*. There are other cross-pueblo similarities and differences. In Zuni, Hopi, the Keresan towns, and Southern Tiwa, but not in the Tewa-Towa area, the kachinas reside in a water source west of the given tribe. The dead take the form of kachinas in Towa, Tewa, Hopi, and Zuni, but the Keresan towns seem to be split on this issue. There are other differences; for example, whether women can be initiated into the kachina cult. Obviously, centuries of evolution and differential acculturation pressure from the Spaniards has caused variations in the cult. Some of the variations, of course, may have been there from earliest times.

The kachina cult is related to Tlaloc, the Mesoamerican god of rain and weather-making. The practice of human sacrifice to Tlaloc—for example, the sacrifice of children to promote rain—had dropped out of the Pueblo kachina cult before the first Spanish conquest. There is indication, especially in the folklore, that such sacrifices were performed in prehistoric times.

Kachinas reached the Pueblos, perhaps moving up the Rio Grande Valley, a little after A.D. 1300. This was a time when rich influences from the Casas Grandes culture of Chihuahua (specifically, the Casas Grandes Medio period) was spreading across southern New Mexico and into western Texas. The very visibility of the kachina ceremonies made them vulnerable when the Spaniards arrived. As we shall see, the missionaries took special aim at these ceremonies, equating them with diabolical behavior. The result was the partial suppression of the cult, especially in the east. Though the Pueblo Revolt restored the kachinas for a time, and the eighteenth-century Franciscans were less vehement in their attacks, eastern manifestations of the cult weakened in the eighteenth and later centuries. It seems likely that alternate and colorful Christian ceremonies were accepted as emotional substitutes. Still, kachinas are found today among the eastern Pueblos, though not the complex panoply seen in the west. Among the Zuni and Hopi, the Christianization agenda of the seventeenth-century missionaries largely failed and kachinas won the day.

In a recent book, I speculated on the great Zuni and Hopi *Shalako* ceremony, an elaborate winter solstice observance that involves spectacular masked dances. I suggested, following earlier work of anthropologist Elsie Clews Parsons, that the Shalako rites had been introduced during the interregnum period that followed the Coronado expedition of 1539–42. Brought by central Mexican Indians who remained in the Southwest, these rites contained incomplete versions of Aztec ceremonies of the twelfth month, Teotleco, interpreted through southwestern iconography, some of it pre-Hispanic in date. If this was the case, Oñate and his men probably saw or heard of the Shalako, especially at Zuni; however, the ceremony was not reported—at least in such terms as to allow it to be identified—until much later historic times.

Other southwestern ceremonial behavior is attested to by archaeology. The cult of the god Quetzalcoatl, associated with the morning and evening star, was certainly part of the ceremonial scene in Oñate's day. Archaeologist Charles C. Di Peso believed that Quetzalcoatl manifestations such as the plumed serpent, use of macaw and parrot feathers for ritual costume and prayer plumes, multifloored structures of adobe (Di Peso refers to "puddled adobe," but in all probability they were coursed adobe), square columns, T-shaped doorways, and stairways appeared as a complex "before A.D. 1050." Of course, Di Peso was relating this complex to Medio period Casas Grandes, and his dates run consistently a century or so too early.

Adjusting Di Peso's dating would probably make the complex too late for Chaco Canyon, although some of these elements, the square columns and stairways, were utilized there, as was the scarlet macaw. On the other hand, coursed adobe is not characteristic of Chaco, although adobe walls are found at the outlier site of Bis sa'ani, east of Chaco Canyon, dating to around A.D. 1130. Nor is the plumed serpent found in Chaco culture. This does not absolutely rule out Quetzalcoatl worship. Ornithologist Charmion McKusick believes that the scarlet macaw itself is a strong marker of Quetzalcoatl worship. The goddess Chalchihuitlicue, "Lady Precious Green," the deity of lakes and springs, and the consort of Tlaloc, was also closely associated with Quetzalcoatl. McKusick suggests that the green plumaged military macaw may have been sacrificed to Chalchihuitlicue. Military macaws, however, seem to be absent from Chaco Canyon and, as said above, are rare in the Southwest outside of Casas Grandes. This might indicate that Chalchihuitlicue worship did not catch on in the upper Southwest, but McKusick points to Chalchihuitlicue depictions at Awatovi as indicating a worship of this complex goddess among the Hopi.

Even assuming that Di Peso's Quetzalcoatl complex is valid for Mesoamerica, certain elements may have spread independently at different times to the Southwest. I suspect that another complex—one that appears in the Mimbres area of southern New Mexico around A.D. 1000, embodying the sun-deer, moon-rabbit complex and the idea of supernatural twins—was the basis of Quetzalcoatl influences in the upper Southwest. *Quetzalcoatl* was a god of merchants and travelers. Under the name *Ehecatl*, he represented the wind. He was also the embodiment of Venus as the morning star, and his name means at least two things: "winged serpent" and "sacred twin." The latter name relates to a twinning with the monstrous Xolotl, the personification of death, represented by the evening star. These twins are fairly clearly related to the divine twins of southwestern religion, and their earthly avatars, twinned religious officers such as the elder and younger bow priests of the bow priesthood in Zuni.

As discussed in chapter 2, sometime in the period A.D. 1150–1200 the various settlements that we collectively call Casas Grandes expanded their influence throughout much of southern New Mexico. A century or so later, certain Quetzalcoatl ideas, including those of the Mimbres, swept into the upper Southwest through Casas Grandes auspices—at about the same time and by the same mechanisms as the kachina cult. If there *was* an earlier Quetzalcoatl manifestation (say, at Chaco Canyon), it was now likely enriched and modified by the new Casas Grandes—based religious ideas.

The Pueblos as of 1598 worshipped a series of deities that appear historically and which can also be identified iconographically from the Golden Age. They include, among others: Sun Father, Moon Mother, the fire god, the twin war-gods (the northernmost extensions of the concept of the divine twins), and the horned or plumed water serpent, which has both Quetzalcoatl and Tlaloc aspects. The association of Quetzalcoatl and Tlaloc actually goes back to Mesoamerica and may date as early as Olmec times. It seems to me that kachinas, at least some of them, are functional equivalents, and perhaps historical descendants, of the *Tlaloco,* the plural form of Tlaloc, sometimes thought of as "helpers" of the primary Tlaloc manifestation.

In any case, Pueblo religion was focused on the kiva or ceremonial chamber and on the courtyard where many of the dances and other ceremonies were held. Kivas were of various sizes and both round and square, partially underground or incorporated in house blocks. Oñate's soldiers reported kiva murals, though they misinterpreted them. The murals most likely related to the ceremonial round.

Unfortunately, we cannot give a detailed coherent description of Pueblo religion as of Oñate's time. The religion of Pueblo Native Americans today has been described in encyclopedic measure by the Pueblo expert Elsie Clews Parsons. Her descriptions of the later historic period probably encode much of what was there in 1598, and, as discussed above, evidence from rock art, mural paintings, and the like give some information on deities and cultic observances such as the kachina organizations. What we lack is specificity of detail, and *that* we probably shall never have.

The political and social organization of the Pueblos was quickly under attack by the Franciscans, primarily because of the close intertwining of religion and political and social organizations. Everywhere the old political order of priests and their helpers was suppressed, even officials with "secular" functions, like the bow priests. As we shall see, the newcomers imposed on the Pueblos something akin to the Spanish *cabildo* structure: a town governor, counselors, and officers with police duties. Eight years before Oñate, Castaño de Sosa had attempted to form cabildo-like governments in the Pueblos, but Castaño's authority did not last long enough for much to be accomplished. Oñate likely started from scratch.

Evidence from rock art suggests that along with the kachina cult in the four-teenth century, the various Pueblos had organized warrior, hunt, and medicine societies. These sodalities still exist, though they were much changed in the Spanish period—the war societies, especially, serving the Spaniards' need for mercenary warriors to fight against the surrounding nomads. It seems likely that the Spanish-Pueblo office of "war captain" in the seventeenth century was held by the head of the war society of a given Pueblo. However, to a lesser or greater degree, all the societies, because of their association with Pueblo religion, came under missionary attack. In Oñate's time this had not really begun.

Lacking any coherent evidence of the sociopolitical situation in the pueblos in 1598, I can only make broad generalizations. Archaeological and distributional evidence suggests that many of the Pueblos had some sort of clan structure. The term *clan,* as used classically in anthropology, referred to matrilineality; that is, it represented a group of people who had (or at least, claimed) common descent in the female line. Clans were important in various social and ceremonial ways, functioning, for example, to organize and control marriage.

Among modern Pueblos the nearest to the classic definition of clan is in the west, where matrilineal clans are found among the Hopi and Zuni. Marriage in Hopi is exogamous, meaning that it is necessary to marry outside the clan, and it also is matrilocal, which is to say that the bridegroom moves to his wife's home—in the case of the Hopi, to a house block where the clan matriarch resides. Hopi clans are also grouped into exogamous larger divisions that the anthropologists call phratries. Crosscutting these clans are societies concerned with various ceremonial activities including kachina initiation. A number of kiva groups also crosscut both clans and societies. Among the Hopi, both boys and girls are initiated into the kachina society, something rather atypical in the Pueblo world.

At Zuni, clans are also exogamous and matrilocal. Houses are owned by women. The man moves in but is always somewhat of a "visitor." If the marriage fails, he returns to his mother's or sister's home. The father's clan of any given individual is ceremonially important, and marriage into this clan, though not actually forbidden, is discouraged. The Zuni have six kiva groups generally restricted to men. All male members of Zuni society between the ages of eight and twelve join a kiva group, usually one chosen by the father or mother at the child's birth. These are not immutable; an individual can choose another group later in life. All boys are initiated into the kachina society, but women normally do not join this society. The Zuni also have curing societies, which are for the most part open to both sexes.

In modern times, the Keresans have matrilineal clans that function to regulate marriage. Ceremonialism is largely in the hands of the religious sodalities. Sometimes called "medicine societies," these also included war and hunt groups. There are winter (turquoise) and summer (squash or pumpkin) kivas with associated Koshare and Quirana, two clowning groups that have management roles in the ceremonial round. These groups are called "clowns" because part of their function is burlesque and satire, but among the Keresans, as elsewhere in the Pueblo world, they are primarily religious in nature. In addition, one finds masked kachinas (whose organization varies somewhat from pueblo to pueblo), weather-control figures who dance primarily in the summer. The head religious officer in the nineteenth and twentieth centuries is called a *cacique*. This name is a Spanish-introduced word, having been picked up by them from the Taino speakers of the Greater Antilles. The office itself may be old. In some Keresan pueblos, the cacique was also head of the Flint Medicine Society. Other officers included the two war priests and various lesser figures.

The Towa (now the single pueblo of Jemez) have matrilineal exogamous clans, though at present the family structure is patrilineal, and the father normally owns the family dwelling. This may be due to centuries of Spanish influence. There are the two kiva moieties (a moiety is a division of a society into two parts), Turquoise and Squash, the membership of which is patrilineal, and a number of societies involving curing, hunting, and war. Kachinas are called *katsana*, a variation of the Hopi name. The cacique heads the political organization; under him are officials, who originally may have been war chiefs, and their assistants.

The Tewa have summer and winter moieties corresponding to the Squash and Turquoise moieties of the Keresans; in these groups the cacique is a moiety head. Kachinas are associated with these summer and winter moieties, and all boys belonged to one or the other of these kachina societies. The moieties were patrilineal, though there is considerable flexibility in membership. There are "clans," but they serve no marriage function.

The Northern Tiwa towns have so-called clans that are actually kiva groups and are assigned to moieties, the northside kiva groups and the southside kiva groups. The Southern Tiwa also have summer and winter moieties and what are sometimes called clans, the corn groups with color-direction associations. At present, kachinas are very weakly developed in both the northern and southern Tiwa.

The anthropologist and Tewa Native American Edward P. Dozier believed that the clan system in the eastern pueblos, Jemez and Tewa, represented a late (presumably historic) borrowing from the Keresans. I suspect that elements of the kachina cult were also reintroduced in historic times from the west, in this case from Hopi. I say *reintroduced* because it seems clear that as of the time of Oñate and for some centuries before, kachinas were an integral part of eastern Pueblo ceremonialism. The new kachina system that arose after the seventeenth-century repression by the Franciscans was a mixture, terminologically and in ceremonial content, of the old Rio Grande Pueblo cult and cultic practices from Hopi and Zuni.

Historian Ramón A. Gutiérrez, in a recent publication, has suggested that aboriginally the Pueblo Indians were all matrilineally oriented.

> . . . suffice it to say that all of the Puebloans were matrilineal at the time of the conquest, and that those Puebloans who were in closest contact with Spanish towns became patrilineal or bilateral. Those Pueblos who most resisted Christianization—the Hopi, the Zuñi, and the Keres at Acoma—remained matrilineal. Among those people we still find a vibrant array of women's fertility societies, spirited ceremonials to vivify the earth and a host of descendant earth-bound symbols that celebrate femininity. Among the Puebloans who became most acculturated to European ways—the Tewa and the Keres (except Acoma)—women's fertility societies were suppressed.

This is an intriguing idea, and a Spanish-introduced "patrilinealization" may indeed have been a factor in the acculturation process among the eastern Pueblos, though I suspect the situation may be somewhat more complicated than a simple transfer from matrilineal to patrilineal status. In any case, hard evidence for this—or any other specific system—is very scanty.

The ceremonial headships of modern Pueblos probably represent somewhat similar offices as of the time of Oñate. What seems to have happened is that the Spanish-introduced cabildo officials replaced certain religious officials, and/or perhaps took over certain functions originally performed by members of the religious hierarchy. It seems clear that a distinction between "religious" and "secular" among the Pueblos could not have been made as of Oñate's time.

If we know little for sure about the Pueblos in 1598, our information on the Jumano and Apachean neighbors of the Pueblos is even less secure. The Jumano had headmen and probably some sort of band structure, but as to the composition of Jumano bands and how such basic social organizations as the family and extended family were organized, we have no real information. Coronado (who called the group Teya), Espejo, and Castaño all visited the Jumano but tell us next to nothing. Fray Alonso de Benavides, in New Mexico during the 1620s, was very interested in the Jumano, but his goal was conversion. His account is heavy on Christian miracles, but it gives no information on the indigenous religious life of the group.

The same problem exists when considering the religion of those hunting and gathering, and sometimes agriculturalist, neighbors of the Pueblos, the Navajo-Apache. Even the scanty evidence from the Spanish documents is mainly later and may represent some sort of accommodation of native systems to the new European power in the Southwest. Documents that describe the situation up to, say, the 1620s are mainly silent on religious and ceremonial matters. The Querechos, later called Apaches, were visited by Coronado, Chamuscado, Espejo, Zaldívar, and Oñate. These Indians had Benavides's enthusiastic attention for he was eager to convert them, but aside from saying that the Apache worshipped the sun and moon, he gave no religious information about them.

Common to all the Apachean groups today are two monster-killing culture heros associated with sun or fire and with water, respectively, and there are also trickster tales with Coyote as protagonist. Sun and moon are important throughout the Apachean world. All Apachean groups have an important role for the shaman, a religious entrepreneur who heals by manipulating spirit power or by reestablishing the ceremonial balance of the universe. Certain Apachean groups—the Navajo, Western Apache, Jicarilla, and Lipan—tell a story of emergence from the underworld that is most likely Pueblo in its genesis. The Navajo, in particular, are rich in ceremonialism, costumes, color-direction concepts, and mythology that seem to be drawn from the Pueblo world. It is unclear just when these elements appeared, but some of them may be prehistoric. Several of the Apache groups utilized masked dancers. These god impersonators likely derive from the Pueblos. The well-known *Yeis* of the Navajo are certainly Puebloan in origin; though not specifically kachinas, they probably borrowed from the kachina cult.

The Apachean basic social unit was the matrilocal extended family. A series of these families stayed together on the annual round and formed what is often referred to as a *local group,* each with its own leader. A confederation of local groups who lived in more-or-less contiguous areas formed a named "band" with a prestigious local group headman functioning also as band leader. Originally these were civil chiefs, but in later days war chiefs were added, though they usually were subordinate to the highest civil authority. At least in historic times, the named bands were weakly developed among the Navajo, perhaps because of the

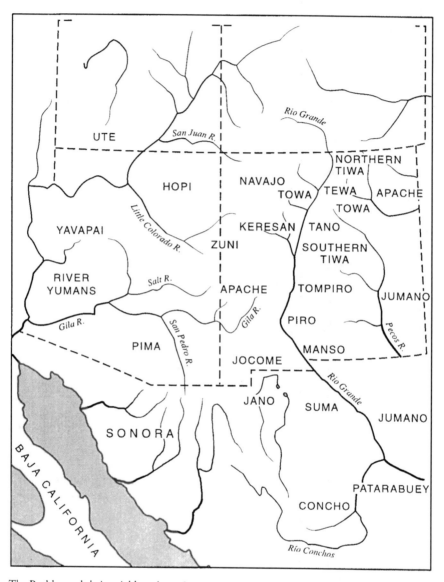

The Pueblos and their neighbors in 1598

differential distribution patterns imposed by sheep herding, which the Navajo had picked up from the Spaniards by the end of the seventeenth century. Or quite possibly sheep herding was diffused to the Navajo from the Pueblos either during the seventeenth-century mission days or in the interregnum period after

1680. The loom itself was presumably a Pueblo import into Navajo life, though just when it came is not known. In 1583, what I take to be ancestral Navajo in the Acoma area were *trading* for cotton cloth. In any case, the tribes and nations of the modern Apachean world are a latter-day phenomenon, dating from the American period and the Bureau of Indian Affairs.

Perhaps beginning in pre-Spanish times but continuing on during the historical period, the Western Apache and the Navajo had developed matrilineal clans, most likely from western Pueblo neighbors. The Jicarilla of north-central New Mexico today have a moiety system that was borrowed from the northern Rio Grande Pueblos. Some of this borrowing was post-Conquest in nature, though in many cases it is very difficult to sort out the date, whether early or late, of a given trait.

The Espejo party saw "Querechos" in 1583 in the area around Hopi and at Acoma. The Querechos were probably among the Jemez during this same time period. The descriptions of Espejo and of Luxán clearly indicate a flourishing trade between Pueblos and Querechos, whom Espejo refers to as "mountain dwellers." There was an active trade with the Acoma and probably the Jemez people, the Querechos providing salt, various game (deer, rabbit, and hare are specifically mentioned), and dressed "chamois" skins. Espejo describes a rather Puebloan-sounding ceremonial dance and implies that it was performed by the Querechos. However, Bernardino de Luna, a member of Espejo's party, seems to identify this particular dance as Pueblo, probably Acoma.

In any case, it sounds as if the Querechos had been living in the region between Hopi and the Jemez Mountains for some time. It is generally assumed that they were *not* there in Coronado's day because of the lack of mention in documents of that period. However, negative evidence is somewhat risky, and it simply may be that the Querechos were intimidated by the large Coronado party and hid in their mountain fastnesses. Even if these Apacheans were post-Coronado, they surely were in the western regions a generation or so before Espejo.

The Querechos were still in the Acoma area during 1598 and 1599, for after the destruction of Acoma by the Spaniards, some of the older Acoma Indians were farmed out to them. It seems to me that the evidence on the "western Querechos" of Espejo and Oñate indicates that they were Navajo. A group on the Little Colorado south of the Hopi, identified by Oñate in 1605 as the Tacabuy, were also probably Navajo. The Navajo were operating in the Jemez Mountains in the seventeenth century, and they were united with the Jemez Indians in various anti-Spanish activities in 1614 and again in 1639. In 1630 Benavides mentioned people, whom he specifically identified as Navajo, residing fifty leagues north of the Xila Apache of the upper Gila drainage.

Zárate Salmerón, who arrived in New Mexico in 1621, was among the Jemez some time before 1623 and contacted the Navajo there. By 1626–27 he had already coined the term *Apaches de Navajo*. From Zárate Salmerón's description, it would seem that the Navajo lived near Zuni and Hopi, perhaps also in the region around Mount Taylor and, possibly, on or around the San Juan River. They clearly extended eastward to the Jemez Mountains, for in 1629 they threatened the pueblo of Santa Clara on the eastern edge of these mountains. Benavides said that the Navajo territory stretched from east to west some 300 leagues, "and we do not know where it ends."

As we have seen, the first mention of the Navajo, using that term, comes in the writings of Zárate Salmerón, likely dating to the early 1620s. To Fray Benavides at the end of this decade, the word *Navajo* referred to the "great planted fields" of the Apaches de Navajo. Assuming that the Espejo period Querecho were Navajo, they may already have been experimenting with agriculture, even though they were still described as hunters in Espejo's day. Agriculture surely did not come to them without the ceremonialism that both donors and recipients would have regarded as essential. I think it very likely that the heavy religious and ceremonial influence on the Navajo (and to a lesser degree other Apaches) came before the Spanish missionaries put an end to the overt practice of Pueblo religion. This is probably especially true of the Navajo, for at least by the early seventeenth century, these people were becoming sedentary and agricultural as well as the inheritors of much Pueblo ceremonialism and social organization. Agriculture, loom use, animal husbandry (turkey), matrilineal clans, color-direction symbolism, sand paintings, masked dances, and much other religious and ceremonial behavior are probably of Pueblo origin. My own belief is that much of the Pueblo flavor of Navajo life appeared before Oñate's time, and probably before Coronado's time. The Navajo continued to borrow Pueblo cultural items during the seventeenth century, especially through contacts with Jemez but likely with other Pueblos as well.

In other words, by 1598 the Navajo were already well on their way to being acculturated. Had the Spaniards not come to the Southwest, the Apaches de Navajo would have—within a century or so—become the first Athapascan Pueblos. The Spanish introduction of sheep and the adaption of sheep herding in the seventeenth and eighteenth century led the Navajo onto another path. It was one they continued to follow throughout later historic times.

CHAPTER SIX

The First Decade in Spanish
New Mexico

The main Oñate party arrived on August 18, 1598, to find that the governor, using fifteen hundred Indians as laborers, had already begun construction of an irrigation ditch for the new colony. The settlers immediately started to move into part of the house blocks of the Tewa pueblo of Okeh (or Oké) and began to construct a church, San Juan Bautista, which was consecrated on September 8. Okeh was part of the pueblo complex now known collectively as San Juan. It was sited on the east side of the Rio Grande, while its other half, Yungue, was west of the river. A few months later the Spaniards began calling their settlement San Gabriel del Yungue, though it is unclear whether at this time they actually physically shifted the settlement across the river. According to modern information from the San Juan people, Okeh was the home of the winter moiety, while Yungue housed the summer division.

In early August Oñate had visited the Towa pueblos of the Jemez River drainage and found one of the village leaders in possession of a silver paten (a shallow plate used to hold the consecrated wafer during Mass). A small hole had been drilled in the middle, and the Jemez native was wearing the paten around his neck. Believing it to have originally belonged to one of the martyred missionaries from Chamuscado's time, Oñate traded for it with the idea of making it a sacred relic at the altar of the new church.

Just days after the arrival of the main party, a rebellion broke out involving some forty-five men who were plotting to return to New Spain. It is difficult to explain why, at the end of a long but generally successful trip to the Southwest, there was this sudden revolt involving a third of the fighting power of the colony. We do not have the rebels' version of events, but Oñate claimed that they expected to find silver strewn around and that they also resented the fact that he

San Gabriel del Yungue (courtesy of the Museum of New Mexico, neg. no. 25)

did not allow them to abuse the Indians. Perhaps, in Oñate's absence, there had been growing discontent among the people in the wagon train. It is possible that certain members of Oñate's party thought in terms of a slaving operation, something still going on along the northern frontier in spite of the colonization laws of 1573. It also may be that enemies of Oñate who had contested his colonization plans were still operating. At any rate, Captain Pablo de Aguilar, who had already clashed with Oñate (see chapter 4) was one of the three ringleaders. The governor sentenced the three to death but was persuaded by the Franciscans and the army to pardon everybody. On August 21 Oñate staged what he called a "day of merciful punishment . . . the occasion of the famous sermon of tears, and of universal peace." Not to be reconciled were four men who on the twelfth of September deserted and fled southward. Oñate promptly sent two of his captains, Gaspar Pérez de Villagrá and Gerónimo Márquez, with three soldiers to apprehend the fugitives. They were eventually overtaken far to the south in Nueva Vizcaya, and two of them killed on the spot, the other two being allowed to escape. This action had little effect on the colony but figured into later investigations of Oñate's governorship.

On September 8 the new church of San Juan Bautista was dedicated and its altar consecrated by Fray Alonso Martínez, the Franciscan commissary. A sermon was preached by Fray Cristóbal de Salazar, one of the missionaries and cousin to Oñate. The church, finished as quickly as it was, must have been of rather flimsy construction, probably some sort of jacal structure plastered over.

Today its location is unknown. The following day, Indians from various pueblos were assembled in "the main kiva" at San Juan Bautista and an Act of Obedience and Vassalage was read to them and accepted by them. Two months earlier (July 7), the Keresan Pueblos had agreed to a similar act at Santo Domingo.

Missionaries were now assigned by Oñate and the father commissary to various pueblos. Francisco de San Miguel was given Pecos, the Salinas region, the Apache region east of the Sierra Nevada (the Sangre de Cristo Mountains), and the Jumano settlements. Francisco de Zamora had as his assignment Picurís, Taos, and the Apaches west of the Sierra Nevada. Juan de Rozas received the Keres pueblos, and Alonso de Lugo, the Jemez group, Zia, and the Apaches of the surrounding area. Andrés de Corchado received Acoma, Zuni, and Hopi. Father Juan Claros was given Tiguex and the Piro pueblos. Cristóbal de Salazar was assigned the Tewa pueblos and was also to be the resident priest for the new Spanish city. The father commissary, Alonso Martínez himself, was not given a specific assignment and presumably intended to remain at the mission headquarters in Santo Domingo.

According to the obedience document, "All of the eight blessed Franciscan fathers volunteered joyfully to go to the nation and tribe assigned to them, not valuing their own lives when it was for the service of God and the king." With such large and diverse areas assigned, it is obvious that from the beginning additional missionaries were expected. When the serious work of missionization began in the post-Oñate years, a considerable number of missionaries were added.

The viceroy had given Oñate instructions to locate the survivors of the Gutiérrez de Humaña and Leyva de Bonilla expedition. According to the account of Humaña's Mexican Indian servant Jusepe, who had escaped and who was now with Oñate (see chapter 3), Humaña had murdered Leyva de Bonilla. To investigate this illegal expedition and to replenish his dwindling food supplies with a buffalo hunt, Oñate sent his nephew, Vicente Zaldívar, with a party of sixty men to the bison area of the southern Plains. Zaldívar left the headquarters on September 15; meanwhile, back in Spain, all unknown to the colonists, a momentous event had taken place. On September 13, the long reign of Philip II ended, and his son became king as Philip III. This had no immediate effect on the colony, though it may have been a factor in Oñate's later legal troubles, the new king being, perhaps, somewhat less sympathetic to the governor than his father had been. However, it *was* Philip III who confirmed Oñate's appointment as adelantado in 1602.

The Zaldívar party went by way of Pecos Pueblo, where Fray Francisco de San Miguel and the Towa-speaking lay brother Juan de Dios were left to begin the work of missionization. Zaldívar and his men then contacted the Apaches, whom Zaldívar referred to as "Vaqueros," probably somewhere in northeast New Mexico or the western part of the Texas Panhandle. They did not locate Humaña but did kill a number of bison—food for the colonists who were chronically short of supplies. The expedition returned on November 8, 1598.

While this was going on, Oñate, taking only thirty soldiers, made a trip to various Pueblos, receiving their submission and investigating mineral and other wealth in the new province. He visited the Tompiro pueblos in the Salinas area, east of the Manzano Mountains, then turned westward, apparently with the idea of finding a route to the Pacific Ocean. Oñate stopped briefly in the Tiwa region and from there marched to Acoma, where he was received with apparent friendliness, though Villagrá later claimed that there was a plot by one of the war society heads, a man the Spaniards called Zutacapán, to isolate and kill him. Considering what happened a few days later, this may well have been the case. The pueblo of Acoma is at the top of a high isolated rock, or *peñol*, extremely difficult to attack. The Indians may have felt that it was invulnerable.

From Acoma, Oñate went on to Zuni, where he met Alonso, a son of the Mexico City native, Gaspar. Alonso—it is unclear how or why he had this Spanish name—"used a few Mexican words but did not understand any." Oñate's captain, Marcos Farfán de los Godos, was sent to explore the Zuni Salt Lake, some forty miles south of the pueblo. About the same time, Villagrá joined the group, having returned from the expedition to capture the deserters and pushed on alone to catch up with Oñate. In transit, Villagrá ran across an Acoma war party under Zutacapán and narrowly escaped with his life.

On November 8, Oñate and his party continued on to the Hopi pueblos where he had heard there were rich mines. Sending Farfán de los Godos with another officer, Alonso de Quesada, and a party of seven soldiers southwestward to explore for mines, Oñate returned to Zuni. He had left instructions for his deputy at Okeh, Juan de Zaldívar, to join him there as soon as brother Vicente returned from the buffalo plains. On December 11, Farfán de los Godos, leaving his small band of soldiers at Hopi, returned from his exploration of central Arizona. He had reached the Verde River and had investigated the mining possibilities in the region around modern Jerome. This area had been previously explored by the Espejo party, from information given by Hopi Indians. It most likely was one of the sources of mineral pigment used by the Hopi for various decorative purposes. The Spaniards never exploited this section of Arizona, though in the nineteenth century Jerome became a copper mining center, and there are gold, lead, and silver deposits in the general region.

December 9 brought desperate news. A small Spanish party under charge of Bernabé de las Casas reached Oñate thirty miles east of Zuni and told the governor that the maestro de campo, Juan de Zaldívar, had been ambushed at Acoma. He and twelve of his party were dead, and other Spanish soldiers were wounded. The first serious Pueblo challenge to Spanish rule of New Mexico had begun.

Juan de Zaldívar had left to join Oñate on November 18, ten days after his brother's return from the Plains. With a party of around thirty-one men, he reached Acoma on the first of December, stopping over for supplies. Initial contact was reasonably friendly, the Acoma Indians giving him wood and water. However, they asked for more time to collect and prepare cornmeal, so Zaldívar made camp at a small stream about five miles from the pueblo. On December 4, Zaldívar led a party totaling nineteen individuals to Acoma in order to collect provisions. Later witnesses stress that the camp master was willing to trade for the cornmeal and had a number of hatchets, hawks' bells, and other objects to offer the Indians. Left in charge of the camp was Captain Gerónimo Márquez, who had only recently returned from Mexico.

Once he reached the top of the peñol, Zaldívar divided his little party into at least three groups to more efficiently collect food from the various houses. This, however, proved to be a mistake for it made the Spanish party extremely vulnerable. The fighting apparently was set off when a Spanish soldier named Martín de Vivero (or Ribero) took two turkeys from one of the terraces, perhaps against the understood agreement. He was set on and killed, and the Acoma flared into attack. Only five of this provisioning party escaped, jumping from lower portions of the rock and rescued by Bernabé de las Casas, who had remained at the bottom with the expedition's horses.

The surviving Spaniards reacted promptly to this crisis. After an initial party under Captain López de Tavora became lost and returned to camp, Márquez sent Bernabé de las Casas with seven men to warn Oñate, while the captain, with the rest of the group, retreated to San Gabriel. On hearing of the threat to Spanish control, Oñate pulled up stakes at Zuni and also returned to Okeh-Yungue, avoiding the rebellious Acoma Indians on the way. His great fear was that the outbreak at Acoma would trigger a Pueblo-wide rebellion. The Spaniards were outnumbered something on the order of a hundred to one, and they were spread rather thinly, with one group of soldiers at Zuni, a few at Hopi, and the major army in the Rio Grande area.

Oñate now consulted the Franciscans and gathered evidence that the attack had been unprovoked and that a Spanish counterattack would be, in Spanish terms, a "just war." On January 12, 1599, the sargento mayor, Vicente de Zaldívar, brother of Juan, was dispatched with seventy-two men plus two pieces of artillery and carts for supplies. With Zaldívar were the interpreters, Cristóbal and Tomás. These two Mexican Indians had lived at least for a time at Santo

Domingo and probably spoke some eastern Keresan, though they may not have known the western, Acoma dialect. However that may be, many individuals in the pueblos must have been fluent in two or more languages, and probably the two native Mexicans managed to interpret reasonably well.

Because of Gaspar de Villagrá we have a fairly complete, if one-sided and flowery, description of the battle for Acoma. Another account by the treasurer of the colony, Alonso Sánchez, is somewhat more prosaic but adds additional information. Still further details come in the various judicial hearings in later years.

Zaldívar and his soldiers reached Acoma on January 21, 1599, and through the interpreters called for the Pueblo to surrender. When that failed, as expected, he camped in the vicinity and worked out a plan for an attack the following day. It was to be a frontal assault. The leader, however, with eleven men would steal behind the peñol and attempt to scale the summits of Acoma from the rear. On the afternoon of January 22, the frontal attack began, and Zaldívar with Captains Villagrá and Aguilar and nine soldiers established a foothold on the peñol. What happened after that is not clear, but Zaldívar and his party seem to have held on during the night of January 22. On January 23, the Spaniards launched a major two-pronged attack, and Acoma was overwhelmed. Many Indians were killed, and seventy or eighty warriors and some five hundred women and children were captured. This is the official account. In 1601, Captain Luis Gasco de Velasco, who was listed in the muster roll of 1598 as treasurer of the expedition, gave another version. According to Gasco de Velasco, the Acoma Indians surrendered and gave up blankets, maize, and other food, but then Vicente de Zaldívar ordered the Indians seized and thrown off the cliffs. Women and children, who had fled to the kivas and houses, had their hiding places set on fire, burning many of them alive. Although Gasco de Velasco had supported Oñate in a letter from the army to King Philip in March of 1599, he later became an outspoken critic.

Whatever the truth of how the Acoma Indians died, certainly several hundred of them perished, including Zutacapán and the other war leaders. A three-day trial beginning on February 9, 1599, was then held for the survivors at Santo Domingo Pueblo. An advocate for the Indians, Alonso Gómez Montesinos, was appointed to meet the requirements of Spanish law, but a guilty verdict was a foregone conclusion. Punishment of the Acoma Indians was announced by Oñate.

No one was to be executed. Of course, a large number of Indians had already been killed, clearly including at least some women and children. Of the captives, males over twenty-five years of age were condemned to have a foot cut off and twenty years of slavery; twenty-four individuals received this sentence. Two

Hopi Indians found at Acoma were ordered to have their right hands severed and were then sent back Hopi as an advertisement of Spanish resolve. Males aged twelve to twenty-five were not mutilated but were also sentenced to twenty years of servitude, as were women over twelve. Girls under twelve were turned over to the commissary, Fray Martínez, and boys under twelve to Vicente de Zaldívar with instructions that they be given a Christian upbringing. According to Villagrá, the poet himself helped escort sixty female children to Mexico, where they were divided out among the various convents. It is not clear where the remainder of the children were sent.

Interestingly, according to Oñate, "Old men and women, disabled in the war, I order freed and entrusted to the Indians of the province of the Querechos that they may support them and may not allow them to leave their pueblos." These Querechos were the Apaches—most likely Navajo (see chapter 5)—living in the vicinity, probably in the Cebolleta region north of Acoma. It does indicate the close relations of the two groups, something noted by Espejo sixteen years previously.

The mutilations, no doubt chosen for their shock value, seem monstrous to the modern reader. It might be said, however, that in the context of late-sixteenth-century European penal practices and attitudes, Oñate did not inflict particularly harsh punishments. Even the enslavements were for a sharply limited period, and children were not to be punished. Of course, permanently removing children from their parents might disturb our sensibilities, but from Oñate's own point of view his actions were hardly excessive.

Still, even in terms of the contemporary moral code, Oñate's actions at Acoma returned to haunt him. In 1614 he was condemned by the viceregal court on a number of counts. One of these concerned the Zaldívar attack. "After the Indians of the town of Acoma had killed Oñate's nephew, the maese de campo, Juan de Zaldívar Oñate, and other soldiers of this company, he sent Vicente de Zaldívar, brother of the deceased, to punish them, which he did with great severity, injuring many innocent people and causing the death of many natives; and the adelantado exercised the same severity with those taken alive in the said pueblo." Politics may well have entered this condemnation of Oñate, but by contemporary Spanish law, Oñate was judged to have exceeded a reasonable response to the Acoma "rebellion."

This was, of course, in the future. As of the beginning of 1599, Oñate had strengthened his position by his firm treatment of Acoma. He quickly made plans to expand the area under his control. First, however, it was time to report to the viceroy, so on March 2, 1599, he wrote a long letter to Monterrey sketching out the events of the past year. Oñate described the new province in enthusiastic terms; there was a variety of rich ores, abundant salt, and, in the mountains, large deposits of sulfur. Game was plentiful, and the area was bountiful in terms of plants. The Rio Grande and other streams had ample fish. The Pueblo Indians were of "good disposition," the Apaches and Cocoyes were extremely numerous, the latter people perhaps to be identified with the Pai people of Arizona. Certain Apache groups lived not in rancherías but in pueblos, one of which was eighteen leagues (about forty-five or fifty miles) from the Spanish capital, a pueblo of fifteen plazas. If this settlement was Navajo, it was likely west of Okeh and may be identical to the Navajo town visited by Benavides's party in 1629.

Not only was New Mexico rich in its own right, but the South Sea was near, and thus the possibility of trade with "Peru, New Spain and China." The region was also suitable for the production of "wines and [olive?] oil." Bison hides represented an important potential trade item. It was a very upbeat report.

A second, short letter enclosed with the first and written on March 5 asked that the viceroy send irons with the royal stamp to mark the silver ingots. Oñate continued to tout the silver mines of New Mexico and was said to have actually constructed an ore crusher at a pueblo called El Tuerto. This town was described as six leagues from San Marcos in the Galisteo country, and seven leagues from the first pueblo of the Salinas—that is, the Tompiro group. Perhaps it was one of the Tiwa-speaking towns east of the Sandias. Possibly it was the San Buenaventura, where Juan Martínez de Montoya reported mines in 1607 or 1608. There is no evidence that any silver, stamped or otherwise, ever reached Mexico from mines discovered by Oñate, but in 1599 hopes were high. As late as 1601 there were persistent reports of mines in the San Marcos region.

The letters were sent with a party that contained Fathers Martínez and Salazar and Captains Gaspar Pérez de Villagrá, Juan Pinero (or Piñero), and Marcos Farfán de los Godos, three men who were deeply trusted by Oñate. Villagrá was given the task of putting together a relief expedition. Meanwhile, the Spanish town of San Gabriel del Yungue was organized as the governmental center and remained the capital of New Mexico until the move to Santa Fe in 1610. At Yungue was constructed the first permanent church in New Mexico, an east-west-oriented edifice built of blocks of volcanic tufa, collected from the edge of the Pajarito Plateau only a few miles away, and set with mud mortar. The foundations of the San Gabriel church were uncovered by Florence Hawley Ellis in the 1960s; its destruction came in the Pueblo Revolt of 1680.

Hard times were ahead for the New Mexico colonists. The years 1600 and 1601 saw serious drought in the Rio Grande Valley, something that affected the Pueblo Indians more than the Spaniards since the latter could and did seize food from the natives. An attempt by Zaldívar to get food and cotton blankets from the Tompiro pueblos, some time around midyear 1600, led to an uprising that was put down with considerable brutality. Zaldívar was on his way to the "South Sea" (that is, the Gulf of California, a trip for which no records whatsoever remain) and so notified Oñate of the problem before pushing on. Oñate marched to the Salinas area, but the fighting was inconclusive, for early in 1601 he found it necessary to send Zaldívar back in force. According to later testimony (admittedly by a hostile witness, Gasco de Velasco), this led to hundreds of people being killed, though in which of these three operations is not clear.

Meanwhile, the relief expedition arrived from the south with seventy-three officially listed colonists, a considerable amount of supplies, and seven missionaries, including a new commissary, Fray Juan de Escalona, and additional friars, Damián Escudero, Lope Izquierdo, Alonso de la Oliva, Luis Mairones, Gastón de Peralta, and Francisco de Velasco. The colonists included mostly Europeans but also Indians and blacks in various mixtures. The expedition reached the New Mexico capital on Christmas Eve. However, all three of the captains sent by Oñate—Pinero, Farfán, and Villagrá—had defected, Pérez de Villagrá actually taking refuge in a church to avoid being forcibly returned to New Mexico. Nor did the two missionaries return. Fray Cristóbal de Salazar had died on the way to Mexico, and Martínez was reassigned. Whether the Franciscan commissary actually requested this reassignment is not clear, but he did suffer from gout (see chapter 4), and perhaps the hardships of New Mexico were becoming too much for him.

In spite of new blood, the situation at San Gabriel continued to be tense. Oñate, leading a party of retainers, did rid himself of one enemy, Captain Pablo de Aguilar, by ambushing him and fatally stabbing him. A second officer, Captain Alonso de Sosa, who tried to return to the south, was attacked and killed by Zaldívar.

Although feelings must have been running high in the colony, Oñate now prepared for a major expedition to the Plains. He set out from San Gabriel on June 23 with seventy or more men (possibly as many as ninety-four), several hundred animals, and six carts. Second in command was Vicente de Zaldívar, who now combined the titles of camp master and sargento mayor. Along was Fray Francisco de Velasco, who reported on the journey, and who like the late Fray Cristóbal was a cousin to Oñate. A second religious on the journey was Fray Pedro de Vergara, a lay brother who had been in the original group of Franciscans in Oñate's New Mexico. The group took the route by Galisteo and then probably south and east via the Cañón Blanco to the Pecos. This stream was called the Cicuye by Coronado, while the Espejo expedition in 1583 renamed it—reasonably enough, considering the bison herds in the vicinity—the Río de las Vacas. To Castaño de Sosa, the stream was the Salado, a name also reflected in the Martínez map of 1602. Oñate, curiously, gave the river yet another name, Río San Buenaventura. Gradually, both the river and the pueblo of Cicuye became known as Pecos.

The day following the crossing of the Pecos River, Oñate and his group reached a river they called the Bagres because of the many catfish. This was likely the Gallinas. The party pushed on slightly north of east and reached the Magdalena (Canadian), following its course eastward. Eventually the group met Apaches, who gave them a friendly reception. Then the party pushed on into the Plains, still following the Magdalena River. They gradually pushed north by east reaching into present-day western Kansas. Here Zaldívar discovered a very large village of seven thousand people, a group Oñate called *Escanjaque*. It is not entirely clear just who were the Escanjaques. They might have been Caddoan-speaking or perhaps Apachean or even Tonkawa. At any rate, they do not seem to have been Quiviran, the modern Wichita.

Oñate did reach a Quivira settlement and described it as consisting of clusters, thirty or forty houses a quarter of a mile apart, with the larger comprehensive set-tlement extending over three leagues (seven or eight miles). This village may have been on Walnut Creek near the present Kansas-Oklahoma border, and Quivira territory seems to have extended into the Great Bend of the Arkansas. In the course of exploration, Oñate came across a Quiviran chief named Catarax. The term *catarax* is a Wichita word for "chief" and is obviously the same word for the leader Tatarrax, mentioned by López de Gómara for the Coronado expedition.

While this expedition was going on, there was trouble back in the Rio Grande Valley. The new Franciscan commissary, Fray Juan de Escalona, was crit-ical of Oñate, and the newcomers were shocked by the lack of food and the bit-ter cold of a northern New Mexico winter. From the descriptions, the winter of 1600–1601 seems to have been exceptionally severe in the San Gabriel region. In 1601 the settlers at San Gabriel, in an attempt to alleviate the food crisis, planted about 100 fanegas (around 880 acres) of wheat, up from 50 the previous year. By this time they also had a mill for grinding wheat.

But the affairs of the colony were in a turmoil, and the murders of Aguilar and Sosa added to the tension. A mutiny quickly flared up at San Gabriel, led by the friars who argued that Spanish settlers' callousness to the Indians was making conversion impossible. A number of senior officers joined them, claiming that New Mexico was not worth the troubles and hardships of colonization. Oñate's loyal followers—twenty-five soldiers, some with families and servants—refused to leave the new province. With them stayed the lieutenant governor, Francisco de Sosa Peñalosa (whose sympathies seems to have been with the rebel group but whose office made it impossible for him to depart) and the Franciscan Escalona, who also felt duty-bound to remain. But the remainder of the colonists, around the beginning of October, moved southward to Santa Bárbara. Sosa Peñalosa sent a self-pitying letter to the viceroy, and Escalona one with scathing criticism of Spanish misdeeds toward the natives. The loyalists sent their own representative, Captain Gerónimo Márquez, to present the case for Oñate.

The outcome of all this was further confused by Philip III's actions. In early 1602, before the turmoil in the colony was known in Spain, the king had granted Oñate the position of adelantado. The king now vacillated, ordering Viceroy Monterrey to investigate and report on the situation in New Mexico. There was considerable maneuvering, with Vicente de Zaldívar being sent to Spain to help argue Oñate's case. A new viceroy, Marquis de Montesclaros, who had arrived in Mexico City in the summer of 1603, was directed by the king to continue the investigation.

Meanwhile, Oñate, perhaps trying desperately to find new sources of income for his colony, decided to make the long-planned trip to the Gulf of California, or as the Spaniards referred to it, the South Sea. Leaving some fifty soldiers to hold San Gabriel, Oñate departed with thirty men and a new Franciscan commissary, Fray Francisco de Escobar, on October 7, 1604. The Oñate party traveled by way of Zuni and Hopi, then southwestward through the Verde region and the Bill Williams River valley to the Colorado. There they explored the lower Colorado region, with its heavy population of Yuman-speaking Indians. The Spaniards failed to find any sort of riches, however; although the Colorado River natives traded in shell and coral, they had no silver or gold. The silver vessels reported by Fray Francisco, which he said were obtained from the California coast, most likely were vessels of steatite, perhaps traded from Santa Catalina Island.

One of Oñate's reasons for going to the coast was to establish a seaport from which New Mexico could be supplied by ships from New Spain and Peru, and which would provide even a closer and easier access to China. This had been discussed in his letter to Viceroy Monterrey dated March 2, 1599. Again it showed the woeful ignorance of the Spaniards as to the actual geography of the Southwest. The trip from the Southwest to the lower portions of the Colorado finally made it clear to Oñate that the dream of a southwestern seaport was a chimera.

Indeed, it was not until the American occupation of the old Spanish Southwest that a maritime presence was established on the Colorado River. The treaty of Guadalupe Hidalgo (1848) allowed Americans to enter the Colorado without paying the heavy Mexican duty, and shipment by sea and river was important until the arrival of the railroads beginning in the late 1870s. Yuma became a transshipment point for supplies and machinery, especially mining equipment, but shallow-draft river steamers could reach as far north as Hardyville, three hundred miles upstream from Yuma.

On his return from the lower Colorado in 1605, Oñate decided to touch base with authorities in Mexico City. With him was the Franciscan commissary, Francisco de Escobar, who in October 1605 presented his report on the large populations of the Colorado River to the viceroy. Montesclaros, however, was not impressed, and the Crown was already thinking of replacing the adelantado. In June 1606, the king ordered Viceroy Montesclaros to recall Oñate and to appoint a new governor for New Mexico. The following year, Oñate sent a letter of resignation to the incoming viceroy, his old friend Luis de Velasco, who had returned from Peru to take charge in Mexico. In 1608 Velasco appointed as governor Juan Martínez de Montoya, who had come to New Mexico in 1600 and was a magistrate on the cabildo, or town council, of San Gabriel. Martínez de Montoya is interesting in that he seems to have established some sort of settlement in the vicinity of the later Santa Fe between 1605 and 1607. In fact, by 1608 there may have been a discussion as to the advisability of moving the capital from the Chama–Rio Grande junction to the relatively empty Santa Fe Valley.

Martínez de Montoya never served as governor; indeed, quite possibly, he never wanted to be governor. The cabildo, perhaps at the behest of Oñate, rejected Martínez, choosing instead Cristóbal, the young son of Juan de Oñate. A much later petition by a descendant of Martínez de Montoya suggests that Cristóbal may have been a sort of shadow official for a few months. It also states that Martínez de Montoya actually took part in an expedition against the Apaches led by young Oñate. There is also some slight evidence that Cristóbal was titular acting governor during his father's trip to the lower Colorado regions in 1604–5. A later poetical book of tribute, the *Canciones Lugubres,* does call him lieutenant governor and captain general. The young man, however, had no future of any sort for he was soon dead. Lansing B. Bloom claims that he was killed by Indians in 1610 while traveling with his father southward from New Mexico. Bloom cites no evidence for this statement, and it seems more likely that Cristóbal died of natural causes, probably after the return to Mexico. One of the writers of the *Canciones,* Alonso de Salas Barbadillo, says that he died at the age of twenty-two. If this is true, it would put Cristóbal's death around 1612.

In any case, this "appointment" of a youth (Cristóbal was seventeen or eighteen at this point) was never taken seriously in either Mexico City or Spain. In fact, by 1608 the whole enterprise of New Mexico was at a crisis point. In March of that year the viceroy advised the king to bring the entire colonization scheme to a stop.

The missionaries had not been successful, there were virtually no precious metals, and the distances involved made it hard to reinforce and defend New Mexico. The serious remaining question was the disposition of Christianized Pueblo Indians, and on this matter King Philip (in a letter dated September 3, 1608) instructed the viceroy to use his own judgment.

At this critical juncture, Father Lázaro Ximénez, who had given an earlier negative report to the viceroy, returned a second time from San Gabriel. Arriving with him was Friar Isidro Ordóñez, and the two brought news that seven thousand Indians had been baptized. Apparently, faced with the shutdown of the colony, the Franciscans were now frantically performing baptisms. Philip III, with that underlying piety so characteristic of the sixteenth- and seventeenth-century Spanish kings, now reversed his decision and decided to make New Mexico a royal province, and one in which missionization would be the primary purpose. A new governor, Pedro de Peralta, was appointed in 1609 although he probably did not actually arrive in New Mexico until early 1610. With him came a new contingent of missionaries and a new direction for New Mexico.

In spite of the considerable documentation on the Oñate period, it is hard to objectively evaluate Juan de Oñate. He had certain leadership traits: he was tenacious, brave, and generally decisive in his actions. Nevertheless, Oñate had difficulty in maintaining loyalty among his followers. By the end, most of his original circle of officers had deserted him, and the missionaries were generally hostile. In fact, Oñate's support among both missionaries and the army seems to have been anchored in relatives such as Velasco and the Zaldívars.

But regardless of his personal virtues and faults, Oñate's efforts were probably bound to fail. His colonists came to New Mexico expecting rich mines and a docile native population. They found neither, and in addition had to suffer through the harsh winters and scorching summers of a northern mountainous region. Many of them felt betrayed by Oñate, and their resentful actions reflected that fact.

Oñate was eventually tried by a new viceroy, the Marquis of Guadalcázar, and found guilty of a number of charges including the use of excessive force in the attack on Acoma. The penalties included perpetual banishment from New Mexico and the payment of a considerable fine. Oñate spent much of the rest of his life attempting to have the penalties expunged and to obtain new honors. He stayed on in Mexico for a time, but after the death of his wife, Doña Isabel, around 1620, he decided to return to Spain. In 1622 the volume of *Canciones lugubres*, mentioned above, was published in Madrid. Purporting to be a memorial to Oñate's son, now dead for a decade, it had very little information on

Cristóbal and was basically a propaganda piece for the glorification of Juan and the Oñate family. The book and his other efforts met with some success, for Oñate obtained the important office of mining inspector for Spain in 1624. The following year he was made a *caballero* of the Military Order of Santiago, a firm sign of royal favor. Oñate died around the first of June, 1626, and his family never regained importance in the affairs of New Mexico.

CHAPTER SEVEN

Church and State through Mid-Century

The situation in the province of New Mexico during the seventeenth century had some unusual features. As pointed out a half century ago by the great Southwest historian France V. Scholes, it seems to have been a period of almost constant stress and turmoil, a struggle to the death (sometimes literally) between church and state, between the Franciscan missionaries and the civil governors and their retinues. Was what *seemed* to be happening in the Southwest typical of Spanish governance in the New World during that period? Was New Mexico unique? Or do the documents give a skewed picture of events?

This last point is certainly true to some degree. Most of the New Mexico governmental archives and the Santa Fe cabildo documents, stored in Santa Fe, were lost in 1680. They were, of course copied, thanks to Spanish bureaucracy, and more and more are coming to light. It was with the Mexican and Spanish repositories of documents, and especially with the voluminous Franciscan documentation, that France Scholes, unquestionably the premier researcher on this period, worked in creating his detailed picture of the seventeenth-century province of New Mexico. His extensive use of mission records has led some modern historians to challenge Scholes's overall picture and to suggest that he introduced a strong pro-Franciscan bias and tended to stress negative aspects of the civil government of the province.

First of all, I doubt this alleged bias on the part of France Scholes. It is possible by picking and choosing isolated pieces of Scholes's work to find pejorative statements about the governors and their parties. It is, however, equally easy to find statements critical of the missionaries and of the settlers. As stated in the preface, I was a student of Scholes and knew him quite well during a time when he was still working and publishing on southwestern matters. Although I discussed the politics of seventeenth-century New Mexico with him a number of times, I never got the impression of a pro-mission bias. Scholes had a healthy objectivity in his approach to all sources—missionary, secular, or whatever.

Was New Mexico, then, different from the rest of Spanish America in its violent church-state controversy? Actually, I suspect that it may have been so. Even a casual reading of the fate of New Mexico seventeenth-century governors gives the feeling that something was very wrong in that province. One governor was murdered, and one died in prison. Others were imprisoned, and most of them bore scars from their New Mexican experience.

The situation, I believe, was the result of a combination of factors that made New Mexico unique in Spanish North America. First of all, the colony was extremely isolated. It was connected to the heartland of New Spain by a supply train that made a round trip from Mexico City to Santa Fe, along what became known as the *Camino Real,* approximately every three years, a long and dangerous route largely controlled by the Franciscans. News traveled very slowly, and even official letters to and from New Mexico did not reach their destinations for months.

A second factor was that by around 1608, New Mexico had been essentially written off by the Spanish Crown as a profit-making colony. It was to be a royal mission province, and secular Spaniards were to be essentially a support group for the Franciscans. However, neither the settlers, some of whom had come with Oñate in the heady and highly optimistic days of first settlement, nor the various governors ever fully accepted this state of affairs.

A complete Franciscan hegemony could only operate in the absence of a large Hispanic population, and the numbers of colonists did remain very small throughout the century. But, however few in numbers, the settlers were determined to get the maximum advantage from encomiendas and *estancias* (ranches), and they naturally tried to exploit the Pueblo population whenever possible. One source of power for the settlers was participation in the city government of Santa Fe.

The governors, also, expected to gain *something* from their time in this rude and isolated area. In spite of the high hopes of Oñate and of such early churchmen as Benavides, no mineral industry developed. In fact, according to a 1638 letter of the commissary-general of the Franciscans in New Spain, not a single mine had been opened up to that date. Lacking mineral wealth to exploit, the Spaniards had relatively few options. One important possibility was trade, which to a greater or lesser degree involved Pueblo Indian labor in the production of cotton and wool goods and other natural products for export to Mexico or to the Plains. This was a source of constant friction since the missionaries felt they had first call on Indian labor for their own Mexican trade. Help from the Crown was not always generous, and the missions for the most part were expected to support themselves.

An even quicker way of gaining wealth was the securing of captives from the surrounding nomadic groups, especially the Apache. Such slaving expeditions usually had as a pretext the attack by Apaches on Pueblo or Spanish towns or estancias. But often the Spaniards attacked first, and the Apaches, thus provoked, tended to retaliate, especially on the outlying Pueblo towns. This state of affairs generally outraged the missionaries, who blamed any loss of converts on the governors and their associates. But slaving became an increasingly important factor in the economy of the Southwest, not only to the governor and settlers but also to the Pueblo Indians themselves. Captives, especially pubescent boys and girls, brought large sums of money in central Mexico and in the mining outposts of Nueva Vizcaya. For a Pueblo Indian operating within the restrictive mission system, it was a chance to function militarily under the governor's patronage. With luck and skill, a given individual might become relatively affluent, but it did tend to undercut the Franciscan control over native populations.

Another aspect of New Mexico life was the intensive conversion program of the missionaries and the governors' reactions to it. A few governors, over a period of several decades, resisted the mission attack on native ceremonials. I am not entirely clear on the reasons for this resistance. However, the seventeenth century in Europe was a period in which folk dances and other ceremonies were popular and accepted. These folk dances seem to have met little opposition from the Church, assuming that they were not part of "devil worship." It may be that governors, who generally had a certain sophistication, saw the Pueblo masked dances as also basically harmless. Still, considering how the clergy felt about such matters, it seems an inadequate explanation as to why certain governors actively promoted the native ceremonials. Perhaps the governors, who generally were very sensitive to what they considered the rights and prerogatives of the civil government, were simply trying to establish their authority. Alternatively, they may have worried about the "public safety" factor, fearing that tensions and turmoil, produced by the missionaries' all-or-nothing religious acculturation, would eventually produce a violent Pueblo reaction. Whatever their reasons, which probably varied from governor to governor, there *was* a violent reaction— on the part of the Franciscans.

Given all this, one would expect a certain amount of friction, but probably one in which the secular and religious powers were in reasonable balance. However, another factor in the power struggle quickly became evident. This was the Holy Office of the Inquisition, aimed at maintaining moral censorship and purity of the Catholic faith. The Holy Office was introduced into the New World in 1517. It quickly spread to the great viceroyalties, at first under control of the bishops, then via separate tribunals established in 1569 and set up in Lima and Mexico City within a year or so after that date. The Inquisition operated largely independently of both the secular and religious authorities in the New World. It was a tribunal with extraordinarily broad powers from which only Indians were excluded—and a powerful and dreaded weapon to use against secular authorities. A commission from the Inquisition was claimed by the Franciscan commissary Fray Isidro Ordóñez perhaps as early as 1613. As it happened, Ordóñez was not a commissary of the Inquisition, although that office would be introduced into New Mexico a decade later. At first this authority was employed with a certain moderation, even gingerly at times. However, it eventually became a powerful weapon in the hands of the friars and was used recklessly and ruthlessly by them, especially in the 1660s. With such broad and essentially undefined powers, the New Mexico missionaries might well be expected to have fought the governors tooth and nail. And the latter officials generally felt obligated to defend the secular power, sometimes at great cost to themselves. The use of the Holy Office upset the already delicate and imperfect power balance and made conflict inevitable.

As discussed in chapter 6, Pedro de Peralta arrived in New Mexico sometime in the winter of 1609–10. The province by that time had shrunk to probably fewer than two hundred people, huddled at San Gabriel. With Peralta came twelve soldiers and a new contingent of eight Franciscans including a new commissary, Fray Alonso de Peinado, who replaced Father Escobar. Peralta had a mission much more sharply focused than had Oñate. He was to move the capital from San Gabriel, where the Spaniards competed for scarce resources with the large Tewa-speaking population. The Santa Fe Valley had already been chosen, and settler Martínez Montoya had done some building there possibly as early as 1605. As discussed below, it may be that the Analco settlement of Mexican Indians also predated Peralta by a year or two. It would at least explain why the desirable heights on the south side of the Santa Fe River were off-limits to the earliest Spanish families. It looks as if the Franciscans had established a prior right to the southern side of the river, and continued to exercise this right throughout the seventeenth century. The missionaries, however, continued to headquarter at Santo Domingo Pueblo, somewhat nearer the center of action as far as the Rio Grande Pueblos were concerned.

Peralta was directed to concentrate on missionization and defense of the Pueblo area. The Apaches, especially those east of the Rio Grande, were to be left to their own devices until the Pueblo region itself was firmly secured. A system of tribute was set up, and encomiendas were established. Directions were given Peralta for the new settlement of Santa Fe. He was to establish cabildo officers and, with their help, deal out lots to the inhabitants of the new villa—apparently by a lottery working off some sort of plat. Each family was to have land for a house, garden, vineyards, and olive groves. The mention of olive groves brings home the point that Peralta was working from a standardized set of instructions. Olives are unsuited to the harsh climate of mountainous northern New Mexico. Irrigation water was to be provided, and settlers were obligated to remain continuously for ten years (for a further discussion of the founding of Santa Fe, see chapter 9).

The core of the colony was a group of families who had remained with Oñate through thick and thin. Perhaps the most important of these were members of the Baca and Barela families and Gerónimo Márquez, who had been Oñate's ambassador in 1601 when most of the colonists had deserted. These were individuals who were determined to make something of New Mexico, and they and their fellow colonists formed one of the factions that jostled and struggled for control of the province along with the governor and his party, the Franciscans, and the Indians themselves during the next seventy years. Some thirty-five of these settlers were awarded encomiendas, the right to the labor of specific Pueblo Indian groups. People awarded encomiendas were called *encomenderos,* and they were required by law to maintain a dwelling in the capital. In fact, many of them lived in Santa Fe, perhaps all of them at least seasonally. The encomenderos technically were not allowed to reside in the towns they held in encomienda, though this rule was sometimes violated in New Mexico. Encomenderos were normally soldiers, and one of their duties was to raise arms when needed to defend the colony. A good portion of their military manpower came from the Indians they held in encomienda.

The encomenderos also functioned directly in the governance of the colony. New Mexico was divided into six to eight subdivisions called jurisdictions, which included all the province except for Santa Fe and its surrounding area. Each jurisdiction was headed by an officer called an *alcalde mayor* who functioned as military commander for his district, local judge, and general overseer for both settlers and Pueblo Indians. The alcaldes mayores were therefore in constant contact with the missionaries, and with an overlapping authority that often caused friction. One of the major sources of power for colonists was a place on the Santa Fe city cabildo either as *regidor* (counselor) or *alcalde* (magistrate). In certain situations, the cabildo officers actually managed to seize the executive power of the provincial government. It was sometimes a dangerous activity, as in the aftermath of the Rosas murder (discussed further below).

Musketeer from de Gheyn's arms manual, 1607 (courtesy of the Museum of New Mexico, neg. no. 20279)

Peralta had been in New Mexico for hardly more than a year and a half, and was still in the process of setting up his new capital, when events occurred that were to destroy his governorship. In late August of 1612, Fray Isidro Ordóñez arrived from Mexico with a twenty-wagon supply train and a new group of Franciscans. Ordóñez had been sent south the previous year to recruit new clergy. He seemed already—for reasons unknown—to have been an enemy of the governor, and once back in New Mexico he moved swiftly. Ordóñez was clearly very much a loose cannon. On his arriving back in the colony, he presented the commissary, Fray Alonso de Peinado, with a letter from the Franciscan commissary-general in Mexico removing Peinado and appointing Ordóñez to the prelacy of the New Mexico custodia. There is a good chance that this letter was forged, making Ordóñez's actions over the next several years totally illegal. His purpose seems to have been the complete subordination of New Mexico's secular authority to Franciscan control.

By a relentless attack on Peralta and by clever manipulation of both the settler contingent and the Indians, Ordóñez managed to undermine Peralta, eventually arresting the governor and holding him prisoner. This situation eventually resolved itself with the arrival of another governor, Bernardino de Ceballos, in 1614 and a new Franciscan prelate, Esteban de Perea, in the winter of 1616–17. Perea had originally come to New Mexico as part of the missionary group that accompanied Peralta in 1609. On his return, the New Mexico mission structure was raised to custodial status, the Custodia of the Conversion of St. Paul. Perea was the first missionary to hold the title of *custos,* or custodian (see chapter 8). It is unclear what happened to Ordóñez, but he seems to have been disciplined in some manner by the order.

Ceballos was not particularly friendly to the Franciscans, but he made relatively few waves. The same could not be said of his successor, Juan de Eulate, who came to New Mexico in 1618 and soon became involved in a violent controversy with Custodian Perea. Partly this was over Eulate's willingness to allow native ceremonials, but in large part it reflected still another chapter in the struggle for authority in the province.

In early 1621 the viceroy issued new decrees, sent both to Governor Eulate and Custodian Perea, that delineated the separate spheres of influence of the lay and religious authorities. Essentially it cautioned the two powers to support each other in appropriate ways but not to intrude on each other's rights and privileges. Probably the Pueblo Indians were the main beneficiaries of these new regulations. The governor and the Franciscans had accused each other of violating Pueblo rights. Now both were forbidden to interfere with Pueblo elections of tribal officers or even to be present when such officers were chosen. Certain restrictions were made on tribute and use of Indian labor by both the missionaries and the civil authority. Labor that caused native hardship, labor of women in the houses of Spaniards except under very strict supervision, and labor at the convents except "with the greatest moderation" was forbidden. Indians were to be paid a half-real plus their food. If food was not forthcoming, the pay would be one real. The missionaries' egregious habit of cutting the Indians' hair for frivolous reasons was strictly forbidden. Apparently, victims of this treatment were fleeing to the Acoma peñol, where a colony of unconverted natives had been forming for some years.

Long hair was and is of great ceremonial importance in the Pueblo world, and the missionaries obviously were aware of this. Hair cutting was another in the mission arsenal of weapons against Pueblo religion. The viceroy was probably *au fait* of the religious aspect of the practice, but he obviously felt that the disruption caused by hair cutting was not worth it. Forced hair cutting, however, continued, regulation or not.

The period of the 1620s was one of relative quiet. The Franciscan custodian, Miguel de Chavarría, moderated the missionaries' relations to the governor, though the rivalry between church and governor flared up again with Chavarría's successor, Vice-custodian Ascencio de Zárate, who at one point excommunicated Eulate.

The governor was recalled in 1625 and soon faced charges for illegally bringing slaves to Mexico. As I indicated earlier, trafficking in slavery was a major economic factor in seventeenth-century New Mexico, but the slaves were supposed to be taken from Apaches and other nomadic groups in warfare. The friars accused Eulate of raiding neighboring peaceful nomadic groups for slaves, some of whom were shipped off to New Spain. Even worse in Spanish eyes was the habit allegedly practiced by Eulate of seizing orphans from the converted Pueblos and selling them in Mexico. Technically, these youngsters were probably not slaves, but in actuality they functioned as such.

In 1623 a new custodian, Fray Alonso de Benavides, was chosen for New Mexico. He departed Mexico City in early 1625, but because of duties in the Santa Bárbara region, he did not reach the custodia until nearly the end of that year. His traveling companion, the new governor, Felipe de Sotelo Osorio, pushed on ahead to Santa Fe, where Benavides joined him with additional missionaries in late January 1626. With Fray Benavides, the mission agenda intensified. Not only were there additional missionaries to expand the process of conversion, but Benavides himself was designated commissary of the Holy Office of the Inquisition, and so formally introduced that powerful position into New Mexico.

Benavides did not actually use his Inquisitorial powers against the civil authorities, concentrating instead on witchcraft, demonology, and bigamy, crimes that had no great political implications. There was a period of relative cooperation between the two power structures in the province. Benavides was an ambitious man, determined to promote the Franciscan influence in New Mexico. He was, however, also very much a politician, and one who obviously preferred to work with Governor Sotelo Osorio. Benavides's great dream was the founding of a Franciscan province in New Mexico with diocesan powers and with himself as the first bishop. It was in pursuit of this dream that Benavides, on leaving New Mexico in 1629, wrote his two Memorials (1630 and 1634), with their invaluable, although not totally dependable, information on the colony.

Benavides was replaced by the former custodian, Esteban de Perea, who also became commissary of the Holy Office. With him came twelve soldiers, nineteen missionary priests, and two lay brothers, plus "nine others, at the cost of the said Provincia [the Franciscan Province of the Holy Gospel, mother organization for the New Mexico Missions]." Perea took charge of the New Mexico missions in April 1629 and set about assigning mission stations. There were now forty-six missionaries in New Mexico, and the work of conversion, already enthusiastically promoted by Benavides, continued with new vigor. Perea stayed on in New Mexico, dying there in 1639. Although he was replaced as custodian in 1630, Perea seems to have held the Holy Office title for a number of years, perhaps until his death. He and his successor, Juan de Salas, were instrumental in a new thrust of missionization, expanding the missions to their maximum extent. During this period, mission stations were set up at Zuni and Hopi. A mission was established at the resettled pueblo of Acoma, and the mission effort among the Tompiro towns was upgraded. Under missionary Andrés Suárez (or Juárez), the great mission church at Pecos was completed during this period. Begun in 1621, it was certainly one of the larger European buildings in North America of the time.

Chililí had a mission established in 1613 with Father Peinado stationed there. The mission station at Abó probably dates a handful of years later. In 1627 Benavides made an establishment at Las Humanas (the present Gran Quivira). Benavides had also been very interested in the Jumanos, having determined—at least to his own satisfaction—that a contemporary nun named María de Jesús (sometimes called the "Lady in Blue") from the Spanish town of Agreda had miraculously appeared and preached to this group.

Juan de Salas, who would become custodian in 1630, had founded the Isleta mission in 1613 and from there had numerous contacts with the Tompiro and Jumano. The Jumano actually came to Isleta to trade in the midsummer, after

Mission ruins, Abó Pueblo (courtesy of the Museum of New Mexico, neg. no. 6395)

probably wintering over in the Tompiro area and before moving out to their hunting territories in the southern Llano Estacado, perhaps in the region around Blanco Canyon where they lived in Coronado's time a century before. In the late summer of 1629, Salas and another missionary, Diego López, made a trip onto the Llano Estacado to missionize the Jumano, presumably at the request of the Indians. Although the Indians were suffering from a drought that affected the southern Plains that year, the missionaries managed to baptize a considerable number of people. The Franciscans were unable to establish a permanent mission in the Llano country, but they seem to have maintained some contact with the Jumano through their mission station at Humanas, which was put on a firmer foundation in the early 1630s.

In Perea's and Salas's time, the Jumanos were increasingly coming under attack by the Apaches and often were finding the long-established trade with their presumed linguistic kinspeople in the Tompiro area disrupted. This Apache threat, which within a few decades would drive the Jumano from their Llano Estacado base, made their association with the newcomers desirable even if it meant accepting the Spanish religion. The María de Jesús story must be seen in the context of that political and economic situation.

Governor Francisco Manuel de Silva Nieto (1629–32) cooperated with the Franciscans. In fact, church and state relationships were relatively quiet until the late 1630s, though in 1632 Perea did denounce Governor Francisco de la Mora y Ceballos for going back to Eulate's practice of seizing children as servants and for establishing estancias on both Pueblo and mission lands. The missions had their ups and downs. For example, at Zuni the resident priest was killed in 1632, and a second friar, traveling down the trade route from Zuni to Sonora, was murdered by his Zuni guides. The Zuni fled to the protection of their fortified mesa, Dowa Yalanne, and a punitive Spanish expedition failed to dislodge them. By 1635 the Indians were beginning to trickle back to their towns, and plans were made for remissionization. The following year, the custodian, Friar Cristóbal de Quirós, demanded that the governor of that period, Francisco Martínez de Baeza, use soldiers to escort the missionaries back to Zuni. The governor refused, and the Zuni mission was probably not reestablished until a number of years later (see chapter 8).

In 1637, Luis de Rosas was made governor, and he remained officially in office for the next four years. The Rosas period brought the quarrel between the Franciscans and the governor's party to a boil, with consequences that kept New Mexico in turmoil for the next forty years. It is curious that the Inquisition was relatively little involved during the Rosas period. The reason seems to be that Fray Perea continued to exercise the office of commissary, but he was now old and sick. He was also increasingly taken up with on-the-ground missionization efforts, having been assigned the recently established mission station at Cuarac (Quarai) in the Salinas region.

Governor Luis de Rosas was, in Scholes words, "an outspoken, hard hitting soldier, fearless in action. He made his decisions quickly and executed them ruthlessly." In the ever tense situation of New Mexico, this was a recipe for disaster. Rosas set himself to diminish the power of the Franciscans. This included undercutting their authority among the Pueblo Indians and, with the help of the Santa Fe cabildo, subverting one of the missionaries, Friar Juan de Vidania. Apparently, Rosas and the cabildo had hopes that Vidania would be appointed custodian, thus bringing the missions under more direct control of the civil authorities.

Since the documents on the Rosas period come mainly from the missionaries, it is not always possible to establish the truth behind the various accusations and counter-accusations. Rosas established a workshop in Santa Fe, neither the first nor the last such operation in the seventeenth century. The governor used the shop for weaving cloth, and he supposedly forced both Christianized Pueblo Indians and captive Apaches and Utes to work as slaves. Rosas was also accused of raiding the Apaches for slaves but then not providing the frontier pueblos with protection against counter-raids. This was probably not the case; whatever his faults, Rosas seems to have been an able military leader. But the main Franciscan objection to Rosas was probably that he ignored their traditional immunities and flouted their authority, especially among the Pueblo Indians.

The Rosas period was one of tumult. The priests at Taos and Jemez were killed by the Indians, and the three Tewa missions of Santa Clara, San Ildefonso, and Nambé were without missionaries for a whole year from the spring of 1640 to the spring of 1641. The Franciscans accused the governor of sending soldiers to expel the missionaries and steal the mission herds. Rosas and Vidania retorted that the missionaries had deserted their posts, and the soldiers simply went to rescue whatever equipment and livestock remained. Since San Ildefonso was being fortified by the natives, Rosas established a short-lived presidio there. To add to the confusion, what seems to have been a smallpox epidemic spread during 1640, killing an estimated three thousand Pueblo Indians. Apache raids were said to have destroyed some twenty thousand fanegas (fifty thousand bushels) of maize. According to the missionaries, Pueblo Indians in desperation were increasingly turning to their old religion.

Disease had already become a serious problem in the Pueblo world. In a 1638 letter to King Philip IV from Juan de Prada, the Franciscan commissary-general in New Spain, the churchman estimated the Pueblo population at forty thousand and mentioned that smallpox had ravaged the area, reducing numbers of Pueblo Indians by about a third. If my own estimate of Pueblo population in Oñate's time is correct, this is too high a percentage of loss, but even so, the reduction was drastic.

According to the commissary-general, the Pueblo area extended from Senecú to Taos, and from Pecos to the Hopi towns. Prada also tallied the Spanish lay population at two hundred, with an additional fifty Franciscans. He indicated that the population lived in Santa Fe, which had approximately fifty houses, though from the account of ex-governor Francisco Martínez de Baeza, writing the following year, it would seem that there were two hundred able armed fighting men (see chapter 9 for a more detailed discussion of the non-Pueblo population).

By 1640 the church-state battle in New Mexico deepened, with excommunications flying in every direction and at least one of the pro-Rosas faction murdered. By the beginning of 1641 the settlers began more and more to swing to the Franciscan side of the quarrel, and the viceroy was also becoming greatly concerned. Juan de Salas had been reappointed as custodian in 1639. He was given

Taos Pueblo, 1880 (courtesy of the Museum of New Mexico, neg. no. 16096)

the Inquisitionary authority in the spring of 1641, at the same time that Fray Hernando Covarrubias replaced him as custodian. A new governor, Juan Flores de Sierra y Valdés, arrived in April of that year to relieve Rosas of his office and, through a *residencia,* to investigate his activities as governor. Friar Vidania was arrested and sent to Mexico for trial with the fall 1641 mission supply train. He escaped, but apparently died within a year or so.

Rosas's residencia had barely begun when Governor Flores died. By this time, new elections had given the Santa Fe cabildo an anti-Rosas majority. With Flores's death, the cabildo became for a time the power center in the province. Rosas was imprisoned and in January 1642 was murdered by a settler named Nicolás Ortiz who accused the governor of a liaison with his wife, María de Bustillas, or Bustillo, a niece of Antonio Baca, alcalde of the Santa Fe cabildo. Although María readily confessed to a longstanding affair with Rosas, there seemed a real possibility that the whole story was a fabrication. Whatever the case, Ortiz was acquitted by the cabildo court on the grounds that his honor demanded Rosas's death. That was not the end of the story. Ortiz was later retried in Nueva Vizcaya and condemned to die, though, like many other condemned individuals on the wild frontier of Mexico, he escaped and disappeared from history. Meanwhile, Rosas's body had been denied burial in consecrated ground since he had died excommunicate.

Even though Rosas was largely discredited, the viceregal officers in Mexico could hardly overlook his murder at the behest of the Santa Fe cabildo. In 1642, a new governor, Alonso de Pacheco y Heredia, was sent to New Mexico. He had certain secret instructions to deal with the situation, and on July 21, 1643, he suddenly arrested and immediately executed eight of the ringleaders opposed to Rosas, including three members of the 1641 cabildo. No action was taken against the Franciscans, who conceded a minor point and gave the dead governor absolution so that he could be reburied in Santa Fe. The fate of María de Bustillas, who had also been arrested in New Mexico, is unknown, but she may have quietly returned to her natal family.

Although the missionaries had trouble with Pacheco, and the situation with governors in the latter half of the century was often (perhaps *usually* would be a better word) thorny, there was a general lowering of the tension in the period immediately following Rosas. New Mexico had gone to the brink, and none of the various parties wanted to risk disaster. The various custodians and vice-custodians for this period—Tomás Manso, Tomás Alvarado, Laurence de Rivas, Antonio de Aranda, Francisco de Salazar, and Antonio de Ibargaray—pushed on with the business of missionization. The several governors who followed Pacheco—Fernando de Argüello Carvajál, Luis de Guzmán y Figueroa, Hernando de Ugarte y la Concha, Juan de Samaniego y Jaca, and Juan Manso de Contreras—had their differences with the Franciscans and with the settlers, but the next really violent episode of this continuing power struggle did not come until the brilliant but ill-starred Bernardo López de Mendizábal arrived on the scene. There were tragicomic scenes. Juan Manso, governor from 1656 to 1659, was the relatively young brother of Tomás Manso and somewhat of a ladies' man. He established a liaison with a local woman, Margarita Márquez, the wife of one of his captains. Margarita gave birth to one and probably two children sired by Manso. For one of them, Manso's friend, Fray Miguel Sacristán (stationed at the Santa Fe, Analco, district convento), was said to have performed a mock funeral, the child being quietly transported to Mexico to be raised as a part of Manso's family. The Inquisition eventually became interested in this affair, especially after the suicide of Sacristán in 1661. Their investigation eventually came to nothing, though it did highlight, as Scholes pointed out, the "ignorance, superstition, and moral laxity [that] characterized the life of the Hispanic community, and the governors—and even the clergy."

A consideration of the first half century in the new province of New Mexico would not be complete without discussing the role of Mexican Native

Americans in Santa Fe. Operating from their base in central Mexico, the Spaniards quickly began to use friendly native populations to help strengthen and buffer their conquests along the northern frontier. Some of these Indians were Aztecs and Tarascans, but the majority seem to have been from the city state of Tlaxcala, that early and important ally of the Spaniards. Tlaxcalans were sent to a number of places in northern New Spain. By around A.D. 1600, there were colonies in present-day San Luis Potosí, Zacatecas, Durango, Chihuahua, and Coahuila.

It is not clear just when central Mexican Indians were introduced into New Mexico, but I have suggested that they may actually have antedated the Spaniards at Santa Fe. It is not clear how many of them were actually Tlaxcalans, though it is often assumed that at least a portion were. Their church was San Miguel—as far as we know, the earliest church in Santa Fe—which may also have been used for a time by the Spanish settlers. San Miguel still exists at more or less the same site, though of course it went through a number of rebuildings. As mentioned earlier in this chapter, the central Mexicans were settled in a *barrio,* or district, just south of the Santa Fe River; a district named *Analco,* a Nahuatl word meaning "across the river." In the Pueblo Revolt of 1680, this Indian contingent remained loyal to the Spaniards, and Analco was attacked by the Pueblo military forces. It is not known just how many Mexican Indians were transplanted to New Mexico, but possibly there were several hundred. I have suggested elsewhere that they were counted with the fleeing Spanish settlers when the colony was evacuated in the latter part of 1680. Some of the central Mexican natives may have returned with the Spaniards, for there is a possible reference to them at Analco as late as 1728. Following that time, they fade from history.

CHAPTER EIGHT

Missionization

Before turning to the details of the Franciscan missionization of New Mexico, perhaps some more general problems should be considered. What were the long-term effects of the new religion, and how did it
compare with the native religion, especially that of the Pueblos? Historians looking at the events of the seventeenth century have generally assumed that
Christianity, because of its perceived superiority over the native religions, would
gradually swamp the aboriginal beliefs. Some students of Spanish southwestern
history, even today, apparently do not realize that this conversion failed to occur.

Even in the high tide of missionization, during the seventeenth century, it is
not entirely clear to what extent the Pueblos actually understood what they
were being taught. As Ramón Gutiérrez has pointed out, the friars in one sense
took over the role of rainmakers and magicians, and much of their success was
due to charismatic domination over the Indians. Certainly, some of their messages became transmuted when transferred to the linguistic conceptual world of
the Pueblos. The cross, for example, was reinterpreted as a prayer stick or a star
symbol, and the calendric rhythms of Franciscan Christianity were assimilated
to the solstice ceremonies of the Pueblos. The Franciscans in the seventeenth
century wanted more; they planned to reorganize the sociopolitical and religious life of the Pueblo Indians to make them "true" converts. What they got
was at the most an incomplete fusion of the two religious traditions, and, more
often, a sullen hostility that led finally to the Pueblo Revolt of 1680. Although
aimed at all Spaniards, this retaliation was clearly directed primarily against the
missionaries.

What were the fruits of missionization? Among modern Pueblo Indians, the
Hopi and Zuni are basically outside the sphere of Christianity. There are, indeed,
modern missions to these groups, and individual Hopi and Zuni may profess
either Catholic Christianity or one of the various Protestant sects; however, most

people in the western pueblos are deeply involved in the "old religion," and it is central to any understanding of these two groups.

In the Rio Grande, where the Spanish presence was more pervasive, the various Pueblos are often considered "Christianized." The Pueblo Native Americans have long been eclectic in their ability to absorb new religious ideas, as evidenced by the widespread acceptance of the kachina cult in the fourteenth century. Many Christian elements have entered the native religion, and indeed, a vigorous folk Christianity is practiced side by side with that religion. However, the traditional religious ceremonies and beliefs are at heart autochthonous. They are carried on in dances and kiva ceremonials quite apart and separate from the Catholic mission churches and the parallel Protestant organizations. So, basically, the Pueblo religion in the east may be said to be the real core of Pueblo life, just as it is in the west.

Was Christianity in any way a "superior" religion to that of the Pueblos when it was introduced into the Province of New Mexico at the end of the sixteenth century? To some degree this is a pointless question, since religion—any religion—obtains its validity from internal acceptance and not from any external "proof." Nonetheless, it may be worthwhile to compare the worldviews and moral imperatives of these competing systems.

Not surprisingly, we know far more about the formal attributes of seventeenth-century Christianity than we do about seventeenth-century Pueblo religion. For the latter, it is usually necessary to extrapolate from nineteenth- and twentieth-century beliefs, something not easy to do.

As far as cosmology is concerned, the Franciscan missionaries in seventeenth-century New Mexico likely saw the earth and heavens largely in Ptolemaic terms. The ideas of Copernicus, Kepler, and Galileo had not penetrated the wilds of New Mexico; in fact, the Church had declared the heliocentric model of the solar system heretical in 1616 and officially maintained that position for many years. Although the Jesuit order had shown an early interest in Galileo's telescopes and had introduced one into China in 1634, the Franciscans in New Mexico were not particularly interested in science. My own guess is that the sun, moon, planets, and stars represented to these unsophisticated friars some sort of mystical emanations. In all likelihood, they hardly thought about such things at all. The missionaries accepted the Gregorian calendar as a practical matter but likely had no clue as to the calculations that went into it.

At that, the Franciscans represented the literate elite of the time and place. Probably the great majority of seventeenth-century laypeople in New Mexico could neither read nor write (see also chapter 9). And there is no evidence, and no real likelihood, that even literate people had available the written texts describing the advances in astronomy or other sciences. Most books that reached New Mexico in the seventeenth century were religious tomes. In the extant lists, there is nothing much that could be called science, perhaps with the exception of a few medical texts and one on "astrology, natural secrets and curious things [?]." Friar Juan de Vidania, one of the missionaries involved in the Rosas affair, wrote a number of letters in 1640–41 concerning that controversy. In them he quotes various classic authors, including Aristotle. It is not clear to what extent these books were actually available to Vidania in Santa Fe. Books actually listed as belonging to the missionaries include mainly missals, breviaries, and manuals of instruction.

In some ways Pueblo Indian cosmological beliefs tended toward the practical. They attempted to establish the solstices and probably the equinoxes, and there is some evidence that they attempted to match full moons with the winter solstice. Since the Indians had no real understanding of celestial mechanics, they apparently never caught on as to why this particular undertaking was often unsuccessful.

The Christian belief in the origin and history of the earth is contained in Genesis and involves the creation of all things within a relatively short time, perhaps a handful of days. The rest of the universe, sun, moon, stars were put in place after the earth was created, and presumably all was done for the special benefit of humans, the last created beings. This happened only a few thousand years before the beginning of the Christian era.

At least in historic times, the Pueblo Indians had rather indefinite ideas about the primal earth. It was thought of as damp or soft, later hardening into rocks. There were spirits, but as yet, no human beings. The great central event in the Pueblo origin stories are the *emergence* of men and women from a series of underworlds to the earth's surface.

The mission period in the Americas, especially the Spanish mission effort, always seemed to have a strong tinge of Manicheism, and the missionaries saw themselves on the front lines in the eternal struggle of light against darkness. The good deities of the Franciscans were a trinitarian god, a divine virgin, and a host of lesser beings including angels and, especially, saints, many of whom were originally living men and women but who became power figures after death. Countering God and his angels and saints were the dark deities of the underworld led by the ex-angel Satan. The devil's adherents (in the eyes of the missionaries) included the gods, goddesses, and spirits of the Pueblo world, one reason why the Franciscans were so adamant in their struggle against Pueblo religion.

Within the Pueblo world there was a more confused situation, for different towns and groups of towns had somewhat different categories of supernatural

beings; at least, this was true in historic times. In chapter 5, I have already speculated as to the Pueblo religion at the beginning of Spanish colonization.
Important in the divine grouping was Coyote, a kind of Promethean figure and
trickster who, along with Sun Father, was instrumental in introducing human
beings to the surface of the earth. Also figuring were the moon, certain of the
stars, the divine twins or twin war-gods, various ancestral beings (kachinas),
cloud beings, earth spirits, wind spirits, water beings, and others. In fact, in the
Pueblo way of thinking, all parts of nature—including inanimate objects such as
stones, water, houses, and pots, not to mention plants and all animals—have
some sort of spirit reality. Although there was not a neat hierarchy of beings, it
might be argued that Sun Father was somewhat of a "high god."

In ideal Christian theology, all people have souls of presumed equal worth; all
human beings are brothers and sisters. In practice, the seventeenth-century
Franciscans made pejorative racial and class distinctions, as did the secular society of the time. There was an indifference to animal and plant life, and to the
earth generally, Christian dogma teaching that human beings were given domination over the earth to use and exploit. Only through Christianity would men
and women find a satisfactory afterlife; non-Christians, and Christians who did
not practice the doctrine of a particular sect (in this case Catholicism), were
doomed to eternal punishment. This was also true of people who accepted favors
from Satan and his minions; witches, warlocks, and the like. This attitude led to
zealotry and to a certain callousness on the part of the clergy, though probably
less so among the New Mexican Franciscans than among their contemporaries
in, say, seventeenth-century Puritan New England.

We are on rather uncertain ground when discussing the moral theology of the
Pueblo religion of the seventeenth century. Today, both the Pueblos and the various Apachean groups see human beings as striving not for domination over their
environment but for harmony with the natural universe. This idea is so widespread that there seems to be a good chance that it has roots deep in antiquity. It
was not borrowed from Christianity since it is antithetical to the Christian idea
about humanity's place in nature. Pueblo religion in the historic period is tightly
focused on group welfare, providing rain for the crops at the appropriate time,
and promoting the health and well-being of the people as a whole. It seems a near
certainty that such an attitude was also true in the seventeenth century, and probably for many hundreds of years before. A dark side of Pueblo supernaturalism
today is the widespread belief in witchcraft and the savage attitude toward people
believed to be witches. Part of this attitude may have derived from the Spanish
culture, in which fear of witches was a very old tradition. It seems likely, though,
that a belief in malevolent spirits predated the Spaniards in New Mexico. But

whereas Pueblo Indians still hold very strong views about witches, the Christian attitude has softened somewhat since the seventeenth century. That is to say, certain modern Christian sects may give lip service to witchcraft and demonic possession, but generally they do not see witches around every corner.

Taken all in all, there seems to have been no particular superiority of seventeenth-century Christianity over Pueblo Indian religion—though from a purely objective point of view the reverse might be argued. Both religions had views of cosmology and of human origins not supported by modern scholarship, and both had destructive elements, especially a belief in witchcraft. The Pueblo faith, however, offered specific solutions to immediate and pressing problems, relating especially to the growing of food, something Christianity did not do as efficiently, at least in Pueblo eyes. Both religions granted something to believers after death, but the Pueblo idea of the dead becoming kachinas and continuing—on a supernatural plane—to function in Pueblo life was more emotionally satisfying. Among many Pueblo Indians, it remains so today.

The Order of Friars Minor, or Franciscans, who were given New Mexico as a mission field, had been founded by Giovanni Francesco Bernardone, known in the English-speaking world as Francis of Assisi (ca. A.D. 1181–1226). Devoted to poverty and good works, Francis collected a group of disciples and formed them into an order in 1209, further authenticated by a Papal Bull in 1223. A second order for nuns was formed in 1212, and a tertiary or third order for laymen and laywomen in 1221. Francis was canonized in 1228, less than two years after his death. After a somewhat stormy period following Francis's death, the Franciscans became an extremely influential order within the Catholic Church. Originally functioning as ministers to the poor, the order quickly adapted itself to missionization. Franciscans were among the first missionaries in Asia, Africa, and especially the New World.

Although we sometimes think of the Jesuits as the "intellectuals" of the Catholic clerical world, the Franciscans, particularly during their formative period, were extremely important in the development of Western science. Note, in particular, Robert Grosseteste (ca. 1175–1253), Roger Bacon (ca. 1220–ca. 1292), and William of Occam or Ockham (ca. 1285–1349), the latter man giving us the famous phrase now called "Occam's Razor."

By the time the Spaniards began exploring America, the Franciscans were organized into a series of *provinces*, with their chief officer, the *provincial*. In newly missionized areas, however, the convents were organized into custodia headed by a custodian. These, in turn, formed *convents*, groups of friars who lived together, the smallest unit of the order. In New Spain, a Custodia of the

Holy Gospel was set up in Mexico City in 1523. Outlying custodiae were organized in Michoacán, Yucatán, Tampico, and Guatemala, and other areas as the need for them arose. In 1535 the custodia in Mexico City was raised to the status of the Province of the Holy Gospel, and eventually various other custodiae were elevated to provincial status, with a commissary-general of New Spain as the chief officer over them all.

In New Spain, the only two exceptions to the evolution of custodia to province were the organizations in Tampico and New Mexico. Although the seventeenth-century New Mexican custodia may possibly have had as many as sixty-six friars, it remained under charge of the Province of the Holy Gospel in Mexico. Also, contrary to the usual pattern of local election, the custodian throughout that century was elected not by the local group but by the mother province. Indeed, the New Mexican custodia never did receive provincial status.

As mentioned in chapter 7, the New Mexican custodia was probably formally established in 1617 with Friar Esteban Perea as the first custodian. Before that time the head of the New Mexico missions had been given the more general title of *comisario,* or commissary. Shortly after the establishment of the custodia, one of the friars, often but not always the custodian, was given the separate title of Commissary of the Holy Office of the Inquisition, Alonso de Benavides being the first Franciscan to receive this title. This powerful office became important in the struggle between church and state, although it was not fully utilized until after mid-century (see chapters 7 and 10).

The first two decades of Spanish control saw only a modest increase in missionization. During the Oñate period, only the area of the Rio Grande near the Spanish settlement was missionized. Oñate's interests, after all, were focused primarily on the economic development of the area. Although friars were assigned to most of the Pueblos, there were only eight missionaries (a number that dwindled during the Oñate years), and the assignments were for the most part on paper only. The headquarter pueblo of Santo Domingo received a mission, as did San Ildefonso and San Juan (Yungue), though the San Ildefonso mission may not have been put on a firm footing until the arrival of Fray Andrés Bautista in 1609. There was some small building activity at Jemez by Fray Alonso de Lugo, but this failed, probably by 1601. Pecos had a missionary as early as 1598 but seems to have been a rather insecure foundation until around 1619 or 1620. The first permanent church in the province, as mentioned in chapter 6, built probably in the year 1600, was at Yungue. It functioned for both the Spanish settlement and for the nearby Tewa Indians of San Juan but may have been deserted when the Spaniards moved their capital to Santa Fe, being reestablished after A.D. 1640.

Visita at San Cristóbal (photograph by the author)

The arrival of Peralta brought additional missionaries and new pressures to spread the missionization program. With Peralta, New Mexico changed from a proprietary to a royal colony with a primary role for the missionaries. Sandia in the old Tiguex region was missionized in 1610, and Isleta received a missionary (Juan de Salas) and convent around 1612 or 1613. Puaray and Alameda, however, were relegated to the status of *visita*—a chapel visited at more or less regular intervals by missionaries stationed elsewhere. Also, between 1610 and 1612, a convent was established at Zia with Cristóbal de Quirós as missionary, and a year or so later a convent was built at Nambé with Fray Pedro Haro de la Cueva in charge.

At some point between 1610 and 1612 a permanent mission was established at the pueblo of Galisteo in Tano country, but the missionary is unknown. A mission station at San Lázaro, set up in 1613, had been turned into a visita by 1621. Meanwhile, a mission was built at nearby San Cristóbal, though soon it, too, became only a visita. As mentioned in chapter 7, Chililí, the first mission east of the Manzanos, was set up probably in 1613 with Fray Alonso de Peinado as the missionary.

In 1616 there were sixteen friars (thirteen of them priests) in New Mexico, and at the end of that year seven additional missionaries arrived in the province.

Mural on the east wall of Giusewa Pueblo in the Jemez area (courtesy of the Museum of New Mexico, neg. no. 6430)

In the next decade, the mission effort was expanded to San Felipe in the Keresan region, the Jemez towns, Taos, Picurís, and a more permanent mission at Pecos. During this same period the first Tompiro pueblo, Abó, received a missionary when Fray Francisco Fonte was assigned there in 1622. A mission at Picurís was founded between 1621 and 1625, and the one at Taos, with Pedro de Ortega serving as missionary, in 1622. Gerónimo de Zárate Salmerón, whose book on New Mexico has made him better known than most Franciscans of the period, founded Giusewa near modern Jemez Pueblo in 1621 or 1622, perhaps originally as San José. The church was destroyed around 1623 and then rebuilt a year or so later under the name of San Diego. The great church at Pecos, in its time one of the most ambitious European structures in all of North America, was begun around 1621 and completed, perhaps in 1625, by Andrés Suárez.

Several missionaries were reassigned during the period 1616–21, but six additional Franciscans arrived in the fall of 1621. The mission effort, however, had its next great leap forward in 1625 with the coming of twelve new missionaries led by Alonso de Benavides, bringing the total number to twenty-six. Benavides, the new custodian, was especially interested in the Manzano Tiwa, the Tompiro, and in the Jumano groups to the east, and he extended the missionization program

Crucifix found in mission ruins, Giusewa Pueblo, Jemez area (courtesy of the Museum of New Mexico, neg. no. 15424)

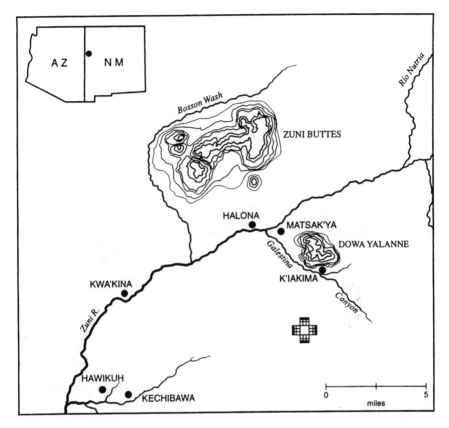

Zuni towns in the seventeenth century. All of the pueblos except Halona (modern Zuni) were probably deserted by 1692. (Modified from Riley, *A Zuni Life*, 1998.)

in that direction. There were foundations at Quarai, briefly at Humanas, and probably at Tajique. There were also refoundations at Jemez (San Diego de la Congregación), and at Picurís. For the first time the Spaniards turned to the Piro area, a rather strange oversight considering that the mission supply trains—in fact, all contact with Mexico—came through Piro country. Between 1626 and 1629 Benavides, with the assistance of Fray Martín de Arvide, established missions at Sevilleta, Socorro, and farthest south at Senecú.

The next surge in missionization came in 1629 when the new custodian, Father Perea, returned from New Spain (see also chapter 7). With Perea came thirty friars, but one died on the trip northward and a second shortly after the caravan arrived. A few friars in New Mexico returned to New Spain, but in the fall of 1629 there were forty-six Franciscans in New Mexico: thirty-five priests and eleven lay brothers.

The next few years saw the missionization program extend to its farthest extent in the New Mexican province. Fray Roque Figueredo spearheaded the Zuni mission at Hawikuh, founded in 1629, and that same year Francisco de Porras established a station at Awatovi in Hopi country. The following year a second convent was set up at the Third Mesa village of Oraibi by Fray Bartolomé Romero. The Zuni missionization effort was deserted in 1632 when the missions at Halona (modern Zuni) and Hawikuh were destroyed. Hawikuh was rebuilt in the 1640s, and Halona probably about the same time. The Hopi missions were maintained until the Pueblo Revolt, which effectively ended missionization in Hopi land.

As mentioned in chapter 7, the mission at Taos was burned and the missionary killed in a rebellion of 1639. The pueblo was "pacified" in 1641, but the church was not rebuilt for more than a decade. As of 1638, the Franciscan commissary-general of New Spain, Father Juan de Prada, could report that mission New Mexico extended like a cross from Senecú in the south to Taos in the north, and from Hopi in the west to the Tompiro settlements in the east.

Senecú is a somewhat mysterious place. It was located on the west bank of the Rio Grande, not too far from San Pascual and Qualacú, but even though a mission was built there, the ruins have never been definitely identified. Possibly they are now buried under Rio Grande sediments. In fact, information on the whole southern Piro area is somewhat confused. Testimony taken by a viceregal commission in 1601 indicated that Qualacú (Cuelaquí) was the southernmost pueblo reported by Oñate, although the adelantado himself called it the "second pueblo." It seems probable that the first settlement was San Pascual, which in spite of its size was deserted by the time of Otermín's attempted reconquest of 1681. It seems to me that there may have been a gradual consolidation of the Piro towns just north of Black Mesa, one that was accelerated when a mission station was begun at Senecú.

A few years after Prada's report, the Franciscans began a mission program among the Mansos of the El Paso area. The mission of Nuestra Señora de Guadalupe was occupied in late 1659, and a permanent structure was built between 1662 and 1668. Administratively, the Guadalupe mission was under control of the New Mexico custodia, but the secular situation is not altogether clear. The Rio Grande at El Paso had, during the course of the seventeenth century, become the boundary line between Nueva Vizcaya and the province of New Mexico. As the mission was south (at El Paso, actually more west) of the river, it logically lay within the jurisdiction of the governor of Nueva Vizcaya. This, however, did not seem to be a particular problem during this period.

Several families of Indians from the Piro pueblo of Senecú were brought in by the missionary in charge, Fray García de San Francisco, to help with the conversion. A half-dozen young Manso men and women, servants in Spanish households, were also recruited to help with the mission effort. This missionization effort at Guadalupe was not without problems; for example, in 1667 there was a flare-up of rebellion. This was quickly extinguished and it was to a reasonably secure El Paso area that the Spaniards fell back during the dark first weeks of the Pueblo Revolt.

As far as the major New Mexico missions were concerned, the second half of the seventeenth century saw the missionary effort stemmed and a retreat begun. Although the Hopi missions held firm until the revolt, Zuni was a constant problem. The mission at Hawikuh (but not the town) was sacked by the Apaches in 1672 and does not seem to have been reopened. During this period, several of the Zuni towns may have been deserted, and after the Pueblo Revolt, only Halona was left.

The Towa pueblos of Jemez presented a constant problem. This was certainly due in part to the interaction of the Jemez and Navajo to the west and north, creating a volatile situation that kept the Jemez region in turmoil. On the eastern side of the mission area a steady attrition took place. Partly due to the drought conditions of 1667–72, and partly to the increasing pressure of Apache nomads, the entire Tompiro region and part of the Manzano Tiwa region were deserted between 1672 and 1680. The same pressures caused the desertion of the southernmost Piro town, Senecú, during that same period. In the crucial year of 1680 only some thirty-three Franciscans were stationed in New Mexico.

How did one go about the business of missionization? The first missionaries no doubt made do with such housing as their hosts could provide, but the plan from the first was to build churches and convents, the latter serving as both administrative and living quarters for the missionaries. Although the first permanent church was constructed at San Gabriel in 1599–1600, the great period of church building came later. For one thing, until some years after 1610 there simply were not enough missionaries to staff any large mission effort. A serious building program really got under way in the 1620s.

How did the handful of missionaries approach the task of convincing some tens of thousands of Native Americans to give up their traditional and tried-and-true religious methods and embrace a puzzling alien code? They could, of course, use force if necessary. Spanish soldiers led by the civil government and by encomenderos were ready to back up the mission program with armed intervention. This, alone, was not enough because the Spanish forces were small and scattered over a very large area. And in fact, rebellions like those of Jemez, Zuni, and Taos continued to flare up during the course of the century.

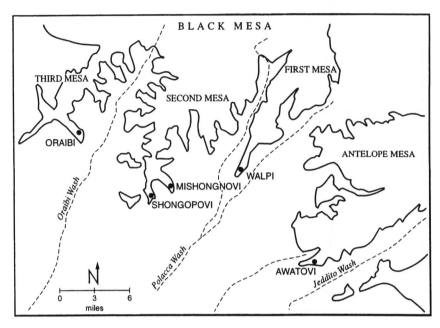

Hopi pueblos in the seventeenth century. Towns were originally on the lower slopes of the mesas.

But from the first, the Franciscans seem to have introduced a powerful moral authority that for the most part worked in the seventeenth-century province. Totally certain of the truth of their faith and their own superiority as human beings, the missionaries acted with great boldness and decision. Unfortunately, with this mind-set the friars saw little or nothing good in Pueblo culture. They quickly realized that this culture was a seamless whole, and that the most effective way to attack Pueblo religion was to pull down the whole social edifice. The Franciscans in central Mexico, during the previous century, had concentrated on the young people, especially the young men, producing a cadre of fanatical Christians who were willing to desert parents and family to follow the missionaries. In New Mexico the Franciscans utilized the same strategy and concentrated on the youth. This produced great bitterness on the part of Pueblo Indians, struggling not only for their religion, but for their total culture. This experiment in rapid forced acculturation on the part of the missionaries began to meet a growing resistance on the part of the Indians. Whenever the military and political pressure against native religion relaxed (as it did in the time of López de Mendizábal), such forbidden ceremonies as the kachina dances, practiced in dangerous secrecy, again became public. Their violent suppression, especially after López's time, was surely one of the factors that led to the Pueblo Revolt.

In the sixteenth century, Franciscan missionaries in central Mexico had thrown themselves into the learning of the native Aztec or Nahuatl language, and this idea of preaching to converts in their own tongues was quickly extended into other parts of Mexico; for example, the Tarascan region. By the time of the New Mexican missionaries, however, the emphasis was on teaching of Spanish to the native groups. Because New Mexico has several very different languages— Zuni, Hopi, Northern and Southern Tiwa, Tewa/Tano, Towa, Piro/Tompiro, and two branches of Keresan—and the missionaries moved around quite a bit, it was undoubtedly simpler to concentrate on Spanish. Still, it did mean that inter-action between a missionary and a parishioner had to be through an interpreter. In an *auto,* or edict—in this case, a questionnaire dated September 4, 1699— Governor Pedro Rodríguez Cubero asked a number of old settlers in pre-revolt New Mexico their understanding of the mission effort. There seemed to be a general agreement that, with very few exceptions, the Franciscans depended on Spanish and on interpreters.

What were these New Mexico Franciscans like? It seems probable on the basis of the evidence we have today that most of the missionaries were humane men, dedicated to their Indian neophytes, albeit only on Franciscan terms. There were exceptions, to be sure. For example, a number of individual missionaries were accused of seducing their female Pueblo parishioners. One recent scholar has claimed that the Pueblo women readily made themselves sexually available to the Spaniards in order to "cool their passions" and to transform and domesticate them. This sort of female behavior does not really fit the Pueblo pattern, at least not in later historic times. In any case, as far as the missionaries are concerned, the claims of sexual irregularity mostly focused on outlying pueblos like Taos and the Salinas area. The Franciscans emphasized celibacy, and sexual miscon-duct does not seem to have been a regular thing. Certainly it was not acceptable behavior in the eyes of the provincia officials in Mexico.

More serious was the charge of cruelty. One notorious example was that of Salvador de Guerra at Hopi, who was charged with having a man flogged to death and who administered whippings followed by applications of hot turpen-tine to boys and girls, often for very flimsy offenses. Guerra was condemned in 1655 to be sent to Mexico City for disciplinary action, although the major charges—first, that he was "incorrigible, overbearing and arrogant and a revealer of the secrets of the Order," and second, that he lacked "modesty and deco-rum"—seem to ignore the main issue of the case. It is unclear if Guerra actually went to Mexico. If so, he soon returned to the province, his sadism apparently forgotten or ignored, and in 1661 he was appointed notary to Father Alonso de Posada in the latter man's capacity of Commissary of the Inquisition.

Miracles were the order of the day. In chapter 7 I mentioned the "Lady in Blue" whose mission to the Jumano so fascinated Benavides, but this apparition was only one of many miraculous events. The missionaries healed the sick when challenged by native leaders. They brought rain to drought-stricken areas where the rain-priests had failed. Francisco de Porras at Hopi made a blind boy see.

The Franciscans personalized their enemies in the struggle for Indian hearts and souls. The native weather-control priests, called "sorcerers" by the Franciscans, were considered active agents of the Devil, whose actions could be seen every day in the Pueblos. God occasionally took a direct hand. At Taos, a sorceress gathered a small group of women around her and was attempting to persuade them to give up their Christian marriages when a lightning bolt from a clear sky struck and killed her. The other women were unharmed and, in the minds of the Franciscans, strengthened in their new faith. At Acoma, baptism of a dying baby caused the infant to instantaneously recover her health.

Miracles were a stock in trade, and to recite one was usually to have it accepted at face value. Usually, but not always! The Porras cure of a blind boy at Hopi seems to have met with some skepticism at a higher level. The Franciscan commissary-general Francisco de Apodaca noted that the miracle was not authenticated and discouraged its publication in Mexico. Generally, though, this was a time and a place where the miraculous was commonplace and the struggle to save souls was waged against real and immediate agents of Satan.

One thing the Franciscans faced throughout the mission period in New Mexico, as did the Jesuits in northwestern Mexico, was a general lack of work-men acquainted with European construction. This was perhaps not as serious as might have been expected, at least in the Pueblo area. Pueblo houses were made of stone and mud mortar or, in some towns in the Rio Grande Valley, of coursed adobe. There was considerable use of wood for such things as door lintels and kiva roofs. But something as massive as a church was outside the experience of Pueblo builders.

A second, more serious factor was the shortage of master builders in the Southwest. The fact that one or two missionaries might be alone in an area made it necessary for them to have a variety of skills, not least of which was the construction of churches and convents. By the seventeenth century, church construction in Europe was on a very sophisticated level. From the Romans, medieval Europe had inherited the idea of the barrel vault to roof the nave, the main portion of the church that extends from the entryway to the chancel or altar area. Early in medieval times, church builders had developed what is called a groin vault, two semicircular arches intersecting at right angles and supported by massive columns. Another solution for the weight of the barrel vault was also quickly introduced: a row of arches running across either side of the nave. And as churches grew higher (especially with the coming of the Gothic order), there were introduced pointed (ogival) arches and the graceful flying buttress, which braced the nave vaults at their points of greatest thrust and which could be carried over side aisles of the church. The result of these engineering principles was broad naves and churches that towered majestically toward the heavens.

None of these things were available in seventeenth-century New Mexico. The laborers, largely or wholly Indian, under the direction of one or two missionaries, had to work with what was doable. There might be some advice and help from missionary experts in other areas or from trained Indians like the Pecos carpenters discussed below. For most of the missions there were nearby estancias with Hispanic families in residence. Still, the major responsibility rested on the shoulders of one or two missionaries. The result was a building in stone (or occasionally adobe) and timber that generally stood the test of time and produced attractive, albeit primarily functional, structures.

The first problem in these simplified buildings was to attain a width of nave sufficient to house a sizable congregation. Using neither the arch nor the vault, the Franciscans fell back on an ancient building technique, employed in the Near East and Mediterranean regions for ten thousand years or more, in which heavy walls support a flat beamed roof. This wall-and-beam type of construction not only spread widely in the arid portions of the Mediterranean Basin but also was in use, long before the Spanish came, in various of parts of arid America. In the Southwest this kind of building dated from the early Pueblo period. Basically it involved the building of rectangular walls, with roofing beams (to which the Spaniards gave the name *vigas*) supported by the heavy walls and forming the foundations for a flat or low-angle pitched roof. The stones were roughly shaped by hammering, and in some areas adobe—crudely constructed blocks of clay placed in irregular courses—was used. Although the mission churches were more elaborate, the basic techniques had been known to the Indian parishioners for centuries.

When a mission station was established, the friar involved was sent out with a standardized kit of materials, including such tools as axes, adzes, hoes, saws, chisels, planes, and augers. Also included were large numbers of nails and tacks, and hinges and locks, plus various raw materials such as iron. The use of raw iron supposes a blacksmith, but it is not clear if the missionaries did their own blacksmithing or whether itinerant smiths, perhaps from Santa Fe or from one of the estancias, made their rounds of mission stations.

The missionary, often newly arrived from New Spain, first requested a tract of land from the Pueblo officials on which to construct a church. Usually the friars preferred to build a mission and convento on suitable flat land near a main plaza, and this often took considerable negotiation with the town leaders. It was preferred that the church be oriented to the cardinal directions, and this was done either with a compass or by observation of the pole star, or of the sun using a gnomon, the shadow-casting element in a sundial. A simple gnomon (without its marked sundial base) was no more than a rod set vertically in the ground. The friar made a circle around this rod using a cord tied to the rod so that it served as a center point. He then marked the shadow of the rod where it intersected the circle at sunrise and again at sunset. The midpoint between these lines, sighting from the rod, would be a fair approximation of north.

Carpentry skills had diffused to the Indians very early in the Oñate period. At Pecos Pueblo, Fray Andrés Suárez introduced Spanish craftsmen to teach the natives, and Pecos quickly became recognized for the skills of its woodworkers. This, like other craft skills, seems to have spread rapidly among the Pueblos, though individual Pecos workmen were in demand for work on mission churches in other pueblos as well as in Santa Fe.

The basic ground plan of a church called for a rectangular nave and associated altar area that was raised above the level of the nave. Sometimes transepts, flanking buildings extending out from the sides of the nave, were used, giving the church a cruciform shape. The churches were usually built with a core-and-veneer construction, a rubble core with facing sandstone blocks set in mud mortar, or, as at Pecos, the construction material might be large adobe bricks. The walls were squared off using primitive measuring instruments, primarily a plumb bob, measuring line, and what was called a *nivel de albañil,* a device made of wooden arms and an attached plumb bob to establish true horizontal lines. Considerable attempt was made to ensure that walls forming the long axis of the nave were parallel, though this depended on the skill of the individual friar— thus producing a certain amount of variation from one church to the next. In any case, walls were quite thick, averaging three or more feet, for they carried the weight of the roof vigas.

The vigas that formed the support and underpinning for the roofs were usually about thirty-five feet long. The preferred wood for vigas was spruce because of its lightness and strength; however, ponderosa pine was easier to obtain in many mission stations. In the missions of Abó and Quarai, for example, ponderosa could be found five or six miles away in the Manzano Mountains. Ponderosa worked quite well, but it tended to twist as it cured, and so ponderosa vigas needed to be seasoned for a year or more. They were usually left in the spot

Model of Abó Pueblo mission, 1943 (courtesy of the Museum of New Mexico, neg. no. 14461)

where they were felled for a period of seasoning, then roughly shaped to lighten them before being transported on carts to the mission. At the building site they were further trimmed and often decoratively carved. When the walls had been built up to their desired height, the roof beams were lifted into place with a primitive block-and-tackle device. Smaller poles were placed on the weight-carrying beams, and a layer of clay over that. Floors were usually of packed earth. Over the entrance door was a choir loft reached by a stairway, for the Franciscans in New Mexico stressed music as an adjunct to sacred instruction. A bell room was normally constructed high at one or the other end of the church. The bells were supplied from bell makers in Mexico (see below).

While supervising the church and the associated convento, the missionary normally took rooms in the adjacent pueblo, where he also set up a temporary altar. After completion of the convento, he moved into relatively spacious quarters. The convento was often built around a central patio surrounded by a covered walkway called the *ambulatorio*. Included in the convento structure was a *portería*, or reception hall, a kitchen and pantry, an infirmary, storerooms, and several *celdas*, or sleeping rooms, one of which might have an office attached for the use of the friar. The convents often included privies; the ones at Abó had a primitive flushing arrangement via a small stone-lined drain. Near the convento structures were the orchards and gardens cultivated by the friars. The orchard at Guadalupe produced "grapes, apples, quinces, plums, peaches, and figs." Gardens contained both native Southwestern and European-introduced plants for the mission kitchen and infirmary.

Mission ruins, Quarai Pueblo, fall 1937 (courtesy of the Museum of New Mexico, neg. no. 8086)

As the seventeenth century wore on, the missions obtained tremendous herds, many tens of thousands of stock animals, especially sheep. It is not entirely clear how the large amounts of land necessary to grazing animals were allotted or administered. By 1663 at least sixty mission estancias were in use, though some pueblos (for example, Abó and Quarai) did not have assigned estancias, the missionaries and the Indian population apparently using lands granted to the pueblos for grazing and agricultural purposes. There were also private estancias within a league or so of some of the Pueblos; to what extent these operated cooperatively with the missions is unclear. Often there seems to have been friction, as in the protest of the Quarai missionary in 1638 about the encroachment of cattle from a neighboring estanciero.

Keeping the missions supplied was a major reason for the supply trains up and down the Camino Real. Although these trains were organized by the Franciscans and were primarily for upkeep of the missions, they also became very important as the basic lifeline of the colony. I shall therefore treat the supply trains in the next chapter, discussing supplies in the context of the province as a whole.

Each of the missions was supplied with sacramental wine (forty-five gallons every three years, the interval between supply trains), olive oil for votive lamps, cloth, and paper. Each friar received two blankets every three years, a hat and two pairs of wool stockings. For the mission infirmary there were bed clothes, various condiments, and instruments such as syringes, cupping devices for bleeding, lancets, scissors, brass basins, grindstones, and stills for water distillation. The kitchen received various cooking utensils including metates, iron spoons, sieves, graters, and spits. There were barrels for water, table cloths and napkins, and tallow candles. Ecclesiastical equipment at the missions included altar cloths, missals, gilded chalices, crucifixes, copal incense, chant books, carved Christ images, lamps, ciboria, and damask to cover the altar. Paper was a standard item, and ink for the locally produced quill pens also seems to have come from Mexico. It was made of tannic acid mixed with iron oxide, and when supplies ran low, it was increasingly diluted with water, making the color weaker and weaker. At some point the missionaries and probably also the governmental officials began to manufacture their own ink made with pulverized charcoal. It is not clear if this practice had begun by the seventeenth century.

Music was not neglected by the missionaries. In fact, the training of native choirs was considered very important in the missionization effort. Musical instruments included trumpets, flutes, and organs. For example, we know of a "fine organ" installed at the mission of Abó sometime around 1660, but organs were common well before that date.

A portion of the interior heating was done, as in Mexico, by use of braziers filled with burning charcoal. Corner fireplaces, and occasionally fireplaces in the middle of walls, were used in the conventos, the fuel generally being wood. At Hopi, where wood was scanty, there may have been some use of coal, although the Franciscans generally were rather negative about the smelly, sulfur-laden local coal.

Each mission has a small signal bell and a two-hundred-pound bronze church bell. These latter bells were not tolled in the later sense of the word but were rung by pulling on the clapper with a rope or thong or by striking the outside of the bell. The bells were usually made in Mexico City, and many of the ones intended for the New Mexico missions were cast from the same mold.

The largest mission church in seventeenth-century New Mexico was built at Pecos during the 1620s by Andrés Suárez. Constructed partly on bedrock and partly on a rubble fill faced with sandstone, the adobe structure had a nave of 133 feet. Its width was even more amazing, tapering from 41 feet at the front of the church to 37.5 feet in the altar area. The thick, heavy walls were protected by buttresses, and there were several bell towers. Plastered white, the church seen by the traveler coming along the trail eastward from Glorieta Pass must have been a most impressive site. This church was so completely dismantled by the Pecos people during the Pueblo Revolt that it was lost until 1967, when National Park Service archaeologist Jean Pinkley rediscovered the footings outside the extant eighteenth-century church walls.

One interesting and still controversial aspect of early missionization was the use of Pueblo Indian kivas. In the patio or convento areas of Abó, Quarai, Pecos, and Awatovi are kivas that have been filled in. Various interpretations of these kivas have been given; that they represent superposition, building a Christian church over a native place of worship; that they were built during temporary absences of the friars by defiant factions in the pueblos; or that they were built by Indians after the Pueblo Revolt to celebrate the return of the kachinas. The kivas at Abó, Quarai, and Pecos, however, seem to have actually been incorporated into the patio area of the churches. Park Service archaeologist and historian James Ivey has pointed out that there is archaeological evidence that the convento kivas were built early in the mission period. He suggests that they represent examples of "halfway houses" where Pueblo Indian leaders could absorb elements of the new religion in settings that were hallowed and sacred in their own tradition. In all cases the kivas were later discarded. As might be expected, however, kivas were also constructed in the ruins of mission buildings after the Pueblo Revolt. In December 1680, at Sevilleta in Piro country, Governor Otermín's men came across a kiva in the chapel area made from wood from the chapel roof.

The courtyard kiva at the pueblo of Quarai is somewhat of an anomaly. It is atypical, being rectangular rather than round as are other kivas in the Tompiro and Manzano Tiwa country. Exactly what this means is not clear. Perhaps it represented an idiomatic choice by Juan Gutiérrez, the missionary in charge. Whoever introduced the Quarai structure included such standard kiva features as the ventilator shaft, a central firepit, entrance through the roof, and possibly a *sipapu,* the shallow depression that symbolizes the entry to the Pueblo underworld. This feature, however, may actually have been the footing for the entry ladder. Although not typical of the area, rectangular kivas would not be unknown to Salinas Indians because there was trade being conducted with the western Pueblos, who used this kind of kiva. I have no doubt that traders from Abó and Quarai occasionally visited Zuni and Hopi, and that these visits were reciprocated. One bit of evidence is the practice of cremation, used primarily at Zuni, which turns up in the Salinas area in contexts dating to the fifteenth or sixteenth century. There was also a certain amount of western Pueblo pottery in the Salinas area.

Although the Abó, Quarai, and Pecos convento kivas are the only ones to date that have been investigated with the idea of Spanish instruction in mind, it seems likely that the early kiva D at Las Humanas (Gran Quivira) and the convento patio kiva at Awatovi excavated by J. Brew were also used for this purpose. It is possible that a number of other early missionized pueblos also had this type of kiva.

Along these lines, it is interesting that the pre-Spanish Pueblo kivas continued more or less in use without mission interference until the furious anti-kiva campaign that followed the López de Mendizábal period. There was a continuous series of attempts by the Pueblo Indians to practice native ceremonials, especially the masked kachina dances. Also, the ceremonial game of *patol,* which I have suggested came from Mexico with Coronado's Mexican Indian allies, was documented for the early seventeenth century as playing a part in baptismal ceremonies. After López de Mendizábal's time, however, there was a concerted attempt to wipe out the more obvious symbols and centers of Pueblo religion. The intolerance of the missionaries became more intense, and it shortly led to the Pueblo Revolt.

If the missionaries in New Mexico constructed pseudo-kivas for instructional purposes, it follows a line of thinking utilized by the Franciscans in central Mexico during the first part of the sixteenth century. For example, Pedro de Gante and his fellow missionaries wrote catechisms using native Nahuatl pictographs. Because of the similarities in certain Aztec religious practices (confession and penance for example) and Christian rituals, the missionaries attempted to use the old practices to effect the new. They also established a college at Tlatelolco based on the pre-Hispanic Aztec *calmecac* schools, the idea being to train noble Aztec youths to the clergy. For a time the Franciscans followed this practice, though there probably was some resistance from the earliest period. Eventually, and perhaps inevitably, given the innovative nature of the program, there was a reaction against this "nativization" of the mission program later in the century. In 1555, for example, the order came from Spain that sermons should not be written in indigenous languages. At the same time, native ceremonial displays of the Christian faith were regulated to guard against any pagan content, and the ordination of Indians was forbidden. By the time New Mexico was colonized, the nativization of religion had ceased to be a normal part of the Franciscan agenda.

Still, one suspects that this tradition, even though subversive, may have maintained itself on the edge of the Franciscan New World. In the province of New Mexico, individual friars may have continued to experiment with it. Certainly, Oñate himself was not hesitant to use the kivas for meetings with members of the Pueblo Indian power structure. If kiva-like structures were built to explain the new religion in a setting reminiscent of the old, the practice had died out (or was felt no longer necessary) by mid-century. After the López de Mendizábal period, it likely would have been totally rejected.

CHAPTER NINE

Spanish Society in New Mexico

The colony of New Mexico grew very slowly during the seventeenth century. There were some 560 people with Oñate, counting the families of soldiers and the numerous drivers, herders, personal servants, and slaves (see chapter 4), but this number likely fell during the next few years. It was not until Peralta's time, after the Spanish Crown had made a firm decision to maintain the colony as a mission province, that the new province began to expand. Even then, Hispanic settlement of the area was slow and sporadic with only one chartered town, the villa of Santa Fe. In addition to its permanent population, a certain number of people lived in the villa seasonally. These included the thirty-five encomenderos and their families as well as many of the estancieros, the owners of ranches and farms scattered throughout the region.

Various population figures have been given for the province of New Mexico during the seventeenth century. An estimate by Oakah L. Jones for 1630 suggests "perhaps seven hundred and fifty Spaniards, mestizos and converted Indians living in Santa Fé." This number may be somewhat high unless the author meant that a significant portion of these people were converted Pueblo Indians working for their encomenderos in Santa Fe. In 1638 the Franciscan commissary-general, Juan de Prada, spoke of about fifty homes and some two hundred Spaniards in the town of Santa Fe. In the petition of former governor Francisco Martínez de Baeza the following year, it was noted that from Senecú to Santa Fe there were "ten or twelve farms of Spaniards who plant wheat and maize by irrigating with water which is obtained from the Río del Norte." In Santa Fe, according to Martínez, there were "a few more than fifty inhabitants." However, Martínez de Baeza added that the entire province contained "two hundred persons, Spaniards and *mestizos*, who are able to bear arms." Counting families and perhaps servants, this would mean a total population of several hundred people.

France V. Scholes believed that "during the first three or four decades after the founding of the province the total was probably less than one thousand." In Scholes's view, the province as a whole never exceeded 2,500 and may have been fewer in the revolt year of 1680. According to the *Autos tocantes* documents for 1680–81, there were 1,946 individuals (including at least 500 servants, some who have may have been Pueblo Indians or Apaches) counted at La Salineta just before the party reached Paso del Norte. Scholes added to that number the 401 settlers and friars recorded as being killed and comes up with a figure of 2,347. C. W. Hackett considered this to be an underestimation. He believed that the La Salineta tally was not a full count, and that the earlier estimate—that Governor Otermín had 1,000 people with him and Lt. Governor García from Río Abajo had 1,500— was more nearly correct. This would make the population in the colony in 1680 around 2,900 individuals, less those Pueblo and Apache Indians who may have been included in the count. The Mexican Indians of Analco were probably listed with the Hispanic settlers, but we cannot be sure of that. The fact is that Spanish population in New Mexico in 1680 still cannot be estimated with any certainty.

The New Mexican Hispanic population was ethnically mixed from the beginning. It is true that the power elite of the colony—which consisted of the governor and other royal officials, the encomenderos, and the missionaries—were mainly Europeans or *crioles* (American-born individuals of European ancestry). These were primarily of Spanish descent, though there were Portuguese, Flemish, and French foreigners in the group. Probably the most important family in the latter part of the seventeenth century was that of Domínguez de Mendoza. The key member of this kin group, Juan de Domínguez de Mendoza, was an important administrative officer and soldier during this period. A partial list of other leading families includes Baca, Durán y Chávez, Gómez Robledo, Lucero de Godoy, and Márquez.

From Oñate's time, however, there had been *castas:* various mixtures of European, Native American, and African. The numbers of blacks, and diverse combinations of black with Indian and European ancestry, had grown rapidly during the sixteenth and early seventeenth centuries. By 1650 individuals with some African admixture were estimated to form 13 percent of the non-indigenous population in New Spain. In New Mexico, individuals of mixed ancestry seem to have been accepted for the most part, and many became solid citizens. For example, a partly black freedwoman named Isabel Olvera, or Olivera, came to the colony in 1600, and one of her sons, or perhaps a grandson, was sent to bring back Nicolás Ortiz to Nueva Vizcaya in the aftermath of the murder of Governor Rosas. A number of the provincial officials were of mixed blood: captains Diego López Sambrano (called a "half-mulatto"), Alvaro García Holgado, Juan Francisco, and

Alonso García; and alcaldes mayores Francisco Ortega, Luis López, Juan Luján, and Joseph Nieto. The wife of the Spaniard Juan de la Cruz, who held the rank of *alférez,* was a central Mexican Indian. Nicolás de Aguilar, perhaps López de Mendizábal's most influential lieutenant, and alcalde mayor of the Salinas area, was several times referred to in official documents as a mestizo. These individuals were sometimes highly regarded. In a letter to the Tribunal of the Inquisition on April 1, 1669, the commissary Fray Juan Bernal mentions a number of witnesses in a case against Cristóbal de Anaya Almazán, a former adherent of Governor López in the early 1660s (see chapter 10). In the letter, Bernal lists the mulatto captain, Francisco de Ortega, a man whom Father Juan considered to be "truthful," "honorable," and "entirely satisfactory." A second mulatto captain, Joseph Nieto, was in Bernal's opinion, "a truthful man and a good Christian." A 1689 document from Mexico City, a legal dispute between Governor Jironza and ex-governor Reneros, describes Captain Roque Madrid, head of the El Paso presidio and a soldier of extraordinary importance in the reconquest period, as a mulatto. I have been unable to find any other evidence for this status, though Angelico Chavez describes Roque and several other members of his family as swarthy or dark.

Only in the turbulent Rosas period did chauvinism and race prejudice become strongly overt. In October of 1641, Fray Bartolomé Romero, in a letter to the Franciscan commissary-general, said that the Rosas-packed Santa Fe cabildo contained "four Mestizo dogs." Even more vehement was a November 1643 statement of Alonso Baca (whose brother, Antonio, had just been executed for his part in the murder of ex-governor Rosas). He declared that the governor's followers included mostly "a foreigner, a Portuguese, and mestizos and sambohijos, sons of Indian women and negros and mulattoes."

Ramón Gutiérrez believes that the eighteenth-century documents show a strongly layered society with the Spaniards, among whom personal honor was an important component of social status, forming an elite class. At the top of the social pyramid were the upper-class "white" Spaniards, government officials, owners of estancias, military officers, and other members of the elite group. Below them were the Spanish or largely Spanish freeholders. At the bottom of the pyramid were Pueblo Indians and slaves, the latter mostly genízaros.

Whatever the situation in the eighteenth century, it is clear that such a rigid system did not hold in the seventeenth. As Scholes points out, despite occasional violent denunciations, various people with mixed ancestry—Indian, white, and black—held important offices in seventeenth-century New Mexico. This was inevitable because of the relatively small in-migration to the colony, resulting in an estimated 80 percent born-in-the-colony population in 1680–81. There was a considerable blurring of ethnic lines in part because the castas tended to marry outside their groups. Although New Mexico was hardly a paradise of racial harmony, there was a potential for substantially good living for mestizos and mulattos during the seventeenth century. It was, perhaps, a harbinger of the racial and cultural diversity that New Mexicans are proud of today.

Life on the frontier, "remote beyond compare," as Diego de Vargas later called the region, was crude, limited, and introverted. Following the initial colonization by Oñate there was a slow spread of individual families up and down the Rio Grande Valley in isolated farm or ranch steads or estancias. As already mentioned, the only town (*villa* in Spanish) was Santa Fe, where the government had been moved from the original town of San Gabriel near the mouth of the Chama, across the river from present-day San Juan Pueblo. Santa Fe was laid out in regular Spanish cabildo form with government buildings, a church, and as indicated above, homes for the various citizens, which included encomenderos and estancieros. South of the Santa Fe River was a district called Analco where a number of central Mexican Indians were settled under charge of the missionaries. But Santa Fe was not really a city in any realistic use of that term. In 1776, more than a century and a half after its founding, the Canonical Visitor Fray Francisco Atanasio Domínguez was sent from the Franciscan mother province in Mexico to inspect the New Mexico custodia. His comments on Santa Fe are revealing.

This villa . . . lacks everything. Its appearance is mournful because not only are the houses of earth, but they are not adorned by any artifice of brush or construction. To conclude, the Villa of Santa Fe (for the most part) consists of many small ranchos at various distances from one another, with no plan as to their location, for each owner built as he was able, wished to, or found convenient. . . .

In spite of what has been said, there is a semblance of a street in this villa. It begins on the left facing north shortly after one leaves the west gate of the cemetery of the parish church and extends down about 400 or 500 varas [1,100 to 1,375 feet]. Indeed, I point out that this quasi-street not only lacks orderly rows, or blocks, of houses, but at its very beginning, which faces north, it forms one side of a little plaza in front of our church. The other three sides are three houses of settlers with alleys between them. . . . The entrance to the main plaza is down through these. The sides, or borders, of the latter consist of the chapel of Our Lady of Light, which is to the left of the quasi-street mentioned . . . and faces north between two houses of settlers. The other side is the government palace, which, with its barracks, or quarters for the guard, and prison, is opposite the said chapel facing south. The remaining two sides are houses of settlers, and since there is nothing worth noting about them, one can guess what they are like from what has been seen. The government palace is like everything else here, and enough said.

Although unimpressive in the eyes of the Visitor, the Santa Fe of Domínguez's time was considerably larger than the seventeenth-century town. It stretched for two or three miles to the west along the Santa Fe River, extending to the village of Quemado (Agua Fría), and with Quemado had nearly fifteen hundred inhabitants. Although Domínguez tallies forty-two families of genízaros (the descendants of enslaved Apache or other nomadic Indians), there is no mention of Analco nor of central Mexican Indians. In fact, according to a study of Marc Simmons, few if any of these central Mexican natives returned after the reconquest of New Mexico in the 1690s. The last known mention of what could be a central Mexican at Analco was in 1728 by an Indian named Juan de León Brito, who petitioned the viceroy for lands in the Analco region "which had belonged to his father." Mentions of Analco during the eighteenth century indicate that genízaros were in occupation of that region, and Simmons thinks that such central Mexicans who did return were simply swamped by the newcomers.

One thing that seems to have been a factor in the founding of Santa Fe was that it had no nearby Pueblo population. This was in keeping with the *Ordenanzas de Descubrimiento* of 1573, promulgated by King Philip II, though of course the Spanish settlement at San Juan had pretty much violated these ordinances which prevented the Spaniards from impinging on Indian settlements. The competition for land that the Spaniards faced in the lower Chama drainage did not apply at Santa Fe. And this is a little surprising! Nestled at the edge of the mountains where the Santa Fe River flows from the Sangre de Cristo foothills, the area was once a region of considerable settlement. As late as early Classic or Pueblo IV times (see chapter 2) there were settlements in or near the present-day city; at Pindi Pueblo and the Schoolhouse site on opposite sides of the Santa Fe River in the Agua Fría area, the Arroyo Negro site in the southern part of the modern city, sites around the later Fort Marcy, at La Garita just north of the modern plaza, and at Arroyo Hondo south and east of the city. Not all of these sites were contemporaneous, but they were all deserted by the middle of the fifteenth century, and some, like the Fort Marcy Hill site, ceased occupation much earlier.

It is true that there was some falling off of population among various Rio Grande Pueblos after the middle decades of the fifteenth century. Several areas were partly or wholly deserted, including the middle Chama, Tijeras Canyon, Pottery Mound on the lower Puerco River, and sites in the Pecos region. But why these desertions involved the Santa Fe River is not clear, for it was a major stream flowing westward into the Rio Grande, and the mountains with their stands of trees and other natural resources were nearby. Possibly the heavy populations of the thirteenth and fourteenth centuries had stripped off the vegetation cover—but by Peralta's time the area had been depopulated for at least a century and a half, and fresh stands of trees would have long since appeared. It may also be that the region was too wet; the Spaniards had to contend with swamps along the river itself. The coming of the "Little Ice Age," a cooling in northern latitudes that began in the thirteenth century, may have been a factor. This period lasted, with some fluctuations, for several hundred years, with maximum cooling in the period 1600–50 and a final flurry a bit before 1750. Possibly it was a slight difference in microenvironments that allowed the less-productive Galisteo River, a few miles to the south, to maintain a considerable population in its upper course throughout much of the seventeenth century.

As discussed in chapter 6, Juan Martínez de Montoya probably had an estancia on or near the site of Santa Fe by 1607 or perhaps a year or two before that. Since Benavides considered that Oñate had founded the villa, it may be that Santa Fe was originally established as a paraje, or stopping point, on the trail running from the south to the lower Chama. The son of one of Oñate's original settlers, Juan Griego II, claimed many years later that he was born in Santa Fe in 1605. Whatever the condition of this original settlement, Governor Pedro de Peralta was instructed in 1609 to make a formal foundation of the town. As part of this formalization procedure, Peralta followed detailed instructions set down in Mexico and Spain. There were supposed to be at least thirty families, and each settler should have breeding stock in cows and bulls, oxen, a broodmare, sows, hens and a rooster, and ewes. Presumably the population quota was met and at least some of the domesticated animals were available in the original settlement. In terms of human occupation, however, we have the names of only sixteen family heads, not including Peralta himself. The area chosen was on the north side of the Santa Fe River, and there were separate blocks for the settlers as well as a block for government buildings. These first citizens of Santa Fe were assigned two sections of land for house and orchard, plus additional land for gardens, vineyards, and olive groves (but see chapter 4). Each received a generous four *caballerías* (more than a hundred acres) of cultivatable land suited for irrigation. In the governmental square was the Casa Real, or government house (the present-day Palace of the Governors), and other governmental buildings, including an arsenal and a jail. The modern Palace of the Governors lies on the foundations of the seventeenth-century structure, though the earlier building probably extended farther to the east. The Palace has been so extensively modified over the centuries that it is impossible to reconstruct the original appearance.

A letter dated March 10, 1620, from Viceroy Fernández de Córdova to Governor Juan de Eulate is interesting in this regard. It seems that the settlers were opting to move the site of Santa Fe to a better location where they could construct four towers, a church, and government buildings. This was probably an attempt (one of the earliest of several) to shift Santa Fe to the higher ground south of the Santa Fe River. Peralta's original settlement in the swampy region north of the Santa Fe River suggests that the Franciscans had previously staked out a claim to the more desirable high ground to the south. It is possible that Analco was actually under construction before the formal founding of the villa. Even in the eighteenth century the high land south of the river was used mainly for genízaros, who had replaced the earlier central Mexicans.

A chapel was called for in the governmental building instructions, though there is some confusion as to just when and where such a building was constructed. Fray Angelico Chavez believed that the Spaniards used the San Miguel chapel until a permanent building for the settlers was constructed in the late 1620s by Benavides on the east side of the plaza, near the present cathedral. This building was destroyed in the Pueblo Revolt of 1680. Its size and shape are unknown, but Chavez thought it might have been similar to the eighteenth-century church that was built on the same site, segments of which are incorporated in the nineteenth-century cathedral. There is a problem, however, with this reconstruction. It seems very likely that the "church and friary," which according to Benavides "would merit admiration anywhere," were in fact the San Miguel church in Analco. San Miguel may have been utilized by the Hispanic settlers as well as the Tlaxcalans since Benavides says, "There the friars are already teaching the *Spaniards* [emphasis mine] and Indians to read, write, play musical instruments, sing, and to practice all the arts of civilized society."

Building of the St. Francis church is less clear. In the letter to Eulate mentioned above, the viceroy made the following statement: "And as to the parochial church which has been proposed to be founded in that Villa of Santa Fe and as to sending a curate vicar for it there is no occasion at present for it to be done, inasmuch as there is already there a church and a convent of Sant. Francisco [yglessia y conuento de Sant Fran^{co}], which seems sufficient for the number of present residents." This statement seems to be contradictory. If the parochial church is only being proposed, then what of the "church and convent of San Francisco"? Although it makes for curious wording, the viceroy conceivably meant the Franciscan *order* rather than a specific church named St. Francis, and was actually referring to the mission-run San Miguel. Fernández de Córdova may have been trying to say something like "inasmuch as there is already there a church and convent *under the charge of the friars of San Francisco.*" If such were the case, it suggests that the St. Francis church was actually still to be founded in 1620. Of course, an acceptable alternate meaning (and perhaps a more logical one) is that the settlers already had a church of San Francisco but wanted a larger one.

The plaza area in the seventeenth century may have been longer than the modern plaza. Width of the plaza is somewhat in doubt, but certain scholars believe that it extended from Palace Avenue to Water Street, named for the Río Chiquito, which drained in a northwest to southeast direction into the Santa Fe River. If that was the case, it would have made a very unusual "split-level" plaza because of the natural terrace above the river. There is, however, some indication that the prominent (if unfortunate) Antonio Baca had a plot of land described as bordered by the plaza on the north and the Río Chiquito on the south. Unless Baca's family lost the plot after his 1643 execution in the Rosas affair and his steading was absorbed into Crown land, it would cast some doubt on the idea that the plaza was ever extended to the Río Chiquito.

At the time of first settlement, Santa Fe had a very well watered aspect. Around the area of original settlement was a series of swamps, called on the early maps *ciénegas*. North, east, and south of the old plaza area, the ciénega probably followed the 7,000 to 7,200 feet contour line. The swamps covered an area of thirty-five acres or more, there were a number of springs, and much of the region was probably woodland.

When the Europeans first arrived, it seems likely that the Santa Fe River had a heavier flow than it does today. As late as the eighteenth century the river was described as full of trout, which were certainly used to some degree as a food source. In 1610 there had been relatively little timber clearing and no overgrazing by sheep as in more recent times. In addition, from the tree-ring record it looks as if the two decades between 1610 and 1630 had above-average rainfall. As this was a Little Ice Age maximum, certain climatic effects might be expected, and this indeed does seem to have been a period of considerable snow and cold.

As the only villa in the province of New Mexico, Santa Fe was the seat of government and the hub of commercial and cultural activity. The Franciscan power center, however, remained at Santo Domingo Pueblo some twenty-five miles to the southwest. Considering the relations between the governors' party and the Franciscans throughout much of the seventeenth century, it was probably a wise move on the part of the order to keep somewhat apart from the secular authority.

Governors in New Mexico were paid by the viceregal authorities. Oñate received an annual stipend of a fraction more than 8,000 *pesos de oro común* (converting into approximately the same number of silver pesos). This was in the Crown's view overly generous, and subsequent governors, starting with Peralta, were given an annual salary of 2,000 pesos. This salary was never adjusted even though there was inflation during the course of the century. Travel allowances for the period 1609–83 averaged about 1,628 pesos per governor. The governors expected to profit from their office, however—both from trade and from the capture of nomadic Indians during the sporadic warfare that characterized the time and place. Occasionally, they stepped over the line and enslaved Pueblo Indian orphans, selling some of them in Mexico. In the early 1620s, Governor Juan de Eulate was forced by the viceroy to return a number of slaves sold in this way.

Trade was important in colonial New Spain, and there had been trading attempts in the Southwest as early as Coronado. In this area, however, large-scale profit-driven trade began with Oñate, who brought with him to New Mexico large amounts of trade goods, including tens of thousands of glass beads, hundreds of hawk bells, plus rings, earrings, needles, medals, mirrors, knives, whistles, rosaries, tassels for rosaries, children's musical toys, buttons, and other objects. Oñate's contract with the Crown called for 500 pesos in trade materials, and the adelantado fell short of this by more than 144 pesos. Nevertheless, the quantity of trade articles was impressive.

Subsequent governors and the more affluent settlers turned to trade, as did the missionaries. Salt was a commodity utilized by the Parral mines, and New Mexico had large numbers of saline areas, especially in the Tompiro district. As far as is known, the shipments of this commodity were private transactions, involving governors but also individual entrepreneurs. Goods produced by Pueblo Indians were also in demand. Governor Francisco Martínez de Baeza (1635–37) pressured the Indians to collect piñon nuts, to weave cotton *mantas,* and to re-trade hides obtained from the Plains Indians. According to one report, Baeza by 1636 had collected seven wagon loads of such goods to ship south to Mexico. Governor Francisco de la Mora y Ceballos (1632–35) sent knives to the missions with orders that they be traded for hides. Mora y Ceballos also was accused by Fray Esteban de Perea of shipping to Santa Bárbara "eight hundred cows, four hundred mares, and a quantity of 'ganado menor' [sheep and perhaps goats] to be sold in that market, and that as a result the citizens of New Mexico had nothing with which to sustain themselves." In spite of criticism, this shipping of stock animals to Nueva Vizcaya continued throughout the century.

Trade goods both to and from New Mexico were for the most part sent with the mission trains. It was possible to organize separate caravans outside this system, and this was sometimes done, but the dangers from hostile Indians, which became greater with each passing decade in the seventeenth century, made it desirable to have as large and well-protected a party as possible. This generally meant the missionary supply apparatus. The mission trains moved along the Camino Real, a road pioneered by Juan de Oñate in 1598, but following at least in part Indian trails that were already centuries old.

Until the year 1631, mission trains were supplied by the viceregal government in Mexico City, which purchased various supplies at auction. When enough materials were amassed, they were sent to New Mexico at somewhat irregular intervals, usually between two and four years. In 1631 the service was reformed. According to James Ivey,

> The viceregal treasury transferred the total budget due the New Mexico missions to the Franciscan procurador-general, who then arranged for the purchase of goods from merchants and suppliers, usually in Mexico City. The method enabled purchase of the goods in a timely manner and at minimum cost. In addition, the treasury would purchase and outfit the necessary wagons, including all spare parts; hire the drivers, guards and other necessary personnel, and cover the expenses of their upkeep during the journey to and from New Mexico. In return, the Franciscans agreed to pay for the upkeep of the wagons and personnel during the time they were in New Mexico and to keep up a full complement of mules for each wagon. After the return of the supply train to Mexico City, the government agreed to maintain the wagons and mules during the year and a half until the next dispatch, but it reserved the right to use them as needed during this period.

The basic contract vis-à-vis the supply train was amended in 1664 when an ex-governor, Juan Manso, received the contract. Although the actual caravan numbers and times may not have changed very much, the organization and function of the supply train were altered, the Franciscan procurator-general no longer having overall power. Manso held the contract until his death in 1673. The final seven years before the Pueblo Revolt saw a retreat to earlier conditions, with the new Franciscan procurator-general, Fray Francisco de Ayeta, purchasing mules, wagons, and supplies using Crown monies.

In any case, from 1631 until at least 1664 the operation of the train tended to be pretty much the same, trip after trip, as per the arrangements between the viceroy and the Franciscans. There were usually thirty-two wagons divided into two sections of sixteen, which in turn were divided into two subsections making four groups of eight wagons each. Each wagon had a single driver, or *chirrionero.* The wagons were not, however, as implied by this term (*chirrión* means "cart"), two- wheeled. Rather, they were four-wheeled vehicles somewhat like the famous Conestoga wagons used by the American pioneers in the eighteenth and nineteenth centuries. The wagons had iron-tired spoked wheels, and spare parts and appropriate tools were regularly carried. For example, axle trees were listed in the inventories and valued at two pesos each. In 1665 a chirrionero was paid nine pesos per month, not a great sum, but probably meals were supplied, and members of the supply train presumably slept in or near their wagons. A wagon was hauled by 8 mules, and each wagon had two teams, plus an additional 32 mules to replace dead or sick animals, for a total of 544 animals. Wagons were supposed to carry about two tons of supplies, though some were loaded well beyond that capacity. Each friar reporting to New Mexico for the first time was supposed to bring, courtesy of the order, 10 heifers, 10 sheep, and 48 chickens, the latter partly consumed on the road, with any survivors added to the mission supply of fowl. Depending on the number of friars with the mission train, there could be several hundred stock animals moving up the trail with the wagons. Although quantities of the goods were intended for the missions, certain luxury goods such as sugar, chocolate, majolica wares, knives, and other manufactured materials were used by the governors for their private use or for trade purposes.

The procurator-general seems to have normally gone with the supply train and until 1664 was its overall director. Along with the thirty-two drivers there were usually four Indians employed as scouts, drovers, and hunters, and sixteen Indian women as cooks. The standard wage for Pueblo Indians during this period was one-half real per day until López de Mendizábal raised it to one real per day in 1659 (see chapter 10). The drovers (*Indios sabaneros*) received 7 pesos (56 reales) a month each and probably were supplied with food. Each female cook had two wagons to care for and received the miserable pay of 20 reales per month plus food. On the other hand, according to a document of 1677, the "usual pay and salary" for soldiers seems to have been 15 pesos per month. The sergeant referred to in the same document received 17 pesos per month, while a commander of a company of fifty men was allotted 4 ducados per day (amounting to approximately 168 pesos per month).

According to the Manso contract of 1664, the Crown was accustomed to supplying fourteen soldiers and their commander as a military escort for the caravan. Thus, each of these trips would involve at least sixty-seven individuals plus the procurador-general and however many friars were along. Of course, when a new governor was coming to New Mexico, his personal retinue would add to the numbers. There were, after all, twenty-five governors (not counting the irregularly appointed Cristóbal de Oñate), all of whom had to make their way to New Mexico. Many of them, certainly, came and left with the mission train. The wagon trains generally departed Mexico City around midsummer, timed to arrive in the New Mexico settlements in late fall or early winter, when the rivers were low and before the severe winter weather. This schedule was not always kept, however. For example the 1659 train reached Santo Domingo in July and left for Mexico City in the autumn. As Governor López de Mendizábal traveled with this particular mission train, and a sizable number of missionaries also journeyed with it, this may have been an exceptional year.

There were most likely entrepreneurial individuals and groups, merchants primarily, who also attached themselves to the supply caravan, though we know very little about these people. That there were individual traders is indicated by the story of Bernardo Gruber from Sonora. This man, operating in the Salinas area, was arrested by the Inquisition on a flimsy charge in 1668 and held prisoner at Sandia until his escape and subsequent mysterious death on the Jornada del Muerto in 1670. The inventory of Gruber's belongings included 105 pairs of assorted wool socks, as well as 14 pair of understockings and 88 elk skins. The skins and the wool socks were likely produced or collected in New Mexico and intended for shipment down the Camino Real.

Mission trains averaged about 10 miles per day in actual travel time on the 1,600-mile trip. This has to be considered a remarkable speed considering the poor roads, heavily loaded wagons, and size and complexity of the wagon trains with their hundreds of livestock. There was a rest and refitting stop of two to three weeks at Zacatecas, 400 miles north of Mexico City. From Zacatecas the train wound its way through deserty and largely empty country for another 500 miles, finally reaching the oases around Santa Bárbara and, after its founding in 1631, Parral. This latter town soon became the commercial hub, especially for goods returning south on the Camino Real. Here another rest stop was made in preparation for the final seven hundred miles to Santa Fe. The train continued north, crossing the Río Conchos near the mission of San Francisco, and then passed near the site of the later Chihuahua City. Generally, the trains seem to have gone through the great Samalayuca sand dunes some 30 miles south of El Paso, then continued northward to Paso del Norte, roughly following the line of modern Mexican National Highway 45. There was an alternate route, however, for those who wished to avoid the dunes. That was to swing northeastward, reaching the Rio Grande 30 to 35 miles southeast of the Paso del Norte.

On arrival in the El Paso area, supplies for the southernmost mission, that of Guadalupe after its founding in 1659, were presumably off-loaded. The train then crossed the Rio Grande and the wagons continued on the east side of the river, traversing the Jornada del Muerto and crossing again at Senecú the first of the Piro missions. It is not entirely clear which side of the river the wagon trains used going northward from Senecú. There were missions on both sides of the Rio Grande, but at least in the nineteenth century, wagon trains preferred the west side because of better forage and availability of water. It is usually assumed that in the seventeenth century the main trail was east of the river, though a more western alternate trail may also have been used.

On reaching the mission headquarters at Santo Domingo, the wagon trains were split, one group going west to Acoma, Zuni, and Hopi, a second north to

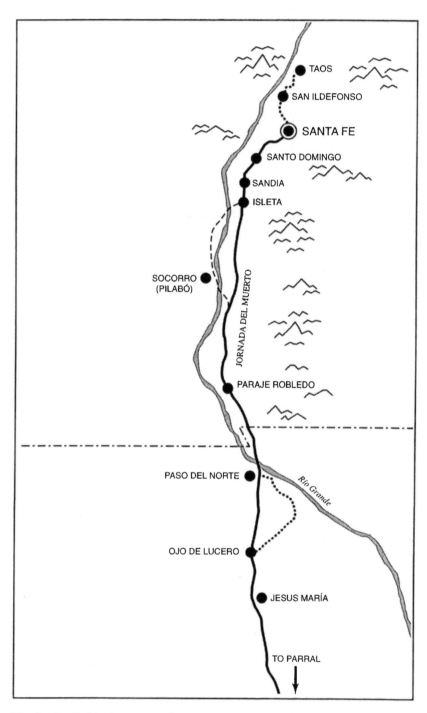

The Camino Real in the seventeenth century

Santa Fe and the upriver missions, and a third east to Galisteo and the Salinas country. The wagons then returned to Santo Domingo where the assembly of a train back to Mexico would take place over the next few months. The wagons were about as heavily laden on the return trip as they had been on the journey north. Trade goods, collected by the governors, and probably influential colonists as well as the missionaries, included antelope, deer, bison, and elk hides, piñon nuts, salt, candles, raw wool, wool woven in the form of mantas and socks, and some maize and wheat. Also shipped south were slaves, including children, captured from the Apaches and other nomadic groups. Large numbers of cattle and sheep were sent with the wagon train in spite of official misgivings about stripping the province of its stock animals. Much of this material was destined for the Santa Bárbara—Parral region, especially the livestock and the salt, which was needed in mining operations.

One of the obsessions of the Spaniards in the New Mexico colony during the sixteenth and seventeenth centuries was mining of precious metals. It was a major goal of the Coronado expedition and one of the basic reasons why the later entradas—those of Chamuscado, Espejo, Castaño, and Leyva-Humaña—were mounted in the first place. By the time of Chamuscado, silver in great amounts had been found stretching in a roughly north-south line from Zacatecas through parts of Durango into present-day Chihuahua. The upper Southwest looked to be the same sort of terrain, and the Spaniards were confident of finding metallic ores in profusion.

Members of the Chamuscado expedition (1581–82) reported mineral deposits in the general region of the Cerrillos range, the Galisteo country, and the Magdalena Mountains. Hernán Gallegos from the Chamuscado party stated that ore samples brought back to Mexico City assayed at twenty marcos (a marco equals about eight ounces) per quintal (a "hundredweight" of roughly one hundred pounds). The "Brief and True Account" says that there were eleven mining areas. Various ores were assayed; one sample was half silver, another was twenty marcos per quintal, and a third one, five marcos per quintal. A letter from the Council of the Indies to the king dated March 14, 1583, mentions an assay of thirty-six marcos per quintal.

Diego Pérez de Luxán with Antonio de Espejo (1582–83) reported mines in the Elephant Butte region, and in the Manzano Mountains. Luxán was on the trip to central Arizona, the region of the Verde Valley near modern Jerome, but he was disappointed in the ores there, finding copper rather than silver. In reality there is both, something that Espejo realized even if Luxán did not. Espejo himself described mines in the Tompiro portion of the Manzanos, the Jemez country, and the Galisteo region. Among the central Arizona mountains, Espejo commented on the mines, the same ones mentioned by Luxán, and "took from them with my own hands ores which, according to experts on the matter, are very rich and contain a great deal of silver."

Gaspar Castaño de Sosa, the lieutenant governor of Nuevo León who led an unauthorized expedition to New Mexico in 1590–91, was also looking for mines. According to his *Memoria,* the lieutenant governor, while at Pecos, showed residents some ore samples that he carried. The Indians told him of several pueblos where he could find similar ore. Eventually, Castaño discovered mineral-rich deposits in the Galisteo region, though he failed to extract any silver. All and all, however, the Castaño expedition found less promise of mineral riches than did earlier expeditions.

This does not seem to have fazed the Spaniards. A major reason why colonization of New Mexico was so desirable was the possibility of striking it rich with silver and perhaps gold. Oñate came prepared with equipment and assay know-how to check out and exploit any mineral deposits. Quite early in the occupation of the new colony, Oñate sent Captain Marcos Farfán de los Godos to investigate the Verde Valley region that had so excited Espejo. They found large veins of ore "so long and wide that one-half of the people in New Spain could stake out claims in this land."

The ores brought back by Farfán were assayed using the quicksilver method. The ore produced some twelve ounces of silver per quintal, though one of the assayers, Contador Alonso Sánchez, believed that the assaying methods were inefficient and that the ore contained a great deal more silver. Not too long after Farfán's return, Oñate wrote the viceroy asking for stamps to label the silver he planned to ship south. It is not clear what silver Oñate had in mind, but perhaps it was the mine near San Marcos where Vicente Zaldívar had built a crushing machine. It may have been this mine that produced a letter by Luis Núñez Pérez in November 1600, talking of a "great [silver] mining discovery."

Unfortunately, Oñate's discovery of silver proved to be a chimera. In a report by the viceroy to King Philip III, dated March 31, 1605, Viceroy Montesclaros commented that ore samples sent by the adelantado had produced copper but no silver. Still, belief in the mineral richness of New Mexico continued. Writing in the 1620s, Fray Gerónimo de Zárate Salmerón claimed that there were mines of all sorts in New Mexico: "silver, copper, lead, magnet stone, coperas [coperas, a green crystalline compound used in dyeing and ink making], alum, sulfur, and turquoise." These mines are not utilized because, as Zárate Salmerón comments sourly, "The Spaniards who are there laugh at all this; as long as they have a good supply of tobacco to smoke, they are very contented, and they do not want any more riches, for it seems as if they had made the vow of poverty, which is a great deal for being Spaniards, who because of greediness for silver and gold will enter Hell itself to obtain them."

Not only Zárate Salmerón but also Alonso de Benavides believed strongly in the mineral riches of New Mexico. In his *Memorial of 1630*, Father Benavides stressed the richness in gold and silver of the province, particularly in the Socorro area and the mountains extending along the Piro country. Especially rich was the hill of Socorro: "Nowhere in the Indies can silver be more easily extracted than from this hill. It will be more profitable to extract one silver mark here than many from other mines, because, while at these mines of Socorro everything is right at hand, at the others all the materials, supplies and even the water have to be hauled a very great distance, thus necessitating expenditures which consume all the yield in silver." This great wealth was going unexploited because there was no one who understood or knew how to properly develop and work the mines. According to Benavides, he had personally sent samples to "some miners in New Spain" who after assaying them were preparing to enter New Mexico in order to develop the mines. The exact location of Benavides's "hill of Socorro" is not known today.

As late as 1638 the commissary-general of the Franciscans in Mexico City, Juan de Prada, mentioned that "mines of gold and silver are not lacking [in New Mexico]". However, the poverty and unfitness of both Indians and Spaniards prevented any mines from actually being worked. Indeed, this seems to have been the case throughout the seventeenth century for there is no evidence that *any* silver or gold came out of New Mexico mines.

It might be well to consider the mining situation in the region south of New Mexico, where enormously rich silver strikes had been made in the latter part of the sixteenth century. The Santa Bárbara area in what is now south-central Chihuahua was settled originally because of the mining potential. This general region, like major mining districts farther south, was on the eastern flanks of the Sierra Madre. The first settlement at Santa Bárbara was actually not the center of great mining activity, but for strategic reasons the town became an important anchor to the northern part of New Spain (and of course the jumping-off point for New Mexico). Around the villa of Santa Bárbara and the Franciscan mission station at San Bartolomé, some thirty-five miles to the east, there developed considerable farming and ranching activity. Mining was only moderately important until 1631, when a major silver strike occurred on the Río San Gregorio about twenty miles north of Santa Bárbara, the site of modern Parral. In 1634 a second strike developed about three miles northwest of Parral at the modern Villa Escobeda. In subsequent years further strikes were made in the general region.

The mines of the region were associated with volcanic activity in Cenozoic times. The silver ore is located in fissure veins that often run for many miles. The ore itself is either argentite (silver sulfide) or is carried as argentiferous galena in galena (lead sulfide). Argentite generally has a much higher silver content and was worked in the seventeenth century by what is called the "patio amalgamation" process. In this process the ore was crushed to a fine powder using a water- or mule-powered stamp mill. Then the finely ground ore was mixed with water and with three reagents: salt, a slurry of mercury, and magistral (chalcopyrite). Occasionally, other materials, lime, and/or iron filings were added in. The mixing was done in a rock-floored outside patio and was stirred usually by driving mules through the muddy concoction. The ore was then put in heaps and allowed to stand for several weeks, or in cold weather even several months. During this period the silver amalgamated with the mercury. The mixture was then washed in tanks or troughs, and the slime was carried away, leaving the heavier amalgam. The amalgam was then pressed into bars and heated, freeing the mercury and leaving metallic silver or a silver-gold alloy.

If the ore to be reduced was galena or if the mercury, which had to be obtained from Spain, was insufficient, another process was used: that of smelting by lead fusion and subsequent cupellation. This was an ancient technique, going back to the days of early metallurgy in the Old World. In this process, the ore, after being crushed into gravel size, was smelted in a blast furnace with lead to separate the silver and gold from the lighter slag and combine them with lead to form an alloy. This alloy was then taken to a cupellation furnace lined with a porous bone ash. At a high temperature the lead in the alloy oxidized and was absorbed by the lining of ash. The more-or-less pure silver and gold were then left at the bottom of the furnace. Forced air was supplied by bellows of goat skin or sheepskin. Bellows, probably similar to these, were part of Oñate's equipment, listed in the Salazar inspection of 1597–98.

Why then did the Spaniards not find silver and gold in the new province? In fact, there is a considerable distribution of argentite in the area. It is found in various places in western New Mexico and in the Río Verde region of central Arizona—though not in the Hopi region, the only part of Arizona with a Spanish presence throughout most of the seventeenth century. Mines in the Río Verde were simply too far from the power center on the Rio Grande to be seriously exploited. However, much nearer Spanish settlements, there were and are argentite outcroppings in the Jemez Mountains, in the Sangre de Cristos, the Magdalena Mountains, the Sandia-Manzano region and in the Cerrillos Hills. Galena also has a wide distribution, as does gold. In the nineteenth century there was a great deal of mining, though there never was the frenetic activity that characterized the California gold rush or the great silver strikes in Nevada.

In the seventeenth century, certain components necessary to a successful mining operation were absent. It is true that chalcopyrite was plentiful, as was salt (the latter material in fact being shipped to the Santa Bárbara–Parral region to use in mining). Mercury, however, is rare or absent in New Mexico. This metal—which is reduced from its sulfide, cinnabar—was shipped to Mexico primarily from Spain. Even in the rich Parral mines there were sometimes shortages of mercury, and New Mexico was even more remote. Mercury was so important that a rumored cinnabar mine in Hopi country created a considerable stir when de Vargas reached that area in 1692. An additional problem, perhaps even more serious than the lack of mercury, was that mining operations were greedy users of water. In New Mexico, as Benavides pointed out, water was generally not immediately at hand.

The major factor in the lack of mining development, however, was the serious undercapitalization of New Mexico throughout the seventeenth century. Income was always very low, and the province had to be massively subsidized by the crown. In fact, France Scholes has estimated that in the period 1596–1683, expenditures for the province exceeded receipts by a greater than ninety to one ratio. There was a low population level and a lack of skilled and motivated workers. In an arid environment with prohibitively high shipping costs for essential raw materials such as mercury, mining in seventeenth-century New Mexico was simply not cost-effective.

The Spanish population in seventeenth-century New Mexico was primarily rural. As said earlier, only one "villa" or town existed—Santa Fe, the capital of the province—and it had a small and partly seasonal population. Both the missionaries and private individuals had estancias, which in the case of the lay population were basically licenses from one or another of the governors for the use of particular tracts of land. These licenses technically became land grants only when registered with the *Audiencia,* either in Mexico City or Guadalajara. This formalization may have occurred occasionally, but as yet no such grants have been found in the archives. Governor Baeza in 1639 spoke of ten to twelve estancias, but during the course of the seventeenth century, their number slowly increased. The central portion of the Rio Grande Basin seems to have had the thickest population. In 1680, for example, on the east side of the Rio Grande, some seventeen estancias extended southward, in one eight-mile stretch, from the Tiwa town of Alameda. There were a large number of mission estancias, sixty or more by the 1660s, although the legal basis of them is unclear. Nor is the legal distinction clear between the mission estancias and Pueblo Indian communally held lands. In any case, the mission estancias produced a great deal, especially stock animals by the thousands. From the reports of the de Vargas expedition during the reconquest of the 1690s, it would seem that certain other areas were relatively heavily populated. The Galisteo Basin had a number of estancias, and there were a dozen or so families in the Santa Cruz region south of the Rio Grande–Chama junction.

The owners of estancias, and to some degree the encomenderos, lived on scattered estates, many of them near one or the other pueblo. In addition, encomenderos sometimes lived within their encomiendas in spite of the strong Spanish laws against this practice. It certainly led to abuses. In one notorious case, the encomendero of Pojoaque, Antonio de Salas, built a ranch house, grazed his stock on Pueblo lands, and drafted Indian labor for a variety of personal services—all forbidden by Spanish law. Governor López de Mendizábal ordered Salas to raze the house and leave the Pueblo land. In the López residencia, Salas sued for damages, claiming that under the special conditions in New Mexico, with constant danger from nomadic Indian raids, the governors had from the first allowed encomenderos to live on their encomiendas. A stepdaughter of Salas, Petronilla, with eight or ten children, was still living near Pojoaque at the time of the Pueblo Revolt, and all were killed in the opening days of the uprising. Antonio de Salas himself escaped south to El Paso, where he died in 1681.

Unfortunately, there has been relatively little archaeology of the outlying seventeenth-century Hispanic settlements in New Mexico. A number of sites have been located, and a few have had a certain amount of excavation. A settlement (LA 34) in the Cochiti area, the largest site known to date, is a building of some twenty rooms with a corral of some 2,100 ft². An estancia (LA 20,000, the Sánchez site), some fifteen miles south of Santa Fe, on Cienega Creek, a tributary of the Santa Fe River, has been excavated in part by students from Colorado College. Here the building is along the south-facing slopes of a ridge, overlooking the small stream. It has ten to fifteen rooms, a corral, a Spanish *horno* (oven), and possibly a torreón (defensive tower) at one side of the building. A certain amount of Mexican majolica and Spanish olive jars were found, as well as the ubiquitous Pueblo pottery. Part of the Indian pottery likely came from the pueblo of La Cienega, which is generally considered to have been nearby but has never been located. The building period at LA 20,000 dates from at least the 1630s and perhaps is earlier. Although the Francisco de Anaya Almazán family held encomiendas in the general area, there is no evidence that this group actually owned or settled the estancia. It has been suggested that it was owned by members of the influential Baca family, a group that was also important in the political life of Santa Fe (see chapter 7). Several other sites can be found in the general Cienega region, including sites LA 16, LA 16,768, and LA 16,773.

East of Tomé in the Río Abajo is another large site, that of Comanche Spring (LA 14,904). This ruin was claimed by its excavator to be early seventeenth century. It contains two complexes of rooms, one on either side of Comanche Creek at a point just a few miles from where the stream devolves from the Manzano Mountains. Archaeologists today do not consider the site securely dated, though more recent, limited archaeological work does suggest that a late-seventeenth-century date is quite feasible.

Dwellings in seventeenth-century New Mexico consisted of square or rectangular rooms made either of stone and mud mortar or of adobes with floors of clay. There was some use of logs, but this type of construction was normally limited to outbuildings. In any case, much of the settlement area was probably somewhat deficient in trees of the size needed for log cabins. Occasionally there would be jacal-type structures but, again, usually in pens or corrals.

The houses were basically home for extended families, and they tended to grow by adding contiguous rooms as time went on and the family grew larger. Sometimes round defensive towers of stone or adobe were added to the cluster of rooms. In the Cochiti area, at Las Majadas site (LA 591), there was a corral as well as outbuildings that may have been used by servants. At Las Majadas, a series of early- to middle-seventeenth-century glazes were found, including pottery made at Pecos, and several sherds of a Hopi Sikyatki Polychrome vessel, probably from a soup plate. A considerable amount of Pueblo culinary wares were found, and sherds of seventeenth-century Mexican majolica. Though privies have been identified in conventos, none have been found in any of the seventeenth-century homesteads. In modern rural northern Mexico, the corral is often the designated latrine area, and perhaps this was the case here. Chamber pots, constructed of pottery or even copper or silver, were likely also used, at least by the upper classes.

One curious aspect of New Mexico demography was the reluctance in both the seventeenth and the eighteenth centuries for colonists to cluster in defensible towns. Governors and regional alcaldes tried again and again to promote such settlements but met constant resistance from the settlers. It is not entirely clear why this was the case, but perhaps the colonists felt that they could exploit the local terrain better in dispersed settlements. This preference for isolated homesteads added to the difficulties of the Spaniards in trying to establish post–Pueblo Revolt settlements along the Rio Grande between Socorro and El Paso, an area highly vulnerable to raiding Indians. In seventeenth-century New Mexico, with its very scanty population spread thinly over the countryside, there was often no realistic alternative to isolated settlements. Of course, in the seventeenth century the estancieros and encomenderos had houses in Santa Fe and lived there intermittently.

Interior walls were whitewashed with a mixture of pulverized gypsum, wheat flour, and water. Not all rooms were heated, but some were fitted with a corner fireplace resting on a hearth six to eight inches high. If a second fireplace was needed, it was placed kitty-corner to the first. The fireplaces were fueled by wood, or occasionally charcoal, and cooking was done with a three-stone arrangement, the stones holding pottery vessels or comales. Doors were fitted with a round wooden peg placed in sockets in the lintel and sill to allow the door to swing back and forth. Iron in the New Mexico colony was much valued and quite scarce, so, understandably, hinges, locks, or latches of that metal were rare. Windows were usually small and might be covered with a cotton cloth or with selenite. Furniture in the rooms was quite scanty. There might be a mealing bin, placed in one of the corners. Crude handmade benches and tables probably made up the balance of furniture. Storage space was created by shelving. This usually took the form of a rough plank, set high above the floor and extending from wall to wall.

In semiarid New Mexico, water was always a consideration. In many cases, building was along or near living streams or springs. The settlement at Comanche Springs had both: a perennial stream, Comanche Creek, and flowing springs that devolved on a headland just south of the southernmost living area. Sometimes it was necessary to utilize temporary pools of water in marshy areas or ones formed by depressions in sandstone outcroppings. We have no evidence for wells in the seventeenth century, although an occasional one might have been dug in the valley bottoms. In any case, water was brought to the houses in Pueblo-made pottery vessels or *tinajas,* or in wooden buckets. Washing of clothing mostly took place in irrigation ditches or along the streams. Soap was somewhat scarce in the seventeenth century, though a certain amount was brought up in the mission trains from the early days of settlement of New Mexico. In the initial Oñate expedition, Captain Alonso de Quesada listed one hundred bars of soap, along with towels and sheets. At some point a local soap industry may have developed, but virtually nothing is known about it. *Yucca glauca,* soapweed yucca, was also used.

Pottery used by the colonists from Oñate's time to the Pueblo Revolt was overwhelmingly produced by Pueblo Indians, though it was often fashioned in non-indigenous forms such as plates, candlesticks, footed cups, goblets, and others. One of the Spanish majolica wares, called Pueblo Polychrome, had designs copied from Spanish lace, originally appearing on women's dresses. These designs seem to have fascinated the Pueblo potters, for they reproduced the semicircular lace patterns in their own pottery. Handled cups are prehistoric in the Southwest, but in the seventeenth century, under Spanish influence, these greatly increased in number.

Food for the Spanish colonists included not only the native maize, beans, and squash but such introduced plants as wheat, barley, plums, peaches, grapes, onions, radishes, lettuce, cabbage, carrots, peas and chickpeas, and other vegetables as well as watermelons and cantaloupes. Condiments included garlic, cumin, coriander, and chile. The turkey continued to be used, and new domesticated animals included sheep, goats, cattle, pigs, and chickens. Dogs were surely used in herding activities as well as to protect the homes, and cats most likely were brought from Mexico to help control the rodent population. There is, however, curiously little information on these animals (see chapter 12 for further discussion).

There was an explosive spread of sheep in New Mexico from herds introduced during the Oñate period, and by the time of the Pueblo Revolt there were certainly tens of thousands of these animals. Sheep are rapid breeders, reaching puberty in five to seven months. A ewe has a gestation period of less than five months, and from birth to the next estrus is only around thirty-five days—thus she can have two pregnancies per year over a productive life span of six to eight years. It seems to be the case that the majority of flocks were owned by the missionaries, but certainly sheep, like other herd animals, were available to the settlers. The popular churro sheep had an adult weight from sixty-five to eighty pounds and produced somewhere between one and two pounds of rough but usable wool per year. Clothing for the less-affluent settler was of wool, and the Spaniards introduced the indigo plant in order to dye the local wool a deep blue. There may also have been some use of cotton, traded from the Pueblo Indians. Aside from cloth, from Oñate's time there was an increasing use of tanned skins of deer and antelope. These were easily available, and skin clothing was warm in the winter. Local tanning skills were encouraged by the fact that these skins, and the clothing made from them, were in great demand farther south in Nueva Vizcaya. An October 1641 inventory of merchandise following the death of a small store owner in Parral brings to light a chamois jacket and two small blankets from New Mexico. The jacket could have been made from sheep or goat hide, or it might have been from a deerskin. The blankets were probably wool. They were handpainted with pictures of the Virgin Mary and of St. Nicholas and perhaps originated in the mission workshops. Although these were the only goods specifically indicated from New Mexico, it seems likely that a number of the other items from that inventory and a second one dated December of that year (from a merchant living about twelve miles from Parral) were from the province. For example, the inventory lists included salt and about two and a half bushels of piñon seeds (nuts). Both items were plentiful in the province and important in the New Mexico "balance of trade," with piñon nuts considered a special delicacy in Mexico. The two and a half bushels mentioned in the inventory would retail for perhaps twenty-five pesos.

The field plots used by the colonists were plowed with a simple wooden plow, aptly described by R. F. Dickey:

> Local farmers constructed a much simplified version of the old European plow, and this type was adopted by both Spaniards and Indians, changing little from the time of the first colony until twenty years after American occupation.
>
> The body of the plow consisted of a short tree trunk with a large limb left attached to serve as a handle, cottonwood being preferred for its toughness. The farmer sharpened the lower end of the trunk and bolted a piece of iron on it as a point. Just in front of the handle a hole was cut in the body of the plow, and equipped with a strong peg on which was hinged the long straight tongue or beam of the plow. The pitch was adjusted by a short upright post set in the body and running through a hole in the beam. By placing pegs in this post, the farmer changed the angle between the beam and the plow body for deep or shallow furrows.

Some forty years ago, I observed a similar plow, drawn by oxen, being used by the Southern Tepehuan, an Indian group living today in southern Durango and northern Jalisco. In regard to ploughs, as with other items of material culture, there was a serious lack of iron in New Mexico. The viceroyalty had a monopoly on iron imported into New Mexico, and as the 1639 report of the Santa Fe cabildo indicates, there was a shortage of iron not only for ploughing but also for horseshoes. According to the cabildo report, no iron had been shipped into New Mexico (at least for the colonists' use) for eleven years.

Although the wagons moving along the Camino Real were four-wheeled, the locally used *carreta* was a two-wheeled, oxen-drawn cart whose wheels were made of sections of cottonwoods with holes pierced in the center to attach to a crude axle. Probably not every homestead had its own cart, for in rough country its use was rather restricted.

Houses of the governors and other "urban" elite in New Mexico were considerably better furnished than those of the ordinary settler. Some furniture was transported over the Camino Real. It was, however, very expensive; for example, a used writing desk might be worth forty to eighty pesos. Bed, bedspreads, pillows, and bolsters were brought over the trail as early as the time of Oñate, as were camp beds, chairs, and tables. Other luxury goods utilized by the wealthier colonists included silver cutlery, salt shakers, pitchers and pots, and several kinds of the popular decorated majolica pottery. Indeed, there was not only majolica but actual Chinese porcelain, obtained by the Manila galleons in their trans-Pacific trade. Some of these Chinese porcelain vessels were already heirlooms when brought to New Mexico, dating from the mid-sixteenth century. The porcelain was incredibly expensive and was said to be worth its weight in silver—and even that may be undervaluating this delicate exotic ware.

Some of the elaborate porcelain cups were likely used to sip chocolate, a very popular drink in Spain and its possessions, including New Mexico. Chocolate was cultivated and much valued by the Aztecs, and the incoming Spaniards quickly picked up the habit of imbibing chocolate drinks. López de Mendizábal was one of the governors who invested in chocolate when he took up the governorship in 1659. In 1541 chocolate in the Parral area could be purchased, at least in large quantities, for one peso per libra, and presumably retailed for something more than that. Parenthetically, the Spanish libra was roughly the same weight as the English pound. Since New Mexico was several hundred arduous miles farther away from the sources of chocolate, it seems very likely that the value in this far northern outpost was considerably greater.

From the Oñate lists we get some idea of the wealth and variety of clothing worn by the upper classes. It included wool outer clothing, silk and wool stockings, ribbons, damask, taffeta cloth in various colors, velvet, lace, and fine cotton, shoes of cordovan leather, and linen shirts, trousers, and underclothing. The upper-class housewife had needles, thimbles, scissors, buttons, and both cotton and silk thread in all colors. A variety of fashionable hats, some with feathers and braid, handkerchiefs, and house slippers were also carried north to New Mexico. There was a great variety of jewelry. Finely ground flour was probably used as a face powder in the seventeenth century, as it certainly was in the eighteenth and nineteenth. From the evidence given by Doña Teresa, wife of Governor López, we see that at least some upper-class people donned clean clothing, and washed their hair every few days and changed their bed linen every two weeks or so. Both sexes tended to wear their hair long, which meant that—given the lack of general washing facilities and no effective insecticides—the problem of head lice transcended sex, age, and even, to some degree, status. Women in the estancias held delousing parties, an activity that they were reluctant to allow men to watch. However, husbands and wives deloused each other, and parents their children. Cosmetics were in considerable demand by all classes, including the flour mentioned above and a rouge made of the alegría plant (*Amaranthus paniculatus*).

We know very little about certain aspects of social life among the various rural dwellers in New Mexico. There was widespread illiteracy, and in any case, books were not available to the general population, and education was almost totally a matter of the family. Still there were amusements, fiestas, saints' days, and birthdays. The governing groups, certainly from the 1630s and 1640s on, set a very low standard of sexual morality, and this attitude seems to have permeated the colony as a whole, even to some degree affecting the missionaries. Playing cards and gambling were well known to the adult lay population. Cards were probably brought to New Mexico as early as Oñate's time. Youngsters also had their childhood games, as similar young people did in Mexico and Spain. However, boys beyond infancy normally would be expected to work at least part of the time with their fathers, brothers, and other male family members. Girls tended to be married rather young and before marriage would have had household chores, including care of their younger siblings. Life, generally, was harsh, and life expectancy past the first flush of youth was not very great.

The practice of medicine in seventeenth-century New Mexico was unsophisticated by the standards set by European medical theory and practice. The seventeenth century saw an upswing in European medicine. There were especially dramatic advances in anatomy, building on the sixteenth-century studies of men like Andreas Vesalius and Hieronymus Fabricius, the latter the mentor of William Harvey, who first described the circulation of the blood. By the mid to late seventeenth century, anatomists and physiologists knew a great deal about the blood, the workings of the nervous, lymphatic, and reproductive systems of the human body, and the function of major organs such as the heart, lungs, liver, and brain. Actual medical practice was somewhat less advanced, and a system of diagnosis and treatment popularized by Galen in the second century A.D. was still followed. Galen considered the body to be governed by four "humors"— blood, lymph, yellow bile, and black bile—each with its own characteristics. Blood, for example, was a hot and moist humor, lymph cold and moist, yellow bile hot and dry, and black bile cold and dry. Diseases were caused by an excess or a deficiency in these fundamental humors.

Although the idea of humors was considerably refined by the seventeenth century, it was still basic to medical practice. Medicines were given to change the humors. A "phlogistic" condition, a kind of inflammation, was considered to be a major cause of illness, and bloodletting was practiced as a sort of overall "antiphlogistic" measure. The purpose of medicines generally was to act as antidotes to the poisons produced by disease. A dream of the times was a universal cure or panacea, a medication that could be used for any disease condition. This, of course, was never found, but drugs that affected specific conditions gradually spread. The seventeenth century saw the first systematic use of metals such as mercury and antimony (the latter often in the form of tartar emetic) in the treatment of various diseases, including syphilis. New drugs from the Americas included ipecac, cinchona (still not properly used for malaria), and guaiacum, the resin from a New World tropical tree, used to treat rheumatic ailments. A number of Old World plant medicines were common in seventeenth-century Europe; for example, digitalis from the figwort family was used as a heart stimulant, and opium from the opium poppy, belladonna, and valerian, all as sedatives.

This, however, was medical development in urban European centers. Spain was actually somewhat backward in medical knowledge and practice. Central Mexico was even more removed, though it should be pointed out that medicine in the newly founded University of Mexico was taught as early as 1553, and a Chair in medicine created in 1575. Subsequently, a *protomedicato,* a regulatory council, was formed in Mexico. Among its other functions it licensed the practice of medicine.

Still, the rude frontier of New Mexico was very far removed from the ideas of European medical practice. A few Franciscans were skilled in medicine and surgery, but for the most part the friars practiced only rough-and-ready medicine. However, individual settlers were expected to know something of the healing arts. Just how many medical books were available in the province is uncertain, but a Spanish-language book of surgery was listed for the López de Mendizábal library.

Under the circumstances, medicine was mainly of the folk variety. By the seventeenth century, an active herbal medicine, a mixture of European and Native American traditions, had developed. The Aztecs of central Mexico had a rather sophisticated system of curing, in some ways superior to European medicine of the time. The Aztecs, as might be expected, were especially skilled in treating injuries incurred in military operations, stopping hemorrhages, setting bones, and applying herbal concoctions to wounds. They also had practical, reasonably efficient quarantine methods to handle infectious disease. The Aztec practice of piping potable water from springs in the Chapultepec area to fountains in various parts of their capital, Tenochtitlan, certainly checked the spread of disease. These aqueducts were reminiscent of ancient Rome and superior to the water supplies of most, perhaps all, contemporary European cities. But the great triumph of the Aztecs was in the experimental approach to herbal curing, the botanical garden in Tenochtitlan being mainly for experimentation and introduction of new medicinal plants. A post-Conquest herbal, the Badianus manuscript written in Latin about 1552, described some of the Aztec medical usage of plants.

The writings of Bernardo de Vargas Machuca discuss the kind of folk medicine that must have been current in the Spanish New World. Though Vargas Machuca was talking about soldiers, and some of his experiences were in South America, many of his medical practices were surely common among the civilian population of New Spain. He specifically gives credit to the Native Americans for certain of his remedies; others were probably European in origin or part of Spanish American folk medicine. As discussed below, at least one copy of the part of Vargas Machuca's book that contains medical information had reached New Mexico by the mid-seventeenth century. His medical practice was basically algorithmic—that is, a set of procedures were set down and, if followed faithfully, could be expected to produce a given result. This writer had a variety of remedies for illness and wounds including the use of plants, minerals, foods, and animal parts for given ailments. Certain of Vargas Machuca's treatments would not be overly appealing today. For disorders of the spleen, the patient mixed his/her own urine with honey and urine-soaked soap and drank this concoction for nine mornings before breakfast. For those with stomach problems, fresh horse manure dissolved in wine, *chicha* (maize beer), or soup—or in water if these were lacking—was strained and given to the patient three mornings before breakfast. For catarrah, the patient was given sulfur mixed with water or, somewhat more appetizing, a small bowl of boiling water with camomile and bee honey. Tertian or quartian fevers were treated with ground snake skin mixed with soup or wine, to be taken three times. Chest colds could be alleviated by smearing the chest with tallow and drinking sulfur during the night. Pelvic pain was cured by taking roasted ground-up *grillos* (this normally means "crickets," though the author may possibly be referring to sorrel shoots) taken with wine or chicha. The writer recommended a tisane of blackberry shoots made into a syrup with honey and urine as an excellent cure for gum boils. Other ingredients used by Vargas Machuca included tobacco, mustard seed (ground and moistened for poultices), sugar, vinegar, maize gruel, gunpowder, white lead, mercury, powdered crab shell, oil of egg(?) (*aceite de huevo*), rosemary, mint, various powdered barks, and lime juice, most of which would be available in New Mexico. Vargas Machuca recommended bleeding and for all his remedies advised holy incantations to increase the efficacy of the cure.

Medicines and medical equipment of various kinds were brought to New Mexico with Oñate and his men. Juan del Caso Baraona seems to have been especially well equipped with "five pounds of medications by recognized masters," as well as two cases of instruments for bloodletting, a syringe and four cupping glasses, plus other surgical instruments. Medicines with the expedition included balsam, sulfur, alum, verdigris (copper treated with vinegar), sarsaparilla, several ointments (including those of lead, mercury, basilicon [resin], and the herbal mixture called "diachylon"), mastic (an astringent resin), molasses, rose honey, rose vinegar, rose extract, rose, myrtle and quince oils, various laxatives and purgatives, turpentine, and an arsenic-based compound called "orpiment." Wine was carried in casks, and oil in large flasks; both had medical but other uses as well. These were typical medications and were replenished by the mission trains throughout the century.

Some of the herbal practices of central Mexico were introduced into New Mexico, and there was also a native tradition practiced by the Pueblo Indians (and perhaps to some degree by the surrounding nomadic groups). Various of these remedies continue today, among both the Pueblos and the Hispanic population of New Mexico. Unfortunately, we have relatively little seventeenth-century documentary evidence for specific medicines. There is an early (1631) report on medicinal uses of the psychoactive cactus root peyote. At that time, both settlers and Pueblo Indians knew of it, which raises the possibility that peyote was pre-Hispanic in the Pueblo world—though it could equally well have been introduced by the early settlers.

In any case, the folk medicine that developed in the seventeenth century was a mixture of Spanish, Mexican, Indian, and Pueblo. From the Spaniards, New Mexican settlers derived their habit of bleeding. This particular treatment was largely counterproductive since it is useful only for victims of hemochromatosis, a rather rare, genetically determined disease that causes an overload of iron in the blood. The treatment for hemochromatosis is to draw blood on a regular basis. For sick people who did not have the disease, blood loss further weakened the body. Strangely enough, bloodletting was a mainstay of European medicine into the nineteenth century. (See "Sources and Commentary" for chapter 9 for further information on bleeding).

There might have been an occasional barber-surgeon in New Mexico during the seventeenth century although, as said above, there seems to be no evidence for them. The economy of the colony was on such a low level that probably such specialists would not have been tempted to make the long journey north. On the other hand, there was an infirmary at the Hermita of San Miguel in the Analco district of Santa Fe, at least by Governor Rosas's time. In fact, it seems extremely likely that all the missions had infirmaries, and medicines of various kinds were part of the supply train traffic into New Mexico.

Education in colonial New Mexico was generally at a very low level. Most of the settlers probably could neither read nor write. This would not have been true of the elite class (the governor and his party, the missionaries, and at least some of the encomenderos and estancieros), but the extant library lists from the seventeenth and early eighteenth centuries do suggest that such reading was somewhat limited. There was a great deal of writing, however, including governmental and ecclesiastic directives, and letters within the province and between New Mexico and Mexico. In the Salazar inspection, Oñate declared some forty-one reams of paper, each of twenty quires, plus an additional thirteen quires. A quire normally has twenty-five sheets, so the governor was carrying over twenty thousand sheets. Moreover, books in the hands of lay individuals also date from the Oñate period. In the Salazar inspection of late 1597, Captain Alonso de Quesada declared that he was bringing to New Mexico "Seven books, religious and non-religious."

As might be expected, books in New Mexico were largely devotional in character; breviaries, missals, manuals, catechisms, *doctrinas,* books of music, and hagiography. There were virtually no books that might be considered "scientific," but there were several histories, including a history of Charles V. The library of López de Mendizábal and his wife Teresa de Aguilera y Roche did contain some popular writings, including Cervantes's *Don Quixote* and a collection of plays published in seventeenth-century Spain. There was also Ludovico Ariosto's *Orlando Furioso,* presumably an Italian-language edition, brought by Teresa, whose childhood had been spent in Italy. López also had the Spanish-language book on surgery, mentioned above, as well as books in Latin and a Latin-Spanish dictionary. His successor, Governor Peñalosa, had the *Milicia Yndiana,* the first part of Vargas Machuca's large work *Milicia y descripción de las Indias,* Gaspar de Villagrá's *Historia de la Nueva México,* and parts of Fray Juan Torquemada's *Monarquía Indiana.* One of Peñalosa's books, a history of the English civil wars, was published in Madrid in 1658, only three years before Peñalosa took office. In the Rosas period, Fray Juan de Vidania made various references to classical works, including Aristotle's *Topics,* Caesar's *Gallic Wars,* Ovid's *Metamorphoses,* and works by Gregory, Augustine, and Aquinas, among others. These works do not appear on any of the known lists, but Vidania may conceivably have had all or some of these books available in New Mexico.

To sum up, the Spanish settlers of seventeenth-century New Mexico had to give up the sophisticated urban life that they might have found in Europe or even in central Mexico. There were no schools, no regular medical facilities, no coinage—in fact, very few of the uses of civilized life. The colonists lived close to the earth, working the estancias for subsistence agriculture and depending on neighboring Pueblos for basic technological needs such as pottery. The extremely small elite group (mainly the governors and their entourages) lived somewhat better. They at least had books to read, their diets were more varied, and some of their personal belongings such as clothing, bedding, and dinner services might have been considered acceptable in high-class circles in Mexico or even in Spain. Such people had servants, although if the problems of the López de Mendizábal family were any guide, the level of service was quite low. It was mainly that of Indian or African slaves or Pueblo Indians serving off minor sentences for misbehavior. The missionaries also lived in reasonably comfortable conventual quarters, eating from majolica ware (*losa de Puebla*), and they, too, had servants, in this case Pueblo Indians. However, all in all, New Mexico was a remote area that developed its own inbred, self-reliant, but woefully undereducated and unsophisticated population. It is no wonder that documents of the time are much concerned with sexual immorality, especially among the elite group. There was simply not enough to do.

CHAPTER TEN

Bernardo López de Mendizábal

By the mid-seventeenth century the Spaniards seemed to be well entrenched in New Mexico. It is true that their numbers were small, and the military force necessary to hold the large Pueblo Indian populations inadequate. However, they depended primarily on the moral power of the missionaries to control the Pueblos, using the military arm in a struggle with the nomadic groups on both the eastern and western borders of the province. More and more the Spaniards were dependent on Pueblo men for military service, acting as auxiliaries in this endless warfare. The Native Americans in this way gradually became acquainted with the uses of war, Spanish style. This does not mean that the auxiliaries were mounted. They generally served as a kind of infantry support force, using native weapons; nevertheless, they slowly became familiar with both horsemanship and with firearms. The Pueblos also learned the rudiments of Spanish tactical and strategic operations.

As Ramón Gutiérrez has pointed out, the Franciscans usurped the functions of Pueblo rain-priests, hunt chiefs, and the medicine societies. In other words, they offered the Pueblo Indians an alternative way of gaining the same supernatural blessings. The icon of the cross, so important to the missionaries, was acceptable because the Pueblos identified it as a star symbol. The liturgical practices of the missionaries, especially those of the Christmas season, fit the ceremonial round of the Indians. Even the lifelong vow of chastity made by each Franciscan would, in Indian eyes, intensify the holiness and spirit power of these strange new holy men.

As pointed out in chapter 8, however, the Franciscans were well aware that their most potent weapon was the indoctrination of children. This "divide and conquer" technique had worked very well a century before in the conquest of Mexico. It became a part of the Franciscan strategy for converting the Pueblos from the very beginning of missionization. As I said in *Rio del Norte*: "For a Pueblo Indian born after about 1630—in some cases after 1610—the mission effort was pervasive. The child attended church services, learned the rites and rituals of Christianity, was taught Spanish, and had constantly drummed into his or her head that the Pueblo fertility and weather-control ceremonies were wicked and depraved."

Still and all, native ceremonies, especially the kachina ceremonies, continued to be practiced. The evidence suggests that repression was sporadic and not particularly effective until the "kachina wars," beginning around 1660. To that extent, it might be said that Spanish occupation of New Mexico could be divided into two periods. During the first sixty years or so, the Franciscans and the Pueblo religious leaders coexisted in a de facto, though rather brittle, truce. There were certainly arrests and attempts to undermine the native ways of doing things, but these tended to be in the less secure outer rings of pueblos, especially Taos, Zuni, and Jemez. In contrast, the last twenty years before the great revolt were marked by explosive attempts to destroy native religion on the part of both missionaries and the secular authorities. There were at least two catalysts for this change in direction (or perhaps one should say "intensification of effort") on the part of the Franciscans. With one or two generations of children with Christian indoctrination having become adults, the Church felt strong enough to be openly hostile toward *any* native religious practice. And, at this very time, a governor, Bernardo López de Mendizábal, appeared; his sympathy for the native religious point of view caused a crisis between the missionaries and their Indian charges. López, though a reasonably devout Christian, believed that the Indian masked dances were "folk dances" best incorporated into the fabric of Christianity. The clerical reaction to López de Mendizábal was swift and violent. Among other things, it signaled the end of the informal uneasy truce between the missionaries and the conservatives among the Pueblos. The various governors before López had developed a working relationship with the church. As discussed in chapter 7, the immediate predecessor to López, Juan Manso de Contreras (1656–59)—a brother of a former custodian, Fray Tomás Manso—formed a close, though somewhat scandalous, bond with Fray Miguel Sacristán of the Santa Fe church and convent. The governor's friendship with the missionaries was cemented when Manso threw the governor's office behind the planning of a mission to the Manso Indians in the El Paso area. Manso's lax morals did disturb Inquisition officials, but nothing much was done and ex-governor Manso became *alguacil mayor,* or chief constable of the Holy Office, in New Mexico and later (1664) was made head of the mission supply service. Still, the Inquisition books were not closed on Manso until after his accidental death in 1673.

As mentioned above, the easy relationship between church and state took a decided turn for the worse with the coming of Governor López de Mendizábal.

On the face of it, one would not expect such problems, for López belonged to a Spanish family that had been upwardly mobile for several generations and had a series of alliances with the Church. Drawing from statements in the *Inquisición* documents, France V. Scholes admirably sums up the ancestry of López and his family.

[López's] father's brother was a Knight of the Order of Santiago and had served as *fiscal* and *oidor* of the Audiencia of Guadalajara, and later as a member of the Council of Castile, *asesor de guerra,* and a member of the *junta* of the Suprema. A cousin was married to an official who had served as a member of the Council of the Indies and later in the Council of Castile. His maternal grandfather was a wealthy Spanish-born merchant of Puebla. López's father was an attorney of the jurisdiction of Chietla. One of López's brothers, Don Gregorio, served as an officer in the Spanish army, and later held several administrative posts in New Spain. Another, Don Juan, was *cura* of the mines of Cimapan. The only blot on the family escutcheon was the fact that one of his maternal ancestors had been tried and convicted by the Holy Office as a Jew.

The "Judaizing" ancestor mentioned by Scholes was Juan Nuñez de León, who was condemned by the Inquisition despite vehement denials on Nuñez's part. López's family was in Scholes's words, "fairly distinguished," but unfortunately for López, not distinguished enough to be exempt from the Inquisition. Having a Jewish ancestor probably was not a great handicap, for the upper class in Spain had a considerable amount of Jewish admixture (usually not acknowledged). This had come largely from *conversos,* individuals and their families who had switched from Judaism to Christianity, their conversions often forced by the authorities. The forced Christianization of Jewish populations in Spain had begun long before the settlement of Spanish America and was in part the outgrowth of a period of intermittent pogroms that began in the late fourteenth century. The famous expulsion of Jews from Spain by Ferdinand and Isabella in 1492 was itself an attempt to Christianize the Jewish population and resulted in tens of thousands of new converts. Thus, by the time of the settlement of New Mexico, Jewish ancestry in Spanish and Spanish colonial upper and upper-middle-class families often went back for many generations. For example, ancestors of Vázquez de Coronado's wife, Beatríz de Estrada, and Juan de Oñate's mother, Catalina de Salazar, were Jewish, and there were indeed many others. However, the charge of Judaizing was a very handy one for Inquisition officials and was widely used in the sixteenth and seventeenth centuries.

Bernardo López de Mendizábal was born in Chietla, a town southwest of the city of Puebla in New Spain, sometime around 1620. His father, Captain

Cristóbal López de Mendizábal, an *hacendado* in that area, was from the Basque region, being born in the town of Oñate, north of Vitoria. Cristóbal's hometown was presumably the same place as the ancestral home of the famous Oñate family. López's mother, Doña Leonor de Pastraña, was born in Mexico. López originally desired to join the Church, and he attended the Jesuit college in Puebla. As López later told the Inquisition officials, he often wore ecclesiastical garb and had taken minor orders. He had actually intended to go into the priesthood but was prevented for family reasons.

From the Jesuit college, López went on to the University in Mexico City. Following his education, López moved to Havana, where he was involved with the galleon service, making a number of voyages. López de Mendizábal then went to Cartagena, in modern-day northern Colombia, where a cousin was bishop. Through this family influence, and probably also because of his clerical training, López was appointed *visitador*, or inspector, to the diocese. In Cartagena, López became acquainted with the governor of Cartagena, Melchor de Aguilera, and eventually married his daughter, Teresa de Aguilera y Roche.

Doña Teresa was born in Allesandra in Spanish Italy. Teresa's mother was an Irish woman who had fled to escape the persecution of Catholics in the British homelands. At the time of Teresa's birth, Aguilera was governor of the Italian province. Though we know relatively little of Doña Teresa, she seems to have been a sophisticated woman, speaking Italian as well as Spanish and perhaps English also.

Following his marriage with Teresa de Aguilera, López spent time in Cuba and Spain before returning to Mexico, where he held the office of alcalde mayor, first in San Juan de los Llanos and then in Guaiococotla. His appointment as governor of New Mexico came in 1658, and López left Mexico City on December 24 of that year to take charge of his new province. He was replacing Governor Juan Manso de Contreras, whose scandalous sexual conduct is described in chapter 7.

With López in the supply caravan was Fray Juan Ramírez. This man was appointed procurator-general of the supply service in 1656, replacing the previous holder of that office, Fray Tomás Manso (Juan Manso's brother), who had been appointed bishop of Nicaragua. Ramírez was quite well educated in spite of relatively humble origins, his father being a miner in Tasco. After a primary education in Tasco, Ramírez was trained in the Jesuit College of Saints Peter and Paul in Mexico City. This *colegio*, founded in 1574, was a boarding school that taught a variety of secular and religious subjects. At the age of sixteen, Ramírez joined the Franciscans, eventually being ordained after further theological studies in Mexico City and Puebla. He had a rather varied experience, serving as vicar-general of the Province of the Holy Gospel and commissary-general of Franciscans in New Spain. In 1655, Viceroy Francisco Fernández de la Cueva, Duke of Alburquerque, appointed him the Franciscan procurator-general for New Spain. A year later he was made procurator-general of the New Mexican custodia. This might be seen as a demotion, though perhaps Ramírez was given the larger office on a temporary basis with the understanding that he would quickly move to the custodia. In 1657, Ramírez took actual charge of the mission supply trains and began the purchases of materials for the missionaries and laypeople of New Mexico. Meanwhile, sometime in 1658, Ramírez was elected custodian of the New Mexico Franciscan custodia.

The supply train bearing the additional missionaries and the new governor, his wife, and retainers began the slow journey from Mexico City to Santa Fe. Because of their somewhat similar backgrounds one might expect López and Ramírez to have had a certain viewpoint in common. From later testimony, however, it would seem that the two men quarreled very quickly and by the end of the long journey north were sworn enemies. Possibly, López with his upper-class family background looked down on Ramírez, a manifestation of the Spanish obsession with honor and social rank. More likely it was a personality conflict between two men, each with an exalted idea of his own worth. By the time López reached New Mexico, he had expanded his dislike to include the New Mexican missionaries, and his statements took on an increasingly violent anti-Franciscan tone. One wonders to what extent López's training by the Jesuits may have affected his attitude toward the Franciscans, or even to what degree he may have considered Ramírez a traitor to his early Jesuit training.

Missionary *policies* were also involved, and the governor and the Franciscans were in conflict from the very beginning about spheres of influence. López considered himself to be the "universal head" of the province, while the missionaries believed that they firmly controlled the spiritual affairs of New Mexico. The difference in the positions may have been largely semantic, perhaps nothing more than an unfortunate choice of phraseology. The Spanish government generally insisted that wide powers be granted to its executive officers, and it seems likely that López was simply trying to say that as governor he had the final authority. But he said so in a way that inflamed the Franciscans.

It was not long before accusations and counter-accusations were being routinely exchanged between the two leaders. According to López, Fray Ramírez had been hostile from the start, failing to provide properly for the governor and his wife and attempting to persuade the viceroy to suspend the López appointment. López documented this unfriendly attitude by sending letters he received from Ramírez back to Viceroy Francisco Fernández de la Cueva as examples of the intemperance of the Franciscans. The viceroy seems to have weighed in on the side of his governor and protested to the Franciscan commissary-general about Ramírez's discourtesy. This further angered Fray Juan, and according to Governor López, he refused all efforts at conciliation. The new governor may have felt a bit outnumbered, for some twenty-four missionaries were in this particular wagon train, making their way to the New Mexico missions. Ten of the twenty-four deserted along the way, and López and Ramírez blamed each other for these defections.

The governor and missionaries had ample time to get acquainted (and to focus on disagreements) because the trip, as always, took several months. At Parral, López, Ramírez, and a few others pushed on ahead to the new Manso mission station near Paso del Norte, arriving there in early June 1659. Moving upriver to Senecú, López de Mendizábal held a series of conferences with the missionary in charge there, Fray García de San Francisco, and undoubtedly with local estancia and encomienda holders in the area. Among other things, the governor discussed with Ramírez and San Francisco the question of Indian labor, something which was quickly to become a sore point among the various factions.

By the time the caravan actually arrived in New Mexico, López and Ramírez were open enemies, and López had solidified his dislike of the entire missionary order in New Mexico. At Socorro, the missionary in charge, Fray Benito de la Natividad, claimed to have welcomed López with arches of flowers and tolling church bells. According to the Franciscans, López greeted Fray Benito rudely, informing him that the missionary should have gone two leagues (five miles or so) to formally meet the governor's party and that the governor should be received "like the blessed Sacrament on the day of Corpus, with pallium and incense." This statement played a part in the later Inquisition investigation of López. The governor flatly denied making any such comment, and it really seems unlikely that López de Mendizábal would have indulged in such inflammatory language. Even later, when the hostilities between López and the missionaries had reached a point of open warfare, the governor generally was careful not to impugn the sanctity of the Church as a whole, only the Franciscan missionaries in New Mexico. Still, López did have a tart tongue when it came to comments on the missionaries. At Socorro he was entertained at dinner by a local estanciera, Luisa Díaz de Betansos and her daughter, Isabel de Salazar. The women complained that they were not always able to attend Mass for lack of riding animals. López assured them that they were "healthier or better" for missing these religious obligations since it meant they could avoid the friars. In later testimony, the ladies claimed to have been shocked by such statements.

López arrived in Santa Fe on July 11, 1659, Ramírez having dropped off at Santo Domingo, the Franciscan headquarters. It was customary for the custodian to make a formal call on the governor at Santa Fe, at which time he normally would be received with considerable pomp and circumstances, and Ramírez therefore sent letters announcing his arrival in the capital. López, however, was still angry because of perceived slights from the Franciscans and replied that although he would assist the custodian, he had no obligation to provide a formal welcome. This kind of behavior formed the pattern of relationships between the governor and the missionaries for the two years of López's governorship.

Several other trouble spots flared up during these first months of López's tenure of office. Even before coming to the Southwest, López had been concerned with the very low pay of the Pueblos. By a viceregal degree of 1621 (see chapter 7) it had been set at a low half-real per day plus food. Forty years later the food provision had been dropped, and there are hints that even the wretched base pay was sometimes not forthcoming. In view of what happened later, it seems likely that the viceregal government wished to adjust the pay schedule, and that López de Mendizábal may have been acting under the orders, or at least with the approval, of the viceroy. At any rate he ordered that the wage be increased to one real per day, with a daily ration of food.

In order to understand this situation, it is necessary to say something about Spanish coins and their different values. First of all, I must stress that we are talking about *equivalents,* for little or no actual money circulated in New Mexico. The basis of calculation seems to have been the peso de plata of eight reales, and a smaller coinage unit called the tomín, ninety-six to the peso and twelve to the real. An "on the ground" unit for calculating value was the cotton or wool manta, a vara and a half (about fifty inches) square. This cloth was reckoned at six reales. A fanega (about two and a half bushels) of wheat was pegged at eight reales, and a fanega of corn at four to six. An ox was worth seven to ten pesos, and a good mule or a slave boy or girl, thirty to forty pesos. According to the Prada letter of 1638, each Indian household, every year, must needs pay its encomendero a fifty-inch piece of cotton cloth and a fanega of maize or wheat, representing on an average perhaps twenty-five wage-days. It does not seem to be excessive, but in lean years it may well have been difficult to meet even those amounts.

The timing of the wage hike was perhaps unfortunate, for the increase came at harvest time in 1659. It produced cries of anger and outrage from the various Spanish encomenderos and estancieros. How much they actually were hurt by the new pricing is uncertain. A number of them complained at López's residencia, some two years later, that they were no longer able to afford Indian labor in harvesting and herding. Another complicating factor may have been the fact that parts of New Mexico were entering a drought cycle that would peak in the late

1660s (see chapter 11). This might have had an intensifying effect on any change in work or wage policy.

Although the raise in wages of the Pueblo worker mainly impacted the land-holding colonists, López's next move was aimed at the Franciscans. In 1648, by order of then Governor Luis de Guzmán y Figueroa, the missionaries had been given rights to the free labor of Indians for various church and convent offices (interpreter, sacristan, bell ringer, cook and porter) as well as for herding and other field tasks. Such Indians were exempt from the normal encomienda tax. After some backing and filling, and only when pressed by the Franciscans to give a definite statement on the matter, López ruled that the new wage laws also applied to these mission workers. He based his ruling on the famous viceregal directive of 1621, which sharply delineated and restricted actions against the Indians by both the ecclesiastical and lay authorities. López also moved against encomenderos who had been in the habit of building on Pueblo land and who also utilized Indian labor, in some cases free labor. The mission labor practices may have been in a gray area, but that of the encomenderos was clearly illegal.

Even before reaching New Mexico there was another flare-up between López and the missionaries concerning the interpretation of a papal bull, the *Omnimoda,* issued by Adrian VI during his short tenancy as pope, 1522–23. This bull stated that in areas where no bishop was in control, monastic prelates were permitted to have the powers of an ecclesiastical judge-ordinary. López insisted that the bull had been revoked by the Council of Trent. This was a murky area of Church law, but during the earlier seventeenth century, the Franciscan custodiae in outlying mission areas of New Spain were generally considered to have judge-ordinary powers. López's reservations were probably sincere, and Scholes, at any rate, believed that the governor did not mean "to deny ecclesiastical authority as such." The Franciscans, however, took that as the governor's meaning and complained vociferously to the Inquisition.

López de Mendizábal began his term as governor by making the customary tour of the province. During his travel and visits, the governor closely questioned various Indians on the activities of the Franciscans. López seems to have had a tradition of being "pro-Indian," at least as far as the clergy were concerned. When serving as alcalde mayor in Guaiocotla, he had assured the Indian leaders that the Church had only limited power over them. Now in New Mexico, he questioned Indians as to the morals of their friars and took steps to limit the ecclesiastical use of Indian labor. In a number of cases he tampered with the actual organization of the missions, dismissing Pueblo servants and denying the missionaries the right to personal service on the part of the Indians.

Custodian Ramírez, because of his duties with the pack train, had returned to Mexico in the fall of 1659, leaving vice-custodian, Fray García de San Francisco, in charge. With Ramírez went a document outlining complaints against the governor, some of them having to do with López's moneymaking proclivities at the expense of Indians, missionaries, and settlers. A second petition was sent by Vice-custodian San Francisco in November. Viceroy Fernández de la Cueva does not seem to have taken any action on the petitions, but he did send copies to the Holy Office. The Inquisitors, in turn, interviewed Ramírez and Joseph de Espeleta, the special envoy who carried the second petition. There the matter rested for the time being.

One of the accusations made against López was that he was trying to enrich himself. He was accused of collecting stock to sell in Parral in spite of his criticism of such activity on the part of the missionaries. He was also charged with forcing Indians from the Tompiro area to collect salt for shipment south. He was supposed to have commandeered some two hundred oxen and pressed Indians into his service to build seven wagons for transporting the governor's goods. López was also accused of taking fleeces from the mission station at Socorro and forcing the Indians there to weave woolen socks for him to sell.

The salary given the governors had been static since the days of Peralta, the second governor, and was increasingly inadequate. There is no doubt that the New Mexico governors in the seventeenth century, like those throughout the Spanish New World, expected to make a profit out of their office, and the governmental structure of the province offered a number of possibilities for profit. One of these was trade, and López had entered on the governorship with trade very much in mind. He invested in large amounts of much-desired goods—chocolate, shoes, hats, textiles, and sugar—and opened a sort of store in the Casa Real when he reached Santa Fe. López collected a variety of goods: cotton and wool cloaks, piñon nuts, antelope and other hides, salt, and slaves. As we saw above, López was also interested in shipping livestock, even though he had criticized the Franciscans for doing the same. It might be said that livestock shipments, though they may have loomed large in the eyes of the colonists, were very much "small potatoes" compared to the vast herds that supplied the central Mexican market from Nueva Vizcaya and other outer provinces of New Spain.

An even more serious accusation concerned López's policy in regard to the Apaches, who flanked the Pueblo country in the high plains to the east. On September 4, 1659, López led a group of forty colonists and approximately eight hundred Indians onto the plains in some sort of punitive raid. This war party collected about seventy captives (worth two thousand to three thousand pesos). According to the claims of the clergy, however, López took the local Indians away at harvest time without making arrangements for their crops (and, indeed, those of the missionaries) to be harvested. They also contended that the raid was illegal, being unprovoked, and exposed the outlying districts of the province to hostile counter-raids. According to testimony by Captain Andrés Hurtado in 1661, there were nomadic raids on the Tompiro pueblos, along the Camino Real in Piro territory, and on the more exposed northern pueblos, Jemez and others. Whether these raids were in retaliation to López's activities is unknown. Indeed, the situation is not at all clear. López may have felt that the colony was under threat and that a preemptive strike was the best strategy. Alternatively, he may simply have been inserting himself into the lucrative slave trade.

Whatever the situation, López did a considerable amount of trading with the eastern Apaches. There had been an annual trade fair at Pecos for some time, with Apaches bringing their hides and other goods. At least in rudimentary form, it probably dated to pre-Spanish times. By López's time, Apachean groups had pushed south and west to the Sangre de Cristos and the line of the Pecos River. The pueblo of Humanas, so named because of the Jumano connection of earlier times, now was the center for trade with these southernmost Apaches. It was also the place where nearby Pueblos brought maize and other goods to trade for skins.

One of the first duties for López when he entered the governorship was to hold an investigation, called in colonial Latin America a *residencia*. In the province of New Mexico, this took the form of a trial hearing conducted by each governor on the affairs of his predecessor. Evidence was collected under the current governor's direction and sent to Mexico City, where the actual ruling was given by the Audiencia, the chief judicial body of the viceroyalty. The retiring governor, Juan Manso, had built up a firm support among leading families within the province. López seems to have developed a prejudice against Manso from Captain Francisco de Anaya Almazán, a well-known encomendero, and other members of his family. Anaya had fallen into Manso's bad graces and was in exile in Mexico City when López first met him. In any case, López de Mendizábal confiscated a considerable amount of Manso's property. Attempts by Manso to bribe the new governor fell through, and eventually Manso was arrested. He finally escaped, in September 1660, through the good offices of friends among the settlers and in the clergy. Ironically, López himself suffered in much the same way during his own residencia two years later—and he was unable to flee.

Within a short time after his arrival, López had created bad feelings by removing certain settlers from various positions in order to make way for his own supporters. For example, the lieutenant governor and captain-general, Tomé (or Thomé) Domínguez de Mendoza was replaced with Tomé's brother,

Juan. This was one case in which a family was split in their loyalties, but for the most part the provincial families lined up on one side or the other. Eventually, this tightly knit, closely intermarried Spanish population of New Mexico became heavily anti-López.

López, however, did have a number of active supporters. For example, the alcalde mayor of the Galisteo pueblos and Pecos regions, Diego González Bernal, enthusiastically backed López's efforts to legalize the ceremonial Indian dances. But when a quarrel developed between the two men, López turned against González, describing him as a "mestizo by birth." Lopéz's change of heart at least had the effect of sparing González the attentions of the Inquisition. Incidentally, this use of ethnic slurs was endemic in seventeenth-century New Mexico, even by such a man as López, whose rather paternal interest in Indians seems to have been sincere and whose main lieutenant, Captain Nicolás de Aguilar, was pretty definitely a mestizo.

The Anaya Almazán family has already been mentioned. The most active López supporter was Cristóbal de Anaya Almazán, who had been a regidor of the Santa Fe cabildo and procurator-general, or city attorney. The death of his father, Francisco, on July 18, 1662, also meant that he was heir to the encomiendas of Cuarac, a part of Picurís and La Ciénega (San Marcos). A second supporter was Francisco Gómez Robledo, son of a Portuguese native named Francisco Gómez who came to New Mexico in 1604. Francisco's mother was Ann Robledo, daughter of Bartolomé Romero, one of Oñate's captains. A third López adherent was Diego Pérez Romero, who had served as *alcalde ordinario* of the Santa Fe cabildo. Diego Romero's father, Captain Gaspar Pérez, was Flemish, originally from Brussels. Diego was actually related to the Romero family through his mother. One of Romero's brothers had an odd physical feature, an abnormal coccyx that produced a "little tail," and which the Inquisitors thought might be an indication of Judaism or diabolism.

An interesting side issue in the Romero trial hearing, discussed below, was the testimony of Fray Nicolás de Freitas in 1661 about a trip to the Plains made by Romero and five others. The group had a commission from López to trade. Reaching the Apaches, Diego Romero reminded the group of his father, who had traded there in the past and who had fathered a son while there. The child was conceived through the agency of a "trader's marriage," probably serving to link the trader firmly with the group. In any event, Diego Romero asked that his hosts arrange the same sort of liaison.

At about four in the afternoon they brought a tent of new leather and set it up in the field; they then brought two bundles, one of antelope skins and the other of buffalo skins, which they placed near the tent. Then they brought another large new buffalo skin which they stretched on the ground and put Diego Romero on it, lying on his back. They then began to dance the *catzina,* making turns, singing, and raising up and laying Diego Romero down again on the skin in accordance with the movements of the dance of the *catzina.* When the dance was ended about nightfall, they put him again upon the skin, and taking it by the corners, drew him into the tent, into which they brought him a maiden, which they left with him the entire night. On the next day in the morning the captains of the rancherias [the Apache settlement] came to see whether Diego Romero had known the woman carnally, seeing that he had known her, they anointed Diego Romero's breast with the blood. Then they put a feather on his head, in his hair, and proclaimed him as their captain, giving him the two bundles of skins and the tent.

There are several interesting aspects to this ceremony. Since Romero's father seems to have gone through with it at an earlier date, it probably was some sort of standard procedure to provide a fictive kinship (adoption?) link between given Apache subgroups and individual Spanish traders. Such ties for the purpose of facilitating trade or other kinds of social relationships are fairly common around the world. The girl given to Romero seems to have been a virgin, at least that is the implication of the story. According to Fray García de San Francisco of Senecú, who reported this episode to Fray Nicolás de Freitas, the Apaches called the ceremony a wedding dance, and said that the action of anointing Romero with the girl's blood constituted a contract of marriage. Certainly, it was not a kachina dance, and probably not an Apache marriage ceremony as such. The archaeologist Donald Blakeslee some years ago suggested that the Romero account represented an early historical example of the Calumet ceremony, a Plains Indian ritual used to establish fictive kin relationships between individuals of different ethnic groups. Even though it seems quite circumstantial, there is always the danger that the account might have been embroidered somewhat by Romero and his companions—or, for that matter, by Fray Nicolás, or by the latter man's informant, Fray García de San Francisco. It seems very unlikely, however, that this story was made up out of whole cloth.

Another loyal follower of López, and in some ways the most interesting of all, was Nicolás de Aguilar. It is not certain where López met Aguilar, but it was probably in New Mexico. At any rate, Aguilar quickly became the governor's most active supporter. This new lieutenant was made alcalde mayor over the Salinas region, which contained Tompiro- and Tiwa-speaking towns. Aguilar was a rather enigmatic but, in many ways, a rather appealing individual. Born in the village of Yurirapundaro some fifty miles south of Querétaro in northeastern

Michoacán, a maternal ancestor was Fernando de Villagómez, one of the conquerors of Michoacán. Aguilar drifted off to Parral at the age of eighteen, working as a soldier and miner. Six years later he killed an uncle in a brawl (presumably by accident) and fled to New Mexico, eventually receiving a pardon from the Crown. There he married a local woman, Catalina Márquez, whose family had been in New Mexico from Oñate's time, and the couple had four children. In their actions against Aguilar, the Franciscans referred to him over and over again as a mestizo, and the description of him in the Inquisition documents as "somewhat brown" also suggested a mixed ancestry. Although there is some indication that Aguilar was illiterate, among his goods inventoried by the Inquisition were four books. One was a printed copy of the four gospels, two others had to do with Catholic religious exercises, and the fourth bore the title *Cathecismo, en lengua Castellana y Timuquana.* This latter book, on the Timucua of Florida, was compiled by the Franciscan missionary Francisco Pareja and was published in 1612 in Mexico. We have no idea where, and under what circumstances, Aguilar came by such a specialized volume and what use he made of it.

There were other adherents to the López cause, but only Anaya Almazán, Gómez Robledo, Romero, and Aguilar were actually tried by the Holy Office. All four men were probably in their mid to late thirties, and with the exception of Aguilar, all were from distinguished New Mexico families. The first three were given relatively light sentences (as Inquisition sentences went in those days). Gómez Robledo was actually acquitted, though he had to bear some of the costs of the trial. This is somewhat surprising because Gómez was accused of Judaizing and very likely had Jewish ancestors through his Portuguese father. Gómez Robledo, however, vigorously defended the father, pointing out that the elder man had come to New Mexico sometime in the first two decades of Spanish rule there and had served long and well. Romero was barred from returning to New Mexico and in 1678 was back in the Inquisition's bad graces, accused of bigamy. He died in prison in Vera Cruz. Anaya Almazán did return to the province (for his further activities, see chapter 11).

Nicolás de Aguilar was López's most active lieutenant in establishing conditions whereby Pueblo Indians could perform their forbidden ceremonial dances. He was, therefore, a main target of the missionaries after López himself. Aguilar made a strong defense, and his preliminary sentence, on a split vote, forbade him to hold public office for a period of six years. Probably, had Aguilar followed the same path as his three comrades, the sentence might have been reduced further. Instead, he decided to challenge the verdict, probably feeling very strongly that he had been wronged. Regardless of the merits of the case, Aguilar seems to have misjudged the court, for his appeal led to a much more serious sentence. Aguilar was banished from New Mexico for ten years and became ineligible to serve in public office for life. Aguilar then disappears from the record. It is not even clear whether or not his family joined him in exile from New Mexico.

France V. Scholes was somewhat of an admirer of Aguilar. Summing up the trial testimony he concluded that:

> Aguilar made a vigorous defense against [charges by the Franciscans] during his hearings before the tribunal. His depositions were characterized by a certain quality of directness that was lacking in the testimony of Diego Romero and Cristóbal de Anaya. It was impossible, of course, for him to evade the major issues, but having taken a stand he usually stuck to it. His nerve—perhaps stubbornness is a better word—never failed him, and he did not humiliate himself, as Romero had done, by coming before the court in hearing after hearing to tell unsavory details of his early life, to admit his guilt little by little, or to testify against his fellow prisoners. During the trial proceedings this rough illiterate frontiersman—this Attila, as the friars called him—displayed greater dignity and self respect than any of the other New Mexican soldiers, with the exception of Francisco Gómez Robledo.

In his two years in New Mexico, López seems to have developed an antagonism to the Franciscans that was matched perhaps only by Governor Rosas two decades before. His concerns, discussed above, that the Indians might be abused by the missionaries and his refusal to allow the Franciscans free Indian labor led to cries of outrage. Indians had tilled mission fields, herded mission flocks, and had performed various menial tasks around the mission convents without pay, and the friars were determined that this policy should stand. In the López residencia of 1662, the Franciscans demanded repayment for 8,317 head of sheep, cattle, and oxen lost due to López's Indian policy.

López and his wife obviously believed that they should live with somewhat of the pomp required by their station as the secular chief and first lady of the New Mexico province. They dressed well and were very aware of the dignity of the office of governor. Inquisition documents that developed out of the later judicial hearings and formal trial of the López pair give some interesting sidelights on the various uses of the time. At the Casa Real, the governor and his wife had their bedroom in one wing of the palace, with the women domestics sleeping in the room beyond. These women were allowed to move through the López couple's bedroom as they liked, even when the governor and his wife were in bed. The men's quarters, however, were in the other direction, and they were forbidden to enter the bedroom of their master and mistress except by direct invitation. Doña Teresa had her own separate drawing room. The rooms were sparsely decorated with two representations of Christ, one in the bedroom and the other in the drawing room. López also commissioned a picture of San Miguel, painted on leather, so clumsily done that his enemies accused him of mockery. It is probably untrue, for López seems to have considered San Miguel a very important figure, perhaps a patron saint. As for the "unskilled" painting, it was done by an Indian who likely was operating under a native artistic tradition.

Unlike most of the settlers, López and Teresa were literate and, as described in chapter 9, had a considerable library that included various religious writings, works of fiction in Spanish and Italian, histories, a Latin text and a Latin-Spanish dictionary. A great deal is known of the couple's personal habits since these were of considerable interest to the Inquisitors, especially when trying to decide if the Lópezes were secret Judaizers. A number of individuals, including four or five actual eyewitnesses, had testified against the two at hearings held by the custodian and Holy Office commissary, Fray Alonso de Posada, in 1661–62. The very practice of sleeping alone in their bedroom, except for a small slave girl, seems to have created some negative talk.

Bernardo and Teresa were also accused of avoiding Mass. This was something that had been of longstanding concern to the clergy, since a similar accusation against the two had been made by the missionary, Ramírez, during the trip north in 1659. The López couple tended to avoid Catholic days of obligation and seldom said grace at meals. When their household members greeted them with pious expressions, they failed to reply. The couple failed in their bedtime devotions and were indifferent to holy images. Antagonistic to piety in others, Teresa had actually whipped a black slave woman who was fasting in honor of Our Lady of Carmén. In addition, Doña Teresa was accused of saving her menstrual blood for ritual purposes, and of using magical potions to attract her husband's sexual attentions. She also treated the bottoms of her feet with onion peel. (Teresa indignantly commented that she had corns, and this was the only remedy available). Teresa de Aguilar was also accused of unusual secrecy in that she kept her writing desk locked. Her reading of a book in an unknown language was considered suspicious by the Inquisitors because of the possibility that it might contain heresy.

In point of fact, heresy and the possibility of Judaizing made up a considerable amount of the later preliminary interrogation undertaken in New Mexico by Custodian Alonso de Posada (see below). Posada learned from servants that both Don Bernardo and Doña Teresa "made a special ceremony" of washing their hair and bathing, with Teresa especially inclined to lock herself in the bedroom at such times. One of the servant women actually attempted to spy on her mistress but without success. Not only did the couple wash themselves on Friday but put on clean clothing and changed the bed and table linen on that day of the week. If they were unable to perform the Friday ablutions, they always postponed washing until the following Friday. And on Saturdays, Doña Teresa was accustomed to primp as if that day was to be specially celebrated.

In the later Inquisition hearings, López, and especially Doña Teresa, made relatively short work of these accusations. The book read by Doña Teresa was Ludovico Ariosto's *Orlando Furioso* in Italian, which the lady read to keep up practice in that language. The couple did not habitually choose Friday for bathing and changing clothing; in fact, Don Bernardo stated that he changed at least his shirt more often, almost every day in summer. Although he might have occasionally have washed his hair on Friday, there was nothing special about the day. Teresa did confess to special attention to her toilet on Saturdays but claimed that this was a common habit of women of her class. It had nothing to do with a day "which the dead law of Moses orders to be observed." Rather, it was because there was not time before Sunday Mass for any but the most superficial makeup.

The black slave woman was not whipped because she was fasting but because she was a troublemaker and had been disciplined for insubordination several times before. In fact, according to Doña Teresa, the servants in the Casa Real were a turbulent group, Apache and black slaves, Pueblo Indians who were serving time for petty offenses, and "low class mestizos." A firm manner and the occasional use of force was the only way the governor's wife could maintain order. Today, we tend to take into account the obvious and often brutal exploitation of these servants and slaves. However, the Inquisitors, operating from the point of view of the master class, seemed to have regarded Doña Teresa's travail with some sympathy.

In any case, the sanitary habits of the couple, their relationships with servants, or even their religious proclivities did not form the major part of the case, at least against López. In order to understand another set of accusations against the governor, it is necessary to consider one of López's own charges against the missionaries—that they habitually violated their vows of chastity both with Indian women and with members of the Hispanic community. The missionary at Tajique was accused of raping a number of his female parishioners, and the Franciscan stationed at Alamillo of having sex with Indian women. More sinister were the activities of Fray Luis Martínez at Taos, who, according to Mendizábal, raped a Pueblo woman and murdered her to keep the news from leaking out. Various citizens were accused of prostituting their wives to the missionaries. The extent to which these accusations were based on fact is not clear. There likely was some sexual misbehavior on the part of the clergy, but the incidences were probably not as widespread as López would have had the Inquisitors believe.

Be that as it may, these accusations infuriated the missionaries, and they struck back, accusing López of sexual liaisons with Pueblo women, mestizo servants, and with wives of settlers. Some he had raped! Certain of these affairs, López cheerfully and rather proudly admitted, listing several of his conquests, though he denied raping anyone. In statements to the Inquisitors, López confessed to having sexual relationships with Ana Rodríguez, the daughter of Alonso Rodríguez, who had close ties with the Anaya family. Ana may have been single at this point, but she soon married Captain Ambrosio Sáez of La Cañada. Another conquest of López was Gerónima Anaya, wife of the younger Francisco de Anaya Almazán, brother of López's loyal captain, Cristóbal de Anaya. López also had an affair with Petrona, daughter of Juan de Gamboa, perhaps at the lady's instigation, an assignation that produced a child. López also admitted other affairs, including one with a mestiza woman named Teresa. In all this, López simply followed the lax morals of the time. If Doña Teresa actually did use love potions, it would be understandable given her husband's casual infidelities.

The missionaries were understandably upset by the governor's interference with the considerable free labor they had been receiving from their Indian parishioners. They argued that without such labor they were unable to till the fields and tend the mission flocks of sheep and cattle. They were also unable to process the goods that went to Mexico, especially cotton and wool products and piñon nuts, trade goods that were often used to buy equipment for the church and convent. For example, sale of piñon nuts had recently financed a fine organ at the pueblo of Abó.

Important as these things were to the clergy, they were essentially technical matters of the division of power between the civil and ecclesiastical authorities. Far more basic, and to Franciscan eyes much more ominous, was the interference by the governor and his alcaldes mayores in the area of missionization, and especially in the continuing practice of native religion. As indicated earlier, there is some evidence that a sort of "don't ask, don't tell" policy regarding the kiva ceremonies of the Pueblos had characterized much of the mission activity through the first six decades of Christianization. By the late 1650s, the missionaries were beginning to tighten the screws. With growing numbers of Christianized and Hispanicized Indians, there was an increasing tendency to outlaw any overtly pagan ceremony. And it was just these ceremonies, lumped by the Spaniards under the name *catzinas* (kachinas), that López now decided to allow, and in some cases even to sponsor.

What the governor had in mind is not entirely clear, but it seems as if he really considered these Indian masked dances to be a harmless folk tradition of the sort that he and his wife had most likely witnessed in Mexico, South

America, and Europe. López's activities in regard to native ceremonialism and the missionaries' reaction take up many pages in the trial and other official transcripts of the later Inquisition hearings. In one way, we can thank the methodical recordkeeping, especially of the Inquisitors, for a flood of information about Pueblo religious practices and beliefs. Many of these data are difficult to interpret, but they do give an unprecedented window on Pueblo life at mid-century.

Fray Nicolás de Freitas, in a January 1661 deposition, divided the kachina dances into two main ceremonies: (1) a direct invocation to the devil by the "false priests" who perform a ritual and offer the fruits of the earth, and (2) a ceremony "with less solemnity but much superstition, in which fathers have intercourse with daughters, sons with mothers, and brothers with sisters, no attention being paid to relationships." He goes on to describe the dances:

> Prior to performing the first variety of the dance, the Indians fast two or three days, and when the fast is ended then comes the day of the dance. They then put on the face a sort of domino, or mask, made with a small hole [probably two eyeholes] through they can see a little. The masks are made of cloth, or of elk skin. They also wear other masks stained black. Those who put on the masks are the most idolatrous. Before going out in public they try them on in the council rooms [kivas] which they have underground. When they come out in public, one of them puts in place where the dance is to be performed the offerings of the things already mentioned. The other dancers perform the dance about it, using a language which is not understood, even by the Indians themselves; or if they do, they are willing to say only that it is the language of the devil. Asked to what end they perform these dances, they say it is to obtain the women they desire, and that the devil gives her to them. Or, they say it is for the purpose of asking him for corn or for other specific purposes. Some of them taking palm leaves, cruelly beat, until the blood flows, this or that one of the dancers who wishes to make this blood sacrifice to the devil. They all become so frenzied that they appear beside themselves, though no drinking has taken place whereby they may have become intoxicated. Sometimes they go from this dance and enter any house which they wish and take pleasure from any Indian woman they desire. In the second variety of this dance there is no fasting; sometimes there is the ritualistic performance already mentioned, but always with the masks on. They perform the dance while singing in that unknown tongue. After dancing they go to whatever house they will, and have intercourse with women of the near relationship mentioned.

A few weeks later Freitas commented that López de Mendizábal had allowed the dances to be held on a hill near Isleta. He then basically repeated the description of the dances given above.

In a deposition in September 1660, Fray Nicolás de Chávez stated that:

He had heard it said publicly in New Mexico that Don Bernardo López de Mendizábal had given his permission for the Christian Indians to perform their ancient and modern dances, among them that of the *catzinas*, which is a dance of the heathen in which the Indians dress themselves in peculiar garments, concealing only their private parts, smearing their entire bodies with earth, and covering their faces with masks like hoods, leaving only a small hole through which they can see a little. Only the men perform this dance, and when they dance it some of them beat the others with palm leaves over their entire bodies until they draw blood; they then go from house to house, entering them and bringing out with blows the Indian women, whom they carry away terrified and frightened to see those demoniac figures to certain rooms which they call *estufas* [kivas], which are underground. There the men and women have sexual intercourse in bestial fashion, fathers with daughters, brothers with sisters, and mothers with sons.

Fray Diego de Santander on November 30, 1660, quoted Don Esteban Clemente, the Indian governor of Las Salinas and Tanos, who wrote in the missionary's presence:

I certify and make oath that some [of the Indians] have very ugly painted masks; certain of the Indians put them on and go to dance in them, and make the people think they come from the other life to speak to them. There are other dances in which they fast; they fast as many days as they can, and afterward the one who has fasted distributes some feathers to those whom he knows, who are the fortunate ones. On the day on which the *catzinas* are to be danced they sweep the plaza of the pueblo, and the faster, as an acolyte, places on the ground some feathers and flour, and he who fasted stands upon it; they do the same thing when they reach the north, west and south sides of the pueblo. Then they lead him to an underground room to give him certain drinks; all this they do in order to have good fortune and to be brave. There are other dances called *catzinas*, in which many people come out with masks on, to dance in the costume of men and women, all of them being men. The purpose for which they do this is not known. They perform other dances, in which they worship an idol, and each one offers him whatever he likes, and they set up an altar. These are the *catzinas* which I know to be evil, although I have heard that there are others; but as I have not verified these superstitions I do not certify more than this.

Santander went on to remark that Clemente was "a very capable interpreter of six Indian languages of this kingdom." Clemente was, indeed, an interesting character. An influential Indian leader, he could read and write as well as speak

Santo Domingo corn dance (from Century Magazine, 1890, courtesy of the Museum of New Mexico, neg. no. 109020)

Spanish. He worked with the missionaries but also was often called on by Alcalde mayor Aguilar. For a time he seems to have been successful in balancing various of the contending forces in seventeenth-century New Mexico: the Franciscans, the governor's party (Clemente was a partner to López on trade ventures into the Plains), and both Christianized and traditional elements within the Pueblos.

This statement by Clemente—if indeed it was not fabricated by the missionaries—was self-serving. A few years later, during the administration of Governor Villanueva (1665–68) Clemente attempted to lead a revolt. He was hanged, and after his death large amounts of native ceremonial gear were found in his house.

In May of 1661 the retired alcalde mayor, Tomé Domínguez de Mendoza, deposed that at Isleta in the fall of 1660 the Indians of the pueblo petitioned Governor López to be able to perform their dances. "The governor gave the permission freely and without any objection." Warned by Domínguez that the dances were considered idolatrous and diabolical, López replied that

> the people did not know what they were talking about; that the *zarambeque* and other dances which the Spaniards dance were not prohibited, and he had not

observed that there were any superstitions connected with the catzinas; he also asked the deponent whether he had observed any. The deponent replied that he had never seen them performed in his life because the religious had prohibited them as being evil, and always mentioned the *catzinas* when they spoke against the superstitions of the Indians.

López thereupon ordered the Isleta Indians to continue with their dance, which Domínguez then described.

> The Indians went out to dance the *catzinas* before the governor and the Spaniards who were with him, among whom the deponent recalls were Juan Domínguez brother of the deponent, Miguel de Noriega, who was secretary of government and war, Juan Griego Naguatlato of the Teguas nation [probably a translator], a resident of the villa of Santa Fe, and one Artiega, whose first name he does not know. The Indians went out wearing various evil costumes; one of them especially had an ugly costume, like a devil, with horns on the head and a bearskin which he dangled by two fingers thrust through the eye-socket—a horrible thing. They sang something which sounded like "Hu-hu-hu,'" at which the governor said "look there, this dance contains nothing more than this 'Hu-hu-hu,' and these thieving friars say that it is superstitious." The deponent knew from the faces of those who were present that they were much affected by this action, but offered no opposition to it because the speaker was their governor and captain-general. Along with the Indians who wore the horrible figure of the devil already mentioned were three others who walked somewhat apart.

After this experience with the governor, Tomé Domínguez became increasingly interested in the Indian dances. At one point he entered one of the Pueblos' underground kivas near the Isleta church and convent. "There he saw hanging up eleven figures, or diabolical masks, with which the Indians dance the *catzinas,* just as we have our holy images; at the foot of one of them was the offering which they are accustomed to make, which was a wreath of flowering grasses. He did not see here any figure which precisely represented the devil."

Francisco Valencia of Isleta, who gave testimony in May 1661, stated that:

> he was in the pueblo of Cuarac [Quarai] in the month of October of last year [1660] when Nicolás de Aguilar, the *mestizo alcalde mayor* of these pueblos, gave the Indians permission to dance their diabolical dances. An old Indian came to say to the pueblo that they should get ready, for the *catzinas* who are their heathen priests, were coming. The Indians of the pueblo went out, taking with them a *mestiza* who lives there to receive the *catzinas*. One of the latter pretending to be the devil, went throughout the pueblo uttering loud cries and saying to the people

that he had been exiled a long time, but that now they might be happy for he was coming to stay with them. He then gave to the *mestiza* a fir branch which he had in his hand, and she took it, and put it in her house. The deponent is ignorant of the significance of this ceremony. Afterwards the *catzinas* walked around about the pueblo shouting, and then went and brought earthen bowls, squashes, and other things, according to their superstitious custom. The deponent alone counted many persons who saw this, and was very deeply moved to see such a thing.

In 1663, Bernardo López de Mendizábal, now in an Inquisition prison, responded at great lengths to the various charges against him. Regarding the Indians' dances, López said:

that the Indians of those provinces are of most diverse nations and tongues. And each one dances according to his custom; they do not all dance the *catzinas* generally. . . . Indians of the pueblo of Tesuque came to the villa of Santa Fé and, as he remembers, with them came their encomendero, Francisco Gómez, and Juan Griego as interpreter. Among other things they asked permission to dance the *catzinas*. The accused [López] asked what dance that was. The *encomendero* having replied, as he recalls, as well as the interpreter and others present, concerning the nature of the dance, stating that it was simply an exhibition of agility, the accused wanted to see it, desiring also that the *guardián* of the villa, Fray Diego Rodríguez, who administered the Indians, should see it. In order that he might do so, the accused sent Toribio de la Huerta to call him. The latter returned, saying that the friar, Diego Rodríguez, was finishing his prayers, or some other employment. The accused, seeing that it was late and that the Indians had to return to their pueblo, told them to dance. They did so after this fashion; ten or twelve Indians dressed themselves in the ordinary clothes which they commonly wear and put on masks painted with human figures of men; then half of them, with timbrels, such as commonly used in New Spain, in their hands, went out to the plaza. The others carried thongs, or whips, in their hands. They placed in the middle of the plaza four or six watermelons. . . . After putting the watermelons in the middle of the plaza, those who were dancing continued to do so noisily, sounding the timbrels crazily, as they are accustomed to do, and saying, "Hu, hu, hu." In this fashion they circled around the plaza and the other Indians with the thongs went along, leaping, watching the watermelons, or prizes, from a distance, and allowing opportunity for other youths and boys, Indians or others, to slip in and snatch the watermelons. The one who did so they chased, and if they caught him they gave him many blows with the thongs, but if they did not catch him, he, being more fleet of foot, carried off the watermelon without receiving any lashes. When several had thus run away the dance stopped, and it contained no other feature. The accused asked them, having noticed that the response, or echo, given by the Indians who were dancing contained no distinguishable word, whether any of it signified or meant anything. The interpreter and the others who knew the language of these Indians said that it meant nothing.

What do we make of the various descriptions of these ceremonial dances? First of all, it is reasonably certain that dances lumped by the Spaniards as *catzinas* were not all kachina dances, although clearly some of them were. Recall, from the descriptions in chapters 2 and 5, that kachina dances, at least in later historic pueblos, were basically weather-control and fertility ceremonies conducted by masked dancers who were avatars of the supernatural ancestral beings lumped under the name *kachina*. These kachinas entered the Southwest, from somewhere farther south, sometime after A.D. 1300. The kachina cult seems to have been basically an outgrowth of the great and ancient Mexican rain deity Tlaloc, and, like the Tlaloc cult, may have originally involved human sacrifice. This aspect had certainly disappeared by Hispanic times.

The seventeenth-century Spanish descriptions of the dances seem, in fact, to be of several ceremonies. Various of the later historic kachina dances are foreshadowed here. This includes such things as ritual whippings with yucca leaves (the "palm" leaves of the missionaries), use of arcane language (probably an archaic form of the Pueblos' own tongue), robing in the kivas, use of masks, the use of sacred corn pollen and feathers, and the ritual number of days. In fact, the "two or three days" fasting mentioned by Freitas is most likely a reference to the four-day ceremonial period of the Pueblos. There seem to be elements of the Chakwena in the dances, and also ceremonies performed by the sacred clowns. Some of the antics of the clown groups sound very much like the later *Koshare,* and the leather masks described in several accounts would fit the historic Zuni mudheads.

The dance specifically described by the governor, however, does not sound like a kachina dance. The Indians were in everyday dress, and there was a strong social element in the dancing. The watermelons, which clearly served as gifts, suggest the gift giving in historic Pueblo dances, whether kachina or not. I get the feeling that what the Tesuque Indians put on for López in Santa Fe was an eclectic dance, perhaps developed to entertain the Spaniards.

One of the elements insisted on by the missionaries (though not mentioned by López) is the widespread incest following the dances. It would be easy to dismiss these allegations out of hand because such incestuous relationships are quite alien to the social or religious uses of the Pueblo Indians. However, I think these claims of widespread incest represent a certain misplaced logic in missionary reasoning. Since the witchcraft mythology in Europe held that incest was an important part of Satan's stock in trade, the evil Pueblo kachina dances, which honored the devil and all his darkness, must also have this element. It may well be that the Franciscans believed these incest charges, for certainly the credulity level in seventeenth-century New Mexico was very high. Still, it should be pointed out that such accusations helped wonderfully in blackening the character of the "Indian lover" López.

The resistance of the Franciscans and their supporters among the colonists had begun even before López had reached his new province. As mentioned earlier, formal accusations against the governor and his followers were sent to Mexico City in the fall of 1659 and presented to Viceroy Fernández de la Cueva early in 1660. In the spring of 1660, a second group of accusations was prepared by Vice-custodian García de San Francisco, including the case against Aguilar, who had actually been excommunicated for his actions against the clergy. Custodian Ramírez, who was in Mexico with the supply wagon train, brought a number of these problems before the Inquisition officials. One side issue was that the Franciscan order was becoming increasingly unhappy with Ramírez, who was considered somewhat at fault for the desertion of a number of missionaries traveling north in 1659, and whose financial records as chief of the supply service were suspect. The order decided to remove Ramírez as custodian, although they allowed him to remain in charge of the supply train for the time being. Around the end of 1660, a new custodian was appointed, Alonso de Posada, a man who had served in the Hopi missions in the 1650s. An able zealot, Posada was to prove a deadly enemy to López.

Not only missionaries were pressing charges against López. These were now augmented by ex-governor Juan Manso, who with the help of friendly colonists had escaped New Mexico on the night of September 9, 1660. A few months later Manso filed charges before the new viceroy, Juan de Leiva y de la Cerda. Manso was generally successful, for in February 1661, López was removed from any jurisdiction in Manso's case, and the viceroy ordered a restoration of Manso's property that had been seized by the governor. A few months later, Manso was appointed an officer of the Inquisition and was ordered to place himself at the disposition of the new custodian, Fray Alonso, who had also replaced Ramírez as the commissary of the Holy Office. Manso was to return to New Mexico early in 1662. Meanwhile, a new governor, Diego de Peñalosa, had been appointed in the latter part of 1660 and soon was on his way north, arriving in Santa Fe in August 1661.

López was fully aware of the attacks and tried to counter them with charges of his own. In the fall of 1660 he collected documents to be sent both to the civil authorities and to the Holy Office, which defended his case. The governor had a certain difficulty in getting his side of the story to Mexico City, however. Tomé

Domínguez de Mendoza, who had been appointed procurador, or attorney, was on his way to Mexico on provincial business. Domínguez, who had been replaced as lieutenant governor, had no love for López and flatly refused to take on this task. The governor, according to Domínguez de Mendoza's later account, became enraged and forbade Tomé to leave the province, eventually replacing him as procurador with the more loyal Francisco Gómez Robledo, who at that time was the Santa Fe cabildo alcalde ordinario. With a companion, Juan Lucero de Godoy, Gómez left in November 1660. On his way, however, he met Fray Alonso de Posada, journeying north to take up his post as custodian and commissioner of the Holy Office. Posada instructed Gómez to report to the new governor, who was also wending his way north, though well behind Posada. Gómez and Lucero met Peñalosa at Zacatecas and turned over the various papers to him. Gómez later testified that he wished to continue on to Mexico City but that Lucero and the governor-elect took the papers without his consent. At any rate, Governor López was never able to publicize his own side of the story until far too late.

After Posada's arrival in New Mexico he quickly began to build cases against López's four main lieutenants: Aguilar, Romero, Gómez Robledo, and Anaya. The first move against López, came with the arrival of the new governor, Peñalosa in mid-August 1661. Peñalosa quickly appointed a number of López's enemies to high offices. For example, ex-governor Manso's nephew, Pedro de Valdéz, was appointed lieutenant-captain general, and the treacherous Lucero de Godoy became the governor's administrative secretary. Anti-López elements in Santa Fe captured the cabildo elections. In November 1661, Peñalosa promulgated orders restoring the clergy's rights to Indian service, given them by Governor Guzmán in 1648.

Peñalosa immediately launched an extensive residencia of López de Mendizábal. It included a potpourri of charges, including corruption, interfering with the clergy in their missionizing efforts, allowing the kachina dances, murder of friendly Apaches in order to enslave their women and children, mistreatment of the missionaries and of settlers, and misconduct with women, including rape. One interesting charge was that López sold the office of lieutenant-captain general of Sandia to Juan Domínguez de Mendoza. The Domínguez de Mendoza family was a highly respected one in New Mexico. As mentioned above, López had removed Juan's brother, Tomé Domínguez de Mendoza, from the position of lieutenant governor and installed Juan in 1659. Tomé quickly became a bitter enemy of the governor, but Juan Domínguez de Mendoza seems to have remained loyal to López. This did not hurt his later chances for advancement, and as we shall see, Juan was an important figure during the last decades of the seventeenth century in New Mexico.

The charges against López de Mendizábal were sent on to the Audiencia in Mexico City sometime during December 1661 with Peñalosa's indictment on some thirty-three counts. Meanwhile, from December on, López had been held under house arrest in Santa Fe. On May 12, 1662, the Audiencia delivered its verdict, which did not go wholly against the ex-governor. His Indian wage policy was upheld, perhaps because it was engineered or at least agreed to by the viceroy in the first place. The court also held that the iniquity of the kachina dances needed more proof. The Audiencia did, however, generally defend the prerogatives of the missionaries in their treatment of Pueblo Indians, especially where contractual arrangements were involved. For example, the right of the clergy to free Indian labor was reaffirmed. López was given a rather severe sentence: he was not to hold public office for eight years, and was fined three thousand silver pesos. On posting bond to insure this payment, the governor was to be set free and allowed to return to Mexico City.

By the time this verdict had reached Santa Fe in August 1662, López's main problem was not with the civil but with the ecclesiastical authorities. In early 1661 the Audiencia of Mexico had restored ex-governor Juan Manso's property, and Manso returned to New Mexico in March 1662 acting as chief constable of the Inquisition. With him came orders for the arrest of López's four main lieutenants, and this was done over the next two months. Peñalosa, though the arrests were engineered by the Inquisition, promptly took over the personal possessions of Aguilar and Romero. Although Custodian Posada did not dispute this high-handed action, the brief honeymoon period between Peñalosa and the missionaries had already ended, and the Franciscans quietly began making a case to the Inquisition against the new governor.

The problem of the moment, though, was ex-governor López. The hearings dragged on through the summer of 1662, and in August, Peñalosa received the finding of the Audiencia against López. The same messenger brought orders from the Holy Office for the arrest of López and Doña Teresa and they were brought to Santo Domingo to be placed in separate cells under the charge of Fray Salvador Guerra, whose murderous proclivities at Hopi were by then forgotten and who was an official of the Inquisition. López de Mendizábal could never be accused of tact. While in the Santo Domingo prison, he remarked to Fray Salvador:

Father, is it possible that the Inquisitors should place in such a plight an illustrious man like myself, the representative of illustrious forbears and of a line which has produced bishops, governors, and Inquisitors, and other persons of great importance? Father, who do you think the Inquisitors are? Sons of cobblers and tavern keepers are made Inquisitors, merely because they prove that they are old Christians. But governors have to be gentlemen . . . like myself. By the Virgin Mary, I know I have not erred, either in malice or in ignorance, for I act wisely, being a man of learning and judicious in my actions.

As Scholes remarks, López was no doubt a man very troubled in mind. His remarks can hardly have endeared him to the Inquisitors. Nevertheless, they were insightful as an analysis of the Inquisition. The Tribunal was obsessed with the concept of "sangre limpio." Its members were required to have a genetic purity that could be found more easily in the common people than among the upper classes with their heritage of ethnic mixture with Moors and Jews. And the level of learning among Holy Office personnel may well have been lower than in the nobility.

While at Santo Domingo, López and Doña Teresa were confined separately, in what seemed to be a bit of gratuitous cruelty on the part of the Franciscans, and the governor was frantic with worry over his wife. It was decided by Posada that the important prisoners would be sent to Mexico City with the autumn supply train, which left in October with Ramírez still in charge. López was shackled in a cart, while Doña Teresa was assigned one of the ex-governor's carriages for her personal transport. As he was being chained, López called to Santo Domingo Indians standing nearby, "See my sons, how much the Fathers can do, since they hold me a prisoner." On Posada's protest that it was the Inquisition who held him prisoner, López replied, "Such a thing has never happened except to a God Man and now to me. I swear to Christ that I am a better Christian than all the men in the world. Look, gentlemen [to some Spaniards standing there], there is no longer God or a King, since such a thing could happen to a man like me."

As the caravan rolled southward, López became desperate to get at least a glimpse of his wife. In order to prevent this, Posada had heavy curtains placed at each end of the cart, blocking off the view except for a narrow space in front. Nevertheless, the ex-governor was able to get news of his wife and others of his party in the wagon train. After reaching Mexico, López also managed to get word to members of his own family and to receive replies from them.

It was April 10, 1663, when López and Doña Teresa were formally turned over to the Inquisitors and placed in separate cells at the secret Holy Office prison. Over the next year concurrent trials were held for the two. As per Inquisition custom, the two were allowed attorneys, and they presented vigorous defenses. López, however, was seriously ill. He had long suffered from gout and other physical infirmities, some probably dating from his stay in the tropical lowlands of Cartagena. By the beginning of 1664, the ex-governor's life was obviously in danger. In May of 1664 he petitioned the court to put him in the same cell as his wife. The two had been in contact through an assistant jailer, one Juan de Cárdenas, who had been a friend of Teresa's father in Cartagena. This liaison was eventually discovered, and Cárdenas removed from the scene. Although the Inquisitors refused to join the couple, they did allow López to keep the outer door of his cell open during the day to improve ventilation. His condition worsened, however, and López finally died on September 16, 1664, apparently without having seen his wife for the last two years of his life. He was buried in unconsecrated ground in a corral on the prison grounds.

Doña Teresa, meanwhile, was conducting a vigorous defense, accusing various of the colonists and missionaries of the province of lying about herself and her husband. She scornfully tore apart the hearsay evidence of servants and others about her alleged Judaizing, her reading of forbidden books (*Orlando Furioso!*) and her social and religious habits. Finally, in December 1664, after twenty months in prison, her trial was suspended and she was freed.

Teresa de Aguilera returned to live with family and friends in Mexico City. She made a number of attempts to get back some of the goods and property belonging to her and her husband that had been seized by the Inquisition. This economic aspect of the López family litigation stretched on for a quarter century, and the final disposition is not known. Even though the principal was now dead, the trial of López de Mendizábal continued. It was not until April 1671 that the Holy Office decided not to press further action against López. His bones were taken up, and the following month they were reburied in Mexico City, in consecrated earth under the chapel of the church of Santo Domingo.

What can be said of this prickly man, often proud to the point of delusion? Though very much the Spanish grandee, López was sometimes generous, and he seems to have felt a genuine responsibility for his Indian wards. He could sneer at the low-born mestizos in the colony, yet his most trusted and most loyal lieutenant was a mestizo. Probably the best-educated New Mexican of his time, traveled and urbane, López, when in a rage, was also a master of invective. His financial affairs quickly became tangled, and clearly he could be as venal as other governors (though perhaps less so than his predecessor, Manso, and his successor, Peñalosa). His love and worry for his wife can hardly be doubted, especially in the dark last months and years. Still, this did not keep López from a continuing series of sexual adventures, which he seemed to enjoy hugely. López knew Church doctrine, and there is every indication that he was a devout Christian, yet his contempt for the Franciscans grew with each passing month of his governorship. He was a person who took quick action and doggedly followed through, even when such actions were unnecessarily confrontational. López knew his own mind and acted on it with vigor.

Those are interesting *personal* characteristics, but did López de Mendizábal as governor also have an effect on the direction of New Mexico colonial policy? Here it can surely be said that he did have an effect, but that it was basically negative. He came to the governorship at a crucial turning point in the history of the colony. The first decades in which the missionaries believed it necessary to cautiously feel their way along, compromising with native religious and social customs, were now over. As of 1659, the Franciscans had educated two generations of Pueblo Indians in the ways of the Spanish and Christian worlds. The Crown policy of encouraging native rule by installing native cabildo-like officers among the Pueblos and making them responsible for a part of the local governance had now been in place for almost forty years. The missionaries had not been enthusiastic about this self-rule because it tended to dilute their own authority, but now they used the native-Spanish-oriented power structure to advance their own program of rapid ruthless religious acculturation.

When López arrived, the second, intolerant phase of the great struggle for the minds and souls of the Pueblo Indians was about to begin. Without meaning to, López hastened this new direction in Spanish-Indian policy. By attempting to lighten the harsh economic burden on the Indians, and especially by sponsoring their native dances, López earned the burning enmity of the friars. The Franciscans quickly demonstrated their power over both the office and person of the governor, and over all those unwise enough to try to advance his policies. Because of that, López's personality probably would have made very little difference in what happened. Had he been the soul of tact, and a paragon of rectitude in fiscal and sexual matters, he would still have been hated. And in trying too much, too fast, López succeeded in intensifying the very trends he sought to reverse. It is not at all clear to me to what extent López de Mendizábal saw a danger in the increasing attack on Pueblo Indian culture by the Franciscans. Perhaps he did not envision an actual rebellion on the horizon, but López was a highly trained administrator and must have sensed the tensions building. The static inbred colony of New Mexico desperately needed Pueblo military help against the steadily rising menace of Apaches, Navajos, and Utes. An attempt to lighten the economic burden of this indispensable Pueblo population would have made both good moral sense and good military sense. And to López, it must have seemed ludicrous to repress the popular dances at a time when the good will of the Pueblos was increasingly important.

But López failed, and in his failure caused an acceleration of the factors that he saw as dangerous or undesirable. The Franciscans had determined to make an example of the recalcitrant governor, and they did it all too well. None of López's successors were willing to reverse the mission Pueblo policy, increasingly dangerous as it must have seemed. New Mexico was soon spiraling downward to war.

CHAPTER ELEVEN

The Gathering Storm

In one way, the arrival of Diego Dionisio de Peñalosa as governor of New Mexico opened a new era of church-state relationships. The Franciscans had proved their power when it came to their control over, and relationship with, the native peoples. However, the basic economic structure of the province was not changed, and the need, or at least the temptation, for the governor and his party to turn a profit was still as much in evidence as ever.

Diego Dionisio de Peñalosa Briceño y Berdugo, the man who replaced López, was born in Lima, in the viceroyalty of Peru, sometime in 1621 or 1622, the son of Alonso de Peñalosa, member of a locally important Spanish Creole family. Diego held several offices in the viceroyalty until questions about his conduct of both public and private affairs forced him to flee Peru. Sometime in the early 1650s he made his way to Mexico and served in various military posts. Eventually appointed by Viceroy Fernández de la Cueva to the position of alcalde mayor of the districts of Xiquilpa and Chilchota (in western and northwestern Michoacán), Peñalosa remained in the west for three years. In 1660, the new viceroy, Juan de Leiva, Conde de Baños, made him governor of New Mexico. He left shortly for the province and arrived in Santa Fe in mid-August 1661. Peñalosa immediately and understandably became the rallying point for dissatisfied colonists and, of course, the missionaries. The residencia for ex-governor López was launched at once with Peñalosa and the new custodian, Father Alonso de Posada, working very closely together. Peñalosa's relationship with the Franciscans was very good, and he backed them totally in matters relating to Indian labor. He did fail to get López's new wage scale reversed, in spite of his charge in the residencia that it had beggared the province. Peñalosa accused López of introducing the doubled wage so that he would be the only person able to afford Pueblo Indian labor (for his own trade and manufacturing enterprises). This must have struck the Audiencia officials in Mexico City as a bit too Machiavellian to be believable; at any rate, they sustained the new wage rate.

But aside from that rebuff, the Franciscans were well treated. The new governor returned the friars' privilege of free labor from the Pueblos, and generally backed the missionaries in their rights to discipline individual Pueblo Indians. In these things he was following López's residencia ruling. On the other hand, the Audiencia members, sitting in Mexico City, were somewhat equivocal as to the missionaries' right or need to suppress the native kachina ceremonies. Given Peñalosa's firm backing for a policy of repression, however, this was somewhat of a moot point. For the rest of the pre-revolt period there was no serious government interference in the Franciscan war on native religion. The Pueblo religious leaders for the most part went underground, only to reappear with sudden and explosive violence in 1680.

Although perfectly willing to aid the missionaries when it came to dealing with the Indians, Peñalosa had other ideas in terms of finances. For one thing, he saw the possibilities of obtaining all, or at least a good part, of the various monies resulting from the widespread López operations. Peñalosa moved rapidly in that direction, aiding ex-governor Manso in his claims against López but holding on to considerable amounts of López's property, including some three thousand pesos in silver bullion, the proceeds of goods, mainly Apache captives, sold by López in Sonora. Some fifteen hundred pesos worth of skins and textile goods owned by the ex-governor were also impounded by Peñalosa with the excuse that such monies were intended to pay for the expenses of López's trial and imprisonment. A great deal of López's personal possessions, including livestock worth more than a thousand pesos, were seized under the pretext that they were needed to pay for a Mexico City lawsuit. It seems likely that Peñalosa intended to keep as large a percentage as possible of these funds.

The situation became more complicated with the order of arrest by the Inquisition of the López couple, brought on August 18, 1662, by the same messenger who brought the Audiencia sentence in the López residencia. Along with this order from the Holy Office came the instruction to embargo the López property. This sealed document passed through the governor's hands and was delivered to Custodian Posada on August 19.

It is clear that Peñalosa realized the importance of the document, and he may have also been informed of the contents by Father Nicolás de Freitas, who had befriended the governor. This embargo of the López estate caused Peñalosa to move quickly before the Inquisition action could be formally promulgated. On August 24 he tried to persuade Doña Teresa to arrange that all the López goods be turned over to him in order to forestall Father Posada and the Inquisition.

Teresa flatly refused, and Peñalosa, on the afternoon of August 26, forcibly removed López from his house arrest and confiscated many of his remaining personal belongings. That evening the papers from the Holy Office of the Inquisition were formally served.

As noted above, Peñalosa had already seized a considerable amount of ex-governor López's property, and in the days that followed, portions of this property were sold to meet his creditors, a great deal of it to Peñalosa's agents at knocked-down prices. Posada and Peñalosa were now at swords' points, and the next few months saw a great deal of legal skirmishing. In the early fall of 1663, Peñalosa actually arrested the custodian for infringing on the civil authority, and held him in Santa Fe at the Casa Real for nine days (October 1–9). Again, the Omnimoda of Adrian VI was invoked by Posada and denied by Peñalosa. It was the only recorded action of this kind, the legal incarceration of a Franciscan prelate by a governor in seventeenth-century New Mexico. Governor Peñalosa had intended to actually expel Posada but lost his nerve. Posada, once freed, began a collection of evidence and witnesses that eventually brought the Inquisition into the picture.

Nearing the end of his governorship, Peñalosa made certain attempts to protect himself from the legal investigation that would follow the end of his period as governor. He removed a number of documents that he considered dangerous from the provincial archives and took others to organize his defense against expected charges. Peñalosa attempted to counter the clerical accusation that he had appointed only personal friends to lucrative offices. In late 1663, but back-dated to May 1662, he made appointments of *escudero*, or temporary substitute holder of the encomiendas, vacated by the arrest of two adherents of ex-governor López, Diego Romero and Francisco Gómez Robledo. Cristóbal Durán y Chávez was issued an escudería to the former encomienda, and Juan Domínguez de Mendoza to the latter. Durán y Chávez had, in fact, been jailed by Peñalosa, and Juan Domínguez had been a follower of López de Mendizábal. Of course, Juan Domínguez's brother, Tomé, was faithful to the Church party, and the Domínguez de Mendoza family was influential in New Mexico.

In the early part of 1664, Peñalosa set out for Mexico City, leaving Tomé Domínguez de Mendoza as acting governor. On his way south, Peñalosa met the new governor, Juan Durán de Miranda, who reached New Mexico in the spring of 1664. Meanwhile, Posada continued to collect evidence against Peñalosa. Like Manso and López before him, Peñalosa was somewhat of a Don Juan. In Parral, on his way to New Mexico, Peñalosa had established a liaison with a young woman, María de Barrios, who later bore him a daughter. Peñalosa flaunted his mistress in Santa Fe, establishing her in the governor's palace, and had a number of affairs with other women as well. Peñalosa was also accused of mistreating the Indians and with making fun of religion and of the missionaries. These accusations were presented to the Inquisition; Peñalosa was arrested by the Holy Office on June 16, 1665, and his first hearings were held in late June of that year. The trial dragged on, as Inquisition trials were apt to do, although a part of this was due to an extended illness of the ex-governor.

Peñalosa fought back in the same manner as López, attacking the missionaries. According to Peñalosa, his main accuser, Posada, also had a black record. Peñalosa reported that when he was in Awatovi (probably in 1662), he had been given information by the convent guardián, Father Mompeán, (but also attested to by Friars Joseph de Espeleta, Fernando de Monroy, and Miguel de Guebara) about the scandalous activity of Posada when the latter man was the missionary in charge at Awatovi:

> being fearful that a leading Indian of the pueblo, whose name was Sixto, was making trouble with an Indian woman with whom Fray Alonzo [Posada] had improper relations—the woman's name, according to the deponent's memory being Isabel—Fray Alonzo ordered two *capitanes á guerra* to kill Sixto. When they had killed him, the friar feared that they would reveal the crime, and asked one Salazar, a *mestizo* who was *alcalde mayor* in the pueblo, to bring the two captains to swift and summary trial—in accordance with the practices of war—upon some pretext of disobedience, and hang them, which he did.

Peñalosa went on to say that on the order of Custodian Xeres, Posada was imprisoned at Santo Domingo, but that he had been released by order of then Governor Juan Manso. Peñalosa insisted that the incident was widely known in New Mexico. However, there seems to have been certain discrepancies in Peñalosa's account. It is not entirely clear just when or under what conditions Posada was in residence at Awatovi. At any rate the custodian in this time period—that is, during Manso's governorship, 1656–59—does not seem to have been a missionary named Xeres. Custodians include Antonio de Ibargaray, Antonio de Aranda, (vice-custodian) Juan Gonzalez, and Juan Ramírez. The latter was custodian in 1659; dates on the earlier men are not certain.

In any case, the defense was to no avail. In February of 1668, Peñalosa was sentenced to public penance and levied a fine of five hundred pesos. He was also forbidden to hold political office and was banished from New Spain and the West Indies, the banishment to take place within thirty days after sentencing. In point of fact, Peñalosa remained in New Spain until December 1668. Meanwhile, the Holy Office proceeded with liquidation of any assets of the former governor on which they could lay hands. Peñalosa was a ruined man, unable to stay in Mexico and a fugitive from justice in his native Peru. He now decided to cut his losses, desert Spain, and offer his services to Spain's enemies. He sailed to England to try to interest the English Crown in seizing Spanish colonies in America. Failing to arouse English enthusiasm, Peñalosa moved on to France, where he had a part in promotion of the 1685 La Salle expedition to the Gulf Coast. Peñalosa never returned to the New World, dying in France in 1687.

Peñalosa's nemesis, Father Alonso de Posada, also returned to Mexico, partly to present evidence against the former governor, and was replaced as custodian and as commissary of the Holy Office by Father Juan Paz. Meanwhile, in New Mexico a new governor, Juan Durán de Miranda, took office in the spring of 1664. Relatively little is known of this governor except that he quickly became embroiled in a quarrel with the Santa Fe cabildo and especially with Tomé Domínguez de Mendoza, its most powerful member. The cabildo, in its first major flexing of muscles since the disastrous aftermath to the Rosas affair, seems to have had Durán imprisoned for a time. The governor was removed from office by decision of the viceroy and replaced by Fernando de Villanueva in the summer of 1665. As far as is known, the missionaries were not involved, this being primarily a power struggle between the governor and the local citizenry. That a furious factional fight was going on, one that also involved the new governor, is indicated by the fact that Villanueva in 1665 accused both Durán de Miranda and former governor Juan Manso for suppressing documents, ones primarily concerning commercial transactions.

At about this time the Mexican office of the Inquisition came to the realization that Inquisitorial powers were being recklessly used in New Mexico to promote missionary aims. Father Juan de Paz, who had replaced Posada as commissary of the Holy Office, quickly had a clash with Cristóbal de Anaya Almazán. As we have seen, the latter man, because of his support for Governor López de Mendizábal, was jailed in Mexico City by the Tribunal of the Inquisition but returned to New Mexico relatively unscathed. He was favored by Governor Villanueva, who appointed him as alcalde provincial de la Santa Hermandad, a sort of rural police officer. Father Paz persuaded, or forced, the governor to cancel this appointment. It was arguably an illegal appointment, and Paz was probably within his rights. Cristóbal, by the way, was the husband of Leonor Domínguez de Mendoza, sister of Tomé and Juan. He continued a successful career in spite of the Franciscans until 1680 when—during the first days of the Pueblo Revolt—Cristóbal, his wife, and six of their children were killed at the family estancia near San Felipe Pueblo.

Another case at about the same time was brought against the popular Juan Domínguez de Mendoza, who in early 1666 was serving as lieutenant governor.

Returning from a raid on Apaches in the Acoma area, Juan Domínguez received a deputation of Acoma Indians who charged their missionary, Nicolás de Freitas, with abuse. Domínguez probably did no more than take evidence in the matter, but Freitas and his companion minister, Fray Diego de Santander, promptly accused him of meddling in the affairs of the Acoma mission. They also brought up the matter of his unrepentant support of the late López de Mendizábal. This case dragged on for some time. The Santa Fe cabildo was drawn into it and petitioned the bishop of Durango to appoint civil clergy who would have jurisdiction in cases that pitted the lay population against the missionaries. Cabildo members were especially exercised by the Franciscan involvement of the Holy Office for the most frivolous of reasons. The Franciscans managed to stave off this power-sharing move, but the Holy Office sharply ordered the Franciscans to drop both the Anaya and Domínguez cases and to be more cooperative with the civil authorities.

In the waning months of 1667, Father Juan de Paz was replaced as custodian by Friar Juan Talabán. He held on to the commissary position for another year, finally being replaced by Fray Juan Bernal, who served for the next decade. That the Inquisition authorities were not totally pleased with Paz can be seen in a letter to his successor, dated October 25, 1669. In this letter, referring to the Juan Domínguez affair, the Inquisitors said that

> because the impropriety and lack of civility with which his predecessor, Friar Juan de Paz, proceeded have been recognized, it has seemed wise to warn our commissary that in dealing with matters which may present themselves in future, he is to take due care not to use the jurisdiction of this Holy Office except in cases for which the instruction given to our commissaries make disposition. Enmities or lack of respect for the friars and the custodian shown by the royal justices or other private individuals are not to be introduced into the fuero of the Inquisition nor are our commissaries to meddle in matters so remote from our office, eager to make every affair and case an Inquisition matter, thus giving rise to much prejudice and hatred against this Tribunal.

Strong words these, but they came too late to save López and Peñalosa. Bernal continued to send reports of malfeasance to the Tribunal, but they mainly concerned such trivia as bad language.

Although the missionaries had some cause to resent Governor Villanueva, and the cabildo opposed Governor Durán de Miranda, there is evidence that, at least as far as the Pueblo Indians were concerned, church and state were now working closely together. Even though their Inquisition weapon had been weakened, the missionaries were now dominant in their control of the Pueblo population, and none of the post-López governors had any inclination to challenge their authority. The brush that Villanueva had with the Church was basically over secular matters, and the governor backed down in the clash over Anaya Almazán. Durán de Miranda seems to have been generally pro-Church, and in spite of clashes with his successor, Governor Villanueva, and with the settlers (or at least with the powerful Domínguez family), he was reappointed in the early 1670s following Juan de Medrano y Mesía, of whom relatively little is known. Medrano does seem to have fallen out with the Domínguez faction; at least, according to documents of a later (1685) trial of Juan Domínguez in El Paso, he actually sentenced Juan to death for his bad treatment of Apaches, though the sentence was commuted. Following Durán's second term was Juan Francisco de Treviño, whose use of force against the Pueblos most likely hastened the revolt, something that Treviño left his successor, Antonio de Otermín, to deal with.

The Medrano y Mesía governorship did coincide with a very grim period in the history of the province. Added to other difficulties—Pueblo unrest, pressure from Apachean groups, and continuing dissension within the colony, problems that were becoming more acute by the year—the period 1667–72 was one of terrible drought and famine conditions throughout New Mexico. In April 1669, the commissary, Juan Bernal, wrote that for the last three years there had been a dramatic shortage of food, with hundreds of Indians dying of hunger (450 at Humanas alone). Not only the Pueblos but the Spaniards were suffering, the latter living primarily on cowhides. Weakened resistance, caused by starvation, may have been a factor in the outbreak of disease, perhaps smallpox, that swept the area in 1671, greatly adding to the turmoil in the province.

The famine started with inadequate harvests in the year 1667, which hit the various pueblos very hard. Fortunately, the mission storehouses were stocked with ample supplies of corn, beans, and wheat, and the missionaries had large herds of sheep and cattle. By early 1668 they were beginning to dip into these supplies to alleviate the food shortages among certain of the Rio Grande pueblos. In subsequent years the famine spread to virtually all the pueblos. The Rio Grande itself seems to have been very low in water, perhaps virtually dry, and both Indians and Spaniards who depended on irrigation agriculture suffered greatly.

The production of food during those dry years was sporadic. Some pueblos and mission estancias apparently brought in crops, even if somewhat reduced ones, and the same thing was true of the colonists. For example, the wealthy Domínguez de Mendoza family was able to donate cattle for famine relief, as did the Valencia and García families. Other Spaniards were desperate for food. In order to supply the missions and the settlers at Santa Fe, the governors organized the *escolta*, or military escort, to the more exposed areas of the province. Some of

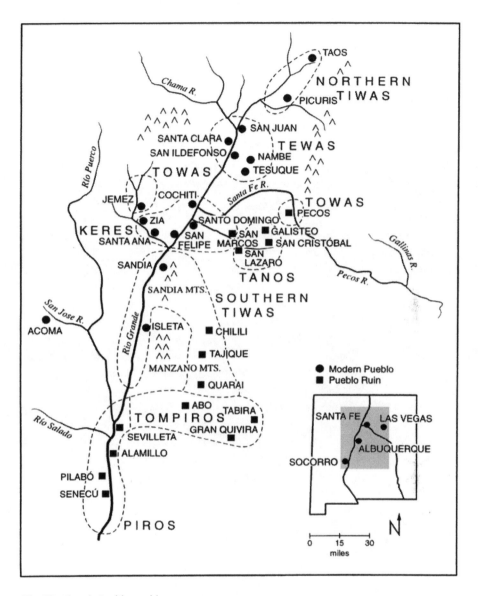

The Rio Grande Pueblo world.

these escorts were stationed for extended periods at threatened pueblos, and it became common for escorts to meet the supply trains coming north out of Mexico.

The drought and the increasing pressure of Apache warfare put great strain on the outlying portions of the province of New Mexico. In the Salinas area, the most affected pueblo was Humanas. This pueblo, built in the semiarid reaches of the southern Estancia Valley, depended on wells and catchments for its water supply. Because of the limited amount of available water, an early attempt by the Franciscans to missionize Humanas in the late 1620s was discontinued, the church there reverting to a visita. In 1659 a permanent mission, San Buenaventura, was established, although the missionaries were unable to organize the full mission estancia system due to the water shortage in the region. Fields to support the Humanas mission were set up at Quarai, and some of the herds were kept at Abó. With the coming of the drought, however, life at Humanas became unsupportable. As mentioned earlier, there seems to have been widespread starvation at the pueblo, and an Apache attack in September 1670 greatly added to the woes of Humanas. It was probably deserted sometime shortly after that date, the converts being moved to the more northern and eastern Salinas towns. But the Salinas and eastern Tiwa regions as a whole were becoming increasingly difficult to maintain, and one after another of the missions closed. According to Fray Francisco de Ayeta, writing from Mexico in 1679, Humanas with five hundred families, Abó with three hundred families, and Cuarac (Quarai) with two hundred families were all deserted in the period 1672–77. Fray Alonso Gil de Avila, forced to abandon Abó, moved to Senecú, where he was killed in an uprising. By 1677 the entire region had lost its missionaries, although apostate or non-Christian Indians may have remained at some or all the towns. An attempt was made in the late 1670s to reestablish a mission presence at Tajique and Quarai. Tajique was briefly reoccupied in 1678, but the effort collapsed two years later with the Pueblo Revolt.

Closing of missions was a complex matter since an attempt had to be made to shift converts to safer locations, nearer the heartland of Spanish control. Desertion of a pueblo had a ripple effect. By wiping out the income of its encomendero, it depressed the economy of the colony, and since the encomenderos functioned as military leaders, it decreased the ability of the Spanish government to maintain a properly working military force.

On the western fringe of the province, there were also desertions. Hawikuh in the Zuni area was under severe Apache pressure, and in 1672 a nomadic attack, probably combined with action by the anti-missionary party in the pueblo, caused the death of the Franciscan Fray Pedro de Avila y Ayala and the destruction of the church and convento. That effectively ended mission control of the western and southern Zuni towns (Hawikuh and Kechibawa), and probably they were deserted by the time of the Pueblo Revolt eight years later.

Mission church at Halona (Zuni Pueblo), late nineteenth century (courtesy of the Museum of New Mexico, neg. no. 14417)

In Hopi country, the famine hit very hard. The missionaries there slaughtered some 4,000 sheep and perhaps 250 cattle and oxen to keep the Indians from starvation. The Hopi, however, do not seem to have been quite as threatened by nomadic Indians, and missionary control of the Hopi towns appeared firm. At the time of the revolt, there were three missions, at Awatovi, Shongopavi, and Oraibi, with two additional visitas. In 1680, there do not seem to have been Spanish soldiers or civilians in the area, and the four priests in residence were killed. This is the one Pueblo area where the Spaniards were permanently swept away.

Apache and Navajo attacks through the last twenty years of Spanish rule in New Mexico increased steadily. Attempts were made to safeguard the Camino Real since Apache groups from the southeastern mountains of New Mexico had begun to regularly infringe, especially on the nearby Jornada del Muerto. For example, in June 1671, Gila and Siete Ríos Apaches attacked a small wagon train in the Jornada, one that was bringing the new governor, Juan Durán de Miranda, to Santa Fe. A rescue mission mounted by Governor Medrano was sent to escort Durán de Miranda to the capital. The Apaches struck again in July, a daylight raid on Senecú that netted a number of horses. It was becoming increasingly necessary in the decade of the 1670s to send escorts to El Paso to meet the mission supply trains.

The Gila Apaches lived in the high country west of and south of the Piro missions, while the Siete Ríos group probably held the east slopes of the Sacramento Mountains, from which stronghold they could raid westward through the Tularosa Basin into the Jornada del Muerto. These and other Apaches to the east of the province, including the troublesome Faraones of northeastern New Mexico, and the Navajos to the north and west, posed more and more of a threat as the century wore on. The dreams of the early missionaries, including Benavides, of massive missionization of the nomads had faded, and well before mid-century a pattern of trade and raid had become the norm. Trade was, and continued to be, important. It was based on earlier trade relationships between the Pueblos and the Querechos (Apaches) and Teya (Jumano). At Coronado's time the most important trading partners to the Pueblo were probably the Teya of the central and southern Llano Estacado. It seems likely that the Pueblo goods trickling into the Wichita and Pawnee country (Quivira and Harahey) in central Kansas went at least in some part through Teya middlemen. As we have seen, the Apaches, during the latter part of the sixteenth century and all of the seventeenth, gradually filtered down the line of the Pecos River, displacing Teya (by then called Jumano) in the western Llano Estacado and penetrating the mountainous area of southeastern New Mexico. Trade was now increasingly to Apaches as the Jumano were squeezed to the east and south. In addition to the earlier maize and beans, shell, pottery, and turquoise that went eastward, the Spaniards added certain European goods, including iron tools, manufactured beads, and holy metals and other religious paraphernalia. In spite of official disapproval, a certain number of guns and supplies of powder also trickled out onto the Plains. Horses were not traded (except perhaps clandestinely), but the Apaches found other ways to obtain this most desirable animal, primarily by raiding the missions and the Spanish settlements.

It is difficult to know which of the parties, settled people or nomads, were the main instigators of the raids, but the fact remains that both benefited greatly by raiding. For the Europeans and their Pueblo auxiliaries, raiding was a quick and easy way to obtain slaves, especially slave women and children who could be sold in Nueva Vizcaya or in central Mexico for a very good profit. The Apaches and Navajos also captured slaves as well as domestic cattle and sheep (in fact, the later large Navajo sheep herds probably had their inception during this period). But, increasingly, the great demand was for horses and horse gear. Sixteenth-century nomads had eaten such horses that fell into their hands. In the seventeenth century the full implications of using the horse as a riding animal, especially to the people on the western Plains, became more and more evident.

The possibilities of Apache as well as Utes, Jumanos, and other wandering tribes receiving horses increased when in 1621 the New Mexico encomenderos were authorized to use Pueblo Indians as herders and teamsters. This was most likely necessary, considering the small number of Spaniards in the province, but it quickly led to horses spreading to the nomadic Indians as apostates among the Pueblos slipped away to join the Apaches and other non-Puebloan tribes, taking with them horses and riding equipment. By mid-century, hostile Indians, especially Apaches, were beginning to be equipped with horses, and this inevitably led to even more effective raiding. By the 1680s the use of horses in warfare was reported for eastern Texas by La Salle. Not only were horses spreading into the southeastern Plains, but attacks on estancias in Nueva Vizcaya were on the increase.

Granted the availability of horses, it is still not entirely clear to what extent the Apaches and Navajos were mounted in the latter part of the seventeenth century. The expedition against the Navajos initiated by Roque Madrid in 1705 did not turn up very much in terms of Navajo horses or other livestock. However, the Navajo were fighting defensive battles from their fortified settlements on the high mesa tops, and cavalry maneuvers would not have been a factor in this kind of warfare.

But certainly to some degree the horse, and war tactics based on horses, had become available to the Apaches before the Pueblo Revolt. This probably did not mean the kind of fighting from horseback that was perfected by the Comanches in the eighteenth century, but rather the use of horses to drastically increase the range and the speed with which a given Apache group could operate. What seems to be a rather steady rise in Apache attacks in the last two decades before the revolt suggests that something had disturbed the balance of power between Spaniard and nomadic Indian. Several things may have been involved—disease and famine with its concomitant population decline among the Pueblos, and tensions within the Spanish community—but the greater flexibility brought by horse use among the Apaches was surely a factor.

The increasing tensions led to attempts to increase the firepower of the provincial armed forces. To counter Apachean and Ute marauders, Pueblo auxiliaries were used with increasing regularity. In 1675, Juan Domínguez de Mendoza was sent with fifty-four Spanish harquebusiers and 250 Indians, presumably Pueblo, with bows and arrows to attack the Faraón Apaches of northeastern/north-central New Mexico and the adjacent Texas Panhandle. Three years later, the same officer was dispatched with a detachment of 50 mounted Spanish soldiers and 400 Christian (Pueblo) auxiliaries to make war against the Navajos to the west of the Jemez Mountains. On the very eve of the Pueblo Revolt, Pueblo Indians were being used in considerable numbers in the Apache wars. The Spaniards do not seem to have realized that they were training Pueblo men for warfare, not only with Apaches but potentially with themselves.

Still, the need for more Spanish soldiers was obviously felt. Custodian Francisco de Ayeta, who in 1677 was also serving as procurator-general of the New Mexican province, managed to persuade the viceroy to send 50 soldiers, 47 of them convicts, to New Mexico, as well as 1,000 horses. Most of the soldiers actually arrived there, though seven managed to escape en route taking with them several saddles, three harquebuses, and 57 horses. Ayeta and the civil authorities in New Mexico quickly realized that these reinforcements were not sufficient, and Ayeta asked for an additional 50 soldiers. This second request was under advisement by the authorities in New Mexico when the Pueblo Indians revolted.

The latter part of the seventeenth century in New Mexico saw the waxing fortunes of one of the prominent families of the colony. A Mexico City merchant named Tomé Domínguez and his wife, Elena Ramírez de Mendoza, were living in Mexico City in the mid-1620s, the mother's family being from Vera Cruz. Their oldest son, Francisco, was born sometime around 1617, and a second boy, Tomé II or Tomé el Mozo, sometime around or after 1620. The most famous member of the family, Juan, came along probably in 1633 or 1634 (or possibly two or three years earlier since he stated his age differently in various documents). The family apparently moved to New Mexico in the train of Governor Pacheco in 1642 and established themselves in the area around Sandia.

Tomé senior was already an old man when he arrived in New Mexico, over eighty years old if later statements of his age are correct. Tomé died in 1656, at the age of ninety-six, and Elena (who must have been considerably younger than her husband) a few years later. There were also several daughters who married into leading New Mexico families. One of them, Francisca, was the wife of Antonio Márquez, presumably a descendent of the powerful Márquez family that had come with Oñate. The Márquez connection was interesting in that one of the female members of that family, Catalina, married Nicolás de Aguilar, and a cousin of Catalina's was the part-Indian Alonso Catití of Santo Domingo, who became famous as a native leader in the revolt period. Juan himself married Isabel Durán y Chávez from a prominent colonial family, and his two sons, Baltasar and Juan, were born around 1660 and 1665, respectively.

Francisco, the oldest of the Domínguez sons, was also the one least known. He was a captain in the Zia-Cochiti area who in spite of his blindness and age survived the Pueblo Revolt with his family. However, he apparently died in the El Paso area, probably by the autumn of 1681. Tomé Domínguez de Mendoza II lived on a prosperous estancia south of Isleta. He was serving as lieutenant governor and captain general when López de Mendizábal took office but was removed because of his loyalty to the missionary party, being replaced by his brother Juan. After López was toppled, Tomé el Mozo held a number of important posts in the government. He was influential in the attempt by the Santa Fe cabildo to get rid of Governor Miranda. In 1666, Tomé was made interim governor of the province during the absence of Governor Villanueva. Tomé and his family escaped southward when the Río Abajo area was deserted by the Spaniards and Piro Indians in 1680. For some reason, not totally clear, he refused to join the abortive Otermín expedition of 1681–82 to recover the Pueblo area, an expedition in which Tomé's younger brother Juan served as lieutenant general of cavalry and maestro de campo.

The most influential son of Tomé senior and Elena was Juan Domínguez de Mendoza. Beginning as a young man, Juan became an important military leader among the Spaniards. As a leading estanciero and encomendero, he commanded both Spanish and native Pueblo Indian forces in a number of raids against the Apaches to the east and south of the colony, and the Navajo to the west and north. He was certainly ambitious, so much so that in later years he produced a number of forged documents to impress the Crown and Council of the Indies. Nevertheless, it is clear that Juan was a premier war leader in colonial New Mexico, and one who had won the trust of a number of governors. His wealth and great variety of family connections apparently saved him in spite of an occasional tendency to back the wrong side, as in the López de Mendizábal case.

In 1684 Juan Domínguez de Mendoza was described in a cabildo certification as being

> tall . . . black haired, of goodly countenance, somewhat dark in complexion and going gray, has a good mustache, and appears to be about sixty years of age. He has three wounds, all on the left side. The first is in a shoulder blade which was broken at the Peñol de Acoma and as a result he has a withered shoulder. The second is in his left hand, the whole span of the said hand being cleft. The third is above the knee on the said left side, across the thigh, and he has another wound on the right side of his head. He received these in active wars and this cabildo knows it was in the royal service of His Majesty, serving him at his own cost and expense.

A list of offices that Juan Domínguez de Mendoza held is given in a Certification of Services, at El Paso, October 13, 1683, by former governor Antonio de Otermín. According to this list, Juan had been, among other things, alférez, captain, sargento mayor, maestro de campo, commander, lieutenant general, and alcalde ordinario of the Santa Fe cabildo. What Juan Domínguez de Mendoza desperately wanted, however, was the governorship of New Mexico, and this office continued to elude him. His dream was probably doomed from the beginning, for no New Mexican governor had ever been chosen from a provincial family. Nevertheless, with son Baltasar in tow, he was on his way to Spain in 1694, still seeking the governorship, when a shipwreck caused the loss of most of their goods. Juan may have been injured in the wreck, for he was hospitalized in Madrid and shortly died. A year later, Baltasar was still trying to get concessions for himself from the Council of the Indies, including the office of governor of New Mexico or that of alcalde mayor of Sonora. His petition does not seem to have been taken seriously, and Juan's family never returned to New Mexico. In fact, the only male Domínguez de Mendoza who went back to the province after the Pueblo Revolt was José, an illegitimate son of one of the Domínguez family, perhaps Tomé II. This individual was with Vargas's army in 1692 and, as will be related below, helped rescue his sister, who had been made captive at the beginning of the revolt.

CHAPTER TWELVE

Fateful Decisions

A Pueblo Indian in the year 1680, especially a religious conservative, must have looked back over the previous eight decades as the epitome
of disaster. When Oñate rode into Pueblo land with his little army and his crowd
of settlers and livestock, he found around fifty thousand Pueblo Indians. There is
no certainty about the number of actual *pueblos* that were inhabited, but there
could well have been as many or more as in Coronado's time, although the overall population had declined by perhaps ten thousand between 1540 and 1598.
And as the seventeenth century went by, Pueblo Indian population continued a
drastic downward spiral.

This downturn the Spaniards in 1680 could see only too well and documented in report after report. Father Ayeta, the Franciscan custodian, in 1679
estimated only seventeen thousand natives, six thousand of whom were able "to
use the bow and arrow"—in other words, warriors. He listed forty-six Indian
towns, but even as he wrote, several of these were in the process of dissolution. In
October of 1680 the Santa Fe cabildo, gathering at La Salineta north of modern
El Paso, estimated that the total number of Pueblo Indian rebels exceeded sixteen thousand (roughly the same number as Ayeta when the Piros and Southern
Tiwas are subtracted). A hundred years after the revolt, Fray Sylvestre Vélez de
Escalante made a series of extracts from the remaining seventeenth-century New
Mexico archives. In an April 1778 letter to his superior, Fray Juan Agustín de
Morfi, Escalante stated that of the forty-six pueblos, seven had been deserted a
few years prior to the Pueblo Revolt: Hawikuh in Zuni, Chililí, Tajique, Quarai
of the eastern Tiwa, and Abó, Humanas, and Tabirá of the Tompiro.

Whatever the case a few years earlier, in 1680 there seem to have been thirty-
two settled towns in the Northern and Southern Tiwa, Tewa, Towa (including
Pecos), and Keresan areas. The main Zuni town was at Halona, and as said earlier,
this may have been the only occupied pueblo. The Hopi, on the other hand, had

Mission ruins at Gran Quivira, July 1916 (photo by Jesse L. Nusbaum, courtesy of the Museum of New Mexico, neg. no. 12864)

five well-documented pueblos. There seem to have been four Piro towns still occupied, but one of them, Senecú, had been resettled in late 1677, following its dissolution after an Apache attack almost three years earlier. It is not certain how many of the Tompiro and east-slope Sandia and Manzano Tiwa towns remained, but the whole area was at the point of collapse, and the Tompiro probably had no viable towns at all. Some of the settlements listed, especially in the Towa and Tewa areas, were very small and perhaps seasonal. The decrease was drastic: for every three inhabitants in 1600 there was only one in 1680. There were a number of reasons for the shrinkage, the most important one surely being the recurring sweep of Spanish disease, especially the dreaded smallpox. The modern Taos Indians have a deity called *Kliwa*, "Refuse Wind," who brings smallpox and other epidemics. I rather suspect that this malevolent spirit, though it may be aboriginal, had taken a new direction and new meaning in the seventeenth century.

There have been revisionist arguments (see notes for this chapter) that Pueblo population losses over the seventeenth century have been overstated and that some of the Pueblos actually had more people in 1680 than at mid-century. This assumed post-mid-century population "rebound" is largely undocumented. There is a possibility that it may have been true in selected cases. For example,

Picurís might have had a population increase, although this has never been quantified except indirectly. During the historic Trampas period (1600–1696) at Picurís there was a considerable increase in the number of artifacts per cubic foot of trash. The excavators believe that during the seventeenth century, Spanish draft animals, the plow, and irrigation led to the opening of heavy wooded and grass-choked bottomlands impossible to cultivate with more primitive tools. In the relatively high (7,300 feet and higher) and cold Picurís area, there is only a scantily overgrown hillside terrain that was possible to cultivate with Pueblo tools. In this case, opening the bottoms may have dramatically increased the arable land and available food resources. Certainly, during the famine period, 1667–72, Picurís was able to trade ewes, wheat, and maize to the missionaries for distribution to harder-hit areas.

Pecos has also been claimed as having a population increase in the latter half of the seventeenth century. With Pecos, it largely depends on which population figures are chosen. The population at Pecos declined from around two thousand in the early seventeenth century to perhaps twelve hundred to thirteen hundred in López de Mendizábal's time. An estimate by Vetancurt for 1680 gives two thousand people, and Vargas in 1692 gave around fifteen hundred people, both sets of figures seeming to show a total or partial recovery. However, I suspect that Vetancurt's 1680 round figures means that he was borrowing from one or another earlier estimate. De Vargas's estimate for the year 1692 was a very rough one, and it flies in the face of Fray Diego de Zeinos's more detailed count of men, women, and children two years later, which gives a total figure of 738. Assuming that Zeinos made a reasonably correct count in 1694, it suggests that—if we believe Vargas's numbers—half the population of Pecos had fled, or died out, in the two years since the governor's reckoning. The far greater likelihood is that Vargas simply inflated the population.

In any event, a Pueblo Indian population "recovery" must have been very shallow because the overall figures quoted above seem to be reasonably accurate. If population in a few selected pueblos did rebound after mid-century, it may have been due to improved agricultural methods, increased resistance to disease during the latter part of the century, or perhaps a slight rise in the birth rate due to a more stable relationship between the Pueblos and their missionary and secular masters. Let me stress again, however, that the Franciscans, whose head counts were crucial in mission planning, indicated a general decline throughout this eighty-year period of Spanish rule. Franciscan estimates were more apt to err on the high side, and to assume that the friars were systematically under-counting their charges in the seventeenth century makes no sense at all.

The eight decades of Spanish rule in New Mexico produced changes that went far beyond the drastic loss in population. The Spaniards, early in their regime, had imposed a new political structure on the Pueblos, mimicking that of New World Spanish towns. This was curiously democratic: a series of cabildo officers in the pueblos, elected by and under at least a limited control of the actual members of a given Pueblo. The missionaries and the Spanish secular authorities were discouraged from interfering in this process, though in practice there was considerable meddling, especially by local Franciscans and by encomenderos. As we have seen, the missionaries had at least a quasi-legal right to demand personal service from the Indians and, except during the López period, had no great difficulty in extracting it. Encomenderos sometimes (perhaps often) utilized Indian labor for personal projects, including the building of private homes on Indian land. This practice was generally forbidden in the encomienda system but was allowed extralegally in New Mexico.

There is no way of knowing the exact relationship of the new cabildo-like offices to those of the old native hierarchy. Indeed, it probably differed from one part of the Pueblo world to the other. Near the center of Spanish secular power, in the upper Rio Grande Basin, it might be expected that the Spanish officials would have somewhat greater importance than in outlying areas. At distant Zuni for example, T. J. Ferguson believes that "the native religious government was not substantially changed or displaced." According to later Zuni tradition, there was a special officer who filled the lieutenant governor slot, the "Spanish Priest," or Tsibolo:wa Shiwani, "to institutionalize a Zuni priest who dealt exclusively with the Spanish people and culture." As far as I know this particular setup did not occur in the Rio Grande Valley.

Through the cabildo and the encomienda system, one office, that of *capitán de guerra* or war leader, among the Pueblos, became more and more important as the century wore on. Threats from marauding Apaches (and toward the end of the seventeenth century, Utes) meant that Spanish military leaders, encomenderos, and/or important estancia holders needed Pueblo Indian auxiliaries, under the command of their own war captains, to flesh out the limited Spanish parties. Such auxiliaries have been discussed in chapter 11, but this important information (crucial to understanding the Pueblo Revolt) is worth reiterating. Native American auxiliaries were chosen from one pueblo or several, fought with native weapons, usually the bow and arrow, and normally were not given horses or European weapons. But they learned the use of these weapons, as well as Spanish tactics and troop organization, and they gradually became aware of Spanish weaknesses as well as strengths. Under Spanish tutelage they slowly became a united fighting force. There is no great amount of information on the

Indian leadership, but I strongly suspect that the Spanish-Pueblo war captains were drawn primarily from chiefs of the pre-Hispanic war societies, thus tying these important officials back into the native ceremonial structure.

What the system meant to seventeenth-century New Mexican Pueblos was a fractured system of authority, with various elements pulling in different directions. The Indian cabildo officers had one set of priorities (no doubt differing from place to place and time to time), the missionaries had another, the encomenderos and estancieros a third, and the secular government a fourth. A fifth set of priorities, about which we have very little direct information and a very incomplete understanding, was that of the old native governmental and religious system. There is no doubt that the Pueblos maintained the moiety and clan headships, and that the religious officers were operating powerfully, if generally in secret. This secrecy became more and more necessary in the last twenty years of Spanish control. After López de Mendizábal, the Spaniards ruthlessly dealt with anything that smacked of "nativism" both in religion and socio-ceremonial organization. Members of the religious hierarchy were stigmatized as agents of Satan, and increasingly the secular authorities were called in to enforce the new order. Hangings, whippings, and general terror became the order of the day.

It seems very likely that the basic structure of Pueblo political and ceremonial life continued on as it had in the Oñate period. Pueblo society and religion in the later historic period seems, to some degree, a continuation of these seventeenth-century structures. As I pointed out in an earlier book on the eastern Pueblos, the native political, ceremonial, and religious life was totally intertwined so that religious versus secular had no meaning in the Pueblo world. Assuming a considerable continuity, the *underlying* politico-ceremonial power in the Pueblo world of 1680 would have been held by a handful of older members of the various groups, men who had been trained from childhood in the various esoteric uses of power and political control. Priests of the highest tier were not war leaders; in fact, they were forbidden to kill or even to observe death. Their function was the promotion of harmony, and the well ordering of relations between the Pueblos and the supernatural world. It was revered men like these, rather than the war leaders (the latter functioning to a greater or lesser degree within the Spanish system), who carried the torch of nativism and gave spiritual underpinnings to the resistance. They were the individuals whom the missionaries attempted to root out. And indeed, the Franciscans were correct in thinking that such persons were the major enemies of the mission system.

The Pueblo religious leaders were hardly creatures of the devil as missionary naivete would have it, but their continued influence made it increasingly difficult for the Christian agenda to be put in place. There is an irony in this, for had the Franciscans been able to compromise, they could have "Christianized" the native religion. Indeed, to some degree this eventually did happen, perhaps even beginning in the seventeenth century. Pueblo religion tends to be inclusive and is strongly goal oriented. The spread of the kachina cult in the fourteenth century is an example of a foreign religion being incorporated into the Pueblo system. Had the missionaries been willing to accommodate the native deities and rituals, they likely could have had a colorful and strongly nativistic Christianity with overt kachina overtones and a gradual evolution of native deities into Catholic saints. But Christian missionaries in the seventeenth century did not work that way. In fact, missionaries (at least the more fundamentalist ones that I have met in various parts of the world) often do not work that way at the end of the twentieth century. For the Franciscans, the result was not accommodation but war.

By the 1670s, the missionaries saw enemies everywhere. The discovery that the highly Hispanicized Esteban Clemente was a secret follower of the kachinas must have seemed to threaten the very foundations of the missionization program. Not only were the "old men," the secret religious leaders, hostile to the Spaniards, but now even the most sophisticated and educated of the natives could not be trusted. There was another source of danger, one that neither missionaries nor settlers seemed to take very seriously. Settled among the Pueblos were numbers of racially mixed individuals with varying genetic mixture of European, Indian, and black. Some of these people, as we have seen, were in the upper echelons of Spanish society, at least in the governmental-military society, and remained loyal to the Crown. Others, including some who were part Pueblo Indian, always had a foot in the other camp.

It seems likely that these mixed-blood individuals were well represented in the *native* military as Pueblo war captains. Such men would be at the heart of any revolt, as important in their way as the charismatic religious leaders, for they had the organizational skills to field native armies. We know that at least some of the Pueblo military leaders in the revolt were drawn from this class. Unlike the religious leaders, the war captains had considerable flexibility. Somewhat like the "free companies" of mercenaries in fourteenth-century Europe, they tended to be sensitive to how the political winds were blowing and able to change sides with relative ease. As discussed below, the Spaniards depended heavily on certain of these Pueblo leaders in the reconquest.

Although we know relatively little about the sociopolitical organization of the Pueblos on the eve of the revolt, there is some archaeological information, especially on material culture, from pre-revolt Pueblo sites. Information from such sites as Hawikuh in Zuni country; Awatovi in the Hopi area; Magdalena, San Pascual, and other pueblos in the Piro country; and Humanas, the modern Gran

Quivira, in the Salinas region is especially useful. These sites were deserted either a few years before the revolt (Gran Quivira and perhaps Hawikuh), during it (Piro towns), or a few years after it (Awatovi). The pueblo of Pecos has been extensively studied and gives considerable information, but Pecos continued to be occupied for a century and a half after the revolt. At the time it was excavated, archaeological techniques were not enough advanced to always differentiate between, say, Pecos in the latter part of the seventeenth century and the same pueblo in the first part of the eighteenth.

One rather curious thing about the archaeology of seventeenth-century sites is that they quite definitely do not show any massive acculturation in architecture and other aspects of material culture. For example, Hawikuh, which was a major mission station for several decades, had very little evidence of Spanish influence except for the mission itself, constructed of form-made adobe blocks. There may have been some increase in room size, but this does not clearly relate to the Spaniards. There was minor use of adobe bricks, and a few beams that seem to show metal axe work. After the rebels took over the Hawikuh convento in 1680, they subdivided the large Spanish rooms. They did include some corner fireplaces in the Spanish style, although they tore out the staircases. The greatest motivation for change seems to have been the introduction of livestock, especially sheep, and of certain European agricultural plants. When the Hawikuh people seized the convento, they turned the interior of the church, the cemetery area, and the patio of the convento into sheep corrals. Even before the revolt, several rooms in the pueblo were used to pen sheep, although at what time during the Spanish occupation (ca. A.D. 1630–80) is not clear. Other than this use, the people at Hawikuh do not seem to have picked up the Spanish habit of specialized rooms, kitchens, dining rooms, and the like. It has been suggested that Hawikuh and other Zuni towns adopted the Spanish-style outside "beehive" oven, or *horno*, during the seventeenth century because of the increasing popularity of wheat and the use of hornos for wheaten bread production. The use of wheat itself is somewhat problematical, however. Archaeologist David Snow believes that wheat may not have been a significant crop among the Pueblos until the late eighteenth century at the earliest.

Among the Hopi, adobe bricks were used to a minor degree in remodeling the mission churches, but the Indians' use of adobes was minimal. In the Piro country, adobe blocks were occasionally placed on masonry footings, but Spanish building techniques were not used extensively. The same was true in the Tompiro region and, generally speaking, in the more northern parts of the Rio Grande Basin. As far as the interior arrangement of houses was concerned, there was relatively little Hispanization. In places where large numbers of Spaniards had lived for a time—San Gabriel del Yungue, for example—there were minor

Horno, northern New Mexico, ca. 1935 (courtesy of the Museum of New Mexico, neg. no. 407)

modifications in rooms and the occasional fireplace, but, in general, Spanish influence in house form and function among the Pueblos was minimal.

Seventeenth-century colonial New Mexico, at the end of a long distribution line, was definitely not a waste economy. At the large site of Humanas in Tompiro country, two sherds of bottle glass and a reworked bottle base, plus a number of "trade" beads, represented the entire glass inventory for the site. Iron tools must have been in great demand by the Pueblos, as they were by Spanish colonists, but there is little evidence of iron. Of course, this is true to a large degree in the Spanish settlements. As pointed out in chapter 9, iron was a government monopoly and very hard to come by. Metal of any sort was in short supply and expensive, and tools were mended and recast whenever possible. All this is reflected in the archaeological data. At Humanas, only fifty-six pieces of metal (more than half were amorphous scraps of iron) were found in the excavations despite a Spanish presence of half a century. This small inventory of metal seems to have been typical of New Mexico seventeenth-century Pueblo sites generally. It is worth stressing again that the Pueblo Indians were in no way averse to iron. In spite of the nativistic aspects of the revolt, discussed below, there was a hard-headed realism that certain Spanish items needed to be preserved. For example, at Sandia in December 1681, a Spanish party led by Juan Domínguez de Mendoza found "a forge, with excellent bellows and the share (of a plow) for an anvil." This forging operation had been set up in the convent.

In the seventeenth century, the Pueblos not only made pottery for their own needs but they also quickly tapped the considerable market of Spanish colonists. To meet the needs of the Spanish settlers, Indian potters began to duplicate Spanish pottery forms. This was especially noticeable at Hopi, where, beginning about 1630, the great Sikyatki tradition began to give way to a coarser ware, San Bernardo Polychrome, with Spanish-derived forms such as soup plates, ring-based saucers, cups, candlesticks, and drain pipes. Spanish decorative elements also appear; floral motifs, rosettes, and eight-pointed stars. There was a reaction to this kind of pottery after the Pueblo Revolt, and Payupki Polychrome (1680–1780), though it melded Hopi and eastern Pueblo styles, made a conscious effort to eliminate Spanish elements both in vessel shape and in decoration. Meanwhile, the brilliant Jeddito potteries dwindled and disappeared, perhaps in part to a Spanish aversion to the coal firing that led to a switch in firing methods. Vetancurt, writing at the end of the century, indicated that the missionaries strongly disliked the foul-smelling sulfur-laden coal available in the area of the Hopi mesas. At some point, dung from domesticated animals became the favored firing method for Hopi pottery. This practice might have been introduced by the missionaries in the late seventeenth century or by eastern Pueblos moving into the Hopi area at the end of the seventeenth and beginning of the eighteenth century. In any case, its full development falls outside the period discussed in this book. The date of disappearance of Jeddito and Sikyatki wares at Hopi is uncertain. They appear as trade wares at Picurís and were being used as late as 1650. Such a date does not necessarily mean that Jeddito wares were being produced at Hopi as late as mid-century. The excellence and elegance of the pottery make it likely that it was treasured and preserved for decades by individual households at Picurís.

A vigorous series of handmade pottery traditions persisted among the Pueblos during the first century of Spanish rule. The competent but not particularly well made San Bernardo Polychrome doubtlessly served the Spanish market, but there is no particular indication that it was in any great demand in other pueblos. But as said above, Jeddito and Sikyatki wares, produced earlier in the century, continued to be prized in the eastern Pueblos.

At Zuni an important seventeenth-century pottery was Matsaki Polychrome, which actually originated sometime around or before A.D. 1500 and lasted until the Pueblo Revolt. A second ware, Matsaki Brown-on-buff, was similar to the polychrome but without red paint. These potteries were probably copied from Sikyatki Polychrome but had coarser, softer paste and inferior brush work in the exterior designs. As in mission-period Hopi pottery, there are Spanish as well as native vessel forms. Another ceramic ware was Hawikuh Glaze Polychrome, which extended roughly over the Spanish period at Zuni (1630–80). Hawikuh Polychrome is rather similar to Matsaki Polychrome except that the black or brown element in the pot has been replaced by glazing, perhaps influenced by the Rio Grande glaze tradition. After the Pueblo Revolt, Ashiwi Polychrome appeared. This pottery was a variant on Hawikuh Polychrome, but without the glazing. Vessel shapes in Ashiwi Polychrome seem to have been affected by Rio Grande forms, and it led directly to later Zuni historic pottery.

For mission-period Rio Grande, the late glazes continued to be popular through the seventeenth century, but there was considerable variation in pottery. In the glaze sequence there were a number of variants on Glazes E and F, including Puaray Glaze Polychrome (1600–1650) and its descendant, Kotyiti Glaze Polychrome (1650–1700 or later), in the central Rio Grande area. Glaze V is found in Pecos during the seventeenth century. Tewa Polychrome in the more northern reaches of the Rio Grande Basin originated in the early part of the century and continued on throughout the period. At Picurís a simple bichrome pottery, Trampas Black-on-white, was made throughout the seventeenth century and may have been involved in trade with the Spaniards. Picurís glazes, including Glazes E and F, persisted until at least the middle of the seventeenth century and perhaps until the temporary abandonment of Picurís Pueblo in 1696.

Although the colonists obtained large amounts of Pueblo pottery, the opposite was not true. Spanish ceramics are rarely found in Pueblo contexts. This is not too surprising considering that the Pueblos seemed to have ministered to the ceramic needs of the ordinary citizen, Pueblo Indian and Spaniard. Pottery shipped up the Camino Real tended to service the elite trade with majolica from central Mexico and even, occasionally, exotic East Asian porcelains and other ceramic items. Governors and their families might have need of majolica and Chinese wares, but no Indian of which we have any knowledge belonged to that elite consumer group. Possibly a man like literate, polylinguistic Esteban Clemente could have had a hankering for—and the wherewithal to purchase—Spanish luxury trade wares, but such a situation surely was exceptional. Also, Pueblo Indians normally cooked and served in the same vessel, the table settings of the Spaniards not being a culinary tradition of the Pueblos. But an acculturated Pueblo Indian, like Clemente, might have opted for the Spanish mode of serving and eating.

Another way in which the Spanish presence modified Indian life was in the introduction of new animals and plants. There were several European-derived animals. Sheep (and to a lesser degree, goats) spread rapidly from the herds brought by Oñate and later colonizing parties. They belonged mainly to the clergy, but as the century went on, more and more of the estancias were stocked with sheep. These animals fell into the hands of the Pueblos, by whom they were enthusiastically welcomed. The situation with cattle was similar. Herds grew more slowly, but certainly cattle were in sufficient numbers for a lively, if not entirely legal, trade to the Nueva Vizcaya mining settlements. Probably both sheep and cattle were trickling to the Apachean groups even before the Pueblo Revolt. Among the Navajo in the eighteenth century, sheep became a veritable way of life, shifting this Apachean group from an incipient agricultural society to a herding one.

The prestige domesticated animal in the seventeenth-century Southwest was the horse. Indians were discouraged from owning and using horses, though it seems unlikely that they were absolutely forbidden to ride. They did, after all, serve as herdsmen, and clearly the Pueblos did learn horsemanship during the course of the century. At the same time horses began to spread to the nomadic tribes both east and west (see chapter 11). By 1680 horses were much valued by the Pueblos, and large Spanish herds fell into their hands at the revolt. Both horses and guns were used enthusiastically by the Pueblos during the revolt, the horse utilized by Pueblo military leaders, obviously as a prestige item. Although there is no great amount of evidence for this, it seems very likely that the Pueblos were middlemen for the additional spread of horses to the nomads. Mules and burros were also used, probably extensively, by both Spaniards and Pueblos, though less is known about them.

Two other animals brought by the Spaniards into the Southwest were pigs and chickens. Evidence for pigs is not great, though we know that large herds of them were in northwest Mexico by the 1530s and were brought to the Southwest by Coronado either "on the hoof" or as salted meat (see chapter 3). One of the inventories of small merchants' stores in the Parral vicinity in 1641 listed two "hides" of lard totaling more than 122 pounds as well as 40 pounds of salt ham. Pig bones have also been found at Awatovi in seventeenth-century midden deposits. It was a regular practice for missionaries newly assigned to New Mexico to bring chickens with them north on the Camino Real. Even though it filled a niche similar to the domesticated turkey, the chicken caught on among the Pueblos. Pueblo gifts to Governor Treviño, discussed below, included both chickens and eggs.

The dog was, of course, an aboriginal domesticate, but the Spaniards introduced their own brand of dogs into the Southwest. Attack dogs called *galgos*, rather like a greyhound, came with Coronado. It also seems likely that Coronado brought herding dogs since he had fairly extensive herds of sheep and cattle on the trail. There is no direct evidence of this, but sheep dogs were routinely used in Spain during this period, and it is difficult to see how large flocks could be moved for hundreds of miles without them. It is very likely that some of these dogs interbred with the local animals as early as Coronado's time, though we have no information on this one way or the other. The early Spanish Southwest had at least two varieties of native dogs: one a small spaniel-like animal and the other, larger with longer hair, analogous to a collie. There also may have been a distribution to the more easterly pueblos of the sturdy Plains travois dog, noted by Coronado only a few days' travel from the Pueblo area.

Cats are another likely Spanish import in the seventeenth century, for these animals were valuable in protecting grain storage areas from mice and rats. They are not mentioned in any of the accounts I have seen, and there has not been enough archaeology on seventeenth-century sites, Spanish or Indian, to shed much light on this situation. However, domestic cat bones were found in a seventeenth-century context at Awatovi. Part of the head and neck of a more-or-less life-sized figurine of a cat with a mouse in its mouth was found, supposedly in the convento area at Pecos, in 1915. This ceramic figure is mold-made, suggesting an origin in Mexico, but the decorations are in bands of glaze paint, *somewhat* reminiscent of the Pueblos. Its date is unclear; it could be seventeenth (or conceivably even sixteenth) century, but it might also be later.

As discussed in previous chapters, a number of new plant foods were also introduced by the Spaniards. Certain ones, such as melons, probably predated Oñate and may have come in with Coronado, but most Spanish domesticates date from Oñate's time or later. They constituted a considerable range of plants, including various fruit trees. Peaches are especially well documented, having been found in seventeenth-century contexts at Awatovi, Abó, Puaray, Paa-ko, Picurís, and (probably seventeenth-century) at Pecos and in the Jemez area. Other fruit trees, especially plum, apricot, and cherry, also appear in the seventeenth century. To what extent they were utilized by the Indians (compared to the missionaries and settlers) is not known, but there certainly was some use. The chile pepper was brought to New Mexico, possibly even before Oñate, where it competed with and largely replaced the native wild chiles. Wheat was planted in the lower Chama area almost immediately by Oñate's settlers. The use of wheat spread to the Rio Grande Pueblos and, today, has religious implications. How much of this took place in the seventeenth century is unknown, for it did involve a new method of milling using hand-, water-, or animal-powered millstones. The Spaniards introduced *molinos* for grinding wheat, but to what extent they spread to the Pueblos in the first eight decades of Spanish rule is not securely known. In any case, a number of garden crops came to the Pueblos via the Spaniards, including cabbage, peas, turnips, onions, garlic, radishes, and cucumbers.

"Pecos cat" figurine (photo by Blair Clark, courtesy of the Museum of Indian Arts and Culture/Laboratory of Anthropology, 31505/11)

Along with the material culture, Pueblo Indians learned a number of craft specialties from their Spanish overlords. These included carpentry (see chapter 8 for the special carpentry skills at Pecos), iron and leather working, new techniques of weaving, and a new material, wool, from the domesticated sheep. As already discussed (and something that would be extremely important during the revolt), the Pueblo men learned new tactics and strategies in warfare, and, as auxiliary soldiers, had considerable practice in the chronic struggles with Apaches and Utes. In addition, large numbers of Pueblo men, women, and children learned to speak Spanish, and at least a few learned to read and write the language. All Pueblo people had been indoctrinated into Catholic Christianity. Some of them, indeed, became Christians in the Spanish sense of the word and, during the revolt, threw in with the Spaniards.

One interesting aspect of the Pueblo Revolt was the millenarian mystique that surrounded it. There can be no doubt that the uprising was the result of a long period of nativistic agitation, brought on by the attack on Pueblo religion and society (much the same thing) and by the suppression of revered religious leaders and the life-enhancing ceremonials. The terrible drought years of the late 1660s and early 1670s exacerbated the situation, as did the increasing attacks by nomadic Indians. Infectious disease, which swept over the Pueblo world and which Spanish medicine was totally incapable of alleviating, added to this crisis feeling. The Spaniards were, more and more, beginning to look like evil creatures, monsters out of Pueblo folklore. The nativistic aspect of the revolt was clear in the promises of the revolt leader, Popé, for a return to health and prosperity when the polluting influence (the Spaniards) had been removed from the scene.

There had been, from Oñate's time, rebellions against Spanish rule. As the seventeenth century wore on, these tended to be on the frontiers of the province; Zuni in 1632, Jemez in 1623, and again in the 1640s and 1650s. Taos rose in 1639, and the missions at Zuni and Taos were both abandoned for a time. A very ugly revolt at Jemez during the governorship of Fernando de Argüello Carvajál (1644–47) led to the hanging of twenty-nine Jemez Indians and the imprisonment of others. The Apaches (in this case probably Navajo) were also said to be involved. An uprising of the Keres, Jemez, and Tiwa Pueblos took place during the governorship of Hernando de Ugarte y la Concha (1649–53). As part of this revolt, a herd of mares was turned over to allied Apaches, though most of the horses seem to have been recovered. A revolt among the Piros occurred between 1665–68, and one in the Salinas region a short time later, both during the administration of Fernando de Villanueva. The Piros were in league with the Apaches, and six of them were hanged after their defeat. The Salinas revolt, of which we know all too little, was headed by the Hispanicizing Esteban Clemente, discussed in chapter 10, and there is reason to think that it had roots in a number of the pueblos.

Another Indian governor of all the pueblos of Las Salinas, named Don Esteban Clemente, whom the whole kingdom secretly obeyed, formed another conspiracy which was general throughout that kingdom, giving orders to the Christian Indians that all the horse droves of all the jurisdictions should be driven to the sierras in order to leave the Spaniards afoot; and that on the night of Holy Thursday . . . they must destroy the whole body of Christians, not leaving a single religious or Spaniard. This treason being discovered, they hanged the said Indian, Don Esteban, and quieted the rest, and when the property of the said Indian was sequestered there was found in his house a large number of idols.

These various revolts were generally in conjunction with Apaches, who seemed only too willing to back the Pueblos in such endeavors. In 1675 still another rebellion flared up, this one centered at San Ildefonso but containing members from various Tewa towns. This took the form of an attempt to bewitch Fray Andrés Durán, two other Spaniards, and an Indian interpreter, plus the murder of several other persons. Governor Juan de Treviño acted with considerable speed, arresting forty-seven individuals, probably leading religious figures, from the Tewa and nearby pueblos. Treviño ordered four of these *hechiceros,* or medicine men, to be executed, and they were arrested by Francisco Xavier and Diego López Sambrano. Three of these men were hanged, and the fourth committed suicide. That the rebellion had spread beyond the confines of Tewa country is indicated by the fact that one of the hangings took place in Keresan San Felipe and another in Towa-speaking Jemez. Some of the forty-three remaining conspirators were flogged. An armed delegation of some seventy men from the Tewas called on the governor in Santa Fe. Although they brought gifts, offering them in return for the prisoners, they left additional forces in the surrounding hills and clearly intended to force the issue. Treviño backed down, accepted the gifts (eggs, chickens, tobacco, beans, and small deerskins), and released his captives. Among the released prisoners was the religious leader Popé, an important figure in the Tewa pueblo of San Juan. Popé subsequently moved to Taos, always a hotbed of rebellion, to await more propitious times. They were quick in coming.

It has been suggested on the basis of the Treviño incident that Spanish repression had actually lessened by the 1670s, but this really does not seem to be the case. Rather, I think that a rising tide of Pueblo aggression coincided with increasing Spanish weakness, militarily and otherwise, explaining Treviño's loss of nerve in the affair of the Tewa religious leaders. It also explains the desperate efforts of Father Ayeta to get additional soldiers for the frontier, even if their ranks were largely filled with convicts. The official reason for these additional men was to fight the Apaches. Even granted that the Spaniards were in deep denial, it is impossible to believe that they did not have some clue that a rebellion was fast brewing among the Pueblos.

When did the Indians first get the idea of a pan-Pueblo coordinated movement against the Spaniards? It certainly predated the movements of the late 1670s. According to Pedro Naranjo, an aged Keres rebel leader captured at Isleta in December 1681, the first attempt to unite all the Pueblos was during the governorship of Ugarte y la Concha (1649–53). The center of this early unrest may have been the Keres pueblos or Jemez, and the insurrection failed because the Hopi refused to join. In the words of Naranjo, "The pact which they had been forming ceased for the time being, but they always kept in their hearts the desire to carry it out, so as to live as they are living to-day."

The revolt, carefully coordinated and planned as it was, must have been the work of numbers of people in most if not all the Pueblos. Two groups of individuals might be expected to lead such a movement. One of these was the native elders, the moiety and clan leaders in the various pueblos, the "old men" and hechiceros of the Spanish accounts. The other group of natural leaders, as mentioned above, must surely have been the military leaders, the "capitanes de guerra" who led native troops against the Apaches and who generally formed the backbone of Spanish-led expeditions against nomadic Indians.

Were there acculturated outsiders who served as leaders in the Pueblo Revolt? In a 1967 article, the Franciscan historian Fray Angelico Chavez suggested that one of the leaders of the revolt was the descendant of a black freedman who came to New Mexico in Oñate's time and who married a Mexican Indian woman. This man, Mateo, took the name Naranjo in New Mexico and established himself perhaps at Santa Clara Pueblo. Chavez believed that the Pedro Naranjo whose age in 1681 was given as eighty years, was a son of Mateo.

The previous year, during the first days of the rebellion, Governor Otermín had received information from captured Pueblo Indians that a major player was an "Indian lieutenant of Po he yemu [who was] very tall, black, and had very large yellow eyes, and everyone feared him greatly." Chavez believed that this representative of Pohé-yemo (or Poseyemu, as it is more normally written) was a member of the Naranjo family, perhaps a brother of Pedro who had thrown in his fortunes with the Indians. Chavez's hypothesis rested in part on a model of Pueblo life which saw the Indians as basically passive and peace loving, attracted to the Franciscan theology and too unsophisticated to mount a rebellion. The intelligent and urbane Naranjo, speaking both Spanish and several Pueblo languages, and knowledgeable in the uses of Christianity, Pueblo religion, and that of native central Mexico provided the intellectual underpinning for the rebellion. The description given of him was that of a black individual, taller than the average Pueblo Indian.

Why would Poseyemu have been the deity chosen to help trigger the rebellion? For one thing, this spirit was essentially pan-Pueblo under various names.

Poseyemu is the Tewa name; the god appears as *P'ashayañi* among the Keres, *Puspiyama* among the Southern Tiwa, *Poshaiyanki* at Zuni, etc. Poseyemu has culture hero aspects, and legends about him tell of a despised youth who was reviled but who taught the Pueblos many of the arts of life.

As part of Father Angelico's argument for a strong black/Mexican Indian influence on the Pueblo Rebellion, he cites a bit of information given by Pedro Naranjo to Otermín's soldiers in late 1681. Naranjo described three native deities who appeared to Popé in a kiva in the pueblo of Taos. These three, named Caudi or Caydi, Tilini, and Tleume, told Popé that they were returning "underground to the lake of Copala." They instructed Popé to tie knots in maguey fiber which would signify the days till the rebellion. The three spirits were observed to "emit fire from all the extremities of their bodies." Chavez pointed out that Copala was a bit of Spanish mythology rather than that of the Pueblo Indians, and he further thought that the three spirits were Aztec deities. As said above, he saw this bit of information as being part of the Naranjo intellectual contribution to the rebellion, with a brother of Pedro functioning as the powerful representative of Poseyemu himself. Chavez thought that this man might be Domingo Naranjo, presumably a younger brother of Pedro. If Chavez's theory is indeed correct, I wonder if it might not have been Lucas Naranjo of Santa Clara, who was killed during the revolt of 1696. This Lucas may have been Domingo's son and Pedro's nephew.

The mythical land of Copala is certainly Spanish in origin, and during the period of early Spanish exploration, its location moved from western Mexico to the North American West. Of course, it may well be that Caudi, Tilini, and Tleume were Aztec spirits, perhaps described to Pedro by his Mexican Indian mother. However, the anthropologist Alfonso Ortiz of San Juan Pueblo thought that the spirits might have been Pueblo, that Popé was in fact doing "a very wise and traditional Pueblo thing: invoking sacred culture heroes as his ultimate rationale for the rebellion he was planning." In fact, Ortiz identified Tilini as the revered Tewa culture hero Tinini Povi (Olivella Flower Shell Youth). Ortiz could not match the other two deities to Tewa supernatural figures and thought that they may have been Keresan or Tiwa. It seems to me that Tleume might conceivably have been a Spanish mishearing of the word *Thliwale*, the kachina-like mountain spirit of Isleta. It might even be a misrendering of the term *Tlatsina*, the Taos form of the word *kachina*.

Something else needs to be considered here. A black man with glowing or burning eyes is a fairly typical late medieval and renaissance European iconographic rendition of the devil. In the Spanish New World such a figure was described by Pérez de Ribas for the Sonoran area a half century before the Pueblo Revolt. Poseyemu therefore owes something to Spanish as well as to

Indian imagination. In addition, the three spirits who voided fire from their body extremities could well have been drawn from contemporary European illustrations of the Christian devil. What may be the case is that a merger of the two traditions took place, strained, of course, through the Spanish literary culture. This does not mean that Poseyemu's representative was *not* a member of the Naranjo family, only that mythologies from both culture worlds were involved in his description.

Who specifically made up the leadership of the Pueblo Revolt? There seems little doubt that Popé was a major figure, probably the single most important individual in the revolt. His inclusion in the group of "hechiceros" arrested by Treviño suggests that he was a member of the Pueblo priesthood. Alfonso Ortiz believed that Popé was a priest, perhaps the chief priest, of the summer moiety at San Juan and that his name could be roughly translated "ripe cultigen." The fact that he never appeared with a Spanish name suggests his deep commitment to the native religion and culture. As a religious leader, Popé would not have been involved in the taking of life, so his role in the Pueblo Revolt would have been one of overall strategy and of prayers and meditation instead of fighting. Curiously, Popé was supposed to have murdered (or ordered the killing of) his son-in-law, Nicolás Bua, Indian governor of San Juan, an individual who sympathized with the Spaniards and who might have prematurely revealed the rebellion (see also chapter 13). According to the Spaniards, Popé insisted on the death of backsliders among the Pueblos after the revolt succeeded. These things simply do not fit Popé's priestly role and remain somewhat of a mystery. The information about the murder of Nicolás Bua, however, came from one source, a Tesuque native named Juan who was in the process of apostatizing (or who perhaps had always been a missionary fifth-columnist). Juan may have been misinformed or lying, as indeed may have Pedro Naranjo, who talked of Popé ordering the execution of Indians who tried to remain Christian after the revolt. Still, the possibility remains that Popé decided to adopt a position in society paralleling that of the Spanish governor, giving up his priestly functions for this highly secular role.

What is perhaps more likely is that the revolt was more elaborately structured than the Spanish realized, with a council of religious leaders as well as a group of military leaders working together but with differing functions, something traditional in Pueblo society. Popé was a religious leader, but certain other headmen mentioned in the Spanish accounts—for example, Tacu of San Juan—cannot be identified as to function. Another set of rebel leaders included Pedro Naranjo of San Felipe, his relative (Pose-yemu's representative; perhaps Lucas Naranjo?), Catití of Santo Domingo, Luis Tupatú of Picurís, the Keresan chieftain Antonio Malacate, the Tano leaders Juan of Galisteo, Antonio Bolsas, and Cristóbal Yope,

Saca of Taos, and Luis Cuniju of Jemez—all of them pretty clearly war captains. Curiously, no specific individual from Pecos, whether religious or secular, was identified, though the religious leader Diego Umviro and a Captain Cachina were involved in the revolt of 1696. As of that time, Umviro was referred to as "the old cacique," and he might have been active in the 1680 uprising. Given the complex politics of the time and the tendency of a number of Pueblo leaders to switch from one side to the other, one wonders if Juan de Ye, who appears as a protege of Governor de Vargas in 1692, may not have been originally a Pecos war leader for the rebels. This was true of a number of other members of the rebellion; Bartolomé de Ojeda of Santa Ana, for example, changed sides after being wounded in Jironza's raid on Zia in 1689, not to mention Luis Tupatú, who had served as overall war leader. Unlike the Pueblo religious leaders, these were men who had important and positive values in Spanish eyes and who functioned easily in Spanish society. It seems unlikely that the religious leaders, once committed to the nativistic cause, had much tendency to change sides, and certainly little incentive to do so. The *capitanes de guerra* had something of value to bargain with, and a number of them found great personal profit in selling their military skills to the Spaniards, once they judged that victory against the resurgent Europeans was becoming increasingly chancy. Only in Hopi, which ruthlessly expunged its one Christianized pueblo, did the war leaders and the religious leaders manage to maintain a solid front against the Spaniards. And only the Hopi remained independent of Spanish rule.

CHAPTER THIRTEEN

The Currents of War

In this book I use the Spanish terminology, *revolt,* since it is firmly fixed in the literature of the period. From the viewpoint of the Pueblos, however, this was no revolt but rather a reaction to a foreign invader, admittedly one whose invasion had taken place several decades before. For example, the modern Hopi see 1680 as the beginning of a war of liberation, not a revolt against constituted authority.

Although the Pueblo Revolt broke out in August 1680, it clearly represented at least some months of planning. The Spaniards were obviously becoming worried about the situation in New Mexico, thus the frantic attempts of the custodian and Franciscan procurator-general, Fray Francisco de Ayeta, to obtain more soldiers for the province. As described earlier, Ayeta in 1678 managed to bring approximately fifty (mostly convict) soldiers to New Mexico with horses and equipment, and in 1679 negotiated for an additional fifty soldiers to form a presidio in Santa Fe. This request gradually made its way through the Mexico City bureaucracy, eventually being referred to the Crown. In June of 1680, King Carlos II ordered the viceroy to take such steps as necessary to defend New Mexico, but by the time his directive reached New Spain, the rebellion was already underway.

But Ayeta's concerns over the safety of the province probably related more to the increasing pressures of nomads, especially Apaches, on New Mexico. Until disaster actually engulfed them, the Spaniards did not fully comprehend the real threat to their rule in New Mexico. And it was not only the New Mexico Pueblos who were planning action against the Spaniards; a number of other groups along the northwest frontier of New Spain were restless and would rebel in the 1680s. That the Pueblos did have military clout was demonstrated when Governor Treviño was forced to release the religious leaders arrested in 1675. But the colonists apparently learned nothing from that incident.

It is hard to explain this bizarre denial of reality, which infected the whole power structure of the colony: missionaries, government officials, and military leaders. A large part of it must have been the Franciscans' belief in the efficacy of their missionization program. That a few evil old men—the hechiceros, or agents of the devil—were up to no good was well understood. Their influence clearly had led to the various outbreaks discussed in chapter 12. But the friars seemed to hold doggedly to the belief that the vast majority of the Pueblos were loyal Christians who would never desert their mentors in time of need. In individual cases, these gentle, passive souls might be led astray by diehard adherents of the old religion or by opportunistic Apaches. Their overall loyalty to Christianity, however, and to their missionary overlords could not be doubted. The Franciscans may have had a psychological need for such a belief, but why was it also accepted by the settlers and the governor? Various governors seem to have bought into this point of view, as did at least some of the major Spanish military leaders, especially Juan Domínguez de Mendoza. At least it led to relatively gentle treatment by the Spaniards of those Pueblo Indians captured after the revolt, and of Indian individuals and groups who deserted the rebel cause and fled to the Spaniards.

Treviño was replaced in 1677 by Antonio Otermín, who essentially followed the policy of his predecessors in office. That he and his military officers were woefully unprepared for the revolt seems clear enough, though Otermín acted with considerable skill and strategic good sense once the crisis arrived. But to what extent was Otermín himself responsible for the Pueblo Revolt? In his reports to the viceroy following the uprising, he takes no real responsibility for the events of August 1680, concentrating instead on his skill in holding the colonists together and on his successful retreat from Santa Fe. It was not until a century later that Fray Silvestre Vélez de Escalante, working in the archives in Santa Fe, focused attention on accusations by the Santa Fe cabildo, filed against Otermín following his replacement in the governorship by Domingo Jironza Pétriz de Cruzate. According to the cabildo report, Otermín had largely given up his authority over the province to his secretary, Maestro de Campo Francisco Xavier, described by the Pueblos as "a man of bad faith, avaricious, and crafty." According to the cabildo, the Pecos Indians had warned Maestro de Campo Francisco Gómez Robledo (who spoke some Towa) about the coming uprising. Otermín had two messengers of the uprising arrested at Tesuque but ordered them put into prison until Xavier could interrogate them. Later, at least according to Escalante, the rebels besieging Santa Fe offered to call off the rebellion if Francisco Xavier was handed over to them, for he was the man "whose fault it is that we have risen, and we will remain at peace as before."

Xavier, in 1680, was not only secretary of government and war and maestro de campo but also an alcalde ordinario. He had come to New Mexico at about the age of thirty as part of the military escort to López de Mendizábal. Xavier married Graciana Griego, daughter of Juan Griego II, the son of one of Oñate's original settlers, and he held a number of offices in New Mexico, serving, for example, under Governor Treviño as a leader in the actions against Popé and other traditionalist Pueblo leaders. The couple had six children, but Graciana appears to have died by 1680. In spite of the enmity of the Pueblos, Xavier and his children escaped to El Paso. Xavier went with Otermín in the 1681 attempt to reconquer the Pueblos but left for New Spain the following year. None of the other family members, except for a young granddaughter, ever went back to New Mexico. Two other Spanish leaders, Sargentos Mayores Luis de Quintana and Diego López Sambrano, were also implicated by Pueblo leaders as brutal in their treatment of the Indians. Neither man was allowed by Vargas to return to New Mexico during the reconquest in the 1690s. There seems to be reasonably good evidence that Xavier at any rate was often barbarous in his activities against the Pueblos.

As mentioned above, the Pueblo leaders had been planning revolt for quite some time. It was necessary to contact and enlist the aid of the religious leaders and, more important, the military leaders of the various pueblos. Because the Pueblo area extended for several hundred miles both east and west and north and south, and since the Indians primarily had to make contact by foot, the conspiracy must by necessity have taken time. It also had to be in the greatest secrecy, and this could not have been easy. In the most important pueblos there were mission stations, and numbers of Indians whose adherence to the new religion, Christianity, would have made them suspect. Even some of the leaders who would otherwise have been expected to support the revolt might be suborned by the missionaries or by their supporters. This does seem to have happened with one individual, Nicolás Bua, at some point before the rebellion began.

In the late summer of 1680 the various strands of the coming rebellion were brought together. All of the pueblos with the exception of the Piro were involved in the conspiracy, and contact was made with various Apache and Navajo groups as well. When the fighting began, it is not entirely clear to what extent the Apachean groups were involved, but they do seem to have joined the Pueblos at Taos. The Mansos were also alerted but delayed their involvement in the war for several years, failing to immediately attack the formidable Spanish force once it made good its escape to the El Paso area.

The method of signaling the final attack was later described to the Spaniards. Messengers carried knotted cords, a knot being unraveled each day until the chosen day. Whether this was true in all Pueblos or only in some is unknown, but a knotted cord, somehow signaling the day of the revolt, does seem to have been involved. What kind of cord is not certain: both a leather strap and a plant-fiber cord are mentioned, and perhaps different kinds of cord were used by different messengers.

In fact, Otermín had considerable warning of the revolt, which may originally have been planned for the morning of August 13. As said above, friendly Pecos Indians had warned Maestro de Campo Francisco Gómez Robledo (date not given), and on August 9, Otermín received letters from Taos informing him that a rebellion was to be launched on August 13. That same day, August 9, Otermín was told by certain of the Tano chieftains that two young runners, Catua and Omatua, had given them the same information. Catua and Omatua were arrested at Tesuque on August 9 and were found to have cords with two knots, signifying a revolt date of August 11. For some reason, the date seems to have been shifted at some point from August 13 to August 11. The capture of the two messengers triggered still another change of plan, and the leaders, operating probably in various pueblos, began to notify the Indians to rise at dawn on Saturday, August 10. Isolated outbreaks may have begun at Tesuque as early as the night of August 9. The outbreak flared as news spread up and down the Rio Grande, and up its tributaries, the Jemez and Puerco/San José Rivers. Jemez and Acoma were in revolt on August 10, but the time schedule in the westernmost pueblos of Zuni and Hopi is less clear. The rebellion in those outlying areas perhaps did not break out until August 11 or 12.

In retrospect, it seems fairly clear that the solid core and center of the rebellion consisted of the Northern Tiwa, Tewa, Towa, and the eastern Keresan Pueblos. Acoma, Hopi, and Zuni Indians also joined the revolt, although one Hopi town, Awatovi, had a strong Christian faction. On the other hand, there seems to have been dissension from the very beginning in the Tano pueblos. We know less about Pecos—not even the name(s) of the revolt leaders have survived—but the subsequent history of the pueblo during the 1690s suggests that there was a strong pro-Spanish party there also. The Southern Tiwa were divided, with Puaray, Alameda, and Sandia taking part in the uprising, but Isleta, the southernmost Tiwa town, remaining in the Spanish camp. This may have been because of the large Spanish military presence there, Isleta being used as a headquarters by Alonso García, lieutenant governor and commander of the Río Abajo section of the province of New Mexico. Why the Piro pueblos were not invited to join the rebellion is not clear, but the Piro area had been under siege by Apachean groups for a decade or more. The Tompiro and the Tiwa towns bordering on the Estancia Valley were already deserted, or virtually so, at the time the revolt occurred.

Even in the heartland there seem to have been pockets of disagreement with the Indian cause, not too surprising when the eight decades of intense missionization are taken into account. It was this ambivalence on the part of some of the Pueblos that likely forced Popé and/or the other native leaders to take strong, even savage, action against wavering or disloyal Indians.

In the first days of revolt the Indians killed a large number of Spanish men, women, and children both in the pueblos and at nearby estancias. Some 70 people were put to death in the Taos area, and more than 30 in the Tewa region. The Indians of Santo Domingo murdered all three of the friars at the Franciscan headquarters. Then, on an estancia between the two pueblos, Santo Domingo and San Felipe war parties slaughtered the sargento mayor, López de Mendizábal's old supporter Cristóbal de Anaya, his wife, several of his children, and others—a total of 12. A nearby estancia belonging to Agustín de Carvajál was raided, and Carvajál, his wife, his daughter, and another woman were killed. In the Galisteo region, four friars were killed, one being the guardián at Pecos, Fray Fernando de Velasco, who was visiting the Tano country.

In the entire province, some 380 Spaniards and 21 Franciscans were murdered. The bodies were usually stripped and sometimes mutilated. Incidents of torture of priests at Jemez, Zuni, and Acoma, and of a Christian mestiza woman at the latter pueblo were later reported, but to what extent the civilian population was subjected to torture or rape is not known. There were some captives. At Galisteo, for example, at least four women were taken captive. They included the daughter of Maestro de Campo Pedro de Leiva and three other women, probably the daughters of Joseph Leiva, who had an estancia in the Tano region. This particular group was killed later, apparently in revenge for the heavy Tano losses at the siege of Santa Fe. The Tiwa Indian Lucas, probably in late 1684, reported Spanish women and children living and being well treated in San Juan Pueblo.

Though we likely do not have a complete count, a few Spaniards, originally reported killed, clearly survived the revolt period. Vargas in 1692 lists a number of former captives who were being sent to El Paso to be cared for by relatives. One was Petrona Nieto, née Pacheco, with five daughters and two sons, three of the daughters having been born when she was in captivity at San Juan. Jose Domínguez Mendoza rescued his sister, Juana Domínguez, and her four daughters and a son. Also released were the wife and grown daughter of Pedro Márquez, and two daughters of José Nevares. Juana de Apodaca and a daughter and son, both probably born in captivity, were also rescued. Juana later married a black drummer and herald named Sebastián Rodríguez. In addition to these Spanish and mestizo captives, a mulatto woman named María was freed along with her three daughters and one son. A number of Pueblo Indians were included in the list, as well as a Jumano woman who had been held captive at Pecos. Two of the Pueblo Indians, a brother and sister, probably Tewa, named Tomé and Antonia, were taken in by Sergeant Juan Ruiz de Cáceres, who claimed them as cousins.

Father Vélez de Escalante mentions two other Spanish women in addition to Petrona Nieto who were found by Vargas at San Juan. Both were unmarried, but one had a small daughter. It is unclear whether these are represented in the Vargas list, though they might be the daughters of José Nevares, mentioned above (if so, the child was omitted from the tally). At Pecos, Vargas found Francisco, a son of the murdered Cristóbal Anaya Almazán.

Whatever his failings in the days preceding the revolt, Governor Otermín took bold and effective action following the outbreak of hostilities. Realizing on August 12 the deadly seriousness of the revolt, Otermín began to plan his defenses. On August 13, Otermín called on survivors to cluster in Santa Fe, and that same day the surviving settlers at Santa Cruz de la Cañada, the Spanish settlement near Santa Clara in Tewa country, made their way to the capital. The Spaniards at Los Cerrillos in the Tano area had arrived the previous day. As settlers trickled in, Otermín began to plan the defenses of the villa. He was faced with the problem that not only did the Indians outnumber him, but they had supplied themselves with a variety of Spanish weapons.

The head count at Santa Fe quickly rose to more than a thousand persons, and Otermín made a distribution of animals, food, and clothing "to the Spanish soldiers, to all their families and servants, to the Mexican natives, and to all classes of people."

On Tuesday, August 15, the siege of Santa Fe began. The Tano Indians were under the command of Juan, who rode a horse and was armed with a harquebus, sword, and dagger. A parley with Otermín proved fruitless, and the Indians burned the Analco area and did considerable damage to the San Miguel chapel. A violent battle broke out along the southern outskirts of the city, the Indians using captured Spanish weapons. The Spanish lines held in that area, but by then the Tewa, Northern Tiwa, and Taos Indians attacked, perhaps from the east and north of the city, although that is not entirely clear. They utilized their captured harquebuses to keep up a fire on the Casa Real and burned houses on the outskirts of the villa as well as the church. Presumably this church was St. Francis, which means that probing parties of the Indians were quite near the center of the town. Their most important action, however, was to cut off the ditches that supplied Santa Fe with water. There were some two thousand Indians surrounding Santa Fe, and the Spanish position seemed desperate. Otermín decided on strong countermeasures and on August 20 delivered a successful surprise attack, killing some three hundred of the overconfident Pueblo warriors, "dislodging them from the streets and houses where they were massacred," and capturing forty-seven. Eight harquebuses, various other equipment, and some eighty stock animals were captured. The prisoners were interrogated, then executed. They told of long planning for the revolt and a mandate of an Indian living to the north (presumably Popé), the lieutenant of Poseyemu. According to Otermín's information, the Indians planned to kill all the male Spaniards, even male children at the breast. Nonetheless, a great many of the women and female children were also killed.

Even though they had won a considerable victory, the Spanish situation could not continue for very long. Only five people had been killed—Maestro de Campo Andrés Gómez and four ordinary soldiers—but a number of Spaniards had suffered wounds, both from bow-and-arrow and harquebus fire. The governor himself was wounded twice, in the face and by a harquebus ball to the chest. But the most important thing was the severing of the Spaniards' water supply, which made the situation intolerable for both humans and animals. Something had to be done, and done while the Indians were still reeling from their defeat.

After consulting with his various officers and such Franciscans as were in Santa Fe, Otermín decided to abandon the town and march southward to link up with Lieutenant Governor Alonso García at Isleta in Río Abajo. The secretary of government and war, Francisco Xavier, was ordered to distribute all the goods to the various settlers. It was a mournful retreat through desolate country, a march punctuated by exchanges of harquebus fire. The party reached the Galisteo region on August 23, and Santo Domingo the following day. Here, although all the Franciscans were dead, the church had not been looted, and the various church vessels were intact.

Meanwhile, apparently on August 11, having just heard of the revolt, the commander of the Río Abajo country, Lieutenant Governor Alonso García, with a small body of men attempted to rescue Spaniards in the Keres and Towa areas. He discovered the great devastation left by the rebels and received a report that Governor Otermín and all of the settlers had already been killed. García then retreated to the south, evacuating Isleta, and continued till he reached the Socorro (Pilabó) area. Originally, he seems to have planned to fortify Socorro, but evidences of hostility on the part of local Piro Indians and the continuing uncertainty as to the situation in the north led García to retreat further to Fray Cristóbal, a place some forty miles south of Socorro. On or around September 4, García received word from the commissary, Father Ayeta, that Maestro de Campo Pedro de Leiva in El Paso was marching to his assistance. Ayeta himself was slowly wending his way northward with the mission supply train. At the same time, García heard that Otermín was alive and on his way to the south. He quickly retraced his steps, joining Otermín at El Alamillo, a pueblo probably located on the east side of the Rio Grande just south of the Alamillo Arroyo, about halfway between Sevilleta Pueblo and Socorro. The site has never been found and probably was washed away by the Rio Grande in flood.

When the two met, an angry Otermín ordered the arrest of his lieutenant governor for having abandoned the province. García made a spirited defense and was eventually exonerated. For the moment the two forces were merged and continued the march south, meeting Leiva with his little army of forty men a few miles south of Alamillo. The augmented force arrived in Socorro the following day, September 7, and after a short wait continued on downriver. Meanwhile, Father Francisco de Ayeta was in the El Paso area with twenty-four wagons, loaded with supplies from Mexico. With Pedro de Leiva, Father Francisco pushed on northward to bring supplies to Otermín's group. The two parties met at a place called La Salineta, ten miles or so north of the Guadalupe mission near El Paso. Over the next several months Otermín purchased grain, cattle, and other supplies from the Casas Grandes and Tarahumar areas and "other suitable places." Also, at La Salineta the governor began a head count of survivors, the basis of modern calculations of the New Mexico population. Of the estimated 1,000 people with Otermín and the 1,500 with García, not all were counted at La Salineta, the total head count there being 1,946, which included the 400 or so servants listed in the muster rolls, though the 317 Piro Indians from Senecú, Socorro, Alamillo, and Sevilleta seem to have been counted separately. Only 155 persons of this total were capable of bearing arms, and there were 471 horses and mules. Leiva was listed in this count, but it is not clear if his relief force, 78 men armed with harquebuses, was included. In any case, there seem to have been several hundred individuals who drifted on into Nueva Vizcaya before they could be tallied. A number went to the Casas Grandes area, and others apparently to Parral. Since the Analco Mexican Indians were curiously under-represented in the head count, possibly they were among those individuals moving on to the south.

Otermín now determined to establish his settlers at El Paso, settling them on the southwest side of the river in the area of modern-day Ciudad Juárez and near the mission settlement of Guadalupe. His immediate plans were for a reconquest, but this took about a year to organize. Finally, on November 5, 1681, the governor launched his reconquest attempt. He had 146 soldiers and some 112 allies— Manso, Piro, Tiwa, and Jemez—plus 28 servants, some of them armed. Several of the Spanish captains went on the expedition, the most important being Juan Domínguez de Mendoza. Some officers were absent, a notable one being Tomé Domínguez de Mendoza, brother of Juan, who begged off, arguing that he had both gout and stomach trouble. In fact, there was considerable resistance on the part of the settlers to join the expedition, and, according to Father Ayeta, the majority of those who did join were discontented. Also, the military equipment was somewhat deficient, a number of the soldiers possessing little or no armor. The Spaniards had great hope, however, that Pueblos and Apaches would be at each other's throats, and that the Pueblo Indians, after tasting freedom, would crave to return to the bosom of the Church. They also thought that if they treated captive Indians well, others would flock to them to be pardoned. None of these expectations proved valid.

Except to bring information about the Indians in revolt, the expedition accomplished very little and was badly handled both by the Spanish forces and by the Indians resisters. The Spaniards overran Isleta, capturing more than 500 people who were then absolved by Father Ayeta. Isleta became a temporary headquarters while Juan Domínguez de Mendoza, with an advance party of 60 men, probed northward in mid-December, eventually reaching as far north as the Keresan pueblo of Cochiti. For the most part, the Indians fled before the advancing Spanish army, leaving only old and sick people. Even though they should have been able to anticipate the Spanish march northward, they seemed to have been largely caught by surprise. Significant amounts of foodstuffs fell into Otermín's hand, and even loaded carts. The Indians did manage to remove their herds of cattle, sheep, and horses for the most part.

At Cochiti there was a parley in which Juan Domínguez de Mendoza and Captain Pedro Márquez attempted to persuade Alonso Catití, Márquez's half-brother and a rebel war leader, to surrender. There was another parley with El Cupiste of Santa Ana, an important Pueblo war leader. The Pueblos held out hope of peace, and Domínguez actually felt that an overall peace treaty, one which would include the Hopi and Zuni, was doable. The Pueblo leaders, however, were stalling, partly while waiting for reinforcements and partly in the hope of trading for supplies, especially powder for their harquebuses. A Spaniard, the mestizo named Domingo Luján, did supply some powder to his brother, one of the Pueblo leaders, El Ollita (Francisco) of San Ildefonso. Luján was interrogated, but when it was discovered that he had only given El Ollita one charge from his own pouch, he was admonished and set free. On December 11 Otermín marched north, establishing a field camp in the vicinity of Puaray. Six days later, Domínguez de Mendoza, hearing of a plot to attack his inadequate force, retreated, reaching Otermín's camp the next day. In the following week, the governor heard that Luis Tupatú of Picurís, the overall commander of the central Rio Grande Pueblo forces, was threatening Isleta with a mounted corps of some fifty men. Otermín then decided to withdraw to El Paso. His men were concerned with the families left behind, and the expedition's horses were worn out.

Otermín reached Isleta on December 30, collecting his small garrison there, and the Spaniards vented their frustrations by smashing masks and other ceremonial objects. On January 1, 1682, the Spaniards burned their headquarters at Isleta and, with 385 Isletans in tow, began a removal to El Paso. They left behind eight pueblos in flames, and they had sacked three others. Of the two prominent missionaries with the expedition, Father Francisco de Ayeta agreed with Otermín that the expedition should be aborted. As the Franciscan procurator-general, he began long-term planning to support the El Paso colony. On the other hand, his secretary, Fray Nicolás López, blamed the governor for burning pueblos and believed that Otermín's inclusion of the hated Francisco Xavier in the expedition nullified his chances of bringing about an accommodation with the Pueblos.

Otermín's problem was that he did not have sufficient forces to extend beyond the Rio Grande Valley unless he could be reasonably certain that he had secured the Pueblo heartland. Although the Pueblo armies were unwilling to fight him in the open field, they were becoming increasingly bold, and the governor was unsure he could win a pitched battle. The situation at El Paso was uncertain, and Otermín really had little choice but to return to the main Spanish headquarters on the northern fringe of Nueva Vizcaya.

Otermín and the Santa Fe cabildo made a temporary headquarters at a place called San Lorenzo de la Toma about thirty miles downriver from El Paso. Near San Lorenzo were founded the settlements of Senecú, primarily for Piro and Tompiro, a second town of Corpus Christi del Isleta (del Sur) for Isleta and other Tiwa refugees, and a third one, Socorro, for Piro and a scattering of Tano and Jemez Indians. This latter town was unstable, and in 1683 the transplanted Pueblos attempted to kill their priest, Antonio Guerra, and the family or two of Spaniards who were in the vicinity. Blocked from doing this by nearby Suma Indians (the mission of San Diego de los Sumas was in the vicinity), the instigators fled to the rebel Pueblos with a large herd of stolen horses. In the fall of 1683 a new governor, Domingo Jironza Petrís de Cruzate, replaced Otermín, who, among other things, had been having difficulties with the transplanted Santa Fe cabildo. After some initial resistance, by the fall of 1684 the new governor carried out a plan to move Socorro to a place nearer Isleta del Sur and made a new settlement of San Lorenzo closer to El Paso. The presidio, whose original location is uncertain—if indeed it ever existed except on paper—was then located at El Paso. Meanwhile, settlers, both colonists and Indians, gradually filled in the area between San Lorenzo and El Paso.

One problem, probably a factor in the refusal of a number of Spanish leaders to undertake the 1681 expedition up the Rio Grande, was rising native unrest in southern New Mexico and in Nueva Vizcaya itself. Indian groups all along the

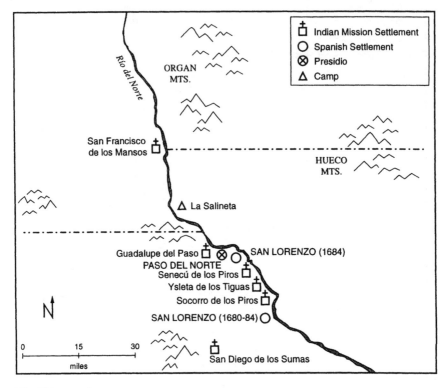

The El Paso settlements, 1680–92

northern frontier were aware of the success of the Pueblos, and the region was extremely volatile. Shortly after the attempted rebellion at Socorro (apparently while Otermín was still in power), there was a rising of transplanted Tiwas and Piros who were in contact with the rebels in New Mexico. This revolt "was suppressed by some gentle measures," according to Vélez de Escalante, though "gentle" must have been in the eyes of the beholder for nine Piros were sentenced to four years' labor in a crushing mill.

Jironza was soon involved on several fronts. In November 1683, he sent a small party up the Rio Grande, reaching a point south of modern Albuquerque. After a skirmish with the Apaches and realizing that the Pueblos had no interest in a Spanish return, the group retreated to the El Paso area. Jironza now decided to concentrate the Spanish population nearer the Manso mission of Guadalupe in the El Paso region. This coincided with, and possibly triggered, a widespread Manso plot which, fortunately for the Spaniards, was discovered in time, with eight ringleaders sentenced to be garroted. This sentence was momentarily held up because an expedition led by Juan Domínguez de Mendoza had gone to the La Junta region, the juncture of the Conchos and the Rio Grande, and the families of his soldiers feared retaliation. Domínguez had taken approximately twenty men, leaving only fifty, seriously under-armed defenders in the El Paso area. The Mansos fled to the stronghold of a rebel Captain Chiquito some fifty miles from El Paso.

Meanwhile, rebellion had flared up among the Sumas, Janos, Jocomes, Chinarras, and Conchos over a large area of what is now western Chihuahua. In part this was caused by the unauthorized influx of Spanish settlers fleeing New Mexico, which put great pressures on the area's resources. Clearly, the population figures for 1684 indicated a continued leakage of people away from the El Paso frontier. A *visita* of the settlements taken in September of that year counted only 1,051 persons, though it is not clear if this count included the resettled Tiwa and Piro Indians. Equipment was also in short supply: the investigators recorded only sixty-six harquebuses, fifty-one swords, and seventy-eight saddles.

At the time of the rebellion, Francisco Ramírez de Salazar was alcalde mayor of Casas Grandes. He had only a dozen men in arms but managed to get an additional thirty (including Indian allies, perhaps Pima or Opata) on loan from the alcalde mayor of Sonora. After a series of inconclusive skirmishes, Ramírez moved his small force to El Paso, joining Captain Roque Madrid, head of the El Paso presidio, in search of the Manso rebels. The two forces of approximately ninety soldiers followed the Manso trail somewhere in the area of the Florida Mountains southeast of present-day Deming. The Mansos were moving farther west, trying to join forces with the Janos. Hearing that Casas Grandes was in trouble, Madrid and Ramírez split their forces, the latter man going to rescue the citizens of Casas Grandes while Madrid pushed on to the Carretas Mountains, some twenty-five miles southwest of Janos, near the Sonoran border. He attacked this stronghold and scattered the Mansos, then turned back to help out in the fighting around Casas Grandes. After a savage battle, the Indian confederates were defeated near Casas Grandes, Madrid reporting that his party had killed forty of the rebels and wounded many others.

By the end of 1684, the situation was more or less under control. Jironza ordered a complete muster of the El Paso presidio, and Spanish soldiers in Nueva Vizcaya gradually gained the upper hand over the various rebel forces. The Spaniards then carried out executions of various ringleaders of the rebellions. Jironza, for example, executed the Manso rebel leaders, by then totaling ten, while at Casas Grandes, forty-three Suma Indians were hanged in 1685.

Meanwhile, the Spanish Crown was coming under increasing geopolitical pressure to reoccupy New Mexico. Shortly after the revolt, the Spaniards learned that France was extending its exploration in the Mississippi Valley. In 1682, the French empire builder, Réne Robert Cavelier, Sieur de La Salle, formally took possession of the entire Mississippi drainage. In part acting on information from ex-governor Diego de Peñalosa, then living in France, La Salle planned an ambitious program of colonization of the vast new area. Named governor of Louisiana, as the new province was to be called, La Salle sailed in 1684 to found a settlement at the mouth of the Mississippi. The following year, after considerable difficulties including the loss of his supply ship to the Spaniards, La Salle landed at Matagordo Bay in present-day Texas, assuming this to be the westernmost mouth of the Mississippi. There he built a fort, St. Louis, and explored inland. La Salle seems to have thought that from Matagordo he would have easy access to New Mexico, and he may actually have intended to challenge the Spaniards. There was certainly no threat to the northern provinces of Spain, for La Salle's tiny expedition had far too little logistical support. In January 1687, the French governor, with some sixteen men (about half of the St. Louis force), made an attempt to go overland to Canada. La Salle was assassinated en route, though a handful of his men reached the Red River, the Mississippi, and eventually a French outpost on the Illinois River. Most of the colonists who remained were killed by Indians.

In 1699, the French began the settlement of La Salle's vast new area of Louisiana. Although they concentrated on the Mississippi River drainage rather than east Texas, a shrewd series of alliances with Indian groups pushed their de facto sphere of influence farther west. Controlling the Mississippi allowed the French in the early eighteenth century to operate trading parties in the Great Plains and to supply guns and horses to their Native American confederates in that region. The effect was to block the Spaniards on the north and east, but the French were never in a position to threaten either New Mexico or the post-seventeenth-century Spanish settlements in southern and western Texas.

By this time New Mexico had a new value in the eyes of the Spanish government, for it was a buffer zone for mineral-rich Nueva Vizcaya. The old missionary value remained, and there was continuing pressure from the Franciscans, who understandably were reluctant to desert their converts in New Mexico. For the moment, however, political infighting between Jironza and the Santa Fe cabildo took center stage. The governor accused Juan Domínguez de Mendoza of attempting to undercut his authority in order to obtain the position of governor. The subsequent trial in absentia (Domínguez being in Mexico City, carrying the cabildo's complaints against the governor) was a field day for Juan Domínguez de Mendoza's enemies, rehashing charges against him going back to Governor Medrano's time. There is no doubt that Domínguez deeply wanted the governorship, and he was vigorously supported by Fray Nicolás López, who was leader of the Franciscans in the La Junta expedition. As pointed out in chapter 12, however, there is no indication that his candidacy was ever taken seriously by the viceroy and the Spanish Crown.

In any case, Pedro Reneros de Posada was given the appointment, arriving in El Paso in September 1686. Reneros is somewhat of a mystery. He first appears as a presidio soldier in El Paso in September 1681, volunteering to go with Otermín on his raid northward. He was listed as a native of Castile, from the Burgos area, a bachelor who owned four horses. Reneros rose to the rank of captain and had been sent by Jironza to Mexico City on some sort of official mission in 1684. I can find no evidence that the new governor had ever been in New Mexico before 1681.

Reneros's regime started off with the execution, for some unspecified crime, of young Juan de Montoya, a member of a family that had come to New Mexico in 1600. The new governor made a series of somewhat rash attempts to tighten the defenses around El Paso. In 1687 he was accused of embezzling the quarterly pay of the presidio for that year. In late summer of 1687, Reneros made a raid northward as far as the Jemez River, where he burned the pueblo of Santa Ana. Returning with four captive Pueblo leaders and with ten others who seemed to have deserted the Indian cause and come to him willingly, Reneros returned to El Paso. There he had the Pueblo leaders executed and the ten other Indians sold into slavery in Nueva Vizcaya. Shortly after his return, Reneros was forced to quell a revolt of Suma Indians in the region southeast of El Paso. Calling the rebels together under a flag of truce, Reneros attacked, killing a number of Indians and capturing others. Nine leaders were immediately shot, and some forty Suma Indians were sold into slavery.

But Reneros's tenure of governor was shortly over. He was replaced in February 1689 by Jironza, who arrived in El Paso with much-needed weapons and supplies. Parenthetically, this ended the hopes of Juan Domínguez de Mendoza for further influence on the northern frontier. Although he had been cleared by the Mexican authorities of the various charges brought by Jironza, he was found guilty of leaving El Paso without a license and forced to pay the court costs. Still, Domínguez seems to have maintained some influence in the viceregal court. He received permission from the viceroy for his wife, son, and daughter to join him in Mexico.

Jironza's main ambition with this second chance at governorship was to activate the reconquest of New Mexico. The Spaniards had been collecting information on how things were going in Pueblo land for some years. In 1682, at the beginning of the governor's first term, an Indian named Juan had made his way south after some years captivity among the Apache. Juan reported that the

Pueblos were still bitterly anti-Spanish. The ruler at this time was the war captain Luis Tupatú of Picurís, and his main lieutenant was Alonso Catití. Hopi tried to break free of the federation but was attacked by a force under Catití, who executed ten men and brought back horses and other booty to Tupatú. The major enemy was becoming the Utes, who had attacked Jemez in the summer of 1683.

In February of 1685, a Tiwa Indian named Lucas reported a recent trip to the Pueblo area. According to Lucas, the Utes were the universal enemy, but that the pueblos of Taos, Picurís, Jemez, and Acoma were on friendly terms with the Apache. He was told that Catití had died, probably in late 1684.

Jironza was determined to see for himself, so in August of 1689, with some eighty soldiers, he marched upriver and attacked Zia in a fight that lasted from dawn to ten at night. Some fifty of Jironza's soldiers were wounded, but according to Vélez de Escalante's later account, Jironza killed six hundred Indians, women and children as well as fighting men. Jironza found the Pueblo area in considerable disarray. Some of the Acoma people had joined other Keresan speakers at Laguna and were involved in a struggle with the remaining Acoma who had stayed at the parent town. The Hopi and Zuni were in a war with each other, and the Keres along with Jemez, Pecos, and Taos were in a struggle with the Tewa and Picurís. These accelerating hostilities had mainly come after the loss of power by Popé, which seems to have occurred sometime around 1683. In 1688 Popé was returned to a leadership position, but he died shortly thereafter. Tupatú again became head of the increasingly fragmented Pueblo world, just in time to take the brunt of Jironza's raid.

It seems likely that Jironza could have carried out the reconquest, but events were not on his side. Diego de Vargas had already been given a provisional appointment as governor as early as 1689, and another claimant, Toribio de la Huerta, who had powerful friends at the Spanish court, had also put in a bid. De la Huerta dangled in front of the Crown his supposed knowledge of mines, not only silver but in particular a mercury mine, somewhere in the Hopi area. Although Huerta did not get the governorship, his story of the mercury mine became important in Vargas's later planning for the reconquest. Jironza apparently was planning another entrada into the Pueblo country, but a flare-up of Indians at La Junta in 1690 drew his attention away from the north. By that time, Vargas very much had the inside track.

CHAPTER FOURTEEN

An Era Ends, An Era Begins

Diego José de Vargas Zapata Luján Ponce de León y
Contreras was born in Madrid in November 1643. He was, in the words of a
recent biographer, a member of the "middling nobility," from an old family dating back to the eleventh century, with a long history of military service to the
Castilian kings. The first Vargas to test his fortunes in the New World was
Diego's father, Alonso de Vargas, who in 1650 served as alcalde mayor in Chiapa,
at that time administratively attached to Guatemala. Alonso, whose young wife
had died in 1649, married again in the Indies and started a second family.
Alonso's own death came in Chiapa in August of 1665.

In 1664, Diego was wed to Beatríz Pimentel de Prado, from a well-connected
neighboring family, and the young couple had five children over the next several
years. But Diego did not have the necessary wealth or aristocratic connections to
obtain a really prestigious office, and his lack of judicial training ruled out a
judgeship. Like his father, he looked to the Indies and in 1673 sailed for Mexico.
Diego served as alcalde mayor first in Oaxaca, then in the mining district northwest of Mexico City. A combination of administrative skills and favor from suc-
ceeding viceroys helped to advance Vargas's career. In June of 1688 he was
appointed governor of New Mexico, though he did not actually take over the
post in El Paso until early in 1691. During this period, crucial to Vargas's ambitions, he was considerably bolstered by the marriage of his daughter to an influential royal official and—at about the same time—the arrival in Mexico of a new
viceroy, Gaspar de la Cerda Sandoval Silva y Mendoza, the Conde de Galve, a
former Madrid neighbor and family acquaintance. Galve remained in office
until early 1696 and would support Vargas throughout his tenure as viceroy.

As discussed in chapter 13, there were two other contestants for the governorship. Toribio de la Huerta, a former New Mexican, probably never seriously had
a chance, though his claim of a quicksilver mine in Hopi country did to some

Diego de Vargas Zapata Luján Ponce de León (courtesy of the Museum of New Mexico, neg. no. 11409)

degree dictate the policy of the early reconquest. Governor Domingo Jironza, who was serving his second term as governor, was another matter. He pressed the Spanish government for a reappointment, and his successful attack on Zia in 1689 had given him a certain credence in the mind of royal officials. But in the end, Vargas was confirmed in his appointment. The new governor arrived in El Paso, taking office on February 22, 1691.

Vargas found the exiled colony in considerable disarray. Jironza in 1690 had been forced to march against the Patarabueye Indians of the La Junta area and had further exhausted his very scanty forces and supplies. On his arrival in El Paso, Vargas made an inventory for the viceroy. In El Paso and the other settlements in the Rio Grande Valley there were perhaps a hundred male Spanish citizens capable of bearing arms, with a total population of some four or five hundred—an indication of the gradual loss of Spaniards over the past decade or so. There were less than a thousand resettled Pueblo Indians. Supplies were in very short supply: a total of three hundred horses and mules, no cattle, and only about six hundred sheep, mostly in mission hands. Food was also lacking: for example, wheat flour had to be imported from Nueva Vizcaya. The presidio at El Paso was very short on arms of any sort, as were the civilians.

Vargas asked for additional muskets and other supplies from the viceroy. It seems likely that he had originally planned to march north in 1691, but troubles closer to El Paso kept him there for a time. He was requested to help Governor Juan Isidro de Pardiñas of Nueva Vizcaya in the west, and there were also problems with the Suma and Apache. In exchange for his services to Nueva Vizcaya, Vargas asked Pardiñas to supply him with fifty soldiers, which Vargas offered to help feed and arm. Governor Vargas was determined to push on with his first entry into rebel New Mexico, and with a fine sense of history, he proclaimed the expedition on August 10, 1692, the twelfth anniversary of the Pueblo Revolt. A week later, Vargas left El Paso on the road northward, with Captain Roque Madrid and the fifty soldiers from the El Paso presidio, plus ten armed citizens and a hundred Pueblo Indian auxiliaries. The fifty soldiers expected from Parral had not yet arrived, so Vargas left orders that they were to follow him northward. With Vargas were three Franciscans: Miguel Muñiz, Francisco Corvera, and Cristóbal Alonso Barroso.

This was an incredibly small group to conquer Pueblo Indians who could call on thousands of warriors, but it seems very clear that Vargas had a great deal of information about the weaknesses of the Pueblo position. Spanish expeditions and individual Indians had been going back and forth from the El Paso area to the Pueblo region for the past twelve years. The most recent Spanish expedition, that of Jironza in 1689, had given the Spaniards considerable up-to-date news.

The previously mentioned deserter from the Pueblo cause, Keresan war captain Bartolomé de Ojeda, who had ties with Zia and Santa Ana, provided detailed information to the Spaniards concerning the situation in the north.

With Bartolomé de Ojeda in camp, Vargas no doubt quickly opened negotiations with other Pueblo leaders. A number of them joined the Spaniards, including Luis Tupatú, "El Picurí," formerly the overall leader of the Pueblos; members of the Ye family of Pecos; and Cristóbal Yope of San Lázaro in the Tano country. On the other hand, Luis Cuniju, the Jemez leader, seems to have remained constant to the Pueblo cause and would be a factor in the 1696 rebellion. Francisco Pacheco of Taos offered fealty to the Spaniards under pressure but reverted to the Indian cause. Lucas Naranjo, the mulatto leader of Santa Clara, temporized for a time but was on the Pueblo side in 1696. Antonio Bolsas, the Tano leader, also remained faithful to the rebellion and was executed by Vargas in late 1693.

Why did a significant percentage of the great captains of the Pueblo world join the Spaniards? I have discussed this matter in previous chapters, but it will bear repetition here because winning over the war leaders of the Pueblos was crucial to the reconquest. One reason probably was that—with conditions worsening—the war leaders may have seen their own best interests served by allying with the Spaniards and receiving, from Spanish hands, power in their own communities. Certainly a number of them thrived under newly established Spanish control. This is a bit reminiscent of the "conservatives" versus "progressives" struggle in the nineteenth- and twentieth-century pueblos, in which the Bureau of Indian Affairs tended to take the side of the progressive or anti-traditionalist faction. The late-seventeenth-century war captains in any pueblo could certainly depend on Spanish support against the native religious power elite. They were also honored in certain specific ways. Vargas, for example, consistently referred to his new allies as "Don," the Spanish title of respect.

Another reason that Pueblo leaders joined the Spaniards is that a number of these men had kinship ties with them and their black and mestizo compatriots. Family ties crosscut ethnic loyalties in certain cases. There were probably also the ties of *compadrazgo,* the godfather/godchild relationship. Vargas used this freely, linking various Pueblo war captains to him by becoming godfather to their children. One suspects that this pseudo-familial relationship had been practiced since Oñate's time, though the loss of church records in the revolt period makes it impossible to be sure of the extent.

Religion may also have been a factor. All the war leaders had grown up in missionized pueblos, and at least Bartolomé de Ojeda seems to have been a believing Christian in the Spanish sense of the word. It could have been operative in other individual situations. A more likely case is that the various native military leaders saw in the events of the past decade an indication that the Christian deity was more powerful than their own gods and therefore worth propitiating.

It seems reasonably clear that Diego de Vargas had at least the beginnings of an "arrangement" with some of the war captains before he started for Pueblo country. His march upriver was swift, and on September 9, 1692, he had reached the ruined Mejía hacienda, roughly at the site of modern Albuquerque. The fifty-man Parral reinforcement had not caught up with the governor's party, and Vargas decided that speed and stealth were the order of the day. Leaving fourteen men with one of his captains, Rafael Téllez Girón, to guard and rest the horse herd and the oxen, Vargas moved quickly on. Téllez Girón was ordered to take an additional ten men from the reinforcement party and send the other forty to augment the governor's rather scanty forces.

Vargas then marched on to Cochiti, which he reached on September 11. The pueblo was abandoned, so Vargas backtracked to Santo Domingo, which he also found abandoned, as was San Felipe. Vargas then followed the Camino Real northeastward to Santa Fe, arriving on the morning of September 13. The governor, finding that the Indians had fashioned the Spanish buildings, the "casas reales," into a fortified pueblo, erected his military camp in the nearby fields, "within sight of the fortress, about a musket shot away." He began a complex series of negotiations both with the Indians who held Santa Fe and deputations from other pueblos in the vicinity. And then, on September 16, Luis Tupatú, "El Picurí," overall war leader of the central group of Rio Grande Pueblos, arrived to see the Spanish commander. Vargas greeted the Picurís war leader and his followers cordially, and the entire group was given absolution by the friars for their apostasy. Vargas had every reason to be cordial. It was a great breakthrough for the governor, perhaps the single most important event of this first expedition of the reconquest. The following day, Don Lorenzo, brother of El Picurí and current governor of Picurís, made obeisance to the Spaniards.

Through the good offices of Tupatú, Vargas made a series of contacts with the Tewa and Northern Tiwa pueblos. On September 21, with Tupatú and Lorenzo, Domingo, a Tewa captain, and various Indians from other pueblos, Vargas set off for Pecos. Arriving there on September 23, having meanwhile met up with the Parral reinforcements, Vargas found the pueblo deserted. Over the next several days he cajoled a few members of the pueblo to return to their home, and he collected some captives from there including the son of Cristóbal de Anaya and the Spanish-speaking Jumano woman mentioned in chapter 13. Meanwhile, Vargas sent out a Keres Indian messenger to try to contact the Santa Ana and Zia people, living in the high country behind their pueblos.

Returning to Santa Fe on September 29, Vargas pushed on to Tesuque, where with Domingo's help he assembled the people and had the Franciscans absolve them. In the next few days, Vargas, the missionaries, and the Spanish soldiers moved through various of the Tewa towns, the friars absolving and baptizing. He then traveled to the Tano towns, where the process was repeated. Vargas reached Picurís on October 5, and three days later was in Taos, where the native governor, Francisco Pacheco, swore allegiance, and general absolution was given by the Franciscans.

The latter part of October was given over to visits to the Keres pueblos and to the Towa of Jemez. At the latter area Vargas seems to have been in some danger of attack but managed to pull off a reconciliation. Captain Roque Madrid must have been useful in these campaigns for he spoke Keresan, probably an Eastern Keres dialect. Meanwhile, on October 16, Vargas had appointed Luis Tupatú to be governor of the thirteen pueblos of the Tano and Tewa, Taos, Picurís, and Santa Fe, extracting an oath of allegiance and formally investing Luis with a cane of office.

The governor then planned to visit the western pueblos of Zuni and Hopi. He was especially eager to do this not only to secure the Spanish western flank but also to investigate the various rumors of wealth in that region. According to various tales circulating in El Paso on the eve of the reconquest, there were rich silver mines in Hopi country where both the Zuni and Hopi Indians were involved in mining operations. Even more important was the story of Captain Huerta, mentioned above, of a cinnabar, or mercury, mine in Hopi land. Having found no silver in eighty years of occupying the Hopi area, the Spaniards might have been somewhat skeptical of supposed silver mines. The report on cinnabar, however, was new, and given the great demand for mercury for processing and reducing the silver from the Nueva Vizcaya mines, this was an exciting potential prize.

Vargas had already contacted Hopi individuals whom he found in the Keresan area.

That is, in the entry which I made into the pueblo of the Keres tribe of Sia, Santa Ana, and Santo Domingo, which I subdued, reduced, and conquered on the mesas of the Cerro Colorado, their captain being Antonio Malacate, in the entry and ascent to the said mesa three indians came out to receive me, two of whom are from this province of Moqui, the eldest named Pedro, the second Sebastián, and the third a coyote named Ventura, an intelligent Indian native of the pueblo of Alona and the province of Zuñi. . . . Having seen the said entry into the pueblo of the said Keres tribe, and, on the following day, the entry which I made to the mesas of the hill and canyon of the Jémez tribe, that afternoon all three Indians accompanied me.

Alona, or Halona, eventually became modern Zuni Pueblo. Ventura told Vargas that the Hopi man Pedro was willing to go on to Zuni and Hopi to prepare the way for Spanish reoccupation. Vargas therefore sent messages ahead with Pedro, giving him a rosary and cross, provisions, and a blanket. He then set out for Zuni, taking along Sebastián and Ventura. At Zuni, Vargas found two more Hopis, who announced that the Faraón Apaches had warned the Hopi that Vargas intended to kill them all: "for I was untrustworthy; and for this reason the natives of this said province of Moqui had fled to the mountains, taking with them their livestock and horse herds; whereupon [the two Hopi men] had come to see what I was doing which they had seen, and for which reason they wished to return immediately to tell them to return to their pueblos."

Sending a directive to the Awatovi chief, Miguel, Vargas left a garrison at Zuni and pushed on with two companies numbering sixty-three soldiers. Vargas's hopes were high for he had been extremely successful persuading war captains in the Rio Grande area to switch to the Spanish side, and it looked as if he could also do this in Hopi. Writing the following year, Sigüenza y Góngora stated that a numerous contingent of Pueblo Indians under the leadership of Luis Tupatú marched with Vargas to Hopi. Actually, Luis and his auxiliaries stayed in the Rio Grande area, but showcasing Tupatú at this particular time indicates the importance that Vargas gave to the Pueblo leader's help. Although El Picurí was not to play an important role in the final chapters of the Spanish reconquest, his help in 1692 was one of the major turning points in that struggle.

At Hopi, Vargas flirted with annihilation. He carried off the trip with his customary confidence and courage, but it was a close thing. Miguel and some of the Awatovi people were friendly and wished to see Spanish rule and the missionaries return. But the remaining Hopi towns were universally hostile, and it is a tribute to Vargas's diplomacy that things were kept a degree below flash point. He did manage to baptize 122 children at Awatovi and even a certain number at the other towns. He had planned to go to Oraibi, the westernmost of the Hopi towns, but on advice of his Awatovi friend, Miguel, decided against it. On November 24, after collecting information on the "cinnabar" mine (which in fact turned out to be hematite), Vargas left for Zuni and then for El Paso, arriving there in mid-December. The first phase of the reconquest, dazzlingly successful except at Hopi, was now over. Vargas, however, had no illusions about the work ahead. In order to hold New Mexico he needed more soldiers and several hundred colonists. For the moment, Vargas's star rode high, and he had every hope that his requests would be fulfilled.

The year 1693 was one of frenetic activity as far as the resettlement of New Mexico was concerned. New colonists were recruited in Mexico City and elsewhere, and Vargas pulled together people, provisions, and equipment. Even so, it was October when the first contingent left El Paso for the northern Rio Grande area. With Vargas were seventy families, a hundred soldiers, a number of Indian auxiliaries and eighteen friars. Vargas had three cannons, various supply wagons, and several thousand head of livestock, including horses and mules. The Santa Fe cabildo in exile now returned to New Mexico.

As the expedition moved northward, Vargas learned that the brittle "submission" that he had negotiated the year before had broken down. His main interpreter, the mixed-blood Pedro de Tapia, deserted and informed the Indians that Vargas secretly planned to kill all the adult Pueblos. The Tewa-Tano group, the Northern Tiwa, the Jemez, Acoma, and Hopi had by then decided on independence, and the Tewa-Tano held Santa Fe.

On his way north, Vargas met with various Pueblo leaders who jockeyed for position. The governor was inundated with rumors and counter-rumors about the loyalty of various individuals and the reliability of this or that pueblo. Although he met with Tupatú; his brother, the Picurís governor, Lorenzo; and the Tesuque governor, Domingo, Vargas seems to have lost trust in them. Part of Vargas's suspicions came from information he received from Juan de Ye, who had been appointed governor of Pecos the previous year. Ye met with Vargas on November 25, warning of Tupatú, Lorenzo, and Domingo, among others. Vargas probably did not believe that the three men had actually defected, simply that they had become ineffective. In any case, he took no action. It does seem that Tupatú and Lorenzo had lost their influence in their pueblos and were no longer effective in political affairs. Luis el Picurí died sometime in the mid 1690s, and little more is heard of Lorenzo. Domingo, however, remained active in the Spanish cause and was killed by his own people in 1696.

By the time Vargas was in the vicinity of Santa Fe, he was depending more and more on men like Ye, Ojeda, and Cristóbal Yope of San Lázaro. Vargas had developed a godparent relationship with Yope, and the Tano chief remained loyal; like Domingo, Yope eventually was killed by his own Pueblo group. Ye also counted Vargas as a friend, although in the case of the Pecos leader, fear of the Apaches and their continuing meddling in Pueblo affairs may have been a factor. Pecos was, after all, dangerously exposed, especially to the aggressive Faraón Apaches.

Vargas arrived in the vicinity of Santa Fe in December 1693, and a temporary settlement was made in the area of the Camino de Cuma, probably less than a mile from the center of the villa. The settlers' straits were desperate: by Christmas, some 22 children had died of exposure, hunger, and disease. Attempts to persuade the Indians holding Santa Fe to surrender produced no results, and after receiving

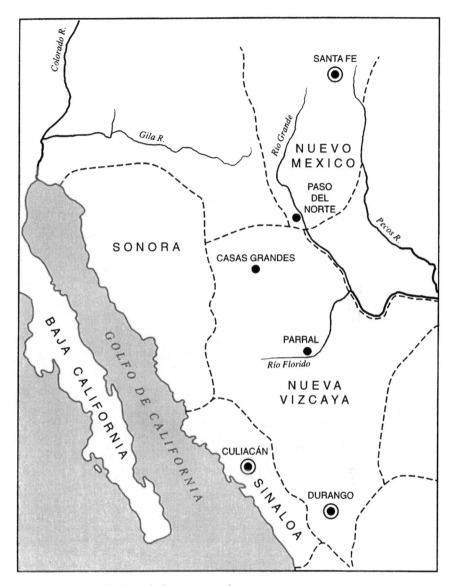

Northwestern New Spain in the late seventeenth century

140 warriors from Pecos, Vargas attacked on December 29. By the following day, the Indian stronghold of Santa Fe was overrun. Some four hundred people of both sexes and all ages, who surrendered voluntarily, were sentenced to ten years of slavery and distributed among the incoming Spanish settlers. Nine of the

Pueblo defenders were killed in battle, and two committed suicide. Seventy others were executed by Vargas's men. The settlers were moved within the walls of Santa Fe.

Vargas had won the battle but war was still ahead. Though he held Santa Fe, only four of the pueblos—Pecos and three Keresan towns, San Felipe, Santa Ana, and Zia—remained loyal to the Spaniards. All the other pueblos were hostile, and a number of them were pulling back into defensive positions and generally making ready for continued struggle. The governor was faced with the task of reducing the enemy, one town at a time. The war also prevented his colonists from following the routine of everyday life, planting fields and harvesting crops. Throughout 1694 the colonists continued to be dependent on looted Indian grain and on the long supply line to Mexico.

Vargas managed to overrun the Cochiti Indians in April but moved cautiously until the arrival of Fray Francisco Farfán in June with an additional 230 colonists forced the governor to step up his food-gathering activities. The Tano towns and Picurís had no extra food, but Taos, where the Indians fled to the mountains at the approach of Vargas, proved to have considerable grain. Through the good offices of some visiting Apaches, Vargas, along with Juan de Ye, met Francisco Pacheco, headman of Taos, urging the Taos to return to their pueblo. After some fruitless negotiation, Juan de Ye offered to spend the night with the Taos Indians and attempt to persuade them to join the Spaniards. Ye failed to return the next morning and at some point in the next few days was murdered.

Vargas then turned to Jemez, where on June 24 he captured a mesa-top refugee town with a considerable amount of foodstuffs. After a summer of warfare, Vargas by early September had subdued all the pueblos with the exception of Picurís and Taos and the westernmost towns of Acoma, Zuni, and Hopi. From September to December 1694, missionaries assigned to the newly reconquered territories moved to take up their posts. By January of 1695 eleven missions had been reestablished, and Spaniards were spreading out along the Rio Grande. In April of 1695, a second villa, that of Santa Cruz in the Tewa area, was inaugurated by newly arrived colonists. This was a region where the pre-revolt Spaniards had held a number of estancias. Another series of settlers, some 44 families, arrived from Mexico in May and were settled in the Santa Fe area. Later that year an additional settlement was made in the region of Bernalillo. The name itself referred to the Bernal family, which had owned an estancia there in pre-revolt times. Parenthetically, the third villa, or chartered town, in New Mexico was founded a decade later in 1706 with the establishment of Albuquerque (originally Alburquerque) at the "Bosque Grande."

Church interior, Santa Cruz (photo by William H. Jackson, ca. 1881, courtesy of the Museum of New Mexico, neg. no. 9785)

By 1695, Vargas had hopes that the province of New Mexico was at last secured. However, the harsh winter of 1695–96 caused desperate hardship both to the Spanish colonists and to the Indians, many of whom had lost their stored grain to Vargas's depredations. In the latter part of 1695 it became increasingly evident, at least to the missionaries, that the Pueblos were ready to make one last effort to throw off their conquerors. As of March 1696, Governor Vargas estimated that there were 276 Spanish families in New Mexico, far short of the 500 he believed were necessary to create a stable province. In addition to the settlers, Vargas had approximately 100 soldiers, but these were considerably scattered, about a quarter of them being on the way to El Paso to bring livestock and food stores back to New Mexico.

In early June, reports of a widespread uprising began to reach Santa Fe. On June 4, 5 missionaries were killed along with 21 Spanish settlers, and all the Pueblos were in revolt with the exception of Pecos and the three Keresan towns (San Felipe, Santa Ana, and Zia) discussed above. Vargas responded by ordering all the missionaries to be withdrawn to safety in the two villas. An attempt by Luis Cuniju and Diego Xenome (war captains at Jemez and Nambé, respectively) to persuade the Pecos Indians to rise was scotched by the new governor, Felipe Chistoe. The Pecos cacique, Diego Umviro, was hanged along with war captain Cachina and two others. A fifth man, Caripicado (Pock Face), escaped but was killed later when he tried to return to the pueblo, and Chistoe sent Vargas his severed head, plus a hand and foot. Cuniju and Xenome were also turned over to Vargas, who had them executed. Pecos supplied 100 warriors to the Spaniards, who also could count on a number of Manso Indians, some of them apparently attached to the missions.

The Tewa towns of Santa Clara and San Juan, led by Lucas Naranjo, were a main focus of the rebellion. Launching a counterattack from Santa Cruz, Vargas crossed the Rio Grande and in late July clashed with Naranjo and his men, who were deployed "in the boulders and the woods of the sierras." The rebel captain was hit in the adam's apple by a lucky shot from one of Vargas's men, apparently killing him instantly. This sudden turn of events demoralized his supporters, who fled the field. Naranjo's bloody head was hacked off by the Spaniards as a trophy. In the opinion of J. M. Espinosa, Vargas's victory in this battle was the turning point of the war. It certainly ended one chapter in the tangled story of the Naranjo involvement in the revolt.

But the Naranjo family maintained a foot in the Spanish camp, for one of their members, José or Josephe, alerted Vargas's most important commander, Roque Madrid, to the 1696 uprising at Santa Clara and subsequently joined the Spaniards. A grandson many years later claimed that it was José who cut off Lucas Naranjo's head, though Vargas reported to the viceroy simply that it was a soldier other than Antonio Cisneros, the man who fired the fatal shot. In later years, José became fairly important in the Spanish government. During the period 1700–1702 he served as alcalde mayor of the Zuni town of Halona. By

1704 he was Vargas's chief scout and captain of the Indian allies. In 1706 he was involved in Ulibarrí's expedition to bring the Picurís Indians back from their western Plains refuge settlement among Apaches at El Cuartelejo in western Kansas. Naranjo continued his command role with the Pueblo Indian auxiliaries until 1720, when he was killed during the disastrous Pedro de Villasur expedition to the central Plains.

With the Santa Cruz area more or less pacified, Vargas gradually reduced all the pueblos, although both Zuni and Hopi remained for the time being outside the Spanish orbit. The inhabitants of Picurís "voted with their feet," fleeing to the Cuartelejo Apache groups on the western Plains, but the Rio Grande Pueblos began to adjust to the post-revolt reality of Spanish rule. Custodian Francisco de Vargas, late in 1696, wrote that there were only thirteen missionaries in New Mexico and asked that the number be increased to twenty-one. In April of 1697, Viceroy Sarmiento Valladares ordered that eight more Franciscans be sent to New Mexico.

The final stabilization of the province in 1696 left the Pueblos with deep internal divisions. At Pecos, the ruthless native governor Felipe Chistoe met continuous opposition but remained firm in his decision to tie his pueblo to the Spanish cause. Those Pecos Indians who did not favor the Spaniards slipped away to the Apaches. The northern Tiwa and Tewa continued to foster Apache alliances for a number of years, as did the Jemez with the Navajo. Curiously, one pueblo that may have welcomed the Spaniards was the lone Zuni town of Halona. The Zuni were in a seriously exposed position, warred on by Apachean groups and apparently at odds with their Hopi neighbors. A Spanish presence gave at least nominal protection from the marauding nomadic tribes. Even so, Zuni was very loosely held in the eighteenth century, and the pueblo had a considerable amount of autonomy, something reflected in the power of the native religion, especially the kachina cult, in modern Zuni.

The Hopi at the time of Vargas's first entrada in 1692 had lined up a number of allies: Utes, Apaches, and Havasupai. Later in the century, the Hopi had troubles, especially with the Utes and Apaches, but for the time being they were friends. Hopi was strengthened by several of the eastern Pueblo groups who fled the Spanish reconquest and reached the Hopi mesas. These included Keresans, Tewa/Tano, and Tiwa, some probably moving to Hopi as early as 1681 in the wake of Otermín's attempted reconquest. Another wave of refugees came to Hopi after the troubles along the Rio Grande in 1693 and 1696. By 1700, there were two separate non-Hopi towns on the Hopi mesas: Payupki on Second Mesa, made up largely of Tiwa from Sandia, and Hano on First Mesa, built by Tano-speaking Indians. The Tewa anthropologist Edward Dozier has suggested that Hano was instrumental in triggering the Hopi attack on Awatovi, described below. Although Payupki was deserted by mid-century, with the Sandia Indians returning to the Rio Grande, Hano remains to this day a Tano enclave at Hopi.

Meanwhile, Governor Vargas, whose term of office officially ended in early 1696, found himself buffeted by shifting political winds. His old friend, the viceroy Conde de Galve, was replaced in 1696 by Bishop Juan de Ortega Montañez. Although Ortega was acquainted with Vargas and probably well disposed to him, it was not the firm friendship that Vargas enjoyed with Galve. To make matters worse, Galve died shortly after returning to Spain, leaving the governor without an important advocate at court. Then Ortega himself was replaced in late 1696 by José Sarmiento y Valladares, Conde de Moctezuma y de Tula, who had no connections to Vargas. Like a number of previous New Mexican governors, Vargas was having increasing difficulty with the Santa Fe cabildo, whose members disliked him for his arrogance and for perceived errors, especially in the handling of the 1693 colonization and the 1696 revolt. In addition, Vargas had a running dispute with the Franciscans, who tended to blame him for the murder of five of their number in the 1696 uprising.

Although Vargas petitioned for an extension of office in New Mexico, King Carlos II had, several years before, granted the governorship of New Mexico to Pedro Rodríguez Cubero, with the understanding that the latter man would take office at the end of Vargas's term. Rodríguez Cubero is a rather interesting person, indicative of how ability rather than ties to the nobility sometimes counted in seventeenth-century Spain. A member of a relatively humble family, Cubero came from Huéscar in southern Spain. This was an area where there were large numbers of converted Moors, and Rodríguez Cubero may have had Moorish antecedents, though he also had influential relatives, two cousins being members of the prestigious military Order of Santiago. Rodríguez Cubero entered the naval infantry service in 1674 as a common musketeer and rose to the rank of captain of infantry. He seems to have had enough family wealth (or collected enough money on his own) to purchase a post in Havana and then the future of the governorship of New Mexico. As was common in that period, he made a donation to the Crown in return for the favor of the office. By 1695 Rodríguez Cubero had changed his mind and petitioned the Spanish authorities to let him out of the contract, pleading that his poor health made residence in such a cold area as New Mexico undesirable. His petition was denied.

Arriving in Santa Fe in early July 1697, Rodríguez Cubero quickly found himself embroiled in a quarrel with Vargas, who simply refused to leave office. The cabildo filed charges against Vargas, and Cubero had the ex-governor imprisoned in Santa Fe, where he remained for almost three years before finally being allowed to journey back to Mexico. During his term of office, Rodríguez Cubero carried out a number of programs originally planned by Vargas. He initiated a building program in Santa Fe and also turned his attention to bringing the western Pueblos back under Spanish control. In 1699, missions were reestablished at Acoma and Halona, and a new mission station set up at Laguna. The following year, the missionary at Halona, Father Juan de Garaycoechea, along with Fray Antonio Miranda, launched an attempt to reintroduce the mission system to the Hopi. They made a short visit to the pro-Spanish, easternmost pueblo of Awatovi, where they were favorably received. Before the Franciscans were able to follow through with their missionization efforts, the other Hopi towns attacked Awatovi, sacking the pueblo and killing many of the inhabitants. In July of 1701 Rodríguez Cubero led a force against Hopi but found that the Indians had retreated to their mesa-top fortresses. Finding water only at ruined Awatovi and unable to maintain a protracted stay in the field, the governor returned to Santa Fe. In spite of repeated attempts to reconquer Hopi during the eighteenth century, this group of pueblos remained permanently outside Spanish control. In the midst of this activity, Rodríguez Cubero's term of office expired, and he was replaced by Vargas. Rodríguez Cubero, whose health was now seriously affected, returned to Mexico City, where he died in 1704.

Meanwhile, his bitter enemy, Diego de Vargas, arrived in New Mexico for a second term as governor. Favored by the king and backed by the new viceroy, the Duque de Alburquerque, Vargas's star was on the ascendant once more. He had won long-drawn-out legal battles with the Santa Fe cabildo and with Rodríguez Cubero. Vargas was awarded the title of marqués and granted an encomienda worth an extravagant four thousand pesos to be collected annually from the Indians of New Mexico. But he was not to enjoy those honors for long. Like Rodríguez Cubero, Vargas seems to have been in rather poor health. In late March of 1704 he began a campaign against the Faraón Apaches, who had recently attacked the new settlement of Bernalillo. Vargas became suddenly ill on April 3 in his field camp south of Bernalillo. He was carried back to that settlement, where he became steadily worse, dying on April 8. The diagnosis was "a severe attack of fever caused by stomach chills," perhaps dysentery or pneumonia.

Though his contemporaries did not fully realize it, the Diego de Vargas years marked the end of an era and a new beginning for New Mexico. Indeed, this new era might reasonably be dated from Vargas's colonization effort beginning in 1692 with its final demonstration that the Pueblo Indians lacked the unity and stamina necessary to hold the region. The old, introverted group of settlers now gave way to the Vargas colonists, people for the most part new to the colony. Eighteenth-century New Mexico was quickly to face very different problems from the mission-dominated colony of the seventeenth century. For one thing, the ratio of

Duque de Alburquerque, Viceroy of New Spain, 1702–11 (oil by Gerald Cassidy, courtesy of the Museum of New Mexico, neg. no. 8780)

Spaniards to Pueblo Indians changed radically over the course of the century. In 1680 the Indians outnumbered Spaniards by a ratio of perhaps six to one. Vargas understood very well that a secure province of New Mexico needed a larger Spanish base, and this was one of the main points of his strategy for reconquest. By the end of the Vargas period, calculating in the loss of the Hopi towns, the population ratio was probably more like one colonist to every four or five Indians. The colonial population continued to grow, albeit rather slowly, throughout the century, whereas the Pueblo population fell, though not as drastically as in the seventeenth century. By the time of Domínguez in 1776, there were more Spaniards than Pueblo Indians in New Mexico. Another important demographic trend was that in the eighteenth century encomiendas were done away with (even the Vargas one was never taken up), and the old order of large estancias gave way to small holdings, family operations that did not depend on native labor. In the eighteenth century, New Mexico, with its growing population and with increased Spanish settlement to the south, became more closely tied to New Spain. Even so, throughout the century, raids by nomadic Indians continued to impact the major routes connecting the province with central Mexico. On the other hand, a route westward to California was gradually forged during this same period.

Following the reestablishment of the missions in the mid-1690s, there was a gradual retreat from the religious certainties of the previous decades. The eighteenth century saw a slow crumbling of mission influence. Much of the Pueblo religion remained underground, and the missionaries did not fully comprehend its continuing hold on the Pueblo people. Commissary Visitor Fray Atanasio Domínguez, writing in 1776, commented on the scalp dance which the Spanish authorities allowed, perhaps even encouraged, as a price for Pueblo cooperation in the continuing fight against hostile nomads. Probably, Domínguez's statement can be taken as indicative of the new missionary attitudes toward Pueblo ceremonies in general: "The contradances or minuets, do not appear to be essentially wicked and are usual on solemn occasions during the year, here in the scalp ceremonial the dances are tainted by the idea of vengeance. The fathers have been very zealous in their opposition to this scalp dance, but they have only received rebuffs, and so the fathers are unable to abolish this custom *and many others* [italics mine], because excuses are immediately made on the grounds that [the Indians] are neophytes, minors, etc."

Eleanor B. Adams and Angelico Chavez, editors of the Domínguez report, assumed—as indeed seems likely—that Domínguez was referring to kachina and other ceremonial dances. By the 1770s, according to Adams and Chavez, "the Pueblos were in full use of their estufas and everything connected with them as they are today."

Although they would not have appreciated the comparison, the approach of the eighteenth-century Franciscans did not differ greatly from people like López de Mendizábal. And in the eighteenth century the Pueblo Indians began to work more and more within the Spanish legal system, using the courts to press their various claims to land and to individual and group rights.

At the beginning of the seventeenth century the Pueblo Indians and their nomadic neighbors were at the very edge of the larger world. Their contact with Europeans and Africans had been sporadic, generally unpleasant, and not particularly coherent. Oñate changed all that, and the seventeenth century was a learning time, a period in which the worldview of at least some of the Southwestern Indians became strikingly broadened with new skills, new languages, and the beginnings of literacy. It was also a time of great tension and increasing bitterness, for the newcomers were determined to destroy the very matrix of Pueblo cultural being. This does not mean that the Spaniards were especially ruthless or cruel. As discussed earlier, Spain, even in the harsher social environments of the sixteenth and seventeenth centuries, treated the New World natives better than any other European colonial power. This was primarily due to the humanizing tendencies of the Spanish Church, and Church influence on the secular power structure. If Spain had the best record, surely the Anglo-Americans had one of the worst, their treatment of Native Americans being marked from the first by cruelty and greed. But for all of Spanish humanity and good intentions, the Franciscans in New Mexico were embarked on an all-or-nothing program of Christianization and Hispanization. Had the friars had their way, the Pueblo Indians of later times would have been turned into a Hispanic peasantry. Other Indian groups in northern and western New Spain became just such marginalized peasants, losing their native languages and cultures. Later, after New Spain was replaced by the independent nation of Mexico, many individuals from such groups were able to make their mark in the political, military, and artistic life of their country. They functioned, however, in a distinctly Hispanic cultural world.

For the Pueblos, things worked out differently: a bloody revolt killed one out of six of the Spanish colonists and sent the rest scurrying back to the edges of Nueva Vizcaya. It took two decades or more for the Europeans to regain control, and even that control was not entirely on their own terms. The eighteenth century was one of accommodation, a period that produced the multilayered structure of the modern Pueblos. In a sense, the Southwestern Indians had won their cultural struggle, but in the process they took sustenance from the dominant Hispanic society. It can be seen today in the Pueblo gene pool, material culture, social and political organization, religion, and to some degree, language. The Pueblos contributed also to their Hispanic neighbors, genetically and culturally. Both groups surely benefited from this interchange.

Sources and Commentary

CHAPTER 1, SPAIN AT THE FLOOD

The situation of Castile and Aragón at the beginning of a united Spain is discussed in J. H. Elliott, *The Revolt of the Catalans: A Study in the Decline of Spain, 1598–1640* (Cambridge University Press, Cambridge, 1963), pp. 1–7. Another detailed discussion can be found in J. Ramsey, *Spain: The Rise of the First World Power* (Office of International Studies and Programs and the University of Alabama Press, 1973), esp. pp. 116–78. For the Nasrids in Spain, see W. M. Watt and P. Cachia, *A History of Islamic Spain* (Edinburgh University Press, Paperbacks, 1977 [first published 1965], Edinburgh, U.K.), pp. 147–50.

Eratosthenes arrived at his estimated circumference of the Earth by measuring its arc between Syene near Elephantine in upper Egypt and Alexandria in lower Egypt. He measured the angle of the sun at noonday in the two places, and decided that they were separated by one-fiftieth of the Earth's circumference. The distance between the two places he estimated at 5,000 stadia, making the circumference of the Earth 250,000 stadia (later "corrected" to 252,000 stadia). Unfortunately, there are several values for a Greek stadium, so modern estimates for Eratosthenes's circumference vary from about 24,000 to almost 29,000 miles, compared to the actual circumference of a little less than 25,000 miles In any case, considering the primitive nature of his instruments, Eratosthenes's figure is remarkable. Consult G. Sarton, *A History of Science: Hellenistic Science and Culture in the Last Three Centuries* B.C. (Harvard University Press, Cambridge, Mass., 1959), pp. 103–6.

For early exploration in the Atlantic, see the two volumes of S. E. Morrison's *The European Discovery of America: The Northern Voyages* (Oxford University Press, New York and Oxford, 1971) and *The Southern Voyages* (Oxford University Press, New York and Oxford, 1974). Also consult two books by C. O. Sauer: *The Early Spanish Main* (University of California Press, Berkeley, 1966) and *Northern Mists* (University of California Press, Berkeley, 1968). See also J. B. Brebner, *The*

Explorers of North America, 1492–1806 (Doubleday and Company, Garden City, N.Y., 1955). Early Spanish contact in the New World is discussed in: C. Jane, ed., *The Four Voyages of Columbus* (Dover Publications, New York, 1988 [reprint of Hakluyt Society publications of 1930 and 1933]); A. R. Pagdon, *Hernán Cortés: Letters from Mexico* (Grossman Publishers, New York, 1971); A. Marrin, *Inca and Spaniard* (Macmillan, New York, 1988); and C. H. Haring, *The Spanish Empire in America* (Oxford University Press, New York, 1947). The Spanish "purification" decree of 1492 that forced the conversion of Jews or drove them from the country is discussed by H. Kamen, "The Expulsion: Purpose and Consequence," *Spain and the Jews*, E. Kedourie, ed. (Thames and Hudson, London, 1992), pp. 74–91. Also consult A. L. Sachar, *A History of the Jews* (Alfred A. Knopf, New York, 1967, 5th ed.), pp. 213–15. A similar decree against the Muslims was proclaimed in 1502. Both laws were aimed more at conversion than expulsion, and in fact the Inquisition had been set up 1478 originally to combat Judaizing tendencies among the converted population, the *conversos*. For a discussion of this, see E. Kedourie's introduction in *Spain and the Jews*, pp. 16–20.

For missionary activity, see Haring, *Empire*, 13, 179–203; J. Lafaye, *Quetzalcóatl et Guadalupe* (Editions Gallimard, Paris, 1974); and J. Cortés Castellanos, *El catecismo en pictogramas de Fr. Pedro de Gante* (Fundición Universitaria Española, Madrid, 1987), especially the introductory sections. There were, of course, Spanish missionary groups other than those I have mentioned in the New World. For example, the government of Hispaniola was given to members of the small Jeronymite order for a short period (1516–18). See H. Thomas, *Conquest: Montezuma, Cortés, and the Fall of Mexico* (Simon and Schuster, New York and London, 1993) pp. 74–75. However, the "big three" made the most powerful impression on Native Americans.

Spanish inflation in the sixteenth century is considered in D. J. Boorstin, *The Discoverers* (Random House, New York, 1983), p. 653. For the relationship of the Spanish government and people with Jews and *conversos* (Jewish converts, often forced converts, to Christianity), see H. Beinart, "The Conversos and Their Fate," *Spain and the Jews*, E. Kedourie, ed. (Thames and Hudson, London, 1992), pp. 92–122. The split with Portugal and the results of the Catalan war are given in Elliott, *Revolt*, pp. 516–18, 523–52. The long-standing weaknesses of the Spanish economy are discussed by Ramsey, *Spain*, pp. 80–83.

CHAPTER 2, THE NATIVE AMERICANS

For a general discussion of the prehistoric cultures, especially in the Rio Grande Valley, see C. L. Riley, *Rio del Norte* (University of Utah Press, 1995), chaps. 3–8. Additional information can be found in A. H. Simmons et al., *Human Adaptations and Cultural Change in the Greater Southwest,* prepared for the U.S. Army Corps of Engineers, Southwestern Division, 1989. See also L. S. Cordell, *Prehistory of the Southwest* (Academic Press, 1984). For Mogollon connections to the western Pueblos, see T. R. Frisbie, "Zuni and the Mogollon: A New Look at an Old Question," *Recent Research in Mogollon Archaeology,* S. Upham, F. Plog, D. G. Batcho, and B. E. Kauffman, eds. (The University Museum, New Mexico State University Occasional Papers, 10, Las Cruces, N.Mex., 1984), pp. 98–114. Oshara is treated in C. Irwin-Williams, *The Oshara Tradition* (Eastern New Mexico University Contributions in Anthropology, 5, 1973). The name *Anasazi* was first used by Kidder in 1936 (A. L. Kidder and A. O. Shepard, *The Pottery of Pecos* [Yale University Press, New Haven], vol. 2, p. 590). For a discussion of its meaning, see "In the News" commentary, *American Archaeology* 2 (2) (1998): 10. For late Hopi archaeology, see E. C. Adams, *Synthesis of Hopi Prehistory and History* (Final Report presented to the National Park Service, Southwest Region, July 31, 1978), pp. 14–16. For the prehistoric distribution of languages in the upper Southwest, see Riley, *Rio del Norte,* pp. 96–105. There have been various classifications of Southwestern cultures. Figure 2 shows the Pecos classification of Kidder, the subsequent Rio Grande classification, and another classification developed in the 1930s by the archaeologist F. H. H. Roberts Jr. of the Smithsonian Institution.

Clearly, glaze wares were diffused from the west, probably from an earlier Mexican homeland. See D. H. Snow, "The Rio Grande Glaze, Matte-Paint, and Plainware Tradition," *Southwestern Ceramics: A Comparative Review,* A. H. Schroeder, ed., *Arizona Archaeologist* 15 (1982): 235–78, 243–48. In addition, M. P. Stanislawski ("The American Southwest as seen from Pecos," manuscript prepared for the National Park Service, Southwest Regional Office, Santa Fe, N.Mex., Feb. 1983, pp. 359–61) sees the possibility of western immigrants into the Rio Grande and Pecos Valleys. Stanislawski thinks that the Pecos Pueblo quadrangle with associated galleries in the upper stories is basically western in form. A discussion of the kachina cult can be found in Riley, *Rio del Norte,* pp. 107–12. See also P. Schaafsma and C. F. Schaafsma, "Evidence for the Origins of the Kachina Cult," *American Antiquity* 39 (4) (1974): 535–45; E. C. Adams, *The Origin and Development of the Pueblo Katsina Cult* (University of Arizona Press, Tucson, 1991), pp. 3–4, 185–91; and E. C. Adams, "The Katsina Cult: A Western Pueblo Prospective," *Kachinas in the Pueblo World,* P. Schaafsma, ed., (University of New Mexico Press, Albuquerque, 1994), pp. 35–46. The importance of Casas Grandes is discussed by C. F. Schaafsma and C. L. Riley, "The Casas Grandes World: Analysis and Conclusions," *The Casas Grandes World,* C. F. Schaafsma and C. L. Riley, eds. (University of Utah Press, Salt Lake City, 1999). The divine twins and solar-lunar animal associations are discussed by M. Thompson, "The Evolution of Mimbres Iconography," in P. Schaafsma, ed., *Kachinas in the Pueblo World,* pp. 93–105.

For the Golden Age of the Pueblos, consult Riley, *Rio del Norte,* pp. 93–118, and for a bibliography on the Golden Age, see pp. 287–291. Foodstuffs, both agricultural and wild, are discussed on pp. 122–26. For the Sonoran statelets, see C. L. Riley, *The Frontier People* (University of New Mexico Press, 1987), pp. 39–96, and Riley, *Rio del Norte,* pp. 199–207. For the home range of the scarlet macaw, consult L. L. Hargrave, *Mexican Macaws* (Anthropological Papers of the University of Arizona, no. 20, 1970), p. 10. For Querechos and Teyas, see Riley, *Rio del Norte,* pp. 190–92; also C. L. Riley, "The Teya Indians of the Southwestern Plains," *The Coronado Expedition to Tierra Nueva,* R. Flint and S. C. Flint, eds. (University Press of Colorado, Niwot, 1977), pp. 320–43.

CHAPTER 3, A CLASH OF CULTURES

For a discussion of Pueblo languages in historic times, see Riley, *Rio del Norte,* pp. 96–105. For Suma and Manso, consult Riley, *Teya,* pp. 320–43. There are many accounts of the Spanish conquest of Mexico; a discussion of sources is given in Riley, *Rio del Norte,* pp. 293–95. One recent and rather detailed study of the Cortés period is Thomas, *Conquest.*

For the early Spanish operation on the west coast of Mexico, see B. C. Hedrick and C. L. Riley, *Documents Ancillary to the Vaca Journey* (Southern Illinois University, University Museum Studies, no. 5, Carbondale, 1976). For the quotes from the Vaca sojourn at La Junta, consult Alvar Nuñez Cabeza de Vaca, *La relación y comentarios* (later referred to as *Naufragios*) (Madrid, 1555), fol. xliii. What is sometimes called the "joint report" has basically the same material; see B. C. Hedrick and C. L. Riley, eds. and trans., *Journey of the Vaca Party* (Southern Illinois University, University Museum Studies, no. 2, Carbondale, 1974), pp. 59–62. This document suggests that the little Spanish party may have gone northwest after leaving La Junta. A discussion of stone boiling in the western Plains can be found in R. H. Lowie, *Indians of the Plains* (American Museum Science Books, New York, 1963), pp. 25–26.

C. O. Sauer (*The Road to Cíbola* [Ibero-Americana, no. 3, 1932]) believed that the Vaca group may have gone far enough north to skirt the southern edge of the Mimbres Mountains and then swung south, perhaps near present-day Douglas, Arizona, and Cananea, Sonora, finally reaching the Sonora River. For a discussion of these matters, see A. D. Krieger, "The Travels of Alvar Nuñez Cabeza de Vaca in Texas and Mexico, 1534–1536" (in *Homenaje a Pablo Martínez del Río*

[INAH, México, D.F., 1961]), pp. 459–74, esp. pp. 463, 469–71. Krieger believed that Cabeza de Vaca ascended the north side of Rio Grande for about 150 miles and then struck out westward. Charles Di Peso (in C. C. Di Peso, J. B. Rinaldo, and G. J. Fenner, *Casas Grandes: A Fallen Trading Center of the Gran Chichimeca* [Amerind Foundation, Dragoon, Ariz., and Northland Press, Flagstaff, Ariz., 1974], vol. 4, pp. 56–74) took the Cabeza de Vaca party generally westward from La Junta, but to the south of Casas Grandes, into the eastern arm of the Bavispe and then the main Yaqui drainage. Di Peso's Corazones, however, is on the Yaqui, which seems a very unlikely location. On the whole I incline to Sauer's route, although the evidence is equivocal for any given route.

Information on the de Soto expedition can be found in J. R. Swanton, *Indians of the Southeastern United States* (Bureau of American Ethnology Bulletin, 137, Washington, D.C., 1946), pp. 39–59. The basic documents of the Coronado expedition have been published in a generally (though not entirely) dependable English translation in G. P. Hammond and A. Rey, *Narratives of the Coronado Expedition, 1540–1542* (University of New Mexico Press, Albuquerque, 1940). For the report of Fray Marcos, see pp. 63–82. For the discovery of gold, see p. 80. Another version of the Marcos report is given in G. B. Ramusio, *Delle navigationi et viaggi. . .*, vol. 3 (In Venetia appressi I Guinti, 1556). This differs from the Spanish version in a description of gold at Cíbola (see fol. 359d).

A collection of Coronado documents appears in G. P. Winship, *The Coronado Expedition, 1540–42* (in the fourteenth annual report of the Bureau of Ethnology, 1892–1893, Washington, 1896). This source is valuable for its reproduction of the Spanish version of the important Castañeda account, done from the one manuscript copy of Pedro de Castañeda's journal known today. This manuscript, in a rather cramped hand, is dated 1596 and is presently in the New York City Library. The Winship transcription generally agrees with the original manuscript, but there are minor differences.

Other documents that shed light on the Coronado expedition are F. López de Gómara, *Historia general de las Indias*, 2 vols., (Calpe, Madrid, 1922 [first published in 1554, twelve years after Coronado's return]). In the mid-seventeenth century the Franciscan friar Antonio Tello, in *Libro segundo de la crónica miscelanea . . .* (Imprenta de La Republica Literaria, Guadalajara, 1891), gives a considerable amount of information about Coronado, and in the mid-eighteenth century, M. de Mota Padilla (*Historia de la conquista de la provincia de la Nueva-Galicia* [Publicado de la Sociedad Mexicana de Geografía y Estadística, Imprinta del Gobierno en Palacio, México, 1870]) also has information on Coronado. The Southwest portions of Mota Padilla's work have been translated by A. G. Day, "Mota Padilla in the Coronado Expedition," *Hispanic American Historical*

Review 20 (1) (1940): 158–70. Two good, popular surveys of the Coronado expedition are A. G. Day, *Coronado's Quest* (University of California Press, Berkeley, 1940) and H. E. Bolton, *Coronado, Knight of Pueblos and Plains* (University of New Mexico Press, Albuquerque, 1964 [first published in 1949]). Both of these authors have a considerable pro-Spanish bias, which makes their comments on native peoples often suspect. Discussions of Coronado's exploration to the Plains can be found in M. M. Wedel, "The Wichita Indians in the Arkansas River Valley," *Plains Indians Studies,* D. H. Ubelaker and H. J. Viola, eds. (Smithsonian Contributions to Anthropology, no. 30, Washington, D.C., 1982), pp. 118–34; see also M. M. Wedel, "The Indian They Called Turco," *Pathways to Plains Prehistory,* D. G. Wyckoff and J. L. Hofman, eds. (Oklahoma Anthropological Society, Memoir 3, The Cross Timbers Press, Duncan, Okla., 1982), and W. R. Wedel and M. M. Wedel, Wichita Archeology and Ethnohistory, *Kansas and the West,* F. R. Blackburn et al., eds. (H. M. Ives and Sons, Topeka, Kans., 1976), pp. 8–20. The discoveries in Blanco Canyon have been discussed in a number of chapters in R. Flint and S. C. Flint, eds., *The Coronado Expedition to Tierra Nueva* (University Press of Colorado, Niwot, 1997), esp. C. L. Riley, "Introduction," pp. 1–28; D. J. Blakeslee, "Which Barrancas? Narrowing the Possibilities," pp. 302–19; C. L. Riley, "The Teya Indians of the Southwestern Plains," pp. 320–43; W. M. Mathes, "A Large Canyon Like Those of Colima," pp. 365–69; and D. J. Blakeslee, R. Flint, and J. T. Hughes, "Una Barranca Grande: Recent Archeological Evidence and a Discussion of Its Place in the Coronado Route," pp. 370–83. D. H. Snow ("'Por alli no ay losa, ni se hace': Gilded Men and Glazed Pottery on the Southern Plains," pp. 344–64) makes insightful comments on the various kinds of pottery that were seeping into the western Plains in Coronado's time. An excellent source on the Coronado and later expeditions to the west Texas area is J. M. Morris, *El Llano Estacado* (Texas State Historical Association, Austin, 1997). For the achievement and especially the failure of the Coronado expedition, consult Riley, *Rio del Norte,* pp. 147–207. The aftermath of the expedition is discussed on pp. 199–224. I suggest that certain things like melons (pp. 214–15), the Mexican game of *patolli* (p. 217), and the Zuni and Hopi Shalako ceremony (pp. 218–20) may date from this interregnum period.

Spanish exploration and settlement in the north interior of Mexico is described in J. L. Mecham, *Francisco de Ibarra and Nueva Vizcaya* (Greenwood Press, New York, 1968). For the Rodrigo del Río settlement of Indé and Santa Bárbara, see Mecham, 188–89. A discussion of the laws of 1573 (which were some years in preparation) can be found in G. P. Hammond and A. Rey, *The Rediscovery of New Mexico* (University of New Mexico Press, Albuquerque,

1966), pp. 6–7. For the explorations of the Chamuscado and Espejo expeditions, see Riley, *Rio del Norte*, pp. 225–39, and Hammond and Rey, *Rediscovery*, especially the Gallegos's relación (67–114), the Pedrosa pueblo list (pp. 115–20), the Luxán account (153–212), and the Espejo report (213–31). In the 1770s, Father Silvestre Vélez de Escalante extracted information from the New Mexico Archives and from various other sources for material on the history of New Mexico. He was mainly concerned with the Pueblo Revolt but has brief comments on earlier periods. According to Escalante, Juan de Santa María, trying to return to Mexico, was ambushed by Apaches while sleeping. Father López was also killed in an Apache raid, while Rodríguez was murdered by the Pueblos themselves. Escalante believed that the missionaries were in Piro country rather than among the Tiguex. See Silvestre Vélez de Escalante, *Extracto de noticias* (Biblioteca Nacional de México, Archivo Franciscano, 19/397, 20/428/1, from a translation prepared by Eleanor B. Adams, ms. in author's possession, n.d.), pp. 3–5. For the Spanish text of the Oñate contract and a discussion of the Patarabueyes in that contract, see C. W. Hackett, *Historical Documents Relating to New Mexico, Nueva Vizcaya, and Approaches Thereto, to 1773, collected by Adolph F. A. Bandelier and Fanny R. Bandelier* (Carnegie Institution of Washington, 3 vols., 1923–37: vol. 1 [1923], vol. 2 [1926], vol. 3 [1937]), vol. 1, pp. 224–55. The Patarabueye comment is on pp. 234–35. Viceroy Monterrey's contract revisions can be found on pp. 263–79.

The Castaño and Morlete journeys are reported in Hammond and Rey, *Rediscovery*, 245–310. A detailed discussion of the Castaño route is found in A. H. Schroeder and D. S. Matson, *A Colony on the Move: Gaspar Castaño de Sosa's Journal, 1590–1591* (School of American Research, Santa Fe, N.Mex., 1965). See also Riley, *Rio del Norte*, pp. 242–45. There is a short seventeenth-century account of the Castaño expedition in Alonso de León, *Relación y discursos del descubrimiento, población, y pacificación de este Neubo Reino de León* (1649), in G. García, *Documentos inéditos ó muy raros para la historia de México: 25* (México, 1909). The Leyva and Humaña expedition is discussed in Hammond and Rey, *Rediscovery*, pp. 323–26; see also Riley, *Rio del Norte*, pp. 245–46, and E. A. H. John, *Storms Brewed in Other Men's Worlds* (University of Nebraska Press, Lincoln, 1975), pp. 36–37.

The Troyano attempt to gain a place in Southwestern exploration comes in a letter to the king reproduced in F. del Paso y Troncoso, *Epistolario de Nueva España, 1505–1818* (Antigua Librería Robredo, México, 16 vols., 1939–42), vol. 10, pp. 262–277. Espejo's petition to be allowed to return to New Mexico can be found in Hammond and Rey, *Rediscovery*, pp. 238–39. Late-sixteenth-century would-be settlers of New Mexico are cited in J. F. Bannon, *The Spanish*

Borderlands Frontier, 1513–1821 (Holt, Rinehart and Winston, New York, 1970), p. 34. See also M. Simmons, *The Last Conquistador* (University of Oklahoma Press, Norman, 1991), pp. 48–49. For a discussion of the native populations of the Southwest in the latter portion of the sixteenth century, see Riley, *Rio del Norte*, pp. 224, 266, 315. See also Riley, *Frontier People*, pp. 177–79, 230–32.

CHAPTER 4, ONATE

The reasons for colonization in the Southwest are discussed in Riley, *Rio del Norte*, p. 246. That the Spaniards actually thought seriously of sailing ships across the Atlantic to New Mexico is indicated by Oñate's contract of 1595. See Hackett, *Historical Documents*, vol. 1, pp. 22–25, and Monterrey's reaction to the project, vol. 1, pp. 270–73. A discussion of the possible relationship of Basque to the Apachean languages can be found in H. C. Fleming, "Dene-Caucasic, Nostratic and Eurasiatic or Vasco—Dene?" *Mother Tongue* 12 (Dec. 1990): 6–12. For the background to Oñate's life, especially valuable works are Simmons, *The Last Conquistador*, esp. chaps. 2 and 3, and D. Chipman, The Oñate-Moctezuma-Zaldívar Families of Northern New Spain, *New Mexico Historical Review* (*NMHR*) 52 (4) (1977): 297–310. Chipman points out (p. 304) that Cristóbal de Oñate's wife, Catalina de Salazar y de la Cadena, had a first husband living in Spain and so might have been a bigamist when she married Cristóbal (at least Chipman believed that there was no evidence for the marriage ever having been annulled). However, D. T. Garate ("Juan de Oñate's *Prueba de Caballero*, 1625: A Look at His Ancestral Heritage," *Colonial Latin American Historical Review* 7 [2] [1998]: 129–73) argues that Catalina's first husband was dead at the time she married Cristóbal de Oñate (p. 158). Garate also presents evidence that Cristóbal de Oñate came not from Vitoria, as is generally stated, but from the small town of Oñate to the north. For Catalina's converso ancestors, see J. A. Esquibel, "New Light on the Jewish-Converso Ancestry of Don Juan de Oñate: A Research Note," *Colonial Latin American Historical Review* 7 (2) (1998): 175–190; also *The Jewish-Converso Ancestry of Don Juan de Oñate* (limited Internet publication, Santa Fe, N.Mex, 1996), esp. sections on the Oñate, Salazar, Cadena-Martínez de Lerma-Mazuelo, Maluenda and Ha-Levi families. Esquibel is uncertain whether Juan de Oñate and his Zaldívar nephews were cognizant of their converso ancestry, seven generations before. However, as the historian Stanley Hordes has pointed out, a generalized memory and practice of Jewish ceremonies among Hispanic Southwestern and northern Mexican families sometime goes back for many generations. See S. M. Hordes, "The Sephardic Legacy in New Mexico: A History of Crypto-Jews, *Journal of the West* 35 (4) (1996): 82–89.

The date and place of Juan de Oñate's birth are still somewhat uncertain. The 1552 date comes from Lansing Bloom, in a letter from Seville dated Nov. 26, 1938 (see L. Bloom in "News Notes," *NMHR* 14 (1) (1939): 115–20). Bloom (p. 118) stated that he had seen a "probanza of 1578" in which a witness stated that Juan and Cristóbal Oñate were born "de un solo vientre" in 1552 in Zacatecas (presumably at the family estate in Pánuco). There does not seem to be any other indication that Juan and his brother Cristóbal were twins, so perhaps the twinship was fraternal (see Simmons, *Last Conquistador*, p. 34).

For a discussion of the Chichimec region, consult P. Kirchhoff, "Los Recolectores-Cazadores del Norte de México," *El Norte de México y el Sur de Estados Unidos* (Sociedad Mexicana de Antropología, Tercera Reunión de Mesa Redonda sobre Problemas Antropológicas de México y Centro America, Castillo de Chapultepec, México, 1943), pp. 133–144. An English version of this important paper appears in B. C. Hedrick, J. C. Kelley, and C. L. Riley, eds., *The North Mexican Frontier* (Southern Illinois University Press, Carbondale), pp. 200–209 (translated by C. L. Riley).

A good, though brief discussion of the problems of Juan de Oñate in getting his expedition together comes in G. P. Hammond and A. Rey, *Don Juan de Oñate, Colonizer of New Mexico, 1595–1628* (University of New Mexico Press, 1953, 2 vols.), vol. 1, pp. 7–15; the contract with Viceroy Velasco is given on pp. 42–57; the Monterrey modifications to the contract are given on p. 10. For Oñate's appointment as adelantado, see Hammond and Rey, *Oñate*, vol. 2, pp. 766–67; for the Ulloa inspection, see vol. 1, pp. 94–168. A cautionary note on certain shortcomings in the Hammond and Rey translation is sounded by J. R. Craddock, "Juan de Oñate in Quivira," *Journal of the Southwest*, vol 40, no. 4, 1998, pp. 481–540. A good summary discussion of the inspection is given in Simmons, *Last Conquistador*, pp. 82–83; see p. 45 for information on the family of Juan de Oñate and Isabel de Tolosa, and on Cristóbal's commission as lieutenant. The boy is not actually cited in the Salazar inspection but, curiously, is listed in the Ulloa inspection (Hammond and Rey, *Oñate*, vol. 1, p. 160). Simmons (*Last Conquistador*, p. 45) states that the daughter of Juan de Oñate and Isabel de Tolosa was born "in late 1598 or early 1599 at the family home in Pánuco." However, unless Isabel was with her husband for the part of the journey northward from Santa Bárbara, any child fathered by Oñate would surely have been born before the end of 1598. The position of Oñate's men as of the end of 1596 is given in Viceroy Monterrey's letter to the king dated November 15, 1596 (Hammond and Rey, *Oñate*, vol. 1, p. 184); for the Salazar inspection, see vol. 1, pp. 199–308. Salazar discusses the reinforcements guaranteed by Juan de Guerra in a letter to the viceroy dated May 4, 1598 (Hammond and Rey,

Oñate, vol. 1, pp. 390–92). A good description of the expedition at launch point comes from Simmons, *Last Conquistador,* pp. 93–97.

For castes in seventeenth-century Chihuahua, see C. Cramaussel, "Ilegítimos y abandonados en la frontera norte: Parral y San Bartolomé en el siglo XVII," *Colonial Latin American Historical Review* 4 (4) (1995): 405–38, 405–10. Chihuahua in the seventeenth century seems to have been a place with a great deal of racial mixture. Not only were there the Indian and mestizo castes, but numbers of Africans lived in the area, both slave and free. See Parral Archives (New Mexico Highlands University and DRSW files and University of Arizona Library), AZU Film 0318, RI. 1647, 1648, 1659 D, Roll 6172 G. 18–535, Roll 6724 R. 201–20.

A good summary of the personnel and equipment that finally went north with Juan de Oñate comes from Bannon, *Borderlands Frontier,* p. 36. Juan de Vasco Velasco (Hammond and Rey, *Oñate,* vol. 2, p. 609) says there were more than five hundred in the Oñate party. The recent analysis of the makeup of Oñate's expedition by D. H. Snow (*New Mexico's First Colonists: The 1597–1600 Enlistments for New Mexico under Juan de Oñate, Adelante and Gobernador* [Hispanic Genealogical Research Center of New Mexico, Albuquerque, 1998]) is an exceedingly valuable source. See esp. pp. 1–6 for a discussion of the makeup of the expedition. Of the domestic animals taken north by Oñate, the sheep are generally considered to be the churro variety, but this is not absolutely certain.

For the march itinerary, see Hammond and Rey, *Oñate,* vol. 1, pp. 309–19. The routing of Oñate is discussed in J. Roney, "Tracing the Camino Real," *El Camino Real del Tierra Adentro,* G. Palmer, ed. (New Mexico, Bureau of Land Management, Cultural Resources Series, no. 11, 1993), pp. 85–99, esp. the maps on pp. 88–90. Roney's comments on the Oñate route north from the Río Carmén can be found on p. 87. For more routing information, see the testimony taken in Mexico in late July 1601 ("Copie de las informaciones, recogidas sobre el estado de la Provincia del Nuevo México," Archivo General de Indias, Seville [AGI], est. 58, caja 3, leg. 15; from a copy in the Bancroft Library, Berkeley, Calif. [cited as *Informaciones,* 1601]). A slightly edited translation of this document can be found in Hammond and Rey, *Oñate,* vol. 2, 623–69 [Valverde Investigation of 1601].

The discussion of the Concho and Suma Indians draws on C. O. Sauer, *The Distribution of Aboriginal Tribes and Languages in Northwestern Mexico* (Ibero America, vol. 5, pp. 59–64 [Concho] and 65–74 [Jumano and Suma]). Additional information comes from W. B. Griffen, "Southern Periphery: East" (*Handbook of North American Indians* [*HNAI*], vol. 10, *Southwest,* A. Ortiz, ed. [Smithsonian Institution, Washington, D.C., 1983]), pp. 329–42. The archaeology of Chihuahua is covered in D. D. Brand, *The Chihuahuan Culture Area (New*

Mexico Anthropologist 6–7 [3] [1943]: 154–55). A valuable general discussion of this Camino Real can be found in M. L. Pérez-González, "Royal Roads in the Old and New World: The Camino de Oñate and Its Importance in the Spanish Settlement of New Mexico," *Colonial Latin American Historical Review* 7 (2) (1998): 191–218.

For the route to and up the Rio Grande to El Paso, see the Oñate itinerary, Hammond and Rey, *Oñate*, vol. 1, pp. 314–15. The official Act of Taking Possession is given on pp. 329–36; see also G. Pérez de Villagrá, *Historia de Nueva México, 1610, A Critical and Annotated Spanish/English Version*, trans. and eds. M. Encinias, A. Rodríguez, and J. P. Sánchez (University of New Mexico Press, Albuquerque, 1992), pp. 131–38. The initial subjection of the Rio Grande and Pecos River Pueblos is discussed in the Oñate Itinerary, Hammond and Rey, *Oñate*, vol. 1, pp. 315–28. For the Doña Inés story and the statements about Pedro Oroz (or as Hammond and Rey transcribe it, "Orez"), see p. 321. J. L. Kessell (*Kiva, Cross, and Crown* [University of New Mexico Press, Albuquerque, 1987], p. 77) points out that Juan de Dios was a *donado*—that is, an Indian "donated" to the Church from babyhood. Oñate refers to him as a "lay brother" (p. 321) and as "the beloved Franciscan lay brother" (p. 343). My arguments that Inés was from the Coronado expedition can be found in Riley, *Rio del Norte*, pp. 205–6, 249–50.

CHAPTER 5, THE PUEBLOS AND THEIR NEIGHBORS IN 1598

For a discussion of population among the Pueblos, see Riley, *Frontier People*, pp. 177–83, 230–32, 259; Riley *Rio del Norte*, pp. 224, 266. Oñate's estimates of 1599 are given in Hammond and Rey, *Oñate*, vol. 1, p. 485; those of Benavides for the 1620s are found in P. P. Forrestal and C. J. Lynch, *Benavides' Memorial of 1630* (Academy of American Franciscan History, Washington, D.C., 1954), pp. 13–34; for the quote on the Apache, see p. 14. See also A. H. Schroeder, "Rio Grande Ethnohistory," *New Perspectives on the Pueblos*, A. Ortiz, ed. (University of New Mexico Press, Albuquerque, 1972), pp. 40–70; on p. 48 Schroeder reaches the same conclusions as do I in estimating Oñate-period Pueblo populations. However, A. M. Palkovich ("Historic Population of the Eastern Pueblos: 1540–1910," *Journal of Anthropological Research* 41 [4] [1985]: 401–26) tends to accept the Oñate figure of 60,000 (p. 406). But a recent intriguing article (H. Roberts and R. V. N. Ahlstrom, "Malaria, Microbes, and Mechanisms of Change," *The Kiva* 63 [2] [1997]: 117–35) suggests that malaria was possibly introduced—at least to Sonoran and Arizonan populations—by Coronado's army. Whether the malaria plasmodium could have maintained itself in the Rio Grande Basin is an open question, but it might have done so on a low level. In addition, D. T. Reff (*Disease, Depopulation, and Culture Change in Northwestern New Spain* [University of Utah Press, Salt Lake City, 1991], p. 109) place both measles and dysentery in the Sinaloa area some six years before Coronado's expedition. As Roberts and Ahlstrom (*Malaria*, p. 123) point out, some of the Coronado contingent was drawn from this very region. If the general conditions postulated by H. F. Dobyns in "Estimating Aboriginal American Population: An Appraisal of Techniques with a New Hemispheric Estimate," (*Current Anthropology* 7 [4] [1966]: 395–416) hold for the Southwest, as I think they surely do, then some population decline between Coronado's time and that of Oñate seems inevitable. For another view of the population problem, see D. Henige, *Numbers from Nowhere: The American Indian Contact Population Debate* (University of Oklahoma Press, Norman, 1998).

The Teya and Querecho are discussed in Riley, *Teya*, pp. 320–343. For the Comanche, see E. Wallace and E. A. Hoebel, *The Comanche: Lords of the South Plains* (University of Oklahoma Press, Norman, 1952), pp. 8, 325–28; G. Hyde, *Indians of the High Plains* (University of Oklahoma Press, 1959), pp. 52–62, 95–98. Hyde (p. 62) thinks the term *Comanche* may come from that tribe's name for itself, *Neuma* with a Ute ending *-ache*. The resultant *Neumache* was distorted by the Spaniards into *Ceumache* or *Comanche*. T. R. Fehrenbach (*Comanches: The Destruction of a People* [De Capo Press, New York, 1994 (first published in 1974), pp. xiii, 90–91) gives the native Uto-Aztecan name as *Nermernuh* ("true human beings"), with the Spanish *Comanche* being a misrendering of the Ute word for these people, *Koh-mats*, "those who are always against us." Another, rather unlikely possibility is that *Comanche* comes from two Spanish words: *camino* and *ancho* (broad road).

For Frederick W. Hodge's comprehensive list of pueblos, see Hammond and Rey, *Oñate*, vol. 1, pp. 363–74. The Martínez map is reproduced as end pieces in Hammond and Rey, *Rediscovery*. For an overall figure on pueblos, see Juan de Torquemada, *Monarquía indiana* (Nicolas Rodriguez Franco, Madrid, 1723, 3 vols. [reprinted from the 1615 edition]), vol. 1, p. 679. For the situation among the Tewa in Castaño's time, see Schroeder and Matson, *Colony*, pp. 130–33. The Zuni situation is described in some detail in *A Zuni Life*, by V. Wyaco, transcribed and edited by J. A. Jones, Historical Sketch by C. L. Riley (University of New Mexico Press, Albuquerque, 1998).

Fray Francisco de Escobar's comments on Zuni population as of 1605 are found in Hammond and Rey, *Oñate*, vol. 2, pp. 1013–14. Hopi towns at the beginning of history are discussed in C. L. Riley, *The Protohistoric Hopi* (manuscript in the files of the Laboratory of Anthropology, Santa Fe, N.Mex.), chap. 1, pp. 8–9. See also J. O. Brew, "Hopi Prehistory and History to 1850," *HNAI,* vol. 9, *Southwest* (Smithsonian Institution, Washington, D.C., 1979), pp. 514–23. A good overview of the Pueblo settlements in the sixteenth century is given in A. H. Schroeder, "Pueblos Abandoned in Historic Times," *HNAI,* vol. 9, pp. 236–54.

For languages of the Southwest, see Riley, *Rio del Norte,* pp. 96–105. Pueblo trade, including that which extended into the Spanish period, is discussed in Riley, *Frontier People,* pp. 190–98, 236–40, 267–77, 302–4, 319–24.

An excellent source on the Manso is P. H. Beckett and T. L. Corbett, *The Manso Indians* (COAS Publishing and Research, Las Cruces, N.Mex., 1992). The relationship between the Manso and the El Paso phase of the Jornada Mogollon is discussed on pp. 39–47, 53–56 (Appendix A, contributed by David V. Hill). Michael Whalen's comments on the doubtful 1561 date can be found on p. 45.

For the term Tanpachoas, see Hammond and Rey, *Rediscovery,* p. 169. Oñate's statement on the Manso can be found in Hammond and Rey, *Oñate,* vol. 1, p. 315. Coronado's contact with the Mansos is discussed in Riley, *Rio del Norte,* p. 166.

For a discussion of the Manso language, see Beckett and Corbett, *Manso,* pp. 32–37. Other speculation on the languages of this region can be found in N. P. Hickerson, *The Jumanos* (University of Texas Press, Austin, 1994), pp. 321–22. T. H. Naylor ("Athapaskans They Weren't: The Suma Rebels Executed at Casas Grandes in 1685," *The Protohistoric Period in the North American Southwest: A.D. 1450–1700,* D. R. Wilcox and W. B. Masse, eds. [Arizona State University, Anthropological Research Papers, no. 24, 1881], pp. 275–81, p. 278) suggests that the Sumas were culturally and linguistically related to several of the Chihuahuan and Texas groups, including the Concho and Jumano (p. 278). He does not deal with the Mansos. An argument that the Jumanos were separate from both the Suma and Manso is given by B. Lockhart in "Protohistoric Confusion: A Cultural Comparison of the Manso, Suma, and Jumano Indians of the Paso del Norte Region," *Journal of the Southwest* 39 (1) (1997): 113–49, p. 141. See also C. F. Schaafsma, "Ethnohistoric Groups in the Casas Grandes Region: Circa A.D. 1500–1700," *Layers of Time: Papers in Honor of Robert H. Weber,* Archaeological Society of New Mexico, 23, M. S. Duran and D. T. Kirkpatrick, eds. (Albuquerque, N.Mex., 1997), who ably summarizes the several positions on ethnic identity in the region (pp. 85–98).

For cultural material on the Manso, see Hammond and Rey, *Oñate,* vol. 1, p. 315; Hammond and Rey, *Rediscovery,* pp. 78–79, 169, 218; and Forrestal and Lynch, *Benavides' Memorial,* pp. 10–13.

Trade in the Southwest both pre- and post-Columbian is discussed in Riley, *Frontier People* (see trade under various chapter headings); see also Riley, *Rio del*

Norte, pp. 112–18. For macaws in Pueblo IV and later times, consult Hargrave, *Mexican Macaws*, pp. 49–54. For the homeland of the scarlet macaw, see E. R. Blake, *Birds of Mexico* (University of Chicago Press, Chicago, 1953). Comments on the military macaw and the thick-billed parrot can be found in D. Creel and C. R. McKusick, "Prehistoric Macaws and Parrots in the Mimbres Area, New Mexico," *American Antiquity* 59 (3) (1994): 510–24, esp. p. 511. P. Y. Bullock ("Are Macaws Valid Indications of Southwestern Regional Trade?" paper presented at the 59th annual meeting of the Society for American Archaeology, Pittsburgh, Penn., 1992, Office of Archaeological Studies, Museum of New Mexico, Santa Fe) has challenged identifications of scarlet macaws found in archaeological contexts. In my opinion, however, Bullock overstates the difficulties in making such determinations.

For origin of the Pecos glazes, see A. O. Shepard, "Rio Grande Glaze-paint Pottery: A Test of Petroglyphic Analysis," *Ceramics and Man*, F. R. Matson, ed. (Viking Fund Publications in Anthropology, no. 41, 1965, pp. 62–87), pp. 69–81. For the Protohistoric pottery traditions in the Rio Grande area, see D. H. Snow, *Rio Grande Glaze Tradition*. A good discussion of the properties of fibrolite is found in A. V. Kidder, *The Artifacts of Pecos* (Yale University Press, New Haven, Conn., 1932), pp. 50–51. For Zaldívar's comments on trade from the Southwest to the Plains, see Hammond and Rey, *Oñate*, vol. 1, p. 400. Trade in the same area was commented on during the Valverde Inquiry of 1602, given in Hammond and Rey, *Oñate*, vol. 2, pp. 836–77; see p. 864.

The influence of the Spaniards on the sixteenth-century Pueblos is discussed in Riley, *Rio del Norte*, pp. 209–24. See also Schroeder, *Rio Grande Ethnohistory*, esp. pp. 47–51. The use of the four-pointed star is discussed in P. Schaafsma, "Feathered Stars and Scalps in Pueblo IV," ms. in library, Laboratory of Anthropology, Museum of New Mexico, Santa Fe, n.d. See also P. Schaafsma, *Warriors, Shields, and Stars: War Imagery and Ideology of the Pueblos, A.D. 1250–1600* (Western Edge Press, Santa Fe, in press).

For agricultural practices among the Pueblos in Oñate's time, see Riley, *Rio del Norte*, pp. 214–15. Hunting in late prehistoric times (presumably much the same as in Oñate's days) is discussed on p. 104. Native plants and animals used by the Pueblos as of Oñate's time, including melons(!), are listed in Hammond and Rey, *Oñate*, vol. 1, pp. 481–82. For the early arrival of melons, see R. I. Ford, "The New Pueblo Economy," *When Cultures Meet: Remembering San Gabriel del Yungue Oweenge* (Sunstone Press, Santa Fe, N.Mex., 1987, pp. 73–91), pp. 77–78. Ford thinks the melons may have spread from the Conchos area in late pre-Oñate times. I think it possible (perhaps even likely) that they were left by Coronado. For the mention of chile by the Espejo party, see M. Cuevas, *Historia de los descubrimientos antiguos y modernas de la Nueva España, escrita por el conquistador Baltasar de Obregón* (Departo. Editorial de la Sría de Educación Publica, México, 1924), p. 304. Castaño de Sosa also mentions chile peppers; see Hammond and Rey, *Rediscovery*, p. 278. Late prehistoric plant and animal use is discussed by K. A. Spielmann and E. A. Angstadt-Leto, "Hunting, Gathering, and Health in the Prehistoric Southwest," *Evolving Complexity and Environmental Risk in the Prehistoric Southwest*, J. A. Tainter and B. B. Tainter, eds. (Proceedings of the Santa Fe Institute, vol. 24, Addison-Wesley, Reading, Mass., 1996), pp. 79–106.

For plant use among the historic Pueblos, see M. C. Stevenson, *The Zuni Indians* (Rio Grande Press, Glorieta, N.Mex., 1985 [originally published as BAE-AR 23, 1904]), pp. 385–86, 390–439. See also M. C. Stevenson, *Ethnobotany of the Zuni Indians* (BAE-AR 30, 1915), pp. 35–102; see pp. 39–64 for medicinal plants, and pp. 65–83 for edible plants or ones used in weaving, dyeing, basket making, pottery decoration, and as cosmetics. For other Pueblos, see L. A. White, *The Pueblo of Santo Domingo* (AAA Memoir 43, 1935), esp. p. 80; A. F. Whiting, *Ethnobotany of the Hopi* (Museum of Northern Arizona, Northland Press, Flagstaff, 1966); C. H. Lange, *The Cochiti* (University of Texas Press, Austin, 1959), esp. pp. 125–41 (hunting and fishing), pp. 145–52 (use of plants); W. W. Robbins, J. P. Harrington, and B. Freire-Marreco, *Ethnobotany of the Tewa Indians* (*BAE Bulletin* 55 [1916]). For comparison with Southwestern Hispanics, consult K. C. Ford, *Las Yerbas de la Gente: A Study of Hispano-American Medical Plants* (Museum of Anthropology, University of Michigan, Anthropological Papers 60, 1975). G. D. Tierney ("How Did Domesticated Plants Come to the Southwest?" *El Palacio* 89 [1] [1983]: 11–17, p. 16) cautions that certain "camp-following" weeds, including plants like purslane, may have arrived with the early Spaniards (p. 16). Animals in the northern Rio Grande Basin are discussed in J. Henderson and J. P. Harrington, *Ethnozoology of the Tewa Indians* (*BAE Bulletin* 56 [1914]).

For astronomical observations of the P-II and P-III Pueblos, see J. M. Malville and C. Putnam, *Prehistoric Astronomy in the Southwest* (Johnson Books, Boulder, Colo., 1989). A discussion of Chimney Rock comes on pp. 45–55. See also R. B. Powers, W. B. Gillespie, and S. H. Lekson, *The Outlier Survey* (National Park Service, Division of Cultural Research, Reports of the Chaco Center, no. 3, 1983), pp. 156–61. A discussion of solar-lunar correspondences comes in J. E. Reyman, "The Predictive Dimension of Priestly Power," *New Frontiers in the Archaeology and Ethnohistory of the Greater Southwest*, C. L. Riley and B. C. Hedrick, eds. (Transactions of the Illinois Academy of Science, vol. 72, no. 4, 1980 [whole volume], pp. 40–55). A useful discussion of the ceremonial calendar among

Southwestern Indians comes in E. C. Parsons, *Pueblo Indian Religion* (2 vols., University of Chicago Press, 1939), vol. 1, pp. 493–549.

A common interpretation of Casas Grandes is that the site itself was the head of a mercantile "empire," the result of settlement by traders from Mesoamerica. This was the thrust of C. C. Di Peso, *Casas Grandes: A Fallen Trading Center of the Gran Chichimeca* (Amerind Foundation, Dragoon, Ariz., and Northland Press, Flagstaff, 3 vols.), esp. vol. 2, pp. 290–95. More recently, there has been a tendency to consider the Casas Grandes area as more diffuse with a number of centers, trading locally and influencing a considerable region in northern Chihuahua and southern New Mexico. See the discussion in Schaafsma and Riley, *Casas Grandes*. For the kachina cult among the pueblos, see P. Schaafsma, "The Prehistoric Kachina Cult and Its Origins," *Kachinas in the Pueblo World*, P. Schaafsma, ed. (University of New Mexico Press, Albuquerque, 1994), pp. 63–79; E. C. Adams, "The Katsina Cult: A Western Pueblo Perspective," in P. Schaafsma, ed., *Kachinas*, pp. 35–46; D. Tedlock, "Stories of Kachinas and the Dance of Life and Death," in P. Schaafsma, ed., *Kachinas*, pp. 161–74, esp. pp. 162–63. Regarding the direction of spread of the original cult, an argument for a diffusion up the Rio Grande from the Jornada Mogollon is given in P. Schaafsma, ed., *Kachina Cult*, pp. 78–79; see also Schaafsma and Schaafsma, "Evidence for the *Origins of the Pueblo Kachina Cult*, pp. 535–45. A diffusion out of Mexico to a more westerly locus is argued by Adams, *Katsina Cult*, pp. 45–46. See also E. C. Adams, *Origin*. The comments on Quetzalcoatl and Chalchihuitlicue are from a manuscript version of C. R. McKusick's *Southwest Birds of Sacrifice*, chaps. 13 and 14 (manuscript at Southwestern Bird Laboratory, Globe, Ariz.) and from personal correspondence with McKusick. For a discussion of sun, moon, and duality symbolism found among the Mimbres and their diffusion to the Pueblo world, see Thompson, *Mimbres Iconography*. On the twin aspects of Quetzalcoatl and its relationship to the twin stories elsewhere in Mesoamerica, see B. C. Brundage, *The Phoenix of the Western World* (University of Oklahoma Press, Norman, 1981), pp. 206, 220–21; also A. Caso, *The Aztecs: People of the Sun* (University of Oklahoma Press, Norman, 1958), p. 24. See also Riley, *Rio del Norte*, pp. 109–12 (kachina cult) and 218–21 (Shalako). Ted J. Warner speculates that in the winter of 1776 Domínguez and Escalante may have lingered at Zuni to see the Shalako, but there is no evidence one way or the other for this. See T. J. Warner, ed., and Fray A. Chavez, trans., *The Domínguez-Escalante Journal* (University of Utah Press, Salt Lake City, 1995), p. 140. For Apache religion, consult Forrestal and Lynch, *Benavides' Memorial*, pp. 43–44. C. C. Di Peso ("Casas Grandes and the Gran Chichimeca," *El Palacio* 75 [4] [1968]: 47–61) discusses the Mesoamerican Quetzalcoatl cult.

M. J. Young ("The Interconnection between Western Puebloan and Mesoamerican Ideology/Cosmology," in P. Schaafsma, ed., *Kachinas in the Pueblo World*, pp. 107–20, esp. p. 109) has tentatively related the ancient Old Fire God of Mesoamerica (called Huehueteotl by the Aztecs) with the Zuni Shulawitsi and the Hopi Somaikoli and Kawikoli. She sees a relationship between Quetzalcoatl, the Zuni Pautiwa, and the Hopi Eototo; while both Quetzalcoatl and Tlaloc may be ancestral to Zuni Kolowisi and Hopi Palölökong, the horned serpent. She also points up the similarity of Quetzalcoatl to the twin war-gods of Zuni and Hopi (p. 115).

For modern (and traditional) Pueblo sociopolitical and ceremonial organization, see E. J. Ladd, "Cushing Among the Zuni," *Gilcrease Journal* 2 (2) (1994): 20–35; also consult E. J. Ladd, "Zuni Social and Political Organization," *HNAI*, A. Ortiz, vol. ed., vol. 9, pp. 482–91). In this Ortiz-edited volume 9 of *HNAI*, see also E. J. Ladd, "Zuni Economy," pp. 492–98; D. Tedlock, "Zuni Religion and World View," pp. 499–508; J. C. Connelly, "Hopi Social Organization," pp. 539–53; A. Frigout, "Hopi Ceremonial Organization," pp. 564–76. For the eastern Pueblos, see various articles in vol. 9 of *HNAI*. Also consult B. P. Dutton, *American Indians of the Southwest* (University of New Mexico Press, Albuquerque, 1983), pp. 9–31; E. P. Dozier, *The Pueblo Indians of North America* (Holt, Rinehart and Winston, New York, 1970), pp. 133–76, 200–212. Dozier's statement on the recent diffusion of Tanoan clans comes on pp. 165–66. For material on the cacique among the Keresan Pueblos, see L. A. White, *The Pueblo of Santa Ana, New Mexico* (American Anthropological Association, Memoir 60, 1942), pp. 96–99. The idea that originally all the Pueblos were matrilineal comes from R. A. Gutiérrez, *When Jesus Came, the Corn Mothers Went Away* (Stanford University Press, Stanford, Calif., 1991), p. 79.

For a discussion of Jumano and Apache culture in the sixteenth and later centuries, see W. W. Newcomb Jr., *The Indians of Texas* (University of Texas Press, Austin, 1961), pp. 225–45 (Jumanos), 103–31 (Lipan Apaches). See also M. E. Opler, "The Apachean Culture Pattern and Its Origins," *HNAI*, A. Ortiz, vol. ed., vol. 10, 1983, pp. 368–92; also R. M. Underhill, *The Navajos* (University of Oklahoma Press, Norman, 1956), pp. 3–32. For a survey of early Apacheans, see Y. R. Oakes, "Expanding Athabaskan Chronometric Boundaries in West Central New Mexico," *La Jornada, Papers in Honor of William F. Turney*, M. S. Duran and D. T. Kirkpatrick, eds. (Archaeological Society of New Mexico, 22), pp. 139–49. Questions as to Navajo origins are certainly unsettled. For the early identification of Apaches de Navajo, see Forrestal and Lynch, *Benavides' Memorial*, esp. pp. 44–52 (for the location of the Navajo, see pp. 44–45, 52); F. W. Hodge, G. P. Hammond, and A. Rey, *Fray Alonso de Benavides' Revised Memorial of 1634*

(University of New Mexico Press, Albuquerque, 1945), pp. 306–10; G. Zárate Salmerón, *Relaciones de todas las cosas que en Nueva México . . . 1538–1626* (Documentos para la historia de México, 3rd sér., México, 1856); an English translation is *Relaciones: An Account of Things Seen and Learned by Father Jerónimo de Zárate Salmerón,* A. R. Milich, ed. (Horn and Wallace Pubs., Albuquerque, N.Mex., 1966); for the material on the Navajos, see p. 94. Identification of the name *Tacabuy* as perhaps Navajo comes from J. D. Forbes, "The Early Western Apache," *Journal of the West* 5 (1966): 336–54, p. 349. For Zárate Salmerón's work at Jemez, consult J. D. Forbes, *Apache, Navajo, and Spaniard* (University of Oklahoma Press, Norman, 1960), esp. pp. 114–15. Apachean contact with the Jemez in the seventeenth century is considered by D. M. Brugge, "Pueblo Factionalism and External Relations," *Ethnohistory* 16 (2) (1969): 191–200, esp. pp. 192–93. The question of Navajo penetration into the Chama area is discussed in C. F. Schaafsma, "The Piedra Lumbre Phase and the Origin of the Navajo," paper presented at the 58th annual meeting of the Society for American Archaeology, St. Louis, Mo., 1993 (copy available at the library, Laboratory of Anthropology, Santa Fe, N.Mex.). C. R. McKusick and J. N. Young (*The Gila Pueblo Salado* [Salado Chapter, Arizona Archaeological Society, Globe, 1997], p. 121) believe for example that the historic Navajo trait of leaving spirit exits (broken lines or other imperfections) in manufactured goods may have Salado (Mogollon) origins, probably transmitted through the western Pueblos.

CHAPTER 6, THE FIRST DECADE IN SPANISH NEW MEXICO

Much of the information in this chapter comes from the various Oñate documents collected by Hammond and Rey (*Oñate*) and found in Villagrá's *Historia.* For background on the Franciscans, see Torquemada, *Monarquía indiana.* Specific information on the Oñate period in New Mexico comes from Torquemada, vol. 1, pp. 672–81. There is also some information in J. de Villagutierre Sotomayor, *Historia de la Nueva México,* A. C. Herrera, ed. (Madrid, 1953). The early settlements at Okeh and Yungue are discussed in F. Hawley Ellis, "The Long Lost City of San Gabriel del Yungue," *When Cultures Meet,* H. Agoyo and L. Brown, eds.; *San Gabriel del Yungue* (Sunstone Press, Santa Fe, N.Mex., 1989), and "San Gabriel del Yungue as seen by an Archaeologist, 1985" (manuscript in the library, Laboratory of Anthropology, Museum of New Mexico, Santa Fe). The "merciful punishment" statement by Oñate comes in the Itinerary of the Expedition, Hammond and Rey, *Oñate,* vol. 1, p. 323. The Obedience and Vassalage document for Santo Domingo is in vol.

1, pp. 337–41; the document for San Juan is on pp. 342–47; see esp. pp. 342–43 for the quote on the missionaries' willingness to go to their various stations. For an excellent secondary source, see Simmons, *Last Conquistador.*

Oñate's trip westward in 1598 and the struggle for Acoma, 1598–99, is to be found in a number of sources, especially Villagrá, *Historia,* and in various of the Oñate documents collected by Hammond and Rey, *Oñate.* See especially the acts of obedience and vassalage at Acoma and Zuni, vol. 1, pp. 354–62; Farfán's trip to the Zuni salines and central Arizona, vol. 1, pp. 406–15; the Sanchez letter of Feb. 28, 1599, pp. 425–27; the various Acoma trial data, pp. 428–79; the Luis Gasco de Velasco report, vol. 2, pp. 608–18; and the Ginés de Herrera Horta account, vol. 2, pp. 643–57, especially the information given Herrera by Fray Juan de Escalona and others about Acoma (pp. 648–50). For the trip to central Arizona mines, see K. Bartlett, "Notes upon the Routes of Espejo and Farfán . . . ," *NMHR* 17 (1): 21–36. For the Zutacapán story, see Villagrá, *Historia,* pp. 167–70, 175–79. Zutacapán's son was named Zutancalpo, which like Zutacapán has somewhat of a Nahuatl or Aztec flavor (see pp. 246–47). A superior secondary source is G. P. Hammond, "Don Juan de Oñate and the Founding of New Mexico" (hereafter referred to as "Founding"), *NMHR* 1 (1): 77; 1 (2): 156–92; 1 (3): 292–323; 1 (4): 445–77 (all 1926); 2 (1): 37–66; 2 (2): 134–74 (both 1927). See esp. 1 (4): 445–62, which discussed the attack on Acoma. Gutiérrez (*When Jesus Came,* pp. 52–53) believes that the immediate cause of the battle was a confusion about goods given the Spaniards by the Indians. The Spaniards looked on these goods as tribute, and the Indians saw them as gifts.

The official story of the battle of Acoma is given in Villagrá, *Historia,* and Hammond and Rey, *Oñate,* vol. 1 (Sánchez's account, esp. pp. 426–27). Alonso Sánchez says that more than 800 people died and about 580 were captured. For the Gasco de Velasco account, see pp. 614–15. Vasco's earlier support for Oñate is indicated by his signature on a laudatory letter (the New Mexico army to the King of Spain) dated Mar. 6, 1599 (Hammond and Rey, *Oñate,* vol. 1, pp. 490–91). For the disposition of the little girls from Acoma, see G. Espinosa, ed., *History of New Mexico by Gaspar Pérez de Villagrá* (Quivira Society, Los Angeles, 1933), p. 32. The statement by Oñate on shipment of the older Acoma Indians to the Querecho is found in Hammond and Rey, *Oñate,* vol. 1, p. 478. The quote on Oñate's conviction in regard to the Acoma war can be found in *Oñate* vol. 2, p. 1111.

In his search for metals, Oñate seemed to ignore the fact that except for marginal use for decorative purposes, the Pueblo Indians did not seem to use or have any. See *Informaciones* (1601), pp. 8, 20, 36, 60; mines in the San Marcos area are reported on pp. 11, 27, 45, where one informant, Jusepe Briendar, claimed to have seen ore that yielded four ounces of silver. For an English translation, see

Hammond and Rey (*Oñate,* vol. 2, p. 630), who identify the soldier as Joseph Brondate. Regarding the settlement in the San Juan area, I have suggested in a previous book (Riley, *Rio del Norte,* p. 250) that the Spaniards actually made the switch from Okeh to Yungue. However, David H. Snow (personal communication) points out that there is no real evidence for such a move. Information on the church at San Gabriel comes from Hawley Ellis, *Archaeologist,* pp. 66–74; also Hawley Ellis, *When Cultures Meet,* pp. 33–35.

The troubles in the Tompiro country are discussed by Gasco de Velasco (Hammond and Rey, *Oñate,* vol. 2, p. 615); see also the Valverde investigation of 1601 (pp. 650–65), and also the report of Fray Juan de Escalona to the viceroy, dated Oct. 1, 1601 (*Oñate,* vol. 2, p. 693). It has sometimes been said that Escalona informed the viceroy that 800 men, women, and children had been killed in Tompiro country. However, Escalona was referring to both the Acoma and the Tompiro (Hammond and Rey, *Oñate,* vol. 2, p. 693). In any case, Vicente de Zaldívar's *Servicios* of 1602 (AGI, Guadalajara 252: 103-3-23) gave another story. Zaldívar claims that the war was concluded peacefully because of the benign attitude of himself and the Spanish forces.

For the murders of Aguilar and Sosa, see the report of Captain Vasco de Velasco (Hammond and Rey, *Oñate,* vol. 2, pp. 612–13). However, Simmons (*Last Conquistador,* p. 159) correctly points out that our only source for these atrocities is Vasco, whose enmity to Oñate was well known. There may have been ameliorating circumstances, though the desertion of three of his most important captains suggests the possibility that Oñate was somewhat unstable.

Identification of the Escanjaques ("una Ranchería de yndos en q avia mas de 7U aminas") includes the idea of N. P. Hickerson (*The Jumano,* pp. 71–72) that they might have been Apachean. M. M. Wedel (*Wichita Indians,* p. 121) suggested Tonkawa, while W. W. Newcomb and T. N. Campbell ("Southern Plains Ethnohistory: A Re-examination of the Escanjaque, Ahijados, and Cuitoas, *Pathways to Plains Prehistory,* D. G. Wyckoff and J. L. Hofman, eds. [Oklahoma Anthropological Society, Memoir 3, 1982], pp. 35–38) believe that they were Caddoan-speaking. A discussion of Oñate in Wichita country can be found in M. M. Wedel, "The Ethnohistoric Approach to Plains Caddoan Origins," *Nebraska History* 60 (1979): 183–96. For Wichita in the Coronado period, see M. M. Wedel, *Turco,* pp. 153–62. For Catarax and Tatarrax (or as Hammond and Rey spell the name, Tatarax), see Hammond and Rey, *Oñate,* vol. 2, p. 754 and 754 n. 15, and López de Gómara, *Historia general,* tomo 2 , p. 236.

Torquemada (*Monarquía indiana,* vol. 1, p. 679) talks of fields of wheat, barley, and maize, all irrigated from the Río Chama, as well as onions, lettuce, radishes, cabbages, melons, and watermelons. For a discussion of wheat planting at San Gabriel, see Hammond, "Founding," p. 51; for comments on the period 1601–4, see pp. 58–61. For problems in the colony, see the Valverde Investigation (Hammond and Rey, *Oñate*, vol. 2, pp. 623–69); desertion of the colony (pp. 672–89); Escalona's letters (pp. 692–700; and the petition of the loyalists (pp. 701–39). For the trip to the South Sea, see Escobar's diary, pp. 1012–34. A later account of this trip is given by Zárate Salmerón (*Relaciones*, pp. 64–76). For comments on the misidentification of steatite as silver, see Riley, *Frontier People*, pp. 151–52.

The various events that led to Oñate's removal and the appointment of Peralta can be found in Hammond and Rey, *Oñate*, vol. 2, pp. 1006–11, 1032–1105. See also Simmons, *Last Conquistador*, 178–95; and F. V. Scholes, "Church and State in New Mexico, 1610–1650," *NMHR* 11 (1) (1936): chaps. 1 and 2, pp. 9–76; *NMHR* 11 (2) (1936): chap. 3, 145–78; *NMHR* 11 (3): chap. 4, 283–94; *NMHR* 11 (4): chap. 5, 297–349; *NMHR* 12 (1) (1937): chaps. 6 and 7, 78–106. For the Martínez de Montoya story, see the collection of Martínez de Montoya papers at the History Library, Museum of New Mexico. This includes various petitions and statements of Martínez de Montoya's descendants documenting their ancestor's deeds in New Mexico. Also consult F. V. Scholes, "Juan Martínez de Montoya, Settler and Conquistador of New Mexico," *NMHR* 19 (4) (1944): 337–42. The statement on the San Buenaventura mines is found on p. 340.

The story of Cristóbal has been related by A. Rey ("Cristóbal de Oñate," *NMHR* 26 [3] [1951]): 197–203). See also the 1953 reprint of the compilation of F. Murcia de la Llana, *Canciones lugvbres, y tristes, a la muerte de Don Christoval de Oñate. Teniente de Governador, y Capitán General de las conquistas del Nuevo México* (Madrid, 1622 [reprinted 1953 in Valencia]). In a "Prologo," Agapito Rey and José M. Blecua analyze the book and discuss the problems of Cristóbal's life. Parenthetically, there is little substantive information on Cristóbal in the actual poems that make up the body of the book. The statement about the younger Oñate being killed by Indians comes from L. B. Bloom, "Oñate's Exoneration," *NMHR* 7 (2) (1937): 175–92, p. 175. The last years of Oñate are described by E. Beerman, "The Death of an Old Conquistador: New Light on Juan de Oñate," *NMHR* 54 (4) (1979): 305–19. Rey and Blecua, in the prologue to *Canciones lugubres* (p. 22), speak of a 1628 document that suggests Oñate was still alive as of that time. This, however, would seem to be an error since Beerman (see esp. pp. 311–12) presents convincing evidence of the death date. It is not clear to what extent Oñate relatives may have maintained themselves in New Mexico, but Fray Angélico Chávez (*Origins of New Mexico Families* [Museum of New Mexico Press, Santa Fe, rev.ed., 1992]) lists neither the Oñate nor the Zaldívar family as continuing on into the later seventeenth century. Parenthetically, Fray Angelico in the latter part of his life preferred not to accent either of his names. This leads to a certain inconsistency in the bibliographic citations. For example, Chavez uses the accent in *Origins* but does not use it in the Warner and Chavez book cited above.

CHAPTER 7, CHURCH AND STATE THROUGH MID-CENTURY

An excellent discussion of the problems in interpreting seventeenth-century history comes from W. H. Broughton, "The History of Seventeenth-Century New Mexico: Is It Time for New Interpretations? *NMHR* 68 (1) (1993): 3–12. Broughton is certainly correct about the unbalanced nature of the materials available; however, for reasons discussed in this chapter, I do not agree that Scholes was particularly pro-Franciscan. A paper by Van Hastings Garner ("Seventeenth-Century New Mexico," *Journal of Mexican American History* 4 [1974] [Santa Barbara, Calif.]: 41–70) makes some good points, but I feel that his critical comments about Scholes are somewhat off the mark.

Information on the beginnings of the Inquisition in the Americas comes from C. H. Haring, *Spanish Empire,* pp. 203–5. For Ordóñez's use (or misuse) of the Inquisition, see Scholes, *Church and State,* chaps. 1 and 2, pp. 46–47; see also F. V. Scholes, "The First Decade of the Inquisition in New Mexico," *NMHR* 10 (3): 195–241, p. 196. The evidence pointing to Benavides being the first Inquisition commissary is given in F. V. Scholes, "Problems in the Early Ecclesiastical History of New Mexico," *NMHR* 7 (1) (1932): 32–74; see esp. p. 53.

A second organization, the Santa Cruzada, also operated in New Mexico but was of minor importance in the church and state controversy. The Santa Cruzada ("bulls of crusade") granted by the pope to Spain for sale of indulgences to finance Spanish wars against the Moors may have dated from the twelfth or thirteenth centuries. They were continued after completion of the Reconquista in 1492, the justification now being the Spanish wars against the Turks and against Muslims in Africa. Sale of these indulgences began in the New World perhaps as early as 1535, with all castas eligible to purchase them except for Indians. A commissary sub-delegate authorized to sell the indulgences was appointed for New Mexico in 1633 (see Haring, *Spanish Empire,* pp. 135, 286–87). The legal status of this commissary in New Mexico quickly became still another bone of contention between governor and clergy (Scholes, *Church and State,* chap. 5, pp. 304–7). The Santa Cruzada was only one more irritant in the struggle between church and state. For the reaction of the Santa Fe cabildo in 1638 to the bulls of indulgences, see Report of the Cabildo to Viceroy, dated Feb. 21, 1639 (Hackett, *Historical Documents,* vol. 3, pp. 66–74).

Information on mining in early New Mexico comes in Hackett, *Historical Documents*, vol. 3, p. 109. For the instructions to Peralta, see the transcription of L. B. Bloom, "Ynstrucción a Peralta por Vi-Rey," *NMHR* 4 (2) (1929): 178–87. See also L. B. Bloom, "When Was Santa Fe Founded?" *NMHR* 4 (2) (1929): 188–201. The founding of the Franciscan custodia in New Mexico is discussed in great detail in Scholes, *Ecclesiastical History*, esp. pp. 52–59. For the numbers of encomenderos, see John, *Storms*, pp. 67–68; also Hickerson, *Jumano*, p. 79. For the organization of the province into subdivisions, see F. V. Scholes, "Civil Government and Society in New Mexico in the Seventeenth Century," *NMHR* 10 (2) (1935): 71–III, pp. 91–92.

Events of the Eulate governorship are told in Scholes, *Church and State*, chap. 3; the decrees of 1621 are discussed on pp. 151–56. See also the letter from Viceroy D. Fernández de Córdova to Governor Eulate dated Mar. 10, 1620 (L. B. Bloom, "A Glimpse of New Mexico in 1620," *NMHR* 3 (4): 357–80, esp. pp. 365–68; for the enslavement of Pueblo orphan children, see pp. 149, 170 n. 21.; see also Scholes, *Civil Government*, p. 83. Scholes doubted that the authorities in Mexico City actually considered the orphans "slaves" in the legal sense of the word. Documents relating to the Eulate investigation can be found in Inquisición, Siglo XVII, Archivo General de la Nación, Mexico City, (AGN), tomo 257. For the Benavides period, see Scholes, *Church and State*, chap. 3, 162–63, 173; chap. 4, p. 283. For a sketch of Benavides's life and ambitions, see Forrestal and Lynch, *Benavides' Memorial*, pp. ix–xxii.

Missionization of the Jumano is discussed in Forrestal and Lynch, *Benavides' Memorial*, pp. 56–62. The María de Jesús story (with commentary by the editors) is on pp. 58–61. See also Hickerson, *Jumano*, pp. 86–102, for general material on the Jumanos, and for Mother María, note esp. pp. 91–94. See also Hodge, Hammond and Rey, *Benavides 1634*.

For the founding of missions in the Perea-Salas period, see John, *Storms*, pp. 78–79, and A. C. Hayes, J. N. Young, and A. H. Warren, *Excavation of Mound 7: Gran Quivira National Monument, New Mexico* (National Park Service, Publications in Archeology, 16, Washington, D.C., 1981), pp. 5–6. The final years of Perea's service are given in Scholes, *Church and State*, chap. 5, pp. 298–99.

For the quote on Rosas's character, see Scholes, *Church and State*, chap. 5, p. 297. The cabildo was still favorable to Rosas in the letter to the viceroy cited above (Hackett, *Historical Documents*, vol. 3, pp. 66–74). For the events of Rosas life, see Scholes, *Church and State*, chaps. 5 and 6; for information on Ortiz and his wife, María Bustillas, see chap. 6, pp. 337–47; see also Chávez, *New Mexico Families*, pp. 10, 83. A summary of the period after Rosas is given in Scholes, *Church and State*, chap. 7, pp. 102–6. For a list of seventeenth-century Franciscan prelates in New

Mexico, see F. V. Scholes, "Mission Chronology" (manuscript in author's possession, dated 1949–50). For Father Prada's petition to the king, see Hackett,
Historical Documents, vol. 3, pp. 106–15; Governor Martínez de Baeza's population
figures are found on p. 119. See also O. L. Jones, *Los Paisanos: Spanish Settlers on the
Northern Frontier of New Spain* (University of Oklahoma Press, 1979), pp. 110, 129.

A list of New Mexico governors for the period can be found in C. W. Polzer,
T. C. Barnes, and T. H. Naylor, *The Documentary Relations of the Southwest,
Project Manual* (Arizona State Museum, Tucson, 1977), p. 95. The events from
the Pacheco governorship through the confused years of López de Mendizábal
and Peñalosa have been documented by F. V. Scholes, "*Troublous Times* in New
Mexico," *NMHR* 12 (2) (1937): 134–74 (chaps. 1 and 2); *NMHR* 12 (4) (1937):
380–452 (chaps. 3 and 4); *NMHR* 13 (1) (1938): 63–84 (chap. 5); *NMHR* 15 (3)
(1940): 249–68 (chap. 6); *NMHR* 15 (4) (1940): 369–417 (chaps. 7 and 8);
NMHR 16 (1) (1941): 15–40 (chap. 9); *NMHR* 16 (2) (1941): 184–205 (chap. 10);
NMHR 16 (3) (1941): 313–27 (chap. 11). The Manso-Sacristán story is found in
chap. 1, pp. 133–39.

For Tlaxcalans in Santa Fe, see M. Simmons, "Tlascalans in the Spanish
Borderlands," *NMHR* 39 (2) (1964): pp. 101–10. See also Bannon, *Spanish
Borderlands,* pp. 30, 73, 99, 177; see also Riley, *Rio del Norte,* p. 253; Hackett,
Historical Documents, vol. 3, p. 331. However, E. B. Adams and Fray Angélico
Chávez (trans. and annots., *The Missions of New Mexico, 1776* [University of
New Mexico Press, Albuquerque, 1956], p. 304 n. 2) are somewhat skeptical of
this Tlaxcalan settlement and—in any case—believe that if there were
Tlaxcalans in Santa Fe, they did not return after the revolt of 1680. David H.
Snow (personal correspondence) points out that there is really no evidence for
Tlaxcalans as such as against more generalized "Mexican Indians" in the early
settlement of New Mexico.

CHAPTER 8, MISSIONIZATION

For religion among the Pueblo Native Americans, see E. C.
Parsons, *Pueblo Indian Religion* (University of Chicago Press, 1939), vol. 1, pp.
170–209. For the Apachean groups, consult Dutton, *Indians of the Southwest,* pp.
89–96, 121–28. The extent of missionization in the seventeenth century is discussed by Gutiérrez, *When Jesus Came,* see esp. pp. 55–82. Information on libraries
in seventeenth-century New Mexico is given by E. B. Adams and F. V. Scholes,
"Books in New Mexico, 1598–1680," *NMHR* 17 (3) (1942): 226–70. Adams and
Scholes say that "the inventories, if we had them, would probably reveal that
some of the friars brought with them a few volumes on medicine, science or

pseudo-science" (228–29). The extant lists, however, give only the ones mentioned in the text.

A discussion of Galileo and his contemporaries and the development of modern astronomy is given in Boorstin, *The Discoverers*, pp. 312–27. Though seventeenth-century Catholics considered all saints to have been living, breathing people at one time, a number of pre-Christian deities also became revered as saints. A well-known example is St. Brigid, the avatar of a Celtic goddess of that name.

"Occam's Razor" (*entia non sunt multiplicanda praeter necessitatem*) refers to the fact that simpler explanations that fit the known facts should be favored over more complex ones, a dictum of modern science.

For the formation of the custodia of New Mexico, see Scholes, *Ecclesiastical History*. Discussion of the first appointment of custodian is on pp. 51–58. For the various mission foundations, see Scholes, *Mission Chronology*, which gives a list of the various missions and their friars as well as names and terms of the various custodians from 1598–1680; see also F. V. Scholes and L. B. Bloom, "Friar Personnel and Mission Chronology, 1598–1629," *NMHR* 19 (4) (1944): 319–36; *NMHR* 20 (1) (1945): 58–82. James Ivey (personal communication) has some reservations as to whether the building identified as the early church at Yungue was actually used for ecclesiastical purposes. I am also indebted to Ivey for the information on the sequence of building at Giusewa. For the names of missionaries in the late 1620s, see Scholes and Bloom, *Friar Personnel*, pp. 69–72. More on the return of Father Perea to be custodian is given by Bloom, *Perea*, pp. 223–35. Dating for the rebuilding of the Zuni missions comes from F. V. Scholes, "Correction," *NMHR* 19 (3): 243–46, p. 246.

Father Prada's comments on the extent of New Mexico can be found in Hackett, *Historical Documents*, vol. 3, pp. 107–8. For problems of San Pascual, Senecú, and Qualacú, see *Informaciones*, 1601, pp. 14–15; see also Hammond and Rey, *Oñate*, vol. 1, p. 318. M. P. Marshall and H. J. Walt (*Rio Abajo: Prehistory and History of a Rio Grande Province* [New Mexico Historic Preservation Program, Santa Fe, 1984], p. 250) (following a suggestion of David Snow) feel that San Pascual may possibly be the first settlement mentioned by Oñate and was actually called Texaamo. Why the Spaniards, three years later, called Qualacú the first settlement is unclear. See also M. P. Marshall, *Qualacú, Archaeological Investigation of a Piro Pueblo* (U.S. Fish and Wildlife Service, University of New Mexico Office of Contract Archaeology, 1987), p. 27. Marshall makes the point that the pueblo was probably already in decline by the early seventeenth century, if not before. It may be that only the northwest quadrant of the site was occupied during the period of Spanish colonization (Marshall, *Qualacú*, p. 73). A small amount of Tewa Polychrome at the site

(p. 81) suggests that there may have been some, perhaps marginal, occupation past mid-century.

For the foundation of the Manso mission, see O. L. Jones, *Los Paisanos: Spanish Settlers on the Northern Frontiers of New Spain* (University of Oklahoma Press, Norman, 1979), p. 112. A very good summary statement on this mission of Guadalupe can be found in V. Walz, "History of the El Paso Area: 1680–1692," Ph.D. dissertation in History, University of New Mexico, Albuquerque, 1951, pp. 11–21. However, Walz (p. 16) is skeptical of the traditional December 1659 founding date. See also W. H. Timmons, *El Paso: A Borderlands History* (Texas Western Press, El Paso, 1990), esp. pp. 15–17, 310–11. Comments on Zuni in the seventeenth century are given in T. J. Ferguson, "Historic Zuni Architecture and Society: A Structural Analysis," Ph.D. dissertation in Anthropology, (University of New Mexico, Albuquerque, 1993), pp. 83–87. The Manso mission and the strategies and problems that beset this effort are discussed in John, *Storms*, p. 92. See also F. V. Scholes, "Documents for the History of the New Mexican Missions in the Seventeenth Century," *NMHR* 4 (1) (1929): pp. 45–58 (docs. 1 and 2); *NMHR* 4 (2) (1929): 195–201 (doc. 3, Testimonio del estado que tiene la conversion de los Mansos y dedicación de su iglesia). See also AGN Provincias Internas, 35, exp. 3 (Scholes Collection, Center for Southwestern Research [CSWR], University of New Mexico, Zimmerman Library).

For the serious drought that began in 1677, see J. E. Ivey, "'The Greatest Misfortune of All': Famine in the Province of New Mexico: 1667–1672," *Journal of the Southwest* 36(1) (1994): 76–100.

The high mark of sixty-six missionaries is an estimate by Scholes (*Ecclesiastical History*, p. 42). No document to my knowledge actually gives that number, and I have some reservations concerning such a large contingent of Franciscans at any one time. Sexual attitudes of the Indians, especially female, are discussed in Gutiérrez, *When Jesus Came*, p. 51. For the missionaries stationed in New Mexico in 1680, see J. M. Espinosa, *The Pueblo Indian Revolt of 1696* (University of Oklahoma Press, Norman, 1988), p. 33.

For examples of miracles, see Forrestal and Lynch, *Benavides' Memorial,* pp. 27–30, 33–34. Gutiérrez (*When Jesus Came,* p. 74) points out that the Taos woman struck by lightning became a cloud spirit, validating to other Pueblo Indians the truth of her position. For Porras's miracle at Hopi, see Riley, *Hopi,* chap. 3. J. O. Brew ("The History of Awatovi," in *Franciscan Awatovi,* Papers of the Peabody Museum, vol. 36, R. G. Montgomery, W. Smith, and J. O. Brew, eds. and authors [Cambridge, Mass, 1949, pp. 1–43], p. 10) suggests that if the Awatovi people believed that a boy was made to see in 1629 by divine intervention, it might help explain why they—of all the Hopi—attempted to reintroduce the Spaniards in 1700. This explanation seems a bit far-fetched to me.

For the period after mid-century, see the various articles in Scholes, *Troublous Times*. Much of the material on the López de Mendizábal period comes from a series of AGN documents, including Inquisición, tomos 587, 593, 594, and 596 (Scholes Collection, CSWR). The Rodríguez Cubero document with its information about language use among the missionaries (Autto en estta Villa de Santa Fee en [Sept. 4–9, 1699], Don Pedro Rodriguez Cubero, BNM 4:29) is courtesy of the Vargas Project, University of New Mexico, Albuquerque. See esp. fols. 5v, 7r, 9r, 11v, 12v, 14v. Concentration on young people by the missionaries is discussed in Gutiérrez, *When Jesus Came*, pp. 74–76; see also Riley, *Rio del Norte*, pp. 261–62. For the Salvador de Guerra episode, see Scholes, *Troublous Times*, chap. 1, pp. 145–46; see also Riley, *Rio del Norte*, p. 262. Guerra's reputation was still very much a matter of public record in the 1660s. For example, Mendizábal's alcalde for the Tompiro area, Nicolás de Aguilar, prosecuted by the Inquisition, repeated the horror stories of Guerra and of Fray Francisco de Velasco of Zuni. See Hackett, *Historical Documents*, vol. 3, p. 141.

Construction of medieval European churches is discussed in F. and J. Gies, *Cathedral, Forge, and Waterwheel* (Harper Perennial, New York, 1995), pp. 129–39. For details of mission and convent construction in seventeenth-century New Mexico, see J. E. Ivey, *In the Midst of a Loneliness: The Architectural History of the Salinas Missions* (Southwest Cultural Resources Center, Professional Papers, no. 15, Santa Fe, N.Mex., 1988), esp. pp. 35–54; G. Kubler, *The Religious Architecture of New Mexico* (University of New Mexico Press, Albuquerque, 1990 [originally published in 1940]; and J. O. Brew, "The Excavation of Franciscan Awatovi," and R. G. Montgomery, "San Bernardo de Aguatubi, An Analytical Restoration," pp. 45–108 and pp. 109–288, respectively, *Franciscan Awatovi*, Papers of the Peabody Museum, vol. 36, R. G. Montgomery, W. Smith, and J. O. Brew, eds. and authors, Cambridge, Mass, 1949). Kubler (*Architecture*, p. 38 n. 1) gives only two examples of the use of the arch in New Mexican churches which have "any antiquity." Of the two, the mission station at Pecos is clearly eighteenth century or later, and the Isleta example almost certainly so.

Discussion of the actual building of a church and mission is drawn largely from the excellent survey by J. E. Ivey, *Midst of a Loneliness*, pp. 35–54. See also F. V. Scholes, "The Supply Service of the New Mexico Missions in the Seventeenth Century," *NMHR* 5 (1) (1930): pt. 1, pp. 93–115; *NMHR* 5 (2) (1930): pt. 2, pp. 186–210; *NMHR* 5 (4) 1930: pt. 3, pp. 386–404. The carpentry skill of the Pecos Indians is discussed by Kessell, *Kiva, Cross, and Crown*, pp. 132–33. See also Ivey, *Midst of a Loneliness*, p. 39; mission bells are discussed on p. 42; for the convento, see pp. 42–43, and also Scholes, *Documents,* pt. 3, p. 199, and J. E. Ivey, "Another Look at Dating the Scholes Manuscript: A Research Note," *NMHR* 64 (3) (1989): 341–47. For mission and other estancias in seventeenth-century New Mexico, see Ivey, *Famine,* pp. 77–79.

For supplies to maintain a mission, see Scholes, *Supply Service,* pt. 1, pp. 100–105. Use of ink in the missions is discussed in M. Simmons, *Coronado's Land* (University of New Mexico Press, Albuquerque, 1991), pp. 26–29. For heating arrangements, see Ivey, *Midst of a Loneliness,* pp. 166, 167, 178, 188, 224; Montgomery, *San Bernardo,* p. 166; Forrestal and Lynch, *Benavides' Memorial,* p. 41. For the missionaries' attitude to Hopi coal, see A. de Vetancurt, *Teatro Mexicano,* vol. 3, *Crónica de la provincia del Santo Evangelio de México* (Colección Chimalistac de Libros y Documentos Acerca de la Nueva España, 10, José Porrua Turanzas, ed. (Madrid, 1961 [first published in 1698]), p. 275. The organ at Abó is mentioned in Hackett, *Historical Documents,* vol. 3, p. 192. There were other organs in New Mexico: see, for example, S. Dougherty, "A Brief Survey of Music on the Camino Real," *El Camino Real de Tierra Adentro,* G. Palmer, ed. (NM-BLM, Cultural Resources Series, no. 11, 1993, pp. 157–68), p. 161.

Most stations had only one missionary. According to Scholes, *Documents,* pt. 2, pp. 52–57, in the mid 1660s, of twenty-five missions listed, seven (Nambé, Picurís, Pecos, Jemez, Sandia, Senecú, and Guadalupe at El Paso) had two missionaries at this time, and only two (Santa Fe and the mission headquarters at Santo Domingo) had three friars in residence. The document, a report to Mexico City on the state of the missions, 1663–66, makes a strong plea for thirty friars (in addition to the thirty-six already serving), most of them to be priests.

The seventeenth-century Pecos church is described in A. C. Hayes, *The Four Churches of Pecos* (University of New Mexico Press, Albuquerque, 1974), pp. 19–28. For a reevaluation of the dating of the various Pecos churches, see C. White, "Adobe Topology and Site Chronology: A Case Study from Pecos National Historical Park," *Kiva* 61 (4) (1996): 347–63. Discussion of the kivas included in convento areas is given in Ivey, *Midst of a Loneliness,* pp. 415–21 (appdx. 5). See also J. Ivey, "Convento Kivas in the Missions of New Mexico," *NMHR* 73 (2) (1998): 121–52. See esp. pp. 140–41 for comments on the Humanas and Awatovi kivas. Information on the Pecos kiva comes from Ivey, personal communication. A Spanish use of kivas as a meeting place to confer with Indian leaders is given in Hammond and Rey, *Oñate,* vol. 1, p. 342. Information on the rebuilding of kivas after the Pueblo Revolt comes from Vélez de Escalante, *Extracto de noticias,* p. 66; see also C. W. Hackett and C. C. Shelby, *Revolt of the Pueblo Indians of New Mexico and Otermín's Attempted Reconquest, 1680–1682* (The University of New Mexico Press, Albuquerque, 1942, 2 vols.), vol. 1, pp.

cxxix, and vol. 2, p. 207. A continuation of native religious practices in the first decades of the eighteenth century is discussed in A. L. Knaut, *The Pueblo Revolt of 1680* (University of Oklahoma Press, 1995), see esp. pp. 72–87. The patol comment can be found in Scholes, *First Decades*, p. 240; see also Riley, *Rio del Norte*, p. 217. Contacts between Zuni and the Tompiro towns is discussed in Riley, *Frontier People*, pp. 246–48.

The sixteenth-century Franciscan practice of utilizing Native American cultural items to better introduce Christianity is discussed in J. Cortés Castellanos, *El catecismo en pictogramas de Fr. Pedro de Gante* (Publicaciones de la Fundación Universitaria Española, Biblioteca Histórica Hispanoamericana, 10, Madrid, 1987). See also W. Browne, "When Worlds Collide: Crisis in Sahagún's *Historia universal de las cosas de la Nueva España*," *Colonial Latin American Historical Review* 5 (2) (1996): 101–49, pp. 110–11.

CHAPTER 9, SPANISH SOCIETY IN NEW MEXICO

A count of settlers with Oñate is found in D. H. Snow, *First Colonists*, p. 3. For an analysis of encomenderos in New Mexico, consult D. H. Snow, "A Note on Encomienda Economics in Seventeenth Century New Mexico," *Hispanic Arts and Ethnohistory in the Southwest,* M. Weigle, ed. (Ancient City Press, Santa Fe, N.Mex., 1983), pp. 347–57. For population figures, see Jones, *Paisanos*, p. 110; Scholes, *Civil Government*, p. 96 and n. 44; Hackett, *Historical Documents*, vol. 3, pp. 108, 119–20, 327–328, n. 133. Additional information is given in Hackett and Shelby, *Revolt*, vol. 1, pp. cvii–cxvii. The 401 Spaniards killed or missing was in fact an underestimate. What Otermín said in his statement of September 29 at La Salineta was that the casualty list included "the Father *Custodio,* the head of this church, eighteen priests, two lay friars, making the number twenty-one, and more than three hundred and eighty Spaniards, men, women and children, together with some servants, among whom were seventy three Spaniards capable of bearing arms." See, R. E. Twitchell, *Spanish Archives of New Mexico,* (Torch Press, Cedar Rapid, Iowa, 1914, 2 vols.), vol. 1, p. 44. The 2,500 figure for escapees is given on p. 39. For estancias in the Alameda area, see Hackett and Shelby, *Revolt,* vol. 1, p. li. This is taken from the Auto of Juan Huarte (Auto Pertenecientes, ff. 18–19; see *Revolt,* vol. 2, pp. 227–28).

A. R. Knaut (*The Pueblo Revolt of 1680,* University of Oklahoma Press, 1995) takes issue with these figures (pp. 133–35). He believes that "the number of people of European background residing in New Mexico on the eve of the revolt stands near one thousand" (134). Knaut also disagrees with the count of 401 settlers killed. Knaut, however, seems to be mainly interested in sorting out the race mixture, or as he calls it, "miscegenation." If he is actually trying to get a count of more or less *pure-blood* Spaniards or other Europeans (as against Indians or the various castes, especially mestizos), a thousand is perhaps too high. Knaut does make a good point that Pueblo Indians may be included in the Scholes-Hackett figures.

For material on black or part-black captains in the period around 1670, see Hackett, *Historical Documents,* vol. 3, pp. 269–72. For blacks in Mexico, see J. Landers, "Africans in the Spanish Colonies," *Historical Anthropology* 31 (1) (1997): 84–103; and P. Stern, "Gente de color quebrado: Africans and Afromestizos in Colonial Mexico," *Colonial Latin American Historical Review* 3 (2) (1994): 185–205. For an extended discussion and list of blacks and mulattos in early New Mexico, consult D. H. Snow, "Afro–New Mexicans in the Colonial Era," *New Mexico Genealogist* 37 (2) (June 1998): 1–11; Snow calls Alvaro García Holgado "a prominent mulato" (3). See p. 1 in "Afro–New Mexicans" for figures on the number of blacks in New Spain in 1650. For lists of specific mixed-blood individuals, see Scholes, *Troublous Times,* chap. 1, p. 140. The comments on Roque Madrid come from Walz, *El Paso,* p. 241. See also A. Chávez, *Origins,* pp. 65–68. The most prominent "mestizo" in early New Mexico history was, of course, Cristóbal de Oñate, great-grandson of a daughter of the Aztec emperor Moctezuma II. In his case royalty obviously overrode *mestizaje.* The genealogist José M. Esquibel (personal communication) points out that a number of prominent seventeenth-century New Mexico families had Indian bloodlines. Notable ones were the Griego-Bernal and the Lucero de Godoy/Montoya-Zamora extended families.

The tendency for Spanish settlers to spread out is discussed by M. Ebright, "Breaking New Ground: A Reappraisal of Governors Vélez Capuchín and Mendinueta and Their Land Grant Policies," *Colonial Latin American Historical Review* 5 (2) (1996): 195–233. Important families in New Mexico are discussed in Scholes, *Troublous Times,* chap. 1, pp. 140–41; see also, Chávez, *Origins,* pp. 9–11, 19–23, 24–27, 59–62. For castas in seventeenth-century New Mexico, see Scholes, *Church and State,* chap. 5, pp. 308–9; Scholes, *Civil Government,* pp. 96–97; Chávez, *Origins,* pp. 10, 82. For a study of castas beginning at the close of the seventeenth century, see A. Bustamante, "'The Matter was Never Resolved': The Casta System in Colonial New Mexico, 1693–1823," *NMHR* 66 (2) (1991): 143–63. Bustamante's comments on blurring of the caste system come on pp. 144–45. For more on Isabel Olvera, see M. J. Cook, "Daughters of the Camino Real," *El Camino Real del Tierra Adentro,* G. G. Palmer, ed. (BLM, New Mexico State Office, Santa Fe, 1993), pp. 147–56), pp. 149–50. The evidence for a caste society is given by Gutiérrez, *When Jesus Came,* pp. 176–206. The quote by Domínguez on the physical appearance of Santa Fe in 1776 comes from E. B.

Sources and Commentary

Adams and Fray Angélico Chávez, *The Missions of New Mexico, 1776* (University of New Mexico Press, Albuquerque, 1956), pp. 39–40. The census figures for Santa Fe are given in Adams and Chávez, *Missions*, p. 42. A slightly earlier anonymous (1765) census (D. C. Cutter, trans. and ed., "An Anonymous Statistical Report on New Mexico in 1765, *NMHR* 50 (4) (1975): 347–52); p. 351 lists 89 families of Indians in the villa (no further breakdown). However, the numbers of "gente de razón" in Santa Fe included 274 families or 2,244 individuals, plus 80 soldiers. This is a family size of more than 8 persons, which seems rather high. The average family size for other parts of New Mexico in this census is about 4.6 persons. If this figure actually held for Santa Fe, the population total would be more in line with that of Domínguez.

For information on Juan de Griego I am much indebted to the manuscript "Another Mexico," by Donna Pierce and Cordelia T. Snow. This was prepared as part of an exhibit with the same name at the Governor's Palace, Museum of New Mexico, 1997, and there is a copy on file in the office of the Director of the Governor's Palace, Santa Fe. For the comments on Griego, see esp. p. 30.

For the Mexican Indians at Analco and their disappearance in the eighteenth century, see M. Simmons, "Tlascalans in the Spanish Borderlands," *NMHR* 39 (2) (1964): 101–10, pp. 108–10. Whether these were actually Tlaxcalans is uncertain, though the eighteenth-century map of Joseph de Urrutia (dated 1766–68 but perhaps copying an earlier map) calls the area south of the Santa Fe River the "Pueblo or Barrio of Analco which owes its origin to the Tlascalans who accompanied the first Spaniards who entered in the Conquest of this kingdom" (Adams and Chávez, *Missions*, pp. 10–11). Still, as Adams and Chávez point out (304), this may have come from a misreading of one of the Otermín documents, and we cannot really be certain that Tlaxcalans, as against other central Mexican natives, were in Santa Fe in the seventeenth century. A discussion of Santa Fe in 1620 comes from a letter from the viceroy to Eulate, in L. B. Bloom, "A Glimpse of New Mexico in 1620," *NMHR* 3 (4) (1928): 357–80, pp. 369–370. For comments on the 1573 *Ordenanzas*, see C. T. Snow, "Hypothetical Configurations of the Early Santa Fe Plaza," (*Santa Fe Historic Plaza, Study I*, L. Tigges, ed. [City Planning Department, Santa Fe, N.Mex., 1990]), pp. 55–56. Parenthetically, the Spanish word for *swamp* is now generally spelled *ciénaga*. For the value of the land unit *caballería*, I am using the 1573 *Ordenanzas*, as analyzed by D. H. Snow, "Review of Agrarian and Linear Land Measurement of Land from Seventeenth Century Documents," *Santa Fe Historic Plaza, Study 1*, pp. 85–107, p. 97. J. P. Sánchez ("The Peralta-Ordóñez Affair," *Santa Fe: History of an Ancient City*, D. G. Noble, ed. [School of American Research Press, Santa Fe, N.Mex., 1989], pp. 27–38) says that 4 caballerías equaled about 133 acres (28). This unit of land measurement seems to have been somewhat variable; for example, Polzer, Barnes, and Naylor (*Documentary Relations*, p. 50) list the caballería as 609,408 square varas or 105.76 acres.

For comments on the sequence of churches in Santa Fe, see Angelico Chavez, "Santa Fe Church and Convent Sites in the Seventeenth and Eighteenth Centuries," *NMHR* 24 (2) (1949): 85–93. The question of Benavides and San Miguel is discussed by Forrestal and Lynch (*Benavides' Memorial*, p. 24 n. 53), as well as by Hodge (Hodge, Hammond and Rey, *Benavides*, pp. 273–74, n. 86). In 1692 Vargas ordered repairs on San Miguel (primarily a new roof) so that it might serve as a temporary church, presumably for the entire population. See J. L. Kessell, R. Hendricks, and M. Dodge, eds. *To the Royal Crown Restored* (University of New Mexico Press, Albuquerque, 1995), pp. 476–77. For a discussion of the Santa Fe situation a decade or so after the founding, see Bloom, *New Mexico in 1620*, p. 370. For the material quoted about the 1620 church situation, see the Spanish transcription, p. 380. In a popular pamphlet, Brother B. Lewis, F.S.C. (*Oldest Church in U.S. The San Miguel Chapel*, published as a guide to the Santa Fe San Miguel Church, 1957, unpaged) believes that San Miguel was built in 1610, though he gives no evidence for that particular year.

The size of the original plaza is discussed by Chavez, "Santa Fe Church." See esp. p. 92, where he says, "the Santa Fe Plaza in its original form, from 1610 to 1680, ran clear up to the middle of the present Cathedral." The question of the overall size of the plaza is still much in dispute. See C. T. Snow, *Configurations*, pp. 55–84, for an argument for a somewhat larger north-south extension of the plaza. An argument that the plaza did not extend as far south as the Río Chiquito is given by S. M. Hordes, "The History of the Santa Fe Plaza, 1610–1720," *Santa Fe Historic Plaza, Study I*, pp. 3–36, esp. pp. 6–7. A good summary of the region west of the plaza can be found in C. T. Snow, "Historical Overview West of the Santa Fe Plaza" (see S. S. Post and C. T. Snow, *Archaeological and Historical Survey for the Richards Avenue and West Alameda Project, Santa Fe, New Mexico* [Museum of New Mexico, Office of Archaeological Studies, Archaeology Notes 62, Santa Fe, 1992], pp. 23–48). For the archaeology of the area, see F. Levine, "Down Under an Ancient City," *Santa Fe: History of an Ancient City*, D. G. Noble, ed., pp. 9–25, pp. 16–18. An excellent summary of the archaeological sequence along the Santa Fe River can be found in Post and Snow, *Survey*, pp. 9–21. It was hoped that a series of excavations in the present plaza in 1990 might shed further light on seventeenth-century Santa Fe. Unfortunately, because of the disturbed nature of the plaza subsoil, relatively little was learned, although a certain number of seventeenth-century artifacts were found. See D. H. Snow and C. T. Snow, *Santa Fe Historic Plaza Study II*,

Plaza Excavation Final Report, Fall 1990, (Cross-Cultural Research Systems for the City of Santa Fe, 1992), pp. ii, 67, 74–80.

For the Palace of the Governors, see B. Bunting, *Early Architecture in New Mexico* (University of New Mexico Press, Albuquerque, 1976), pp. 80–82. M. Simmons ("Spanish Irrigation in New Mexico," *NMHR* 47 [2] [1972]: 135–50) discusses the early attempts at irrigation at Santa Fe. Excavations in the mid-1970s among seventeenth-century deposits in the Casa Real have produced bones of trout, catfish, and the now extinct blue sucker, which was being used as late as the Pueblo Revolt period (Pierce and Snow, *Another Mexico,* p. 43).

Tree-ring information for the period of the founding of Santa Fe comes from J. A. Tainter and F. Levine, *Cultural Resources Overview: Central New Mexico* (USDA, Forest Service and BLM, Santa Fe, N.Mex., 1987), p. 77. See also C. T. Snow, *Hypothetical Configurations,* pp. 56–58. For governors' salaries, see F. V. Scholes, "Royal Treasury Records Relating to the Province of New Mexico, 1596–1683," *NMHR* 50 (1) (1975): 5–23 (pt. 1); *NMHR* 50 (2) (1975): 139–64 (pt. 2), pt. 1, pp. 13–15. For Oñate's trade materials in the final Salazar, inspection, see Hammond and Rey, *Oñate,* vol. 1, pp. 220–23. Interestingly, in the Ulloa inspection undertaken a year or so previously, Oñate listed some 620 pesos of trade goods, 120 pesos over his announced quota (vol. 1, pp. 134–36). Governor Eulate's trade in Pueblo Indians, illegally enslaved, is found in Scholes, *Church and State,* chap. 3, p. 164. The trade situation in the 1630s is reported by Scholes *Church and State,* chap. 4, pp. 285–87. The quote by Perea can be found on pp. 285–86.

The 1631 contract for the supply train can be found in Scholes, *Supply Service,* pp. 96–113; for the 1664 and later arrangements, see pp. 392–401. For information on the mission supply trains, I draw heavily on J. E. Ivey, "Seventeenth-Century Mission Trade on the Camino Real," *El Camino Real de Tierra Adentro,* G. G. Palmer, ed. (BLM, Santa Fe, N.Mex., 1993), pp. 41–67; see esp. pp. 42–48. For the quote on the founding of the service, see pp. 42–43. Additional relevant papers from Palmer, *Camino Real,* include D. Scurlock, "Through Desierto and Bosque," pp. 1–11; C. L. Riley, "The Pre-Spanish Camino," pp. 13–20; M. Simmons, "Opening the Camino Real," pp. 29–34; T. E. Chavez, "North from Mexico and Beyond," pp. 35–40; C. T. Snow, "A Headdress of Pearls," pp. 69–76; J. O. Baxter, "Livestock on the Camino Real," pp. 101–11; and D. H. Snow, "Purchased in Chihuahua for Feasts," pp. 133–46. Various costs for personnel and equipment on the mission trains come from the AGI (Mexico, leg. 42, data for Oct. 12, 1665, in Scholes Collection). Pay for soldiers is given in Hackett, *Historical Documents,* vol. 3, pp. 316–22. For the timing of the López de Mendizábal train, consult Scholes, *Troublous Times,* chap. 2, pp. 155, 163. For the Gruber story, see J. P. Sánchez, *The Río Abajo Frontier, 1540–1692* (Monograph of the Albuquerque Museum, Albuquerque, N.Mex., 1987), pp. 120–28. The route of the Camino Real through Chihuahua is discussed in Roney, "Tracing the Camino Real," in *Camino Real,* pp. 88–90. See also Knaut, *Revolt,* 122–26. For nineteenth-century preferences as to the trail, see A. H. Schroeder, "The Camino Real in 1846–1847," *Camino Real,* pp. 177–86, p. 177.

The search for minerals by the Chamuscado party is reported in Hammond and Rey, *Rediscovery,* pp. 110, 114, 143, 145. The comments of Luxán are found on pp. 170–71, 176, 196–98, and of Espejo on pp. 222, 223, 227 (see quote), and 228. Castaño's search for mines is discussed on pp. 279, 289. For the Farfán trip to the Verde River area, see Hammond and Rey, *Oñate,* vol. 1, 408–15. The quote from Farfán is on p. 413. For the assay results, see vol. 1, pp. 420–24. The request for silver stamps comes from vol. 1, p. 489; for the Núñez Pérez letter, see vol. 1, p. 584. Report of the San Marcos mine is found in vol. 2, p. 630. The discouraging remarks of the viceroy appear in vol. 2, pp. 1001–2; see also p. 1034. For the mining situation in the 1620s, see Zárate Salmerón, *Relaciones,* p. 56. For the comments on mines and mining by Father Benavides, see Forrestal and Lynch, *Benavides' Memorial,* p. 17. Father Prada's remarks are contained in Hackett, *Historical Documents,* vol. 3, p. 109.

For information on mining in sixteenth- and seventeenth-century Nueva Vizcaya, I draw heavily from R. C. West, "The Mining Community in Northern New Spain: The Parral Mining District," *Ibero-Americana* 30 (1949): esp. pp. 1–9, 11–14, 17–39. For New Mexico mining, consult W. W. Long, "A History of Mining in New Mexico During the Spanish and Mexican Periods" (M.A. thesis in History, University of New Mexico, Albuquerque, 1964). See also E. Ramos Garrido, "El papel del azogue en la industria minera en España y en las Indias," *Colonial Latin American Historical Review* 5 (2) (1996): 151–94. The "mercury" mine in Hopi country is discussed by J. L. Kessell and R. Hendricks, *By Force of Arms: The Journals of don Diego de Vargas, New Mexico, 1691–93* (University of New Mexico Press, Albuquerque, 1992), pp. 123–201. An excellent source for distribution of minerals in New Mexico is S. A. Northrop, *Minerals of New Mexico* (University of New Mexico Press, Albuquerque, rev.ed., 1959), esp. pp. 119–20, 182–84, 190–92, 246–49. For the disparity between income and outgo in New Mexico, see Scholes, *Treasury Records,* pt. 2, p. 160.

Information on seventeenth-century estancia sites in New Mexico comes from D. H. Snow, "A Review of Spanish Colonial Archaeology in Northern New Mexico," *Current Research on the Late Prehistory and Early History of New Mexico,* B. J. Vierra, ed. (New Mexico Archaeological Council, Special Publication 1, Albuquerque, N.Mex.), pp. 185–93. I also had the opportunity to tour the Ciénega site with David Snow in the summer of 1996. An insightful survey of living conditions in colonial New Mexico comes from M. Simmons, "Hygiene, Sanitation, and Public Health in Hispanic New Mexico," *NMHR* 67 (3) (1992): 205–25); see also Simmons, *Coronado's Land*, pp. 4–7 (skin clothing); pp. 12–16 (hairdressing); pp. 17–20 (cosmetics); pp. 21–25 (sanitary facilities); pp. 31–34 (games); pp. 78–84 (carts). For clothing of the upper classes, see Hammond and Rey, *Oñate*, vol. 1, pp. 219, 252–53. Domesticated plants introduced by the Oñate settlers are discussed in Torquemada, *Monarquía indiana*, vol. 1, pp. 672, 678. Torquemada lists barley (*cevada, cebada*) twice, but barley was probably not an important crop during this period; however, there is some archaeological evidence for this plant (see Ford, *New Pueblo Economy*, p. 80). Ford also discusses other plants, found both archaeologically and in the early documents; see pp. 76–77, 80. For additional material on cosmetics, see K. C. Ford, *Yerbas*, pp. 124–25. The appearance of New Mexico materials on the shelves of merchants in Chihuahua comes from P. Boyd-Bowman, "Two Country Stores in Seventeenth Century Mexico," *The Americas*, vol. 28 (3) (1972): 237–51, pp. 240, 241, 244, 247, 248. The quote on ploughs comes from R. F. Dickey, *New Mexico Village Arts* (University of New Mexico Press, Albuquerque, 1949), p. 101.

Age at marriage for women is given by Gutiérrez, *When Jesus Came*, p. 272, for the period 1690–1846. By age fourteen, 11.5 percent of all girls were married; by sixteen, 40 percent; and by eighteen, 63 percent. For family life of the López couple, see Scholes, *Troublous Times*, chap. 7, pp. 380–88. Information on estancias comes from Hackett, *Historical Documents*, vol. 3, p. 119. For estancias in the Santa Cruz and Galisteo areas, see J. L. Kessell, R. Hendricks, and M. D. Dodge, *Blood on the Boulders*, vol. 4 of *The Journals of don Diego de Vargas* (University of New Mexico Press, Albuquerque, 1998 [books 1 and 2 paged consecutively]), pp. 609–16. An excellent summary of the estancia situation can be found in Ivey, *Famine*, pp. 77–79. The situation of encomenderos is discussed in H. A. Anderson, "The Encomienda in New Mexico, 1598–1680," *NMHR* 60 (4) (1985): 353–37. For the Salas affair, see Scholes, *Troublous Times*, chap. 3, pp. 388–89; for the Salas family in revolt times, consult Hackett and Shelby, *Revolt*, vol. 1, p. xxxiv, and Chávez, *Origins*, pp. 100–101.

Comments on Spanish and Chinese pottery and on Spanish forms and decoration in pottery produced by the Pueblos in the seventeenth century are made by Pierce and Snow, *Another Mexico*, pp. 34–36. A brief account of the Sánchez or Ciénega site (LA 20,000) was given by O. L. Jones and M. Stoller, *Southwestern Mission Research Center Newsletter* 29 (102) (1995): 11–12. This important site has been excavated over a period of years by students from Colorado College under the overall direction of M. L. Stoller, with archaeologist D. H. Snow and historians M. E. Jenkins and O. L. Jones. An analysis of the pottery found at LA 20,000 using x-ray fluorescence on sherds was published by W. J. Thomas, N. W. Bower, J. W. Kantner, M. L. Stoller, and D. H. Snow, "An X-ray Fluorescence-Pattern Recognition . . . ," *Historical Archaeology* 26 (2) (1992): 24–36. It shows a preponderance of Pueblo sherds, both painted and plain-ware utility ceramics. Among the painted pottery, most of the sherds were Kotyiti Glaze ware, but with some seventeenth-century Teya Matte-paint pottery from farther north on the Rio Grande. For additional information on the Sánchez site, see a series of papers available in the Site Files LA 20,000 in the ARMS area, Laboratory of Anthropology, Museum of New Mexico. They include: S. Dillard and K. Davis, *La Ciénega: Ceramic Artifacts of a Spanish Colonial Rancho, LA 20,000*, Dept. of Anthropology, Colorado College, Colorado Springs, 1980), pp. 34–35; K. Boyer, J. Spradley, and S. Wolfe, *The Material Culture of La Ciénega* (Colorado College, 1982), pp. 1, 16, 21, 25–28, 35, 38; H. Sergeant, G. Carpenter, and B. Beall, *Faunal Analysis of LA 20000, Sánchez Site, La Ciénega, NM* (Colorado College, 1991), esp. pp. 41–43. For background material, consult A. G. Harper, K. Oberg, and A. Cordova, *Man and Resources in the Middle Rio Grande* (University of New Mexico Press, Albuquerque, 1943), p. 49.

The Majadas site is discussed in D. H. Snow, *Las Majadas Site, LA 591* (Museum of New Mexico, Laboratory of Anthropology Notes, no. 75, 1973), pp. 11–12, 14, 18, 24, 34–35. Also consult A. H. Warren, *The Pottery of Las Majadas* (Museum of New Mexico, Laboratory of Anthropology Notes, no. 75a, 1979). For the Comanche Springs site, see F. C. Hibben, B. Benjamin, and M. S. Adler, Comanche Springs, *The Artifact* 23 (3) (1985): 41–58. In 1997 and 1998 there were reports on a reinvestigation of Comanche Springs, with mapping and some limited archaeology. See A. F. Ramenofsky, S. Penman, R. Flint, and W. X. Chávez, *Comanche Springs Report (LA 14904)* (report to the Valley Improvement Association, Belen, New Mexico, 1997); and A. F. Ramenofsky, *Excavation Summary: LA 14904 Comanche Springs* (Report to the Valley Improvement Association, Belen, New Mexico, 1998). Dr. Ramenofsky (personal correspondence, Oct. 5, 1998) stated that she "is revisiting the issue of when the Spanish structures were built, used and abandoned. The ceramics recovered this summer [1998] suggest a mid-seventeenth or even early post revolt occupation."

Room interiors are discussed in Dickey, *New Mexico Village Arts,* esp. pp. 51–52. For additional information on seventeenth- and eighteenth-century *torreones* and room interiors, see Bunting, *Architecture,* esp. pp. 79–83. It should be pointed out that surviving examples of towers are mostly eighteenth century or even later. Bunting (*Architecture,* p. 72) says that the earthen floors were "in some instances sealed with a thin coating composed of clay and animal blood." I could find no documentation on this, and archaeologist Cordelia T. Snow (personal communication) frankly doubts that such floors were in use. Information on sheep and other animals in the sixteenth- and seventeenth-century New World comes from D. K. Abbass, "Herd Development in the New World Spanish Colonies," *Themes in Rural History of the Western World,* R. Herr, ed. (Iowa State University Press, Ames, 1993), pp. 165–93, esp. p. 180, table 6.2. In northern Mexico, cattle herds increased explosively in the latter part of the sixteenth century. According to Abbass (p. 176), by 1579 even small ranchers in Zacatecas and Durango owned 20,000 head of cattle and some ranchers held as many as 150,000. In New Mexico there was never a great expanse of cattle herds in the seventeenth century, perhaps because the country was better suited for sheep. The serious iron shortage in the colony is one of the subjects of the cabildo report to the viceroy in 1639 (Hackett, *Historical Documents,* vol. 3, p. 73).

The amount and variety of goods in seventeenth-century New Mexico, especially the rich clothing and furnishings, are discussed by Pierce and Snow (*Another Mexico,* pp. 33–39). For the price of chocolate, see Boyd-Bowman, *Two Country Stores,* p. 246.

Medicine in seventeenth-century Europe is discussed in C. G. Cumston, *An Introduction to the History of Medicine* (Dorset Press, New York, 1987), pp. 273–317. For texts in medicine, see Scholes and Adams, *Books,* pp. 242, 263. For Mexican medicine, consult G. Schendel, *Medicine in Mexico* (University of Texas Press, Austin, 1968), esp. pp. 45–80 (Aztec medicine) and 85–101 (early Azteco-Spanish medicine). The Aztecs utilized not only plants but animals in their medical practice (38). Medical practices in the military are discussed by B. de Vargas Machuca, *Milicia y descripción de las Indias* (Madrid, Librería de Victoriano Suárez, 2 vols., 1892 [first published in 1599]), vol. 1, pp. 125–40. I have not had a chance to examine the *Florilegio Medicinal* of the Jesuit Juan de Esteyneffer (Steinhöfer), which was published in 1712. Though later than our period, it seems to have contained a variety of information applicable to seventeenth-century New Mexico. For a discussion, see M. A. Kay, "The *Florilegio Medicinal*: Source of Southwest Ethnomedicine," *Ethnohistory* 24 (3) (1977): 251–59.

The great Badianus manuscript was originally written by an Aztec student at the College of Santa Cruz in Tlatelolco. This man, whose Spanish name was Martinus de la Cruz, served as "physician of the College" and seems to have written the first draft of the manuscript in Nahuatl, the Aztec language. Another Aztec student, Juan Badianus, who was proficient in Latin, translated the manuscript into that language. An English edition, translated and annotated by Emily Walcott Emmart, was published as *The Badianus Manuscript: An Aztec Herbal of 1552* (Johns Hopkins Press, Baltimore, 1940). For peyote use, see AGN, Inquisición, tomo 304 (Scholes Collection), which also contains several reports of witchcraft. A possible value for bloodletting is discussed in the "Breakthroughs" section of *Discover* 18 (12) (Dec. 1997): 38. According to cardiologist David Meyers, bleeding might cut the risk of heart attacks, perhaps by reducing the normal iron levels in blood. According to this argument, iron is a catalyst in cholesterol oxidation, producing oxidized cholesterol, a serious irritant which scars the arteries. Removing blood on a regular basis lowers the amount of iron in the blood. Obviously, a great deal more study is needed before anything definitive can be said about Meyers's idea. Meyers believes that might possibly explain why premenopausal women, with their monthly loss of blood, have fewer heart attacks than do men of the same age group. However, a physician colleague of mine, Richard V. Lee, M.D., points out that postmenopausal women treated with estrogen revert to the favorable ratio enjoyed by younger women. Lee doubts that menses have anything much to do with protection against heart attack.

For comments on the San Miguel infirmary, see Kubler, *Architecture,* p. 79. Lists of medicines that were brought by Oñate and his men can be found in Hammond and Rey, *Oñate,* vol. 1, pp. 104–5, 110–11, 219–20, 255.

Books were reported by the Oñate expedition (see Hammond and Rey, *Oñate,* vol. 1, p. 253). Oñate's supply of writing paper is listed in the same volume (218). For books in seventeenth-century New Mexico, see Adams and Scholes, *Books,* pp. 256–70. The comments on Fray Juan de Vidania come on pp. 231–33. Also consult E. B. Adams, "Two Colonial New Mexico Libraries, 1704, 1776," *NMHR* 19 (2) (1944): 135–67, pp. 149–51. A number of books at Zuni were reported by de Vargas in 1692. See J. M. Espinosa, *First Expedition of Vargas into New Mexico, 1692* (University of New Mexico Press, Albuquerque, 1940), pp. 201–3; also listed in Scholes, *Books,* pp. 260–61.

CHAPTER 10, BERNARDO LOPEZ DE MENDIZABAL

See Gutiérrez, *When Jesus Came,* esp. pp. 55–63, for a discussion of Pueblo Indian attitudes toward the Franciscans, and their identification as powerful "Inside Chiefs" (63). For the quotation on the missionary effect on children, see Riley, *Rio del Norte,* p. 262. The continuation of native ceremonies has been discussed in Ivey, *Midst of a Loneliness,* pp. 420–21. See esp. p. 420 n. 13.

Material on Manso can be found in Scholes, *Troublous Times,* chap. 1, pp. 136–39. See also *Santo Officio contra Doña Theresa de Aguilera . . . ,* part 1 of AGN, Inquisición, tomo 596, also Inquisición, tomo 594. A discussion of the Jews in late-medieval Spain and during the reconquest can be found in Kedourie, *Spain and the Jews.* See esp. chap. 1, A. Mackay, "The Jews in Spain during the Middle Ages," pp. 33–50; chap. 2, E. Gutwirth, "Toward Expulsion: 1391–1492," pp. 51–73; and chap. 3, H. Kamen, "The Expulsion: Purpose and Consequence," pp. 74–91. For the ancestry of Beatríz de Estrada, see J. A. Esquibel, "The Jewish-Converso Ancestry of Doña Beatriz de Estrada," *Genealogical Society of Hispanic America Journal* 9 (4) (1997): 135–43. Shirley Cushing Flint (personal communication), who has also studied the Estrada family background, thinks that Beatríz had Jewish ancestors from two different bloodlines. For the Oñate ancestry, note the discussion in chap. 4.

For the order of custodians during this period in New Mexico, consult Scholes, *Troublous Times,* chap. 1, pp. 141–42; for the ancestry of López de Mendizábal, see pp. 152–66. The quotes are on pp. 152 and 164 n. 1. This latter quote, on the ancestry of López, was drawn from the López testimony of April 28–30, *Primera audiencia de Don Bernardo López de Mendizábal,* Inquisición, tomo 594. The age of López comes from an Inquisición document dated April 28, 1663, in which he stated that he was "over forty years old." See Hackett, *Historical Documents,* vol. 3, p. 193. Doña Teresa, López's wife, was perhaps a year or so younger than her husband according to her statement in AGN, Inquisición, tomo 502. López's plan to join the priesthood is given in Hackett, *Historical Documents,* vol. 3, p. 218. Additional biographical data can be found in Scholes, *Supply Service,* pt. 2, pp. 196–200 (material on Ramírez is contained in pp. 191–93); and in Hackett, *Historical Documents,* vol. 3, pp. 119–230. The Jesuit educational activities in Mexico are discussed in Haring, *Spanish Empire,* pp. 228–29. For the uses of personal honor in New Mexico in the seventeenth and eighteenth centuries, see Gutiérrez, *When Jesus Came,* pp. 176–226.

The troubles between López and Ramírez are discussed in Scholes, *Supply Service,* pt. 2, pp. 196–98, and in Scholes, *Troublous Times,* chap. 2, pp. 153–55. This comes mainly from the trial evidence found in AGN, Inquisición documents 587 and 594. Additional material is found in the statement of Fray Nicolás de Freitas (Hackett, *Historical Documents,* vol. 3, pp. 157–58). The quote in which López demanded treatment such as being offered the Blessed Sacrament is found in Scholes, *Troublous Times,* chap. 2, pp. 155, 165, and in the 1660 statement of Fray Joseph de Espeleta in Hackett, *Historical Documents,* vol. 3, p. 147. López's encounter with Doña Luisa and Doña Isabel is discussed by J. P. Sánchez in *The Rio Abajo Frontier: 1540–1692* (Albuquerque Museum, History Monograph, Albuquerque, N.Mex., 1987), pp. 111, 148. Luisa's testimony is taken from AGN, Inquisición, tomo 593 (Apr. 30, 1662). The quote on ecclesiastical authority can be found in Scholes, *Troublous Times,* chap. 2, p. 157. The events brought about by Ramírez's return to Mexico are discussed on pp. 162–64.

For a discussion of different "pesos," see L. H. Warner, "Conveyance of Property, the Spanish and the Mexico Way, *NMHR* 6 (4) (1931): 334–59. Warner points out that, by at least the eighteenth century, several different "pesos" of eight, six, four, and two reales were used (337). Though it is hard to extrapolate from one Spanish province to another, the half-real wage given in New Mexico does seem to have been in the low range vis-à-vis other parts of the Spanish American empire. See R. K. Barber, "Indian Labor in the Spanish Colonies," *NMHR* 7 (2) (1932): 105–42; *NMHR* 7 (3) (1932): 233–72; *NMHR* 7 (4) (1932): 311–47. My colleague Richard Flint has pointed out that in some transactions the tomín was the gold equivalent to the silver real. For more information on cost of living in Spanish New Mexico, consult Scholes, *Civil Government,* vol. 10, no. 2, pp. 103, 109; Warner, *Conveyance,* pp. 337, 339; Hackett, *Historical Documents,* vol. 3, pp. 110, 120. Knaut (*Pueblo Revolt,* pp. 102–4), who generally accepts the traditional view that López de Mendizábal was an unmitigated scoundrel, suggests that the governor raised Indian wages to gain better access to the native workforce. Such an action would seem to me a curiously circuitous way of attaining this goal.

For the cycles of dry and wet years, see S. Herr and J. L. Clark, "Patterns in the Pathways: Early Historic Migrations in the Rio Grande Pueblos," *Kiva* 62 (4) (1997): 365–89, p. 372 (Palmer Drought Severity Indices for selected stations in northern New Mexico).

The decrees concerning the treatment of Indians were issued by Viceroy Diego Fernández de Córdova to both the current governor (Eulate) and the custodian (Perea) in January and February 1621; see Scholes, *Church and State,* chap. 3, p. 151. The Omnimoda argument is discussed by Scholes in *Troublous Times,* chap. 2, 156–57. A good discussion of López in relationship to Pecos Pueblo can be found in Kessell, *Kiva, Cross, and Crown,* pp. 174–84. For the petitions sent to the viceroy, see Scholes, *Troublous Times,* chap. 2, pp. 161–64. Information on López's punitive raid of September 1659 and the counter-raids into Spanish territory is given in Hackett, *Historical Documents,* vol. 3, pp. 187–88. For trade by López, see Scholes, *Troublous Times,* chap. 3, p. 380. Trade in Humanas is discussed in the Inquisition hearings against Nicolás de Aguilar (Hackett, *Historical Documents,* vol. 3, p. 135, drawn from AGN, Inquisición, tomo 512). The *residencia* of Juan Manso is contained in Scholes, *Troublous Times,* chap. 3, pp. 381–84. Kessell, *Kiva, Cross, and Crown,* pp. 178–83 has interesting information on González Bernal, taken in part from the López *residencia.* For identification of the Anaya Almazán encomiendas, see Snow, *Encomienda,* p. 354.

Information on Nicolás de Aguilar and on Catalina Márquez can be found in Chávez, *Origins,* pp. 1, 69–70. The trials of Aguilar and his three colleagues by the Inquisition are discussed in detail in Scholes, *Troublous Times,* chap. 8, pp. 392–414. The story of Romero on the Plains is given in Hackett, *Historical Documents,* vol. 3, pp. 155–56, 161. For comments on Apache marriage ceremonies, at least in later historic times, see Opler, *Apachean Culture Pattern,* p. 370. Speculation on the Calumet Ceremony comes from D. J. Blakeslee, "The Origin and Spread of the Calumet Ceremony," *American Antiquity* 46 (4) (1981): 759–68. Information on the later life of Romero comes from J. L. Kessell, "Diego Romero, the Plains Apache and the Inquisition," *American West* 15 (3) (1978): 12–16. The quote about Aguilar's poise in front of the Inquisition is found in Scholes, *Troublous Times,* chap. 8, pp. 399–400. For the Timucua dictionary, see Swanton, *Southeastern Indians,* pp. 829, 849. Aguilar's alleged lack of literacy is referred to in Hackett, *Historical Documents,* vol. 3, p. 146. Scholes, *Troublous Times,* chap. 5, p. 67, gives the list of livestock claimed lost by the Franciscans. For the fate of the four captains of López who also were tried by the Inquisition, see Scholes, *Troublous Times,* chap. 6, 249–52; chap. 8, pp. 392–401. Chávez, *Origins,* pp. 1–2, 35–37, 69, 87 95–98; Hackett, *Historical Documents,* vol. 3, pp. 137–47. Various of these documents are to be found in AGN, Inquisición, tomo 512. The friars' financial claims against López are discussed in Scholes, *Troublous Times,* chap. 5, pp. 66–67.

For details of the López de Mendizábal library, see Adams and Scholes, *Books in New Mexico,* pp. 262–64. Arrangement of Bernardo and Teresa's living quarters in Santa Fe comes from AGN, Inquisición, 244 and 246; see also Hackett, *Historical Documents,* vol. 3, pp. 224–25. Other evidence is given by López de Mendizábal and Doña Teresa de Aguilar at various Inquisition hearings. See Scholes, *Troublous Times,* chap. 7, pp. 378–88; also see Hackett, *Historical Documents,* vol. 3, pp. 224–25 (material contained in AGN, Inquisición, 594, 243–55). Sexual accusations against both the clergy and against López can be found in Hackett, *Historical Documents,* vol. 3, pp. 214–16, 218, 225. See also comments in Riley, *Rio del Norte,* pp. 262–63. Specific information on López's affairs can be seen in Hackett, *Historical Documents,* vol. 3, p. 225, and in Chávez, *Origins,* pp. 4, 31, 94, 100.

Various descriptions of the "catzinas" by Franciscans, settlers, and by López himself are scattered through the documents. See Hackett, *Historical Documents,* vol. 3, pp. 133, 134, 137, 142, 146, 152, 157–58, 159, 164, 165, 166, 172–73, 174, 176, 177–78, 179–80, 182, 183, 184, 185, 208–9, 222, 223–24. Quotation and paraphrase of the material on kachina dances are drawn from Hackett, *Historical Documents,* vol. 3, pp. 133, 134, 157, 158 (Freitas), 152 (Chávez), 165 (Santander), 177–78, 179–80 (Domínguez), 180 (Valencia), 223–24 (López). Regarding various aspects of the kachina cult in historic times, consult Parsons, *Pueblo Indian*

Religion, vol. 1, pp. 42, 52–53, 87, 108, 150, 155, 236 n., 257, 474–76. Information on Clemente's later tragic career is given in the declaration of Diego López Sambrano (Hackett and Shelby, *Revolt,* vol. 2, pp. 299–300). Also consult J. L. Kessell, "Esteban Clemente, Precursor of the Pueblo Revolt," *El Palacio* 86 (4) (1980–81): 16–17; Sánchez, *Rio Abajo Frontier,* pp. 131–32; and Knaut, *Pueblo Revolt,* pp. 166–67.

For the counterattack on López, see Scholes, *Troublous Times,* chap. 4, pp. 434–39. For Ramírez's own problems with the Church, see chap. 3, p. 442. The escape of ex-governor Manso and his subsequent testimony to the viceregal officials and the Inquisition are discussed in chap. 3, pp. 383–84. The attempts of López to get information to the viceroy can be found in chap. 4, pp. 438–41. The López residencia is discussed in great detail in Scholes, *Troublous Times,* chap. 5, pp. 71–79. For Posada's actions against López and Doña Teresa, see chap. 4, pp. 445–51. For Manso's appointment as chief constable of the Inquisition, see chap. 6, p. 449. López's imprisonment at Santo Domingo and his trip south to Mexico City are vividly described in Scholes, *Troublous Times,* chap. 6, pp. 263–68. The quotations by the ex-governor can be found on pp. 263 and 264–65, respectively. The ethnic purity of the common people compared to the nobility in Spain is discussed by Ramsey, *Spain: Rise of the First World Power,* pp. 98–100. The remarks to Fray Salvador Guerra are taken from Guerra's *Certificación,* dated August 15, 1662, in AGN, Inquisición, 587. The story of the trial of Bernardo and Doña Teresa is brilliantly told in Scholes, *Troublous Times,* chap. 7, pp. 369–91.

CHAPTER 11, THE GATHERING STORM

A discussion of Peñalosa's background is found in Scholes, *Troublous Times,* chap. 5, pp. 63–64; see also P. Gerhard, *A Guide to the Historical Geography of New Spain* (Cambridge University Press, Cambridge and New York, 1972), pp. 386–88; and Hackett, *Historical Documents,* vol. 3, pp. 257–58. The collection of López's assets by Peñalosa is discussed in Scholes, *Troublous Times,* chap. 6, pp. 254–63. The events of late August 1662, are described in Scholes, *Troublous Times,* chap. 6, pp. 255–58. For Doña Teresa's part in these proceedings, see AGN, Exp. 1, Inquisición, 596. The Posada-Peñalosa controversy is detailed in Scholes, *Troublous Times,* chap. 9, pp. 15–40; see also Hackett, *Historical Documents,* vol. 3, pp. 250–54. Parenthetically, Posada's name is sometimes given as Alonzo de Posadas. I have followed Scholes transcriptions here except in direct quotes. For Peñalosa's redistribution of encomiendas, see pp. 33–34. A copy of the document appointing Juan Domínguez escudero in 1662 still exists (see Scholes Collection, CSWR, ms. 360, box 11, folder 1, Baltasar

Domínguez de Mendoza to Council of Indies). For the charges against Peñalosa brought by Father Alonso de Posada, see Scholes, *Troublous Times*, chap. 9, pp. 36–38.

Peñalosa's trial by the Inquisition is found in Hackett, *Historical Documents*, vol. 3, pp. 257–69. For the quote on Posada's alleged misdeeds at Awatovi, see pp. 259–60. For additional information, see Scholes, *Troublous Times*, chap. 10, pp. 184–205. In France, Peñalosa produced a *Relación del descubrimiento del país y ciudad de Quivira* purported to be the journal of a voyage the governor made to the Plains in 1662. Mention of this expedition and its fictitious nature is made in a petition of Baltasar Domínguez de Mendoza to the Council of the Indies, Oct. 1, 1694 (Scholes Collection, CSWR, ms. 360, box 11, folder 1). This document, supposedly written by Fray Nicolás de Freitas, was published in English by J. G. Shea under the title *The Expedition of Don Diego Dionisio de Peñalosa* (New York, 1882; reprinted by Horn and Wallace, Albuquerque, N.Mex., 1964). The publication also included the Spanish text, which was probably taken from a French original. Shea (pp. 8–12) also includes a laudatory and rather doubtful biographical sketch of the ex-governor, apparently written by Peñalosa himself. T. E. Chávez (*Quest for Quivira* [Southwest Parks and Monuments, Tucson, Ariz., 1992], pp. 20, 55) has suggested that Peñalosa borrowed from and expanded on a real (but virtually unknown) journey by Alonso Baca in 1634, an expedition to Quivira and beyond.

The Villanueva-Miranda controversy is contained in Hackett, *Historical Documents*, vol. 3, pp. 280–84. A discussion of the missionary attacks on Anaya and Domínguez de Mendoza can be found in Scholes, *Troublous Times*, chap. 11, pp. 313–23. The quote from the letter from the Inquisitors to Fray Juan Bernal is on p. 320. The original is in A.G.P.M., Inquisición, 590, fol. 513. More on Cristóbal Anaya can be found in Chávez, *Origins*, p. 4; and Hackett and Shelby, *Revolt*, vol. 1, p. 66 (from Auto of Alonso García, La Isleta, Aug. 14, 1680). For other reports to the Holy Office, see Hackett, *Historical Documents*, vol. 3, pp. 271–79. These include the Gruber case with its outcome, unfortunate for all concerned. Governor Medrano's problems with Juan Domínguez de Mendoza are discussed in Walz, *El Paso*, pp. 203–4. Fray Bernal's 1668 statement about Indian attacks and famine, written to the Tribunal of the Holy Office, is reproduced in Hackett, *Historical Documents*, vol. 3, pp. 271–72. An excellent account of those troubled years is to be found in Ivey, *Famine*, pp. 76–100. The situation in the Salinas area from the time of the famine to the Pueblo Revolt is discussed in Ivey, *Famine*, pp. 85–91. Various tree-ring charts for sub-areas in New Mexico are given by Herr and Clark, *Early Historic Migrations*, p. 372. The drought seemed particularly harsh in the northern Rio Grande area and around Chupadero

Mesa. For Humanas especially, see Ivey, *Midst of a Loneliness,* pp. 399–407. Custodian Ayeta's statement of 1679 can be found in Hackett, *Historical Documents,* vol. 3, p. 298. For the outbreak of disease in 1671, see Hackett, *Historical Documents,* vol. 3, p. 302. The situation at Zuni is discussed by Ivey, *Famine,* p. 90; see also Crampton, *Zunis of Cíbola,* pp. 36–38. The fate of Fray Pedro de Avila y Ayala is told in Adams and Chávez, *Missions,* p. 197 n. 2. For conditions at Hopi during the famine, see Mission Report of 1672, Scholes Collection, CSWR, archive 360, box VII—1, item C. The missionization situation at Hopi in 1680 can be found in A. de Vetancurt, *Teatro Mexicano,* vol. 4, *Menologio Franciscano* (Colección Chimalistac, 11, Madrid, 1961 [first published in 1698]), pp. 275–76. For a summary of the events in Hopi during the seventeenth and early eighteenth centuries, see Riley, *Hopi,* chaps. 4 and 5.

The attacks in the Jornada del Muerto are discussed in Ivey, *Famine,* pp. 88–89. See also John, *Storms,* pp. 92–93. My colleague Curtis F. Schaafsma believes that the Siete Ríos Apaches were named for the Seven Rivers area north and west of Carlsbad. They were probably the ancestors of the modern Mescalero. For horses spreading to non-Pueblo Indians, see D. E. Worcester, "The Spread of Spanish Horses in the Southwest," *NMHR* 19 (3) (1944): 225–32, pp. 225–29. The Apaches were interested in mares (surely for breeding stock) as early as 1650 (see Escalante, *Extracto de noticias,* p. 102). For horse-raiding in Nueva Vizcaya, consult Hackett, *Historical Documents,* vol. 2, pp. 219–25. For the Roque Madrid expedition, see R. Hendricks and J. P. Wilson, eds. and trans., *The Navajos in 1705* (University of New Mexico Press, Albuquerque, 1996). The Faraones and Navajo expeditions of Juan Domínguez are given in a commission as maestro de campo, issued on January 5, 1675, and commission as lieutenant captain-general issued July 12, 1678. Both are part of the Scholes Collection, CSWR, ms. 360, box 11, folder 1. For the reinforcements sent from Mexico to New Mexico at the request of Father Ayeta, see Hackett, *Historical Documents,* vol. 3, pp. 326. Information on the request for additional men can be found on pp. 18–19.

For the Domínguez de Mendoza and related families, see Chávez, *Origins,* pp. 1, 3–4, 24–27, 69–70. Also see the Domínguez de Mendoza file in the Scholes Collection, CSWR, ms. 360, box 11, folder 1, esp. documents dated 1625, 1652, 1662, 1665, 1667, 1669, 1675, 1676, 1678, 1684, 1694, and 1695. The 1694 document reports Juan's death in Madrid. Documents for 1675 give information on Juan Domínguez's expedition against the Faraones Apaches, and ones for 1678 describe the Domínguez attack on the Navajos. Tomé's lack of participation in the 1681–82 raid into the Pueblo area is cited in Escalante, *Extracto de noticias,* p. 59. The quotation on Juan's physical appearance comes from a certification document dated June 23, 1684. A commission to the title of alférez real dated Oct. 12, 1643, is a forgery, and a number of the other documents, including a commission as captain in 1652, are suspect, in part or whole. The return of José Domínguez de Mendoza to New Mexico is discussed by Chávez, *Origins*, pp. 169–70.

CHAPTER 12, FATEFUL DECISIONS

For the Pueblo population in Oñate's time, see the "Sources and Commentary" section for chap. 5. The population figure given by Commissary Ayeta for 1679 can be found in Father Ayeta's petition dated May 10, 1679 (Hackett, *Historical Documents*, vol. 3, p. 299). It was taken from the mission registers and includes all the Pueblos plus the Guadalupe mission near El Paso. The cabildo estimate for October 1680 is taken from Hackett and Shelby, *Revolt*, vol. 1, p. 180. B. W. Zubrow (*Population, Contact, and Climate in the New Mexico Pueblos* [Anthropological Papers of the University of Arizona, no. 24, 1974], pp. 12–14) has a considerably higher estimate: some 34,500 Pueblo Indians in the year 1680. In Zubrow's reconstruction, the Pueblo population rose sharply from less than 20,000 in 1630 to a peak in 1680, then fell precipitously for the next eighty years (to somewhere between 5,000 and 6,000) before beginning another, slower rise. It is not clear, however, where Zubrow got his numbers. Certainly, they contradict the various estimates made, especially by the missionaries, at intervals throughout the century. Espinosa (*Pueblo Revolt*, p. 33) gives the population total for the Christianized Pueblos as 25,000, which again seems considerably too high. His figure of approximately 2,900 Spaniards, reflecting Hackett's figures (see chap. 9) is also perhaps a bit on the high side. For a count of eastern Pueblos in the seventeenth century, see Palkovich, *Historic Population*, pp. 409–10. The count of Pueblos by Vélez de Escalante can be found in Twitchell, *Spanish Archives*, vol. 2, pp. 267, 269. Since Escalante knew Zuni well, having been the missionary there, he probably felt reasonably secure in his statement that as of 1680 Hawikuh was deserted.

The possibility of stabilization of the Pecos population after mid-century is found in the population estimates of Kessell, *Kiva, Cross, and Crown*, pp. 489–90. The comment by D. R. Wilcox ("Changing Perspectives on the Protohistoric Pueblos," *The Protohistoric Period in the North American Southwest, A.D. 1450–1700* [D. R. Wilcox and W. B. Masse, eds., Arizona State University, Anthropological Research Papers, no. 24, 1981, pp. 378–409], p. 397) that figures for Pecos "suggest that a population decline in the second quarter of the 1600s had been completely reversed by 1680" considerably overstates the case. A discussion of disease in the early post-Hispanic Southwest comes in A. F.

Ramenofsky, "The Problem of Introduced Infectious Diseases in New Mexico: A.D. 1540–1680," *Journal of Anthropological Research* 52 (1990): 161–84.

For the Taos deity of death, see E. C. Parsons, *Taos Pueblo* (General Series in Anthropology, no. 2, 1936), p. 110. A deity of disease is discussed in Parsons, *Pueblo Indian Religion,* vol. 2, p. 938. For a linkage of sociopolitical and religious leadership among the Pueblos, see Riley, *Rio del Norte,* pp. 125–29, 261. In my comments on twentieth-century missionaries, I do not mean to issue a blanket criticism, for there are innovative and progressive individuals and groups. One excellent example of religious broad-mindedness from the Southwest is the painting of Zuni mythological scenes in the old Franciscan mission church at Zuni Pueblo (see Riley, *Zuni,* pp. 142–43).

For Rio Grande and Pecos River Pueblo towns occupied in 1680, see Hackett and Shelby, *Revolt,* vol. 1, pp. xxix–xlix. For the Zuni, consult Crampton, *Zunis,* pp. 36–39; see also T. J. Ferguson, "The Emergence of Modern Zuni Culture and Society," *Protohistoric Period,* Wilcox and Masse, eds., pp. 336–53. The quotes about Zuni governance can be found on p. 346. For Hopis, see I. A. Leonard, trans., *The Mercurio volante of Don Carlos de Sigüenza y Góngora* (Quivira Society, Los Angeles, vol. 3, 1932). Information on Hopi can be found on pp. 80–88. The 1693 Spanish text for this Hopi visit is reproduced on pp. 118–28 (fols. 13–18 in the original text). See also M. J. Espinosa, ed. and trans., *First Expedition of Vargas into New Mexico, 1692* (University of New Mexico Press, Albuquerque, 1940); see also Kessell and Hendricks, *By Force of Arms,* esp. pp. 611–16. Kessell and Hendricks also speculate (9–11) on the continuity of native war leaders into the Spanish era. For a count of Piro Pueblos, see Marshall and Walt, *Rio Abajo,* pp. 245–56; see also A. C. Earls, "Raiding, Trading, and Population Reduction among the Piro Pueblos, A.D. 1540–1680," *Current Research on the Late Prehistory and Early History of New Mexico* (B. J. Vierra, ed., New Mexico Archaeological Council, Albuquerque, Special Pub. 1, 1992), pp. 11–19. For Spanish influence, or lack of it, in Pueblo archaeological sites that date from the seventeenth century, see Ferguson, *Emergence,* pp. 364–65; and Ferguson, *Historic Zuni Architecture,* 116–21. For material used in the Hawikuh mission church, consult W. Smith, R. B. Woodbury, and N. F. S. Woodbury, *The Excavation of Hawikuh by Frederick Webb Hodge* (Contributions from the Museum of the American Indian, Heye Foundation, vol. 20, 1966), p. 104. For the situation at one Zuni town, consult an excellent paper by P. A. Gilman, "Contact Period Puebloan Architecture: A Study of Culture Change at Hawikuh, New Mexico," (1978, copy in library, Laboratory of Anthropology, Museum of New Mexico, Santa Fe). Comments on the late Zuni glazes can be found in B. J. Mills, "The Organization of Protohistoric Zuni Ceramic

Production," *Ceramic Production in the American Southwest* (B. J. Mills and P. L. Crown, eds., University of Arizona Press, Tucson), pp. 200–230. Mills (pp. 223–24) makes the point that Zuni glazing techniques were reintroduced to that western pueblo from the Rio Grande, probably during the early seventeenth century. The time and place of introduction of hornos is somewhat of a mystery, but R. Swentzell ("An Architectural History of Santa Clara Pueblo," master's thesis, Department of Architecture, University of New Mexico, Albuquerque, 1976) places a Spanish oven at San Ildefonso in 1591, seven years before Oñate. Her source is a rather vague mention in a nineteenth-century government document, and I suspect that such an early oven did not exist. However, it does seem likely that the horno was an early—that is, seventeenth-century—introduction to the Pueblos. Montgomery (*San Bernardo de Aguatubi*, p. 166) felt that friars, settlers, and Pueblo Indians alike made extensive use of the outdoor ovens.

For general comments on the flow of handicraft skills from the Spaniards to the Indians, see Pierce and Snow, *Another Mexico*, pp. 22–23. A. H. Schroeder ("Rio Grande Ethnohistory," *New Perspectives on the Pueblos*, A. Ortiz, ed., University of New Mexico Press, Albuquerque, 1972, pp. 40–70, p. 50) comments on Oñate that following "a short stay in San Juan, his colony moved into a pueblo across the river, adapting it to their use, remodeling some rooms and building others, and in the process introduced into the pueblo new items such as fireplaces, sundried adobe bricks, a church, and associated architectural features as well as the tools needed for construction."

Spanish material in Humanas is discussed by Hayes, Young, and Warren, *Excavation of Mound 7*, pp. 166–67. The rebel forge set up at Sandia is reported in Escalante, *Extracto de noticias*, p. 84; see also Hackett and Shelby, *Revolt*, vol. 2, p. 225. For the Hopi pottery situation, see Riley, *Protohistoric Hopi*, chap. 6, pp. 95–96; see also E. C. Adams, *Walpi Archaeological Project, Phase II*, vol. 1, *Overview and Summary: A Report Submitted to Heritage Conservation and Recreation Service* (Interagency Archaeological Services, San Francisco, in partial fulfillment of the requirements of contract no. C2504, 1979), p. 47.

The Picurís data come from H. W. Dick, D. Wolfman, C. F. Schaafsma, and M. Wolfman, "Introduction to Picurís Archaeology" (ms. in library, Laboratory of Anthropology, Museum of New Mexico, Santa Fe, 1965), pp. 45, 122–23. See also the formal report (H. W. Dick, "Picurís Pueblo Excavations," Dept. Interior, National Park Service, Contract no. DI-14-10-0333-1348, Santa Fe, 1965), which says that San Bernardo Polychrome had been tentatively identified there (p. 146). See also R. B. Woodbury, "Evidence of Prehistoric Farming in the Vicinity of Picurís, New Mexico" (ms. in library, Laboratory of Anthropology, Museum of New Mexico, Santa Fe, 1966). The glaze situation at Picurís is found in Dick, *Picurís*, p. 141. C. F. Schaafsma ("Geology in Archaeology," *Prehistory and History in the Southwest: Collected Papers in Honor of Alden C. Hayes*, N. Fox, ed. [Archaeological Society of New Mexico, no. 11], pp. 5–14, p. 12) says that analysis of the Hopi sherds found in Picurís indicates that the pottery was actually made in the Hopi villages. For Picurís's ability to supply food during the lean year of 1672, see Ivey, *Famine*, p. 85.

The change in fuels at Hopi for pottery firing is suggested by A. de Vetancurt, *Teatro Mexicana*, vol. 3, *Crónica de la provincia del Santo Evangelio de México* (Colección Chimalistac de Libros y Documentos acerca de la Nueva España, 10, J. Porrua Turanzas, ed., Madrid, 1961 [first published in 1698], p. 275) when he talks about "piedras que sirven de carbon aunque el humo es nocibo por fuerte." Zuni pottery in the mission period is discussed in Smith, Woodbury, and Woodbury, *Hawikuh*, pp. 325–34. See also E. K. Reed, "Painted Pottery and Zuni Prehistory," *Southwestern Journal of Anthropology* 11 (2): 178–93. Reed (190) suggests that the seventeenth-century continuation of Matsaki Polychrome be called "Concepción Polychrome," but this terminology has not caught on. For seventeenth-century ceramics in the Rio Grande area, see D. H. Snow, "The Rio Grande Glaze, Matte-Paint, and Plainware Tradition," *Southwest Ceramics: A Comparative View*, A. L Schroeder, ed., *Arizona Archaeologist* 15 (Aug. 1982): 235–78, esp. pp. 257–63. Also consult R. W. Lang, "The Fields of San Marcos," *Soil, Water, Biology, and Belief*, H. W. Toll, ed. (New Mexico Archaeological Council, Special. Pub. no 2, 1995), pp. 41–76.

For a discussion of Spanish animals and plant foods introduced to the Pueblos, see Ford, *New Pueblo Economy*, pp. 75–83; see also Riley, *Rio del Norte*, pp. 214–15. Horse and burro bones turn up at Awatovi; see S. J. Olsen, *Bones from Awatovi, No. 1: The Faunal Analysis* (Reports of the Awatovi Expedition, no. 11, Peabody Museum of Archaeology and Ethnology, Harvard University, Cambridge, Mass., 1978), pp. 19–26. Information on pork products in Chihuahua comes from Boyd-Bowman, *Two Country Stores*, p. 247. For pigs at Awatovi, see Olsen, *Bones*, p. 26. Dody Fugate from the Laboratory of Anthropology, Santa Fe, has given me valuable information on native dogs in the Southwest. Ms. Fugate also pointed out to me the probable sheep dog that hides behind the canine that found water for Oñate's party in the Jornada del Muerto (see Hammond and Rey, *Oñate*, pt. 1, p. 317). The cat skeleton at Awatovi is reported in Olsen, *Bones*, p. 19. I am grateful to Cordelia T. Snow for bringing the cat mask discussed above to my attention, and for her valuable input on what the ceramic figure represented. The story is that the archaeologist Jesse L. Nusbaum excavated the piece, probably from the convento area of Pecos, in 1915. Louise Stiver, curator of collections, MIAC/LA, cautions that there is some confusion in the cataloging system regarding the cat. In the original Museum of New Mexico catalog number it is listed as a clay bead from the vicinity of Mexico City. The artifact, of course, is not a bead, and Stiver points out that there is a great deal of duplication in the early museum catalog system and much of the original catalog is missing. The cat figurine does have the word "Pecos" written on the interior of the cat's head. There is a catlike creature in a group of petroglyphs on the Zuni Buttes photographed by geologist Dennis Slifer. It was probably made by Native Americans, but the date is unknown.

The millenarian aspect of the Pueblo Revolt is discussed by D. T. Reff, "The 'Predicament of Culture' and Spanish Missionary Accounts of the Tepehuan and Pueblo Revolts," *Ethnohistory* 42 (1) (1995): 63–90, p. 70. For the various pre-revolt Pueblo uprisings, including that of Clemente, see the Declaration of Diego López Sambrano, Dec. 22, 1681, in Hackett and Shelby, *Revolt*, vol. 2, pp. 292–303. The quote about Clemente can be found on pp. 299–300. Other Indian trouble in the pre-revolt period is given by Juan Domínguez de Mendoza in Hackett and Shelby, *Revolt*, vol. 2, p. 266. See also the statement in Escalante, *Extracto de noticias*, pp. 101–4. Bannon (*Spanish Borderlands*, p. 81) calls the Treviño conspirators "*hechiceros* . . . meeting at one of the northern pueblos." The sentences carried out in the Treviño affair were documented by Diego López Sambrano (see Hackett and Shelby, *Revolt*, vol. 2, p. 300). Consult Wilcox, *Changing Perspectives*, p. 397, for the idea that Spanish-Pueblo tensions had lessened in the years immediately before the revolt. It is true that officials in New Spain preferred to hear that Apaches were the basic troublemakers in the Southwest. See, for example, Hackett, *Historical Documents*, vol. 3, p. 287. J. P. Wilson ("Before the Pueblo Revolt," *Prehistory and History in the Southwest*, N. Fox, ed., [Archaeological Society of New Mexico, no. 11, 1985], pp. 113–20) has pointed out that certain late-century officially reported "Apache raids" may have been in part Pueblo revolts.

For various aspects of the Pueblo Revolt and the years of turmoil leading up to it, see an important collection of articles published as part of a tricentennial-year observation of the revolt in *El Palacio* 86 (4) (winter 1980–81). These include (in addition to Kessell, "Clemente," pp. 16–17, cited in chap. 10) M. Simmons, "Why Did It Happen?" pp. 11–15; A. Ortiz, "Popay's Leadership: A Pueblo Perspective," pp. 18–22; H. Agoyo, "The Tricentennial Year in Pueblo Consciousness," pp. 27–31; and T. E. Chavez, "But Were They All Natives?" p. 32.

For early attempts of a Pueblo-wide revolt, see Hackett and Shelby, vol. 2, pp. 245–46. Escalante (*Extracto de noticias*, p. 95) extracts basically the same information. For the initial information on Poseyemu, see Hackett and Shelby, *Revolt*, vol. 1, p. 5; see also Fray Angelico Chavez, "Pohé-yemo's Representative and the Pueblo Revolt of 1680," *NMHR* 42 (2) (1967): 85–126, p. 88. For further discussion of

Poseyemu, see Parsons, *Pueblo Indian Religion,* vol. 1, pp. 178–79; and A. F. Bandelier, *Final Report of Investigations of Among the Indians of the Southwestern United States* (Archaeological Institute of America, Cambridge, Mass., vol. 1, 1890; vol. 2., 1892), vol. 1, pp. 310–11; vol. 2, pp. 47–50. See also Ortiz, *Popey,* p. 21. A thoughtful analysis of Chavez's paper on Poseyemu is found in S. Beninato, "Popé, Pose-yemu, and Naranjo: a New Look at Leadership in the Pueblo Revolt of 1680," *NMHR* 65 (4) (1990): 417–35). In the Rio Grande, the stories about Poseyemu were also entangled with the Montezuma myth, the story spread in historic times of the mighty emperor of the Mexica who extended his power to the Southwest. However, this Montezuma aspect of Poseyemu seems to be post-seventeenth century. For an extended discussion of the Montezuma story, see C. H. Lange, C. L. Riley, and E. M. Lange, *The Southwestern Journals of Adolph F. Bandelier, 1889–1892* (University of New Mexico Press and the School of American Research, Albuquerque and Santa Fe, 1984), pp. 513–17. In regard to the three spirits seen by Popé and described by Pedro Naranjo, consult Hackett and Shelby, *Revolt,* vol. 2, pp. 246–48, 385. For Chavez's analysis, see *Pohé-yemo,* pp. 100–101. Beninato (*Popé, Pose-yemu, and Naranjo,* p. 434) tends to accept Fray Angelico Chavez's belief that the three spirits seen by Popé were in fact Aztec deities. For Copala, see J. L. Mecham, *Francisco de Ibarra and Nueva Vizcaya* (Greenwood Press, New York, 1968), pp. 65, 78, 80. See also J. P. Sanchez, *Explorers, Traders, and Slavers* (University of Utah Press, Salt Lake City, 1997), pp. 5, 8, 11. For a Pueblo identification of Popé's spirits, see Ortiz, *Popay,* p. 20, and Parsons, *Pueblo Indian Religion,* vol. 1, pp. 176, 349; and vol. 2, p. 739. Additional information on the Thlatsina can be found in Parsons, *Taos Pueblo,* pp. 109–10. In regard to Popé's political and religious function, Alfonso Ortiz (*Popay,* p. 22) thought that Popé may have seen himself "being needed in a wider leadership role to ensure the long-term success of the Revolt." It must be said, however, that this whole situation remains somewhat murky.

Speculation on the "black man," Poseyemu's representative, can be found in Reff, *Predicament of Culture,* esp. pp. 74, 76–77. Comments on Bartolomé de Ojeda are found in Espinosa, *Revolt of 1696,* p. 240. Not all scholars believe that Popé was primarily a religious figure. J. S. Sando (*Pueblo Nations: Eight Centuries of Pueblo Indian History* [Clear Light, Santa Fe, N.Mex., 1992], p. 177) suggests that he was a war leader. For details on Tupatú of Picurís, see Espinosa, *First Expedition,* pp. 102–7. The curious lack of leaders' names for the Pecos rebels is commented on by Kessell (*Kiva, Cross, and Crown,* pp. 241–42). Kessell (personal communication) thinks that, quite possibly, some of the Ye family at Pecos were involved in the Pueblo Revolt. For details on Pedro Umviro, see Kessell, Hendricks, and Dodge, *Blood on the Boulders,* pp. 748, 749, 751, 854, 879.

Sources and Commentary

CHAPTER 13, THE CURRENTS OF WAR

For the activities of the procurator-general Ayeta, see Hackett, *Historical Documents,* vol. 3, pp. 18–19, 286–89. For the missionary and Spanish governmental attitude toward Pueblo Indians, see the various documents on the attempted reconquest of 1681–82 (Hackett and Shelby, *Revolt,* vol. 2; and Vélez de Escalante, *Extracto de noticias,* for that period). The villainy of Francisco Xavier is discussed by Vélez de Escalante in *Extracto de noticias,* p. 12. For biographic reference on Francisco Xavier, Luis de Quintana, Diego López Sambrano and their families, see Chávez, *Origins,* pp. 58, 89, 113. Concerning the statement of Juan of Tesuque about the murder of Nicolás Bua, see Hackett and Shelby, *Revolt,* vol. 2, p. 234; see also Ortiz, *Popay,* p. 22. The role of Apaches in the rebellion is discussed by Hackett and Shelby (*Revolt,* vol. 1, p. xxiv n. 4). See also pp. 71–72 for the report of Alonso García, who stated that sargentos mayores Sebastián de Herrera and Fernando de Chávez retreated from that pueblo, "leaving their wives and children in the said pueblo, dead at the hands of the Christian Taos and the heathen Apaches." For Manso involvement, see the statement of the Santa Fe cabildo from La Salineta, Oct. 3, 1680 (Hackett and Shelby, *Revolt,* vol. 1, p. 181). For the question of the knotted cords as signals for rebellion, note the discussion by Hackett and Shelby, *Revolt,* vol. 1, pp. xxv–xxvii n. 10. The timing of the revolt is discussed by Hackett and Shelby, *Revolt,* vol. 1, pp. xxix–liii. As per Hackett and Shelby (vol. 1, p. xxvi), more than one kind of cord is mentioned.

For the killing of Spaniards at Taos, consult Hackett and Shelby, *Revolt,* vol. 1, p. 73, and for the Tewa area, vol. 1, p. 10. The slaughter of the Anaya family is reported in vol. 1, p. 66. See also Chávez, *Origins,* p. 4. For torture of priests, see Vélez de Escalante, *Extracto de noticias,* pp. 158–61; see also Walz, *El Paso,* pp. 249–50. For the captivity of the Leiva women, see the declaration of the Tano native Pedro García (Hackett and Shelby, *Revolt,* vol. 1, p. 25). Mention of Spanish survivors at San Juan Pueblo comes from Walz, *El Paso,* p. 181. The list of captives made by Vargas is found in Kessell and Hendricks, *By Force of Arms,* pp. 525, 530–31. A photocopy of the Spanish text appears on pp. 526–28, and further information on individuals involved is on pp. 430, 488, and 621. It is not certain that the Anaya Almazán rescued at Pecos was Francisco, but Kessell and Hendricks (p. 488) think it probable. For other information on survivors, consult also Chávez, *Origins,* pp. 5, 27, 81, and 99; Vélez de Escalante, *Extracto de noticias,* pp. 177, 180; and J. L. Kessell, "The Ways and Words of the Other: Diego de Vargas and Cultural Brokers in Late Seventeenth-Century New Mexico," *Between Indian and White Worlds: The Cultural Broker,* M. C. Szasz, ed. (University of Oklahoma Press, Norman, 1994), pp. 25–43, 304–8. For material on the Pueblo captive Juana de Apodaca, see p. 36.

For the early state of the defense of Santa Fe, see the *Autos* of Antonio de Otermín dated Aug. 13, 1680 (Hackett and Shelby, *Revolt,* vol. 1, pp. 11–12) and Aug. 13–20, 1680 (vol. 1, pp. 12–16). The quote about the counterstrike of Spaniards is on p. 15. Otermín's count of survivors is given in Certification of Departure, Aug. 21, 1680 (Hackett and Shelby, *Revolt,* vol. 1, p. 19). See also Walz, *El Paso,* p. 32. For preparations for leaving Santa Fe, see the certification and notice of departure issued by Francisco Xavier (Hackett and Shelby, *Revolt,* vol. 1, p. 19); information on the march is given by Otermín (vol. 1, pp. 19–27). For the activities of Alonso García consult vol. 1, pp. lxvii–lxx, 54–55, 62–65, 70–75; of Pedro de Leiva, vol. 2, pp. 163–68. See also Twitchell, *Spanish Archives,* vol. 1, pp. 24–27. For the location of Alamillo Pueblo, see Marshall and Walt, *Rio Abajo,* pp. 254–55. Otermín's attempts to supply his refugees at La Salineta can be found in Hackett and Shelby, *Revolt,* vol. 1, pp. 132–33. For the muster at that place, see Hackett and Shelby, *Revolt,* vol. 1, pp. 18, 31, 120, 136–54, and 161. For the Leiva escort, see vol. 1, pp. lxxxvii, 51, 85.

Otermín's reconquest attempt is recounted in great detail by Hackett and Shelby, *Revolt,* vol. 1, pp. cxx–ccvii. For the detailed muster roll for the march north in November 1681, see Hackett and Shelby, *Revolt,* vol. 2, pp. 191–201. Material on Alonso Catití is found in *Revolt,* vol. 1, p. 66; vol. 2, pp. 226, 236, 243, 247, 296, 320, 386, and 388; on El Ollita, vol. 2, pp. 239, 241, 260, 263, 266–67, 304, and 387; on Domingo Luján, vol. 2, pp. 263–64. For Father Ayeta's comment on the unwillingness of settlers to go on Otermín's expedition, see *Revolt,* vol. 2, pp. 313–14. Otermín's evaluation of the threat to Isleta by Tupatú is set forth in an Auto of Dec. 24, 1681; see *Revolt,* vol. 2, p. 337. The differing opinions of the head missionaries on the expedition are detailed in Kessell and Hendricks, *By Force of Arms,* p. 20.

For events in the early settlement of the El Paso area, see Vélez de Escalante, *Extracto de noticias,* pp. 120–21. The movement of the various outlying settlements nearer El Paso after the outbreak of Manso hostilities is discussed by Walz (*El Paso,* pp. 118, 145) and Timmons (*El Paso,* pp. 18–20). For the Manso and Suma struggles, see T. H. Naylor and C. W. Polzer, S.J., *The Presidio and Militia on the Northern Frontier of New Spain: 1570–1700* (University of Arizona Press, Tucson, 1986), pp. 483–88, 506–9, 509–27, 528–47 (these citations contain both translations and transcriptions of original documents). The execution of the Suma rebels is discussed by Naylor (*Athapaskans They Weren't,* p. 276). The visita of September 1684 is recorded by Walz (*El Paso,* pp. 160–61). For the El Paso muster of November 1684, see Naylor and Polzer, *Presidio and Militia,* pp. 511–27. For general conditions in the El Paso area, consult Kessell and Hendricks, *By Force of Arms,* pp. 22–24; see also Beckett and Corbett, *Manso*

Indians, pp. 9–12, and Walz, *El Paso,* p. 172. For additional details, see A. E. Hughes, *The Beginnings of Spanish Settlement in the El Paso District* (University of California, Publications in History, vol. 1, no. 3, Berkeley, 1914). De Salle's role in extending French influence into the southern Mississippi Basin is discussed in Brebner, *Explorers,* pp. 269–78. For the eastern Texas missions and Spanish French interaction along this frontier, see J. R. Swanton, *Source Material on the History and Ethnology of the Caddo Indians* (Bureau of American Ethnology, Bulletin 132, Washington, D.C., 1942), pp. 44–50; for French activities, see pp. 50–51.

The background material on Reneros can be found in Hackett and Shelby, *Revolt,* vol. 2, pp. 63, 134. See also Walz, *El Paso,* pp. 221–22; and Kessell and Hendricks, *By Force of Arms,* p. 24. The Montoya execution is recorded by Walz (*El Paso,* p. 222). Background material on the Montoya family is given by Chávez (*Origins,* pp. 77–78). For the 1687 expedition of Reneros to the Jemez River and for the subsequent Suma revolt, see Walz, *El Paso,* pp. 226–27; and Kessell and Hendricks, *By Force of Arms,* pp. 24–25. The end of the Domínguez de Mendoza story is recited by Walz, *El Paso,* pp. 237–38, 244–45. For the account of the Indian Juan, see pp. 126–27; for that of the Tiwa native Lucas, see pp. 179–82. Vélez de Escalante (*Extracto de noticias,* pp. 156–61) has considerable detail on Jironza's military activities in the Pueblo area. Walz (*El Paso,* pp. 246–52) generally follows Escalante but gives a few additional details. For information on the change of Pueblo leadership, see the 1778 letter of Vélez de Escalante in Twitchell, *Spanish Archives,* vol. 2, pp. 276–77. Other information on Jironza in the upper Southwest comes from J. M. Mange, *Luz de la Tierra Incognita en la América Septentrional, y diario de las exploraciones en Sonora* (AGN, Publicaciones, no. 10, F. Fernández de Castillo, ed., Mexico, 1926), p. 212. A discussion of Toribio and his mercury mine is given in Walz, *El Paso,* pp. 254–57. See also J. M. Espinosa, "The Legend of Sierra Azul," *NMHR* 9 (2) (1934): 113–58, esp. pp. 122–24. The Sierra Azul and Cerro Colorado, somewhere in the Zuni and Hopi area, were supposed to have contained rich deposits of silver and cinnabar (mercury ore), respectively, and rumors about them dated from Peñalosa's time (p. 121).

CHAPTER 14, AN ERA ENDS, AN ERA BEGINS

For the history of the Vargas family, see J. L. Kessell, ed., *Remote Beyond Compare* (University of New Mexico Press, Albuquerque, 1989), pp. 3–46. The "middling nobility" comment comes on p. 24. For the expedition of 1689, see Kessell, *Remote,* p. 51, and Vélez de Escalante, *Extracto de noticias,* pp.

156–58. A comment on Bartolomé can be found in Espinosa, *Revolt*, p. 240 n. 1. For information on various Pueblo leaders, both those who continued to defend the Indian cause and those who apostatized, see Espinosa, *Revolt*, pp. 34, 43, 44, and 270; see also Kessell, Hendricks, and Dodge, *Royal Crown*, pp. 402–3. Pueblo Indians who had kinship ties with the Spaniards include members of the Naranjo family, Alonso Catití of the Márquez family, Ollita of Cochiti, and a number of others. For comments on godparenthood, see Kessell, *Ways and Words*, pp. 36–37, 307. For the march north to the Albuquerque area, see Vélez de Escalante, *Extracto de noticias*, pp. 162–63; Espinosa, *First Expedition*, pp. 29–30; and Kessell and Hendricks, *By Force of Arms*, pp. 368–83. Accounts of the entry into Santa Fe and the events that shaped the ritual repossession during September and October 1692 can be found in Kessell, *Remote*, pp. 56–57; and Kessell and Hendricks, *By Force of Arms*, 406–65. The "musket shot" quote is on p. 391. Arrival of the Parral contingent is mentioned in Kessell, *Remote*, p. 58; and in Kessell and Hendricks, *By Force of Arms*, p. 423. Material on the captive Spaniards and others can be found on p. 430; the full list of captives is on pp. 525–31. For the Jemez trip, see pp. 520–23; for visits to various of the Keresan Pueblos, pp. 508–20, 523–24. Statements about Roque Madrid's ability to translate in Keresan can be found in Vargas's journal entries. See Kessell, Hendrick, and Dodge, *Blood on the Boulders*, pp. 200, 225, and 237. For appointment of Tupatú to control over Santa Fe and various of the Rio Grande pueblos, see p. 509. The initial contacts with Hopi can be found in Espinosa, *First Expedition*, pp. 210–11. For the march to Zuni and Hopi, see Kessell and Hendricks, *By Force of Arms*, pp. 545–84; for the return to El Paso, see pp. 584–97. The statement about livestock and horse herds being moved to safety is taken from Espinosa, *First Expedition*, pp. 211–12. For the comments about Luis Tupatú, see C. de Sigüenza y Góngora, *The Mercurio volante: An account of the first expedition of Don Diego de Vargas into New Mexico in 1692* (Irving A. Leonard, trans., The Quivira Society, Los Angeles [contains both English and Spanish texts], 1932), p. 80. The happenings at Hopi are recorded by Espinosa, *First Expedition*, pp. 216–28.

For the 1693 expedition northward, see Kessell, Hendricks, and Dodge, *Royal Crown Restored*, pp. 398, 439, 440, 444, 457, and 473. A count of the Vargas army and settlers is given in Espinosa, *Revolt*, p. 41. Warnings by Juan de Ye are drawn from Kessell, Hendricks, and Dodge, *Royal Crown Restored*, pp. 437–38. According to Vargas, El Picurí was dead by October 1696 (Kessell, Hendricks, and Dodge, *Blood on the Boulders*, p. 1033). For the attack on Santa Fe, see Espinosa, *Revolt*, pp. 43–44; see also Kessell, Hendricks, and Dodge, *Royal Crown*, pp. 525–35. For the events of 1694 and 1695, see Espinosa, *Revolt*, pp. 44–46. The first part of the rebellion is described by Vargas in a letter to the viceroy dated July 31, 1696 (*Revolt,* pp. 257–80). The missionaries' point of view is given in custodian Francisco de Vargas's letter to the Franciscan guardián in El Paso dated July 21 (*Revolt,* pp. 246–57). Ye's murder is reported in Kessell, *Kiva, Cross, and Crown,* pp. 268–70; for the execution of the Pecos rebels, see p. 289; see also Kessell, *Ways and Words,* pp. 39–40. More on Caripicado can be found in Vargas's campaign journal (see Kessell, Hendricks, and Dodge, *Blood on the Boulders,* p. 1008).

Background information on the Bernal family comes from Chávez, *Origins,* p. 12. For background on the settlements of Bernalillo and Santa Cruz, see R. Julyan, *The Place Names of New Mexico* (University of New Mexico Press, Albuquerque, 1996), pp. 36–37, 324; T. M. Pierce, *New Mexico Place Names* (University of New Mexico Press, Albuquerque, 1965), pp. 16, 148–49. The Cisneros involvement in Naranjo's killing comes from Kessell, Hendricks, and Dodge, *Blood on the Boulders,* pp. 844–45; see also Espinosa, *Revolt,* p. 278. The statement of José Naranjo's grandson can be found in Chavez, *Pohe-Yemo,* p. 107. Hendricks and Wilson (*Navajos in 1705,* pp. 118–20) have a thumbnail sketch of José Naranjo. It has occasionally been argued that there were two Naranjo families, and that the José who featured in the early post-Conquest military action was a Spaniard. Hendricks and Wilson (154) cite the unpublished genealogical manuscript of Epifanio Conrado Naranjo ("Naranjo," 1991, ms. in possession of R. Hendricks and J. P. Wilson) for this particular point of view. I have not had the chance to consult this work, but Fray Angelico Chavez's detailed analysis of the family in *Origins* and in *Pohé-yemo* does seem rather convincing. For a discussion of this controversy, see Kessell, Hendricks, and Dodge, *Blood on the Boulders,* pp. 953–54.

For the return of the Picurís groups among the Apache, see D. A. Gunnerson, *The Jicarilla Apaches: A Study in Survival* (Northern Illinois University Press, De Kalb, 1974), pp. 122–25. Nomadic allies of the Hopi are reported in a letter of Vargas to the king dated May 16, 1693 (Espinosa, *First Expedition,* p. 220). For eastern Pueblo settlements at Hopi, see E. H. Spicer, *Cycles of Conquest* (University of Arizona Press, Tucson, 1962), pp. 191–92. For the Hano involvement in the attack on Awatovi, see E. P. Dozier, *Hano: A Tewa Indian Community in Arizona* (Holt, Rinehart and Winston, New York, 1966), p. 13.

For the missionary counts of 1696–97, see the exchange of letters in Espinosa, *Revolt,* pp. 289–95. Material about Rodríguez Cubero comes from R. Hendricks, "Pedro Rodríguez Cubero: New Mexico's Reluctant Governor, 1697–1703," *NMHR* 68 (1) (1993): 13–39. For the Knights of Santiago connection, see Kessell, *Remote,* p. 75; for Vargas's grant of a title of nobility and of an encomienda, see pp. 68–69. See also L. B. Bloom, "The Vargas Encomienda," *NMHR* 14 (4)

(1939): 366–417. Details of Vargas's later career can be found in Kessell, *Remote,* pp. 83–88. The attempts of Father Garaycoechea (also spelled Garaicoechea) to refound the Hopi missions is described in Crampton, *Zunis,* pp. 44–47. For Rodríguez Cubero's attempts to regain Hopi after the Awatovi fiasco, see Hendricks, *Cubero,* pp. 30–31. The last years of Vargas are discussed in Kessell, *Remote,* pp. 78–88. Population estimates for the eighteenth century can be found in Gutiérrez, *When Jesus Came,* pp. 167–74. Gutiérrez (174) indicates that in 1776 there were 9,742 Spaniards and 8,602 Puebloans. For the scalp dance and eighteenth-century dances in general, see Adams and Chávez, *Missions,* pp. 257–58. The quotes given in the text are on p. 258. The new route from New Mexico to California is covered in J. P. Sanchez, *Explorers, Traders, and Slavers,* esp. chaps. 4–8. For commentary on the relationship of settlers and Indians on the northern frontier throughout the colonial period, consult J. Chávez Chávez, "Retrato del Indio Bárbaro . . . ," *NMHR* 73 (4) (1998): 389–424. Changing conditions in eighteenth-century New Mexico are discussed by C. R. Cutter, *The Protector de Indios in Colonial New Mexico, 1659–1821* (University of New Mexico Press, Albuquerque, 1986), esp. pp. 41–46.

New Mexico Governors, 1598–1704

1598–1608	Juan de Oñate y Salazar
1608–9(?)	Cristóbal de Oñate (not recognized by the Spanish Crown)
1609–14	Pedro de Peralta
1614–18	Bernardino de Ceballos
1618–25	Juan de Eulate
1625–29	Felipe de Sotelo Osorio
1629–32	Francisco Manuel de Silva Nieto
1632–35	Francisco de la Mora y Ceballos
1635–37	Francisco Martínez de Baeza
1637–41	Luis de Rosas
1641	Juan Flores de Sierra y Valdés
1641–42	Francisco Gómez
1642–44	Alonso de Pacheco y Heredia
1644–47	Fernando de Argüello Carvajál
1647–49	Luis de Guzmán y Figueroa
1649–53	Hernando de Ugarte y la Concha
1653–56	Juan de Samaniego y Jaca
1656–59	Juan Manso de Contreras
1659–61	Bernardo López de Mendizábal
1661–64	Diego Dionisio de Peñalosa Briceño y Berdugo
1664–65	Juan Durán de Miranda
1665–68	Fernando de Villanueva
1668–71	Juan de Medrano y Mesía
1671–75	Juan Durán de Miranda

1675–77	Juan Francisco de Treviño
1677–83	Antonio de Otermín
1683–86	Domingo Jironza Petríz de Cruzate
1686–89	Pedro Reneros de Posada
1689–91	Domingo Jironza Petríz de Cruzate
1691–97	Diego de Vargas Zapata Luján Ponce de León
1697–1703	Pedro Rodríguez Cubero
1703–4	Diego de Vargas Zapata Luján Ponce de León

Glossary

Adelantado	Honorific title sometimes given a conqueror of a new area.
Alcalde	Magistrate, often of a cabildo.
Alcalde mayor	Mayor of a town, or the executive officer of a district.
Alcalde ordinario	Member of a cabildo.
Alcalde provincial	Police officer in area outside a villa (chartered town).
Alférez	Lieutenant (teniente) in the army; also, a municipal official attached to a cabildo. It can also refer to a standard bearer in an army group.
Alguacil mayor	Chief constable of a municipality or of the Holy Office.
Ambulatorio	Covered walkway in a convent.
Audiencia	Judicial and legislative council, acting also as an appellant court.
Auto	Judicial or administrative decree or order.
Barrio	Section of a city or town.
Caballero	Gentleman (literally "horseman," equivalent to French *chevalier*).
Cabildo	Officials of a town or city government; sometimes refers to the building in which this government is housed.
Camino Real	Long trail from Mexico City to Santa Fe over which supply trains traveled during the colonial period.

Capitán de guerra	Pueblo Indian war captain appointed by the Spaniards.
Celda	Sleeping room in a convent
Chirrionero	Wagon driver on the Camino Real.
Comisario	Chief regional officer of the Holy Office of the Inquisition in seventeenth-century New Spain; also, head of a Franciscan group that had not yet received custodial status.
Compadrazgo	Connection of a godparent with his godchild and with the godchild's parents.
Convent	A group of Franciscan friars living together, the smallest unit of the order; also, the buildings in which the friars lived and worked.
Coyote	In colonial New Mexico, an Indian and black genetic mixture in which the Indian predominated.
Custodia	A Franciscan mission organization, ranking below that of provincia.
Custodian (custos)	The head of a custodia.
Encomendero	Holder of an encomienda.
Encomienda	The grant of labor and tribute of a given group of Indians.
Escudería	The grant of an escudero.
Escudero	A substitute or temporary holder of an encomienda.
Estancia	A large farm or ranch.
Estanciero	Owner of an estancia.
Fray	Friar; in this case, a Franciscan missionary. Usually abbreviated "Fr."
Genízaro	Indian slave, usually Apache or Ute, living with the Spaniards. Descendants of these slaves formed a special population and, especially in the eighteenth century, were often settled in frontier towns.
Guardián	Friar in charge of a mission and convent.
Hidalgo	Minor title of nobility or gentrification (from *hijo* [son] + *de algo* [of something]).
Horno	Oven, especially an outside beehive oven.
Jornada del Muerto	Desert shortcut in southern New Mexico, east of the Rio Grande.

Maestro (maestre) de campo	In early times, an adjutant officer or the chief field officer (camp master). This was how the term was used both in Coronado's and in Oñate's time. By the end of the seventeenth century, "maestro de campo" was the title given to a field grade officer.
Mestizaje	Condition of being a mestizo.
Mestizo	Individual of mixed Indian-European ancestry.
Mozo	Servant; also, a son whose father has the same name ("junior"), e.g., Tomé el Mozo Domínguez de Mendoza.
Mulato (mulatto)	Individual of mixed African-European ancestry.
Nivil de albañil	Plum bob with attached wooden arm used in building.
Paraje	Camp or stop-over place.
Portería	Reception hall in a convent.
Procurador general	Chief supply officer of a Franciscan province or custodia.
Provincia (province)	An administrative unit of Spanish government, equivalent to a modern state (the province of New Mexico); also, a Franciscan administrative unit above that of custodia.
Provincial	The head of a Franciscan province.
Regidor	Councilor in a cabildo.
Residencia	Official inquiry taken at the end of the term of a governor or other officer.
Sambohijo (sambahigo)	Individual of mixed black-Indian ancestry.
Sargento mayor	Major in the army.
Tinaja	Pottery jar, especially for storage purposes.
Torreón	Defensive tower.
Villa	A chartered town. Santa Fe was the only villa in New Mexico throughout most of the seventeenth century.
Visita	A chapel used for intermittent celebration of the Mass; also, an inspection of a town, area, or encampment by official authority.
Visitador	An official inspector.

General Index

Abalone. *See* Shell

Abó. *See* Tompiro

Abu Abd-Allah Muhammad, 11

Acculturation, pueblos in 17th cent., 206–09; use of adobes, 207; Span. crops, 207; ovens, 207; fireplaces, 207; iron, use of, 208

Acoma: Querechos near, 34; in Oñate documents, 53; clans in, 70; missionaries assigned to, 70; Oñate visits, 78–79; J. Zaldívar killed at, 80; V. Zaldívar attacks, 80; Indians sentenced at, 81; Indians flee to, 96; mission established at, 97; miracle in, 118; wagon trains to, 137; Domínguez raids near, 191; revolt in 23–24, Lucas report about, 234; in reconquest, 242, 244, 249

Adams, Charles, on kachina cult, 21

Adams, Eleanor B. and Angelico Chavez, on eighteenth-century Indians, 251

Adelantadado: Oñate appointed as, 42; Columbus first of in New World, 42

Africans in early New Mexico, 127–28

Agriculture (Native SW), 59–60: during Archaic, 13; cotton in, 13; during Basketmaker-Pueblo, 13; during Pueblo IV, 20; among Suma, 46; among Manso, 46; plants adopted, 207; wheat used, 207; fruit, vegs. chile introduced by Spaniards, 212; introduced by Oñate, 287

Agriculture (Spanish): melons introduced by Coronado, 31; orchards of, 121; of settlers, 147; by Vargas settlers, 244, 287

Aguilar, Nicolas de, mestizo in early New Mexico, 128; supports López, 167–68; trial of 168–69; permits kachinas, 176; arrested, 180–81. *See also* Inquisition, Kachinas, Lopez

Aguilar, Pablo de: scouts ahead of Oñate party, 47; trouble of with Oñate, 76; in Acoma attack, 80; killed by Oñate, 83

Aguilera y Roche, Teresa de: family of, 159; marries López, 159; domestic arrangements of, 169–71; accused of magic and Judaism, 170; Inquisition arrests, 181; imprisoned, 182; released, 183. *See also*, Inquisition, López

Aguirre, Lope de, 6

Alameda during Revolt, 223

Alarçón, Hernando de, 30

Albornoz, Rodrigo de, 40

Albuquerque (Alburquerque) as chartered town, 244

Alexander VI, Pope, Donation of, 5

Alibates. *See* Trade

Alvarado, Fr. Tomás as custodian, 102

Analco (Mexican Barrio of): settlement of, 92, 103; Indians at Salineta, 127; Mexican Indians in, 129–30, 132;

Anasazi: from Oshara, 13; influences during, 14; meaning of name, 15; extent of, 15; building material during, 54. *See also* Basketmaker-Pueblo, individual period names

Anaya Almazán, Cristóbal de: Inquisition case against, 128; supports López, 166;

with García, 227; attempts reconquest, 227–29
Ovando, Nicolás, 9
Ovens: in SW, 60; at San Ildefonso, 299

Pacheco, Francisco, as war captain, 238; confers with Vargas, 238–39, 244
Pacheco y Heredia, Gov. Alonso de: executes ringleaders, 102
Padilla, Fr. Juan de: in Quivira, 31; killed on Plains, 38
Parrot, thick-billed, 58–59. *See also* Animals, Trade
Parsons, Elsie Clews, and Shalako, 65; on Southwestern religion, 67
Patayan, 14
Patol (Patolli): played in New Mexico, 125, 258
Payupki, Tiwa form new town of, 247
Paz, Fr. Juan de, 191
Pecos, Towa spoken at, 25; in Oñate period, 45, 49; macaws in, 58; missionaries assigned to, 73; Zaldívar visits, 77; Oñate visits, 84; in Rosas period, 100; early mission in, 109, 111; carpentry skills of, 119–20, 213; mission at largest in SW, 123–24; convento kiva in, 124; and Castaño, 140; pottery from, 145, 210; trade at, 165; settlement of, 201; population in, 203; Spanish influence at, 212–13; war leaders in, 219; warn Spaniards, 221; Revolt of leaders unknown, 223; guardián killed at, 224; captives at, 225; war of with Tewa, 234; in reconquest, 238–39, 246–47
Peinado, Fr. Alonso de: as commissary, 92; replaced, 95; at Chililí, 97, 110
Peñalosa Diego Dionisio de: replaces López, 179; in López residencia, 180; family of, 186; appointed governor, 186; works with Posada, 187; accuses Posada of murder, 189; sentence of, 189; subsequent career of, 190, 232
Penn, William, 8
Peralta, Fr. Gastón de, 83
Peralta, Gov. Pedro de: appointed governor, 86; takes office, 92; settles Santa Fe, 93, 131–32; arrested by Ordóñez, 95

Perea, Fr. Esteban de: as commissary, 95; replaces Benavides, 97; at Quarai, 99; in formation of custodia, 109; objects to cattle shipments, 139
Pérez de Luxán, Diego: names Manso, 55; doubts existence of silver in Arizona, 139
Pérez de Villagrá, Gaspar: as friend of Oñate, 40; sent after fugitives, 76; in Acoma attack, 80; transports Acoma children, 81; deserts Oñate, 82
Philippines, Magellan killed, 5
Phillip II, King of Spain, 1; death of ends Golden Age, 10; and settlement of SW, 36; death of, 77; Ordenanzas of 1577 of, 130
Phillip III, becomes King of Spain, 77; confirms Oñate's adelantado statue, 77; orders withdrawal from New Mexico, 86
Picurís: in Oñate lists, 54; macaws in, 58; missionaries at, 77, 116, 118; encomienda of, 166; population in, 203; pottery in, 209–10; fruit trees in, 212; Tupatú, leader of, 218–19, 229, 234, 239, 241–42; warfare in, 234; lack of food of, 244; flee to Plains, 247
Piman, Indians and language, 28, 50. *See also* Language
Pinero, Capt. Juan: sent to Mexico, 82; defects, 83
Pinkley, Jean, rediscovers Pecos church, 124
Pinzón, Vicente Yañez, 6
Piro: early expeditions to, 33; Oñate travels among, 48; diseases in, 52; towns in, 53, 93; missionization of as late, 113; missions at, 73, 114–15; absence of in Revolt, 223, 226; settle near El Paso, 227; with Otermín, 230. *See also*, Language
Pizarro, Francisco: in Peru, 5; Franciscans on expedition of, 9
Pleistocene (Ice Age), 12
Pojoaque, macaws in, 58
Ponce de León, Juan, 6
Ponce de León, Pedro (Count of Bailén), 42–43
Popé: leads nativistic movement, 214; release of by Treviño, 215; consults three spirits, 217; identified as priest, 218; actions of against native leaders, 224; death of, 234; leadership role of, 302

Snow, Cordelia T., 300
Snow, David H., 44, 207, 276
Socio-political Life: and Pueblo priests, 67, 214, 215, 218; and kiva groups in Pueblo SW, 68; and Spanish offices in SW, 68; and hunt, warrior, medicine societies, 68–69; and clans in SW, 68–70; and war captains in SW, 68, 214, 217–19, 229, 238–41, 246; cacique in, 69; and Apache organizations, 70–71; among Jumano, 70–71; among Navajo; 70–71; of settlers in Santa Fe, 131; in late seventeenth-century Pueblos, 204; and clans and moieties, 205
Solstice ceremonies, 63–64
Sosa, Alonso de, 83
Sosa Peñalosa, Lt. Gov. Francisco de, 84–85
Sotelo Osorio, Gov. Felipe de, 97
Soto Hernando de, 6, 29
Spanish Armada, 2
Squash. See Agriculture
Stiver, Louise, 300
Stone boiling, 27
Suárez (Juarez), Fr. Andrés, builds Pecos church, 97; at Pecos, 111; introduces carpentry to Pecos, 120; and Pecos mission, 123
Suma: location of, 25; as guide to Oñate, 46; culture of, 46; and Apache, 51; diseases in, 52
Supply Trains: basic contract of, 135; makeup of, 135–39; route of, 136–37; supplies of off loaded at Guadalupe, 137; split up of in New Mexico, 139

Taca of San Juan, as unsure of leadership function, 218
Talabán, Fr. Juan, 191
Tano: towns of in Oñate documents, 53; early missions in, 110; kachina dances in, 174; war leaders of, 218; warn Otermín, 223; Spaniards killed at, 224; settlers flee from, 225; in battle of Santa Fe, 225–26; with Otermín, 230; in reconquest, 238, 240, 242; at Hopi, 247–48
Tanoan languages in SW. See Language

Tanpachoas, 55
Taos: Tiwa spoken in, 24; Coronado explores, 30; in Oñate documents, 50, 54; pottery in, 60; missions in, 77, 111, 114–15; in Rosas period, 100; sexual irregularities at, 117; miracle in, 118; resistance in, 157; murder at, 171; disease spirit at, 202; rebellion at, 214; Popé at, 215, 217; Saca at, 219; in Revolt, 223–25, 234; in reconquest, 238, 240, 244
Tapia, Pedro de, 242
Taracahitan. See Language
Tatarrax, 84
Téllez Girón, Capt. Rafael, 239
Tepiman. See Language
Tesuque: dance in, 177–78; Juan of, 218; in Revolt, 221, 223; in reconquest, 240, 242
Tewa-Tano. See Language
Teya: language of, 21; contacted by Coronado, 21, 50; later called Jumano, 25; Cabeza de Vaca among, 27; during Oñate time, 51, 53. See also Jumano, Language
Thorvald, 4
Tiguex: location of, 25; attacked by Coronado, 30; during Oñate time, 51
Tiwa. See Language
Tlaloc, 21, 65. See also Kachina
Tlaxcalan Indians: trained by missionaries, 9; in early Chihuahua, 31; not listed in Oñate expedition, 44; in Santa Fe, 103; in New Mexico(?), 276; at Analco, 283
Tobacco. See Hunting and Gathering, Medicine
Tolosa Cortés Moctezuma, Isabel de: family of; 39–40, 42; marries Oñate, 40
Tomás: as Mexican Indian in SW, 36; contacts Oñate, 48
Tomé, as Tewa Indian rescued after Revolt, 225
Tompiro and eastern Tiwa: language of similar to Teya, 23, 25; towns of in Oñate documents, 53; Oñate visits, 78; missionized, 97, 111, 115; kachina dances in, 176–77; deserted, 194; with Otermín, 230. See also Language
Tordesillas, Treaty of, 5

Index of Initial Citations

In the Sources and Commentary section of this book the initial citation for each author contains the full bibliographic information. This index gives the page numbers of these complete citations. It does not list archival documents since these are adequately cited at each appearance.